Epidemics and Enslavement

Indians of the Southeast

Series Editors

Michael D. Green

University of North Carolina

Theda Perdue

University of North Carolina

Advisory Editors

Leland Ferguson

University of South Carolina

Mary Young

University of Rochester

Epidemics and Enslavement

BIOLOGICAL CATASTROPHE IN
THE NATIVE SOUTHEAST
1492–1715

Paul Kelton

University of Nebraska Press
Lincoln & London

Library of Congress Cataloging-in-Publication Data
Kelton, Paul.
    Epidemics and enslavement : biological catastrophe in the Native Southeast.
1492–1715 / Paul Kelton.
        p. cm.—(Indians of the Southeast)
    Includes bibliographical references and index.
    ISBN 978-0-8032-2756-9 (cloth : alk. paper)
    ISBN 978-0-8032-2791-0 (paper : alk. paper)
        1. Indians of North America—Diseases—South Atlantic States. 2. Indians,
Treatment of—South Atlantic States. 3. Indians of North America—South
Atlantic States—History. 4. Smallpox—South Atlantic States—Epidemiology.
5. Slavery—South Atlantic States. 6. South Atlantic States—History. I. Title.
    E78.S65K45 2007
    614.4089'97075—dc22   2007014353

Set in Garamond Premiere Pro by Omega Clay.
Designed by Omega Clay.

For my mother
Sue Kelton
and in memory of my father
Bill Kelton

CONTENTS

ILLUSTRATIONS

ACKNOWLEDGMENTS

The ideas for this book have evolved over several years in which I have had the good fortune to have been associated with many exceptional individuals. The book began as a dissertation that I completed at the University of Oklahoma, and I could not have asked for a more generous group of scholars to guide me through a difficult project. I am much indebted to Gary Anderson, Don Pisani, Paul Gilje, Terry Rugeley, Cameron Wesson, and Charles Hayes for their support. I also wish to thank my fellow graduate student colleagues, especially Brad Raley, Kelly Lankford, Jackie Rand, J. P. Leary, Megan Benson, Lorien Foote, Matt DeSpain, and Jay Dew, who gave me a sympathetic ear when I needed it. At Southern Connecticut State University, I was blessed to have a wonderful group of colleagues, especially Troy Paddock, Christine Petto, Michele Thompson, Steve Judd, and Hugh Davis, who read and commented on portions of this work. The University of Kansas offered me a great opportunity to pursue my research, and I especially thank my colleagues Don Fixico and Rita Napier for their support. I presented the first chapter of this book at the Hall Center for the Humanities' Nature and Culture Seminar, and I wish to thank Don Worster, Karl Brooks, Greg Cushman, and other participants in that seminar for their insightful comments. Ernest Jenkins and Ryan Gaston helped with particularly difficult translations involving Spanish documents. My colleague Jeff Moran deserves more thanks than I can possibly give him. He read much of the manuscript, and his suggestions have helped me make the work more accessible to nonspecialists. Jeff is a tremendously generous person and an inspiration to all.

The University of Nebraska Press, especially Gary Dunham, Elisabeth Cretien, Joeth Zucco, and Sarah Disbrow, stuck with me and my project for several years, and their reassurance undoubtedly helped me stick with the project. I appreciate Barb Wojhoski, who superbly copyedited the final manuscript. Theda Perdue read the manuscript twice and offered thorough and thoughtful critiques. I truly appreciate how much work she has put into advancing the field of southeastern ethnohistory and in helping me make my own individual contribution. Mike Green read the first draft, and I benefited greatly from his insight. Marvin Smith read the second draft and proved to be a truly generous scholar, who despite our disagreements, welcomed my interpretation as a way to invigorate the prevailing debates within our shared field. The Porter L. Fortune Jr. symposium at the University of Mississippi in 1998 gave me an opportunity to test some of my ideas, and I appreciate the insights that Charles Hudson, Robbie Ethridge, Vernon James Knight Jr., Peter Wood, John Worth, Chester DePratter, Patricia Galloway, Marvin Jeter, and Helen Rountree offered. At various stages of my career, I have sought the advice and help of other scholars. John Henry offered an interested ear on many occasions, graciously read a draft of the manuscript, and gave me an economist's unique insights into my historical questions. I also wish to thank Jay K. Johnson for sharing his work with me before it had been published; Alan Gallay, who generously sent me photocopies of documents that I had overlooked at the Library of Congress; and Steven Hahn, who provided a crucial piece of evidence as I completed the final draft.

Several organizations and institutions have supported this project as well. I am grateful for the grants that I received from the Hall Center for the Humanities of the University of Kansas; the General Research Fund of the University of Kansas College of Liberal Arts and Sciences; the New Faculty General Research Fund of the University of Kansas Center for Research; the Philips Fund of the American Philosophical Society; the Humanities Center Board of the University of Oklahoma; and the Department of History of the University of Oklahoma. I also appreciate the staffs of Watson and Anschutz Libraries of the University of Kansas, Lawrence; the Western History Collection and Bizzell Memorial Library of the University of Oklahoma, Norman; the Manuscripts Division of the Library of Congress; and the National Archives of Great Britain, London. I also wish to thank Darin Grauberger and Ryan Lash of the University of Kansas Cartographic Services for producing the maps that have enhanced this book.

Members of my family have given me immense support and encouragement. I dedicate this book to my mother, whose own curiosity about history has inspired me more than she knows, and to my late father, whose hard work and determination I admired more than he ever knew. I only wish he could have seen the completed product of my labors. My daughter, Caroline, has spent her entire six years of life with her daddy having the weight of publishing this book on his shoulders. Her smiles, sense of wonderment, and good humor sustained me when I most needed it. My son, Bradley, will not remember when Daddy raced to meet the deadlines for this book, but his entrance into my life gave me an additional reason to be happy and to be done. My wife, Stephanie, has brought immense happiness into my life. Her love and encouragement have contributed immeasurably to the completion of this project, and I cannot express in words how much I appreciate her.

In *Epidemics and Enslavement: Biological Catastrophe in the Native Southeast, 1492–1715,* Paul Kelton addresses important issues in the historiography of Native America: how do we explain the apparently dramatic population decline of indigenous people after European contact, and what impact did that have on the history of relations between Indian nations and European invaders? In his narrative of depopulation in the Southeast, Kelton addresses not only the epidemiological issues but also the historical ones. He sees epidemic disease as an intrinsic part of imperialism, which brought disease, determined its trajectory, and benefited from its deadly impact on Native people. Disease shaped economic relations and precipitated warfare between European colonies and indigenous nations, and it contributed to political struggles and realignment on both sides. The role of disease in cultural and historical change is a complex one, and Kelton masterfully weaves the strands together.

Contrary to popular impressions, Native America was not disease-free, but the European invasion brought new and deadlier germs, which originated in Eurasia with the cultural practice of keeping livestock. Once disease had taken root, Kelton holds the English, not the Spanish, and their insatiable demand for labor responsible for its spread. "[G]erms and captive raids," he writes, "worked synergistically to bring unprecedented and unparalleled depopulation in the Native Southeast." On political and economic levels, however, the two worked in opposition and undermined the relationship, rooted in the slave trade, that English colonies in the South had developed with Native nations. The interplay of disease and culture, of epidemiology and economics makes this an extraordinarily complex and sophisticated work, which will reinvigorate the debate over the role of disease in Native history.

Theda Perdue
Michael D. Green

Since the 1970s, Alfred Crosby's Columbian Exchange concept has made biology central to understanding European success in conquering the Americas. European colonization, Crosby emphasized, included much more than just people moving across the Atlantic. Europeans and indigenous peoples exchanged their microbes, flora, and fauna with each other and in doing so created profound changes that put the two groups of people on different historical trajectories. Europeans benefited by the acquisition of American crops, particularly carbohydrate-rich maize and potatoes, and they found an outlet for their increasing population in the Americas. Indigenous peoples of the Americas meanwhile died at alarming rates from the germs that colonizers carried in their bodies. Lacking acquired immunity to diseases such as smallpox and measles, Natives suffered catastrophic rates of infection and mortality. Scholars debate the numerical extent of Native depopulation, but they nonetheless agree that the Columbian Exchange created an epidemiological tragedy of monumental proportions and that without such a calamity European conquest and colonization would have been much more difficult if not impossible.[1]

Since Alfred Crosby first coined the phrase, the Columbian Exchange has justly deserved the scholarly attention it has received. This book adds to that growing literature and seeks to expand our understanding of colonization's biological impact on indigenous peoples. Specifically, I argue that the disease component of the Columbian Exchange was a mediated process in which the larger aspects of colonialism heightened Native vulnerability to infection and mortality. In other words, epidemics and massive death tolls among indigenous peoples occurred not simply due to their virginity to European- and African-introduced germs. Colonialism created conditions in which many new diseases could spread and in which those diseases produced extremely high fatality rates. Biological catastrophes certainly resulted with the arrival of infected Europeans and Africans in the Americas, but the dissemination of those germs to Natives and their impact on indigenous bodies also depended on nonbiological processes of colonialism.[2]

In the American Southeast, English-inspired commerce in Native slaves was the element of colonialism most responsible for making indigenous peoples across the region vulnerable to newly introduced diseases. Around the middle of the seventeenth century, labor-hungry Virginians escalated their acquisition of captives from their allied Native partners in exchange for manufactured goods. South Carolinians expanded both the volume and the geographic extent of such trade and brought indigenous communities as far west as the Mississippi River into the Atlantic market economy. When smallpox entered the English slave-trade network in 1696, an unprecedented biological catastrophe occurred that I call the Great Southeastern Smallpox Epidemic. This horrific event was not simply the result of a deadly virus being introduced to a previously unexposed population but stemmed from the Native slave trade facilitating the spread of such a lethal germ to communities that had been rather isolated from the outside world. The English quest for indigenous labor continued to shape the contours of epidemics in the early eighteenth century, but ultimately massive depopulation wiped out viable sources of potential captives, undermined economic relations between the English and their indigenous partners, and precipitated the Yamasee War in 1715, a conflict that essentially ended the Native slave trade. Before 1715, however, English commercialization of aboriginal practices of warfare and capture had created the deadliest period that southeastern Natives ever had with epidemics.[3]

While this book draws attention to the biological impact of English colonialism, it also addresses the epidemiological significance of Spanish colonialism on the Southeast. Prior to the advent of the Native slave trade, during a time scholars call the protohistoric period, the Spanish were the only Europeans to have a sustained presence in the region. Beginning in the early sixteenth century, the Spanish sent several exploratory parties into the Southeast, most notably Hernando de Soto's entrada, which entered Florida in 1539, headed north into the Carolina Piedmont, turned west across the Appalachian Mountains, and reached the Mississippi in 1542. Neither Soto nor any other Spanish explorer found the great wealth they were looking for, but the Spanish did establish a permanent outpost at St. Augustine in 1565 and thereafter established a string of Catholic missions stretching northward along the Georgia coast and westward along the Florida panhandle. Before the English even arrived on the scene then, indigenous peoples of the Greater Southeast potentially had experience with Columbian Exchange diseases. Documented outbreaks did occur among mission communities, making it seem possible that undocumented epidemics occurred beyond the purview of Europeans. Indeed, scholars generally date the arrival of the Atlantic world's deadliest diseases to the protohistoric period, while some believe that such arrival caused a population collapse as high as 90 percent before the mid-seventeenth century.[4]

With closer attention to disease ecology, however, this study suggests that the impact of newly introduced germs during the protohistoric period is often misunderstood and exaggerated. Each bacterial and viral species that accompanied Europeans and Africans to America depended on a complex set of ecological circumstances to become epidemic in a new environment. Some diseases, for example, cannot be transmitted directly from person to person without an insect vector. The presence or absence of the appropriate vectors of course determined whether an infected European or African was to spark an epidemic once he or she arrived in a new environment. Epidemics of person-to-person transmitted diseases also depend on ecological conditions such as settlement patterns, intercommunity trade, and hygiene practices. Instead of assuming, then, that the mere presence of the Europeans ignited region-wide epidemics, it must be asked whether indigenous peoples had disease ecologies that made them vulnerable to particular germs. It must also be asked whether the Spanish altered Native disease ecologies in a way to ignite region-wide epidemics. My analysis suggests that the protohistoric period was a time in which Columbian Exchange diseases had only a limited impact on the Greater Southeast. Specifically, malaria had a significant chance of becoming widespread and may have resulted in some demographic disruption, but that disease alone would not have produced the 90 percent population collapse that has been suggested. The deadliest scourges—smallpox, bubonic plague, measles, influenza—had only a slight potential of traveling beyond Catholic missions and into the Greater Southeast. Only after the English built an extensive trade network over the last half of the seventeenth century did conditions emerge that facilitated the thorough spread of the Columbian Exchange's most lethal germs.

Putting the protohistoric period in proper epidemiological perspective is of vital importance to southeastern specialists. Particularly, my analysis cautions scholars who read the archaeological record for evidence of a protohistoric occurrence of depopulation from newly introduced diseases.[5] Many of the population movements, abandoned communities, and collapsed polities that scholars have found in the archaeological record and attributed to epidemic disease can be attributed to nonepidemiological causes, and some can be linked to the tumultuous circumstances related to the Native slave trade. The coalescence of various communities into the historic polities known to us as the Cherokees, the Creeks, the Choctaws, and the Chickasaws, for example, originated with slave raiding rather than conjectured epidemics associated with preceding Spanish colonialism.[6] English colonialism, in other words, played the paramount role in radically transforming the social landscape from the heavily populated one that the Spanish found in the mid-sixteenth century to one inhabited by the smaller number of Native polities more familiarly known to us.

The Columbian Exchange may not have initiated the coalescence of the Cherokees, the Creeks, the Choctaws, and the Chickasaws, but diseases did play a role in their emergence as the most important Native polities in the eighteenth century. Newly introduced diseases, as this book will demonstrate, had a differential impact across the social landscape.[7] Between 1696 and 1715, pathogenic microbes arrived in rapid succession, giving indigenous peoples little reprieve and little chance to recover. Since every disease has a particular nature that distinguishes it from others, though, the combined impact of this onslaught varied across the region. The incubation and contagious periods vary from one germ to another; thus the ones that remain within their human hosts the longest became the most widespread. Natives who lived closer to colonial settlements faced multiple diseases, while those who lived farther away faced fewer and had lower overall rates of depopulation. Colonialism also contributed to epidemics having a differential impact. The slave trade especially heightened its victims' susceptibility to infection and mortality. Fearing gun-wielding slave raiders, Natives often could not maintain their usual subsistence routines and faced malnourishment. They also had to live in compact and fortified settlements where fairly typical germs associated with poor sanitation put their malnourished bodies in an even weaker state. It was, in fact, during the height of the Native slave trade that indigenous peoples suffered the worst biological consequences of colonialism as the deadly synergism of Columbian Exchange diseases, aboriginal germs, and malnourishment took a truly horrific toll. By 1715 much of the Coastal Plain, the Piedmont, the Gulf Coast, and the Mississippi Valley had been widowed of its aboriginal population. Some of the survivors fled into the interior to join the larger confederacies, while others remained near European settlements as either tributary communities or as depleted peoples on the verge of becoming so. The Cherokees, the Creeks, the Choctaws, and the Chickasaws all suffered depopulation from Columbian Exchange epidemics, but they experienced fewer diseases and could use their military power to protect themselves and even bring in captives to augment their sagging numbers.

While this study attempts to move the examination of infectious diseases and their impact on indigenous peoples in new directions, it employs the methodologies of two well-established fields: ethnohistory and environmental history. Scholars in these fields have employed anthropological concepts and epidemiological knowledge to develop a more complex view of European expansion, colonization, and the fate of Native peoples. Ethnohistorians point out that one cannot examine how indigenous groups responded to colonization without knowing what they were like before contact and before written records documented their past. Scholars in this field combine the evidentiary base of anthropology, such as the archaeological record, ethnography, and oral history, with documentary evidence to retell history from a more balanced perspective. They also pay particular attention to the cultures of indigenous peoples, examining cultural change and persistence as they interacted with colonial powers.[8] Environmental historians use ecological knowledge and concepts in retelling history not as a mere matter of people interacting among themselves but as human beings having a reciprocal relationship with all elements of nature, including the simplest of living matter—microbes. This reciprocal relationship continually produced ecological changes, ranging from minor unobservable phenomena to major catastrophes that fundamentally shaped broad patterns of our past.[9]

This book draws from other disciplines, but it remains a work of historical scholarship. It engages the two primary tasks that all historians must fulfill. First, historians must establish the sequence of events that compose the human past. In other words, they create narratives based on known facts arrayed in a chronological format. Second, historians attempt to explain why and how the past has developed. This involves asking questions, interpreting what we believe to be true, and analyzing what it all means. To be sure, the topic of this book necessitates an analysis that utilizes medical and anthropological concepts. Because colonial-era indigenous peoples did not leave written records and the biological forces that European observers poorly understood greatly affected Native actions, interpretation demands an interdisciplinary approach. Every effort, however, will be made to preserve the historian's preference for common language rather than scientific jargon.

Successfully combining narrative, analysis, and interpretation is a demanding task for any historian, but the structure of this book nonetheless attempts to accomplish that goal. Chapter 1 recreates the disease ecology of the Native Southeast as it existed before European contact, assessing how vulnerable indigenous peoples were to infection and mortality from Columbian Exchange germs. Chapter 2 focuses on Spanish colonialism during the protohistoric period. It carefully examines the potential epidemiological impact that exploration and colonization of Florida had on the greater Southeast. Chapter 3 moves the analysis to English colonialism in the last half of the seventeenth century. It reconstructs the development of English-inspired commerce in indigenous captives and then shows how the Great Southeastern Smallpox Epidemic followed the course of the Native slave trade. Chapter 4 continues to explore the ways in which the Native slave trade facilitated biological catastrophe in the early eighteenth century. It specifically focuses on the Yamasee War, a multitribal revolt against South Carolina whose origins lay in the biological catastrophes that the Native slave trade created.

By putting the Columbian Exchange into a larger colonial context, I neither intend to diminish the suffering that countless indigenous peoples went through, nor do I intend to obscure the horrendous legacy that infectious disease has left. Epidemiological disaster still remains vivid in the historical record and should continue to help understand European expansion and Native defeat. As this study shows, however, epidemics should be seen not as the inevitable consequence of biological forces but instead as contingent on the type of colonial system that Europeans chose to impose on the region and its indigenous inhabitants. In the Southeast, the English slave trade gave the Atlantic world's diseases the agency they needed to produce the stunning biological catastrophes that forever changed the historical trajectories of both Natives and newcomers.

Chapter One

Disease Ecology of the
Native Southeast
1000–1492

In 1492, the indigenous peoples of the Americas lacked experience with many of the nasty germs that had plagued Europeans, a fact that has led to both scholarly and popular characterizations of Native populations as "virgin soil." But despite its prevalence in historical discourse, the virginity metaphor is often misunderstood. Most troubling are misinterpretations of Native inexperience that imply indigenous peoples lacked the genetic immunity that Europeans and their descendants supposedly possessed due to years of exposure to common diseases.[1] Also problematic are studies that place such an emphasis on disease that they divorce germs from the larger context of colonialism and give them sole responsibility for the destruction of Native societies and the success of European invaders. Last, the metaphor of virginity, which historians have applied to Natives in general, obscures variable factors such as environment, settlement patterns, preexisting health status, subsistence routines, and exchange practices that mediated the spread of new pathogens and led to differential results among the indigenous population. Depictions of indigenous peoples as virgin soil have thus unfortunately obscured more than they have illuminated.

To appreciate the reality of Europe's biological impact on indigenous peoples in its full complexity, an approach that goes beyond the virgin-soil metaphor is needed. That approach is one of disease ecology. Once having arrived in the Americas, germs entered into a new environment in which potential host populations had a set of ecological relationships that were different from those of former hosts in Europe and Africa. Novel diseases did not spread whenever and wherever they were introduced, and they did not spread like "wildfire" simply because Natives were virgins. Instead, epidemiological results depended on the new and varying environmental circumstances in which germs were deposited and on how other aspects of colonialism disrupted the preexisting disease ecology of indigenous peoples.

To illustrate the importance of disease ecology in understanding the impact of postcontact epidemics, consider the various ways people become infected. Pathogenic microbes are all around, but all do not enter human bodies in the same way; a variety of delivery vectors exists. First, the physical environment—the water one drinks and the soil in which one grows food—can harbor free-living pathogens and those expelled from infected peoples or animals. Such water- or soil-borne germs are especially troublesome for communities with poor sanitation. Second, animals can infect people with some diseases, known as zoonoses. When people share the same habitat with certain wild animals or keep domestic livestock, their chances of becoming infected increase substantially. Feces and urine of animals can pollute water and soil with a variety of pathogenic microbes, and of course, people must always be aware of the dangers of consuming contaminated meat. Humans also must be wary of an animal's bite, such as that of a mosquito, which can potentially deliver a number of different pathogens into their bloodstream. Third, humans themselves serve as a vector for infection. Microbes are transmitted directly from one victim to another through sneezing, coughing, or diarrhea, or through the exchange of blood, semen, or other bodily fluids. Such human-to-human contact varies substantially with population size, density, and settlement patterns. The physical environment, animals, and humans all play a role in determining whether a pathogen, once introduced to a host community, will spread successfully among multiple victims, causing an epidemic.

Once infected, the chances of individuals dying from diseases depend considerably on environmental circumstances. Here one needs to look at nongenetic factors that shape the level of health and well-being of host populations. The connection between malnutrition and infection is widely known, as hungry and famine-stricken people are more susceptible to contracting diseases and dying from them. Nutritional and calorie deficiencies retard the immune response and accelerate mortality among infected groups. Similarly, diseases are known to work synergistically with each other; people suffering from one disease have a reduced ability to fight off infection from another germ. A high pathogen load—numerous preexisting infections—compromises the immune systems of victims of new diseases, causing death rates to surpass what would be expected among an otherwise healthy population. Whether host populations maintain access to an appropriate amount of nutritious food and whether they live in a relatively disease-free or disease-filled environment are key questions in understanding their vulnerability.

The Native Southeast provides a particularly intriguing area to examine how disease ecology shaped the impact of postcontact epidemics. Home to the famous "mound builders," the region has a rich archaeological record from which we can assess how vulnerable indigenous peoples were in their native state. On the surface, the southeastern population may appear to have been especially predisposed to suffer catastrophic epidemics after Europeans brought new germs to the region. The Native Southeast contained some of the largest, most complex, and most densely populated polities north of Mexico. One might be tempted to assume that once deposited anywhere in the region new germs would have easily proliferated and spread, causing major losses throughout the Native population even before sustained contact with Europeans and Africans developed. A closer look at the disease ecology of the region, however, suggests that the nonepidemiological aspects of colonialism had to transform the lives of Natives before they became vulnerable to regionwide outbreaks. An examination of the disease ecology of the Native Southeast indeed leads to a conclusion that biological forces necessarily depended on colonialism's economic aspects, which should receive primacy in explaining Europe's successful conquest of the Americas.

Horticultural Transition

To understand the disease ecology of the Native Southeast, one must begin with the land itself. Indigenous peoples lived over a wide expanse of territory, covering many distinct subregions. At the center of this diverse landscape stands the Appalachian Highlands, whose ancient rounded peaks reach elevations of over six thousand feet and provide the headwaters for the region's many rivers. Down each side of the Appalachian Divide, rivers move swiftly through narrow valleys before emerging out of the highlands. To the east these rivers pour into the somewhat larger valleys of the Piedmont, an area of rolling hills that widens as it arches along the Appalachians from Virginia to Alabama. At the eastern edge of the Piedmont, elevation drops sharply, creating a series of rapids known as the Fall Line, which mark the beginning of the Coastal Plain. This swath of land begins in Virginia, expands south, curves west, and then extends up along both sides of the Mississippi Valley. The region's rivers slow considerably as they move through the Coastal Plain, carving wide valleys with numerous oxbow lakes and swamps before reaching their ocean destination. The coastline itself presents a diverse landscape with its sandy dunes, marshes, reefs, islands, and bays arrayed at seemingly random locations. On the western slope of the Appalachian Highlands, rugged foothills and plateaus compose yet another distinct subregion, known as the Ridge and Valley Province. There various tributaries meet to form the westward flowing Tennessee. This meandering river cuts a broad valley through the heart of the Southeast and serves as a southern boundary to an area of hills, cliffs, and bluffs known as the Cumberland Plateau.[2]

For thousands of years, indigenous peoples had lived in this land and subsisted on a wide variety of wild game and produce. White-tailed deer served as the most important source of animal protein. This species could be found in large numbers in heavily forested upland areas, where it avoided predators and feasted on acorns, but riverine and coastal environments also attracted this ubiquitous animal. Turkeys and raccoons abounded throughout the Southeast as well, yielding a surprisingly large amount of meat. Bears, more difficult to hunt and less numerous, nonetheless drew the attention of hunters. Natives consumed their flesh and rendered their fat into oil, which had dietary, cosmetic, and prophylactic uses. A portion of the Native diet also consisted of smaller game such as squirrels, opossums, rabbits, turtles, and other mammals, which became especially useful when deer hunters had failed in their endeavors. Aquatic-related species provided yet another vital source of food. Fish and waterfowl thrived in the region's numerous rivers, swamps, oxbow lakes, lagoons, bays, and estuaries. In these same places, indigenous peoples found emergency sustenance in the form of clams, oysters, mussels, and other shellfish. Gathering supplied even more nourishment for the Native population. Various nuts, berries, and roots provided valuable additions to the indigenous diet.[3]

While the ancient practices of hunting, fishing, and gathering remained important for all Natives, the Southeast ultimately became a land of farmers. Horticulture in fact has a long history in the region. Sometime between 2500 and 1500 BC, indigenous peoples in the eastern woodlands had successfully domesticated four plant species, including sunflower, sumpweed, goosefoot, and squash. Indigenous peoples may have valued squash more as a container, but they consumed its seeds too. Three other cultivated plants—knotweed, maygrass, and little barley—were added to the Native diet between 500 and 200 BC These crops originated from wild species native to the region that hunting and gathering tribes selected for their edible seeds. Over time foragers learned to plant these seeds near their base camps and to reap a dependable harvest. Nevertheless, indigenous crops never composed a majority of any Native community's dietary intake. These plants, while high in nutritional value, yielded a low volume of edible food and provided little return to farmers for their efforts. The subsistence

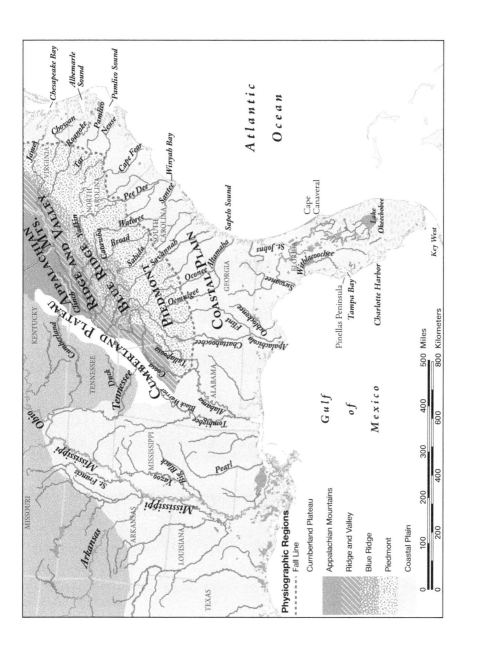

Physiographic Regions

----- Fall Line

Cumberland Plateau

Appalachian Mountains

Ridge and Valley

Blue Ridge

Piedmont

Coastal Plain

0   100   200   300   400   500 Miles
0   200   400   600   800 Kilometers

MISSOURI

KENTUCKY

TENNESSEE

VIRGINIA

NORTH CAROLINA

SOUTH CAROLINA

GEORGIA

ALABAMA

MISSISSIPPI

ARKANSAS

LOUISIANA

TEXAS

FLORIDA

Atlantic Ocean

Gulf of Mexico

CUMBERLAND PLATEAU

APPALACHIAN MTS.

RIDGE AND VALLEY

BLUE RIDGE

PIEDMONT

COASTAL PLAIN

Ohio

Mississippi

St. Francis

Arkansas

Cumberland

Tennessee

Duck

Black Warrior

Tombigbee

Alabama

Coosa

Tallapoosa

Pearl

Big Black

Yazoo

Chattahoochee

Flint

Apalachicola

Ocmulgee

Oconee

Altamaha

Savannah

Saluda

Broad

Catawba

Wateree

Santee

Pee Dee

Yadkin

Chowan

James

Roanoke

Tar

Neuse

Cape Fear

Pamlico

Winyah Bay

Sapelo Sound

Withlacoochee

Suwannee

St. Johns

Pinellas Peninsula

Tampa Bay

Charlotte Harbor

Lake Okeechobee

Cape Canaveral

Key West

Chesapeake Bay

Albemarle Sound

Pamlico Sound

Chattooga

routines of indigenous peoples continued to revolve around seasonal movement to acquire the great bulk of their food through hunting, fishing, and gathering.[4]

Horticulture did not dominate the subsistence routines of southeastern Natives until the arrival of maize. Maize, originally domesticated in Mesoamerica around 3500 BC, appeared in the Southeast as early as AD 200 but did not immediately transform the subsistence routines of indigenous peoples. The first species to arrive were small and provided little more food than native cultigens. Natives did not turn to this new vegetable out of hunger, then, but grew small amounts to augment their diets much as they had native crops. For hundreds of years, hunting and gathering peoples experimented with corn as a supplemental crop, but after much experimentation, indigenous peoples ultimately found maize to be a dependable vegetable. By AD 900, maize species had become much more resistant to drought, larger in cob length, and far richer in carbohydrates than the earliest varieties. Whether these changes occurred due to later imports from other regions or through Natives repeatedly selecting seeds from their hardiest plants is unknown, but what is certain is that agriculture was becoming a much more important activity in the lives of indigenous peoples. By AD 1250, beans, another Mesoamerican domesticate, had been adopted into the agricultural practices of Natives, and the well-known vegetable triad of corn, beans, and squash had become complete.[5]

The transition to horticulture led to important biological changes for indigenous peoples. The higher volume of calories that corn made available resulted in a population explosion. This demographic increase may have been due in part to changes in female bodies that allowed them to have more babies. Much like modern-day athletes, women in hunting and gathering societies lived strenuous lives, keeping themselves lean and consequently less fertile. Female fertility consequently increased as they changed to a more sedentary lifestyle and consumed a higher volume of calories.[6] Changes in the way children were fed more certainly increased the birthrate. Maize when processed into gruel provided an alternative food source for infants, permitting mothers to wean their children at an earlier age than hunter-gatherers. Shortened periods of breastfeeding allowed women to conceive sooner after giving birth and produce more children over the course of their lives.[7] This gradual increase in population, which was probably imperceptible to Natives, created increasing demands for food and thus led people to rely more on corn. Deer consumption had, in fact, fallen well below what earlier peoples had eaten as the growing human population put increasing demands on wild game species.[8] The turn to full-time farming came not with an abrupt crisis but as a gradual development in which indigenous peoples passed an imperceptible point of no return. After they initially experimented with corn, the fertility of women increased, populations rose, and competition for wild resources became fierce, so Natives had to grow more maize. The cycle continued beyond the point at which indigenous peoples could do without horticulture.[9]

Not only did farming increase female fertility, but it also made sex ratios more favorable for increased reproduction rates. Hunters and gatherers placed a premium on male labor, selecting greater numbers of females for infanticide.[10] Hunters and gatherers also consciously attempted to keep population low; pregnant females and infants meant more mouths to feed and inhibited mobility as tribes made their seasonal subsistence rounds. Horticultural peoples practiced infanticide less. Their sedentary life made mobility less important; women and children could stay at home, where food was readily available.[11] Also, female labor was critical in producing this food.[12] With more females surviving childhood, greater numbers of women reached reproductive age than in hunting and gathering societies. When Natives made the horticultural transition, their sex ratios consequently became more balanced. Although the evidence is not clear, it may well be the case that sex ratios among Native agriculturalists were skewed toward more women; men, who still engaged in the hazardous activities of hunting and warfare, most likely had a greater chance of suffering an earlier death and not reaching reproductive age. Regardless of its impact on sex ratios, the spread of maize-intensive horticulture led to population growth throughout the Southeast.

In addition to increases in population, the way Natives physically constructed their communities changed as well. As the transition to horticulture spread across the region, Native groups became more permanently attached to particular locations. Hunter-gatherers often returned to favorite spots where they had good fortune in finding food, and they had seasonal camps where they remained for extended periods, but the Native Southeast took on a new look when people switched the focus of their subsistence routines to farming. People had to remain close to their crops during the growing season to protect them from scavengers and enemies, while abundant harvests made movement during fall and winter difficult. Surplus crops needed to be stored and guarded year around, making permanent settlements necessary to maintain a horticultural-based subsistence economy. Many of these settlements were carefully planned towns, usually consisting of at least one earthen mound, a plaza, and an assortment of public buildings, which together functioned as the ceremonial center for the religious and political activities of a community.[13]

Arrayed near these ceremonial centers were residential dwellings, but the patterns in which they were arranged varied throughout the region. At one end of the settlement spectrum, indigenous peoples constructed nucleated towns, with populations numbering in the hundreds and in some cases in the thousands. Most nucleated towns involved the presence of ceremonial structures, including one or more earthen mounds, public buildings, and numerous individual households, all enclosed behind defensive palisades. At the other end of the spectrum, Natives lived in dispersed communities. Instead of living next door to each other, families scattered their households over the countryside; in some cases, communities stretched for several miles. Members of these households remained linked and came together periodically at their centrally located ceremonial center. Such dispersed communities, although nearly invisible to us today, outnumbered nucleated towns, which have received the bulk of scholarly attention due to their survival in the archaeological record.[14] Native peoples preferred to live in dispersed communities because they promoted the most efficient use of resources. Wood, in particular, became scarce near a nucleated town after a few generations of settlement. Fires for cooking and heating placed the highest demand on this resource, but construction of canoes, houses, palisades, and ceremonial buildings also required significant quantities of wood. Individuals living in long-settled nucleated communities also found themselves traveling increasingly farther to acquire other resources, including clay for pottery, stones for weapons and tools, and wild roots, nuts, and berries. Such long-distance travel was not only tiresome but also dangerous as individuals had to venture well beyond the safe confines of their towns.[15]

Most important, indigenous peoples preferred dispersed settlement patterns because they lessened the risks associated with horticulture. Most communities pooled their labor to cultivate communal fields, but relying exclusively on these fields posed a serious danger. Disasters such as droughts, floods, insect invasion, plant diseases, and enemy sabotage could ruin an entire season's harvest and bring community-wide famine.[16] Garden plots associated with scattered households increased a group's surplus while at the same time providing insurance against crop failure. Except in the case of extreme droughts, disasters usually did not destroy everyone's gardens, giving those who did lose their harvests someone to whom to turn for food. Communal fields also brought the potential problem of soil depletion. Beans, with their nitrogen-fixing abilities, compensated for the high demand for nutrients that maize placed on the soil, but generations of planting at times outstripped this complementary relationship and led to steadily declining crop yields.[17] To survive indefinitely, nucleated towns had to have access to extensive stretches of fertile soil, something that was not always possible because such areas attracted the largest concentration of settlements.

Dispersed communities proved to be more resilient. Their constituent households could make use of areas with spotty patches of fertile soil and could shift locations without causing much friction with rival communities.

While indigenous peoples preferred to live in a dispersed fashion, settlement nucleation did occur periodically at ceremonial centers. In the spring, for example, families congregated to plant communal fields and celebrate rituals to ensure a bountiful harvest. During the growing season, a small resident population took care of a community's sacred space, while people generally remained near their homesteads, tending their fields and gathering wild foods. As maize began to ripen, families again came together at their ceremonial center to celebrate the first harvest. In the late fall, hunting parties left for their seasonal quests for game, leaving a dearth of warriors to protect individual homesteads. Towns then became safe places where agricultural surpluses as well as women, children, and the elderly found protection. As warm weather approached, communities again took on a dispersed look. Early spring was a time of scarcity, necessitating families to scatter, seeking wild plant foods and roots before cultivation could occur. Early spring was also a time in which floodwaters made at least some ceremonial centers uninhabitable. Mound sites are usually located on floodplains, and archaeologists have found a number of these sites prone to seasonal inundation. As spring advanced, the weather warmed, the waters receded, and people again congregated at their community's center, beginning the cycle of dispersion and nucleation again.[18]

Some communities, however, found it very difficult to disperse at all. Despite the disadvantages of nucleation, some towns in the Native Southeast had a large population of permanent residents. To understand why some communities chose such compact arrangements, one only has to look at the physical construction of their towns. Several communities occupied the banks of rivers not simply because of the good soil they found there but because rivers offered a boundary that approaching enemies found difficult to cross without detection. These same towns further surrounded themselves with palisades and even moats to defend themselves against rivals who approached from other directions.[19] Not coincidentally, the bow and arrow made its appearance in the Southeast at the same time that these nucleated settlements popped up across the region. Palisades especially offered a large degree of protection from this new weapon and made siege warfare virtually impossible. High walls with thick poles shielded community members from arrows while at the same time allowing their own warriors to return volleys through small openings against their exposed enemies.[20] Occasionally, rivals breached a community's palisades, subdued its people, and burned its buildings. The difficulty of doing this, though, led Natives to prefer ambushes and raids, battle methods that made living in dispersed settlements especially hazardous.[21]

Nucleated settlement patterns thus reflected the decision of indigenous communities to place more emphasis on defense rather than on efficient resource use.[22] Compact towns, however, should not be linked exclusively with chiefdom-level political organization.[23] It is tempting to conclude that palisades and other defensive structures demonstrate the emergence of a dominant leadership class that could command the labor of commoners and that tribal societies lacked the coercive power to construct such sophisticated works of civic architecture. Settlement patterns, though, remained dynamic regardless of how a polity was organized. On one hand, the most powerful chiefdoms in the Southeast may have built the largest towns with the most numerous mounds, but such ceremonial centers did not necessarily remain occupied year around by a resident population. Rural homesteads remained the preferred settlement type when conditions allowed for dispersion. On the other hand, members of egalitarian communities, when suffering from endemic warfare, were capable of banding together and constructing fortified towns.[24]

Warfare rather than political organization was the most important variable in shaping settlement patterns in the Native Southeast. Geography certainly played a role too, but location did not necessarily bind people to either dispersion or nucleation. As a general rule, living near extensive stretches of fertile soil made it easier for indigenous communities to build compact settlements, while residence where fertile soil was patchier made nucleation more difficult. Compact towns did appear more frequently in the Mississippi Valley and the upper Coastal Plain than they did in the Highlands, the Piedmont, and the lower Coastal Plain, which also did not support intensive maize cultivation. But the land itself did not determine that human settlement would be nucleated; instead, it was competition for these particularly resource-rich areas that put Native communities into a defensive posture. Indigenous peoples favored the Mississippi Valley and the upper Coastal Plain, especially the area just below the Fall Line, because both places offered deep, rich soil that yielded large harvests and oxbow lakes with abundant waterfowl and aquatic species. Those areas also gave indigenous peoples access to broad upland areas that separated the region's major river valleys, where Native hunters pursued the white-tailed deer in seemingly vast forests. Even in this most resource-rich area of the Southeast, though, dispersed settlement patterns remained the preferred option; conversely in areas with patchier soil, indigenous peoples constructed nucleated towns when they seemed the safest way to live. Over the several hundred years before the European invasion, for example, communities in the Appalachian highlands constructed compact towns surrounded by palisades, even though they lived in narrow valleys lacking extensive stretches of fertile soil, while residents of the Mississippi Valley shifted their settlements between nucleation and dispersion, despite the fact that they maintained access to the river's broad floodplains, which could support vast and continuous cornfields.[25]

Any model for aboriginal settlement patterns based on geography or political organization presents a static view of what was a dynamic situation. Nucleation need not be seen as a consequence of location or chiefdom development, and scholars should be cautious in interpreting the dispersion of formerly compact towns as evidence of radical change in the political structure of indigenous societies. Settlement patterns varied over time as warfare waxed and waned. Some communities undoubtedly remained nucleated for several generations but then managed to establish more peaceful relations with rivals, allowing them to live in a more dispersed fashion. Conversely, some communities that had maintained dispersed settlements for years found it necessary to coalesce when an invading enemy made living apart more dangerous. Such alterations in aboriginal settlement patterns, indeed, were of vital significance because they had important health implications for Native peoples both before and, even more so, after the arrival of European colonialism and its germs.

Aboriginal Health

Indigenous peoples must have known that living in nucleated communities provided more safety and that such a decision came at the cost of making resource acquisition more difficult, but they were probably unaware of another detriment associated with living in compact towns—a hidden detriment to the health and well-being of individual community members that would make them even more vulnerable to diseases introduced after 1492. As Native communities became more concentrated and more reliant on maize, indigenous bodies paid a great price. Nutritional deficiencies and aboriginal diseases proliferated among the most nucleated and war-ridden communities, creating health problems across the Native Southeast that would later help shape the contours of death and survival during postcontact epidemics.

The transition to horticulture presents a paradox. Maize production enhanced female fertility and catalyzed population expansion, but at the same time indigenous peoples who depended on farming displayed considerably higher rates of infant mortality and shorter life expectancies than their hunting and gathering ancestors.[26] In AD 950, for example, foragers at the Larson site on the Lower Illinois River were living on average to the age of 26 and saw 13 percent of their infants die before their first birthday. After taking up farming for about one hundred years, these same people could expect to live only to the age of 19 and could expect 22 percent of their infants to perish shortly after birth. Growth rates substantially slowed as well, with 5- to 10-year-old farming children much smaller in stature than their hunting and gathering cohort.[27] Other sites had even shorter life expectancies. Individuals living at Toqua, a horticultural town on the Little Tennessee River, could expect to live 16.1 years.[28] Such a statistic does not tell the full story either. Women probably had a shorter life expectancy than did men. In communities on the Cumberland River dated to AD 1350, for example, males lived on average to 17.4 years of age, while the average age at death for females was 14.6 years.[29] Nine hundred years earlier, when indigenous peoples did not have maize as a major part of their diet, life expectancies had reached as high as 29.5 years.[30]

Shorter life expectancies did not result exclusively from worsening health conditions, of course. People may have died younger due to increasing levels of violence that plagued the Native Southeast during the horticultural transition. Nevertheless, skeletal analyses provide ample evidence that indigenous peoples experienced much higher rates of nutritional deficiencies after becoming intensive maize cultivators. Specifically, archaeologists have discovered numerous southeastern skeletons with porotic hyperstosis, a disorder involving lesions on the cranial vault and eye orbits that indicate iron-deficiency anemia.[31] At the Larson site, one-half of horticultural infants and children displayed porotic hyperstosis, suggesting that the rate of anemia doubled with the transition to intensive maize cultivation.[32] At Cahokia, the largest mound center in the eastern woodlands, the rate of anemia remained substantially lower than at Larson, but even at this most impressive site the percentage of individuals with iron-deficiency jumped from 7 percent in AD 1150 to 25 percent by AD 1400.[33] Physical anthropologists describe populations at other southeastern sites as "severely debilitated" and having anemia in "epidemic proportions."[34] Anemia, as most people know, leads to fatigue, but in severe cases the disorder can result in immune suppression, cardiovascular complications, and shortened life expectancies. It was especially detrimental to the health of women. The shorter lifespan of women in the highly stressed Cumberland communities can be attributed in part to the fact that menstruation and pregnancy increase the need for iron.[35]

The connection between nutritional deficiencies and maize cultivation is not coincidental. Maize is dismally poor in protein and iron, and it lacks two amino acids, lysine and tryptophan, which aid the body in absorbing iron. By processing corn in lime to make hominy, Natives further depleted their bodies of iron by adding excess calcium to their diets.[36] Indigenous horticulturalists, of course, did not live on corn alone, and they attempted to maintain diverse diets similar to those of preceding foraging tribes. They may not have been aware of the detrimental effect of corn or conscious that their ancestors led more robust lives, but they continued to hunt game and gather wild roots, nuts, and berries. They also could rely on beans to some extent to provide some of the nutrients that corn lacked. The archaeological evidence, though, indicates that among some populations compensatory strategies were not enough to stave off anemia; many peoples depended too much on maize.[37] The increasing problem of finding fresh meat during the horticultural transition probably led to this overreliance. With the human population increasing, competition for deer and other game animals became intense. Those tribes that found themselves unable to compete turned more to corn to alleviate their hunger and unconsciously exacerbated their health problems. This solution must have seemed necessary to keep hungry mouths fed, to prevent starvation, and to keep communities intact, but such actions to promote group survival came at the expense of individual health.[38]

Ultimately, horticultural solutions posed challenges to group survival as well. Indigenous peoples must have seen maize as a solution to satiate the appetites of a growing population, but by depending more and more on farming they made themselves increasingly vulnerable to ecological disaster and acute periods of hunger. During most growing seasons, Natives could count on reaping a bountiful harvest from southeastern soils. The region was blessed with abundant rainfall, which usually peaked during the spring and caused annual flooding that left layers of rich soil along the banks of the region's many rivers. The crops derived from this soil could be stored and used to feed a community during the late winter and early spring, typically when game became scarce and wild produce had yet to ripen. This was the season in which hunting and gathering populations suffered deprivation. Horticulturalists, while avoiding these seasonal periods of want, nonetheless exposed themselves to more serious dangers. Sometimes the rains seemed never to stop falling from the southeastern sky, causing summer flooding that washed away an entire season's worth of crops, while other times little rain fell at all, leaving an entire community's corn to wither and die under the hot sun. Crops were also vulnerable to insect invasion, enemy sabotage, and plant diseases. Whatever the cause of crop failure, indigenous peoples went without the food that supplied the bulk of their calories and were forced to rely

on hunting, gathering, and fishing. These activities, which had adequately supplied an earlier population of hunter-gatherers, could not bring in enough sustenance to properly feed large horticultural communities. What followed was not
a normal period of want but a severe crisis that lasted for months on end, causing
starvation and death among community members.

In every event of famine, infectious diseases became more deadly. And horticultural peoples had more diseases to deal with compared to their hunting and
gathering ancestors. Some southeastern communities, in fact, displayed high
pathogen loads and had populations with severely compromised health. This
may be surprising to some students of indigenous peoples, especially after study-
ing the Columbian Exchange. But Natives did have experience with countless
infectious diseases. Many of these were ancient afflictions that had plagued humanity's primate ancestors and continued to infect hunting and gathering peoples as they made their way across the globe. Other germs included fairly typical
ones, picked up from the environment.

Whether foragers or farmers, all Natives suffered from diseases. Relying heavily on game for food and clothing, indigenous peoples exposed themselves to a
number of zoonoses found among the wildlife population. The rabies virus
(*Lyssavirus sp.*) was most likely present in the pre-Columbian environment, and
some unlucky individuals certainly suffered from this fatal disease after being
bitten by an infected wild animal or dog. Animal bites could have also infected
indigenous peoples with dangerous bacteria that cause tularemia (*Francisella tu-
larensis*) and possibly anthrax (*Bacillus anthracis*). Both of these diseases can also
be transmitted through means other than a bite. Tularemia, which was most
likely indigenous to the Americas, results from skinning the carcasses or consuming the meat of infected wild game such as beaver and rabbits.[39] Anthrax,
whose presence in the Americas is debated, usually results from handling hides
and other tissues of infected herbivores.[40] While any case of rabies, tularemia, or
anthrax certainly proved serious and even deadly, all of these diseases remained
rare. All find human beings dead ends in the chain of infection. People cannot
transmit the germs that cause these diseases to others; thus these diseases remained individual afflictions rather than community-wide outbreaks.

Southeastern Natives were also familiar with zoonotic illnesses contracted by
consuming raw or undercooked meat. Diseases such as trichinosis and brucellosis are ancient and nearly global afflictions. The roundworm, *Trichinella spi-
ralis,* causes trichinosis and can be found not only in swine, its best-known host,
but also a number of game animals indigenous to the Americas.[41] This parasite,
as is the case with other worms that humans acquire from consuming animal

flesh, can cause serious damage to the body. At the very least, it robs the body of much needed nutrients, and at worst it prevents the proper function of vital organs and causes death.[42] Bacteria belonging to the genus *Brucella* can also be found in a variety of wild and domestic animals, including bison and deer—the most commonly consumed game among indigenous peoples of North America. Human victims of the disease suffer from a variety of symptoms including fever, headache, chills, and generalized aching. Fatalities from the disease are rare, even in untreated cases, but the bacteria often will affect the joints and cause permanent disabilities.[43] Fortunately, the germs that cause both trichinosis and brucellosis have remained only accidental residents of the human body. Infected individuals cannot transmit the disease to another person. Instead, the parasites remain endemic among other animal species.[44]

Other endemic diseases among animals made the jump to humans through insect vectors.[45] Indigenous peoples of South America certainly experienced two protozoan diseases, American trypanosomiasis (Chagas' disease), spread by blood-sucking bugs belonging to the genus *Reduviidae,* and leishmaniasis, spread by certain species of sandflies.[46] Indigenous peoples of North America did not suffer from those illnesses, but they did contract other zoonoses from insect vectors. Ticks in particular presented a threat for disease transmission. These bugs can carry a number of different bacteria, viruses, and rickettsia (microorganisms more complex than viruses but less complex than bacteria) from animals to humans. One serious tick-borne germ is *Rickettsia rickettsii,* which causes Rocky Mountain spotted fever. Despite its name, the disease occurs throughout North America, with highest infection rates in the Southeast.[47] A vast reservoir of animals, including rodents and dogs, harbors this deadly germ and likely has for thousands of years.[48] Lyme disease, which appears to be new due to recent outbreaks in the eastern United States, also may have a pre-Columbian origin. Ticks acquire the bacteria, *Borrelia burgdorferi,* from white-tailed deer, which probably harbored the disease long before Europeans arrived. With the resurgence of this wild game species in recent times, cases of Lyme disease have consequently increased, especially in wooded suburban areas.[49] Despite the seriousness of many tick-borne illnesses, such diseases involve individuals rather than whole communities. Ticks, of course, attach themselves to their host and feed on a single individual for an extended period of time, rather than biting multiple people over the course of their short lives. And once again, humans are a dead end; people cannot transmit the disease directly to another person and often end up killing the tick that infected them in the first place.

Mosquitoes also possibly served as a vector that infected indigenous peoples with zoonoses. The most familiar mosquito-borne diseases are malaria and yellow fever, which for reasons explained later were certainly not problems for indigenous peoples, but a number of lesser-known illnesses can result from a mosquito's bite. A variety of viruses found in the wildlife population occasionally make their way to humans. Most of these result in mild symptoms that, depending on the particular virus, may include fever, encephalitis, and rashes. Human exposure to mosquito-borne illnesses, of course, increased with the domestication of animals. Herd animals provided an ample reservoir for viruses, and mosquitoes that fed on the blood of these animals certainly injected such germs into the bloodstreams of nearby human herders. Because indigenous peoples in the American Southeast did not keep herd animals, they had a greatly reduced chance of acquiring mosquito-borne diseases. But wild animals still served as a reservoir, and Natives, especially those who lived near mosquito-laden areas, occasionally became infected.

When southeastern Natives made the transition to horticulture, their experience with zoonoses did not change dramatically. If anything, their reliance on crops lessened their exposure to infected wildlife and some insect vectors by lessening the time indigenous peoples devoted to hunting and gathering in wooded areas. The switch to intensive maize production, however, did increase their exposure to a wide variety of other germs and in fact elevated the pathogen load that individuals carried in their bodies.

When humans settled down to live in permanent communities, they made it easier for bacteria to be transmitted from one person to another. Unlike hunter-gatherers, horticulturalists moved away from their filth less often, creating more opportunities for common bacteria, which had always been a problem for humankind, to produce disease.[50] These bacteria include *staphylococci, streptococci, gonococci, pneumococci, diplococci,* and *meningococci,* generally harmless common travelers on and in the human body that may be beneficial but can cause disease when accidentally introduced into areas of the body in which they normally do not live. A number of bacteria, for example, inhabit the human intestinal tract and aid in digestion, but when one ingests these germs into the stomach through fecal-contaminated water or food, the dreaded bouts of diarrhea known as dysentery can occur. *Staphylococcus* and other companion bacteria also can become the source of secondary infection, producing illness when one's immunity has become diminished from another disease or from factors such as malnutrition, trauma, and stress. Pneumonia, of course, is a classic example of this phenomenon. It undoubtedly afflicted the earliest humans, continued to afflict people as they crossed into the Americas, and became even more problematic when an increased pathogen load reduced the immunity of horticulturalists. Equally serious, commensal bacteria can cause septicemia, a dangerous illness more familiarly known as "blood poisoning." This results when *staphylococci* or other bacteria, which normally inhabit the skin, invade the bloodstream through open skin wounds.[51]

Indigenous peoples also became infected by a variety of disease-causing germs that lived outside their bodies. In general, Natives lived cleanlier lives than Europeans did on the eve of colonization, but they did live in a time before water-purification systems, disinfectants, and other measures of sanitation lessened the pathogen load for many human beings, at least those in developed nations. Several types of disease-causing bacteria are ubiquitous in nature and undoubtedly caused problems for indigenous peoples. Clostridia bacteria, for example, live in the soil but infect humans in a variety of nasty ways. These germs will grow on food, leaving the toxins that cause botulism. These same bacteria also can germinate in open flesh wounds, causing the serious diseases of gangrene and tetanus. Similarly, *staphylococci* and *salmonella* bacteria can grow on food and accumulate in porous ceramic pots and inflict individuals with a serious case of food intoxication ("food poisoning"). Not every Native, of course, suffered from these dreaded bacterial infections within his or her lifetime, but such diseases were not rare either. They have been ancient and frequent afflictions of the human species, affecting us from our primate origins to the present day.[52] Indigenous peoples, like all humans before recent times, learned that thoroughly cooking food, bathing, and carefully treating wounds helped to prevent much suffering, but they were never free from the pathogenic and invisible microbes of which they had no knowledge.

Although hunter-gatherers were experienced with bacterial infections, the archaeological record of the Native Southeast bears telling evidence of an increased pathogen load that came with the horticultural transition. Systemic bacterial infections leave their mark on the body by destroying the connective tissue covering the bones or periosteum. At the Larson site, for example, only 26 percent of the skeletal remains of hunter-gatherers displayed periosteal reactions, while 84 percent of a genetically related population displayed bacterial damage several generations after taking up farming.[53] At the Toqua site, 77 percent of the skeletal remains of the birth to one-year-old population had periosteal reactions, probably as a result of pneumonia, septicemia, staphylococcal infection, or gastroenteritis.[54] Such infection undoubtedly increased infant mortality rates, which for Toqua and other nearby sites was one-third of all children dying before they reached five years of age.[55]

Water served as a major source for the contaminants that infected settled horticulturalists. Hunter-gatherers certainly came down with waterborne diseases.
Wherever humans have traveled, they have picked up a variety of free-living bacteria and protozoa from their water supply, causing much misery from dysentery, fevers, and other ailments.[56] Horticultural communities, though, have
been much more prone to such diseases, as their own wastes often circulated
with the water they used for cooking, bathing, and drinking. In the Native
Southeast, many indigenous communities made themselves especially vulnerable to waterborne diseases by locating their settlements along oxbow lakes and
swamps. There, indigenous peoples found ideal soil for growing crops and an
abundance of waterfowl and game fish, but at the same time these nearly stagnant bodies of water served as reservoirs for a variety of pathogens, either free-
living or deposited there through the wastes of nearby human inhabitants.

Typhoid was one possible waterborne illness that afflicted indigenous peoples. The presence of this germ in the Americas before 1492 is uncertain, but
some evidence suggests that it was an aboriginal disease. Typhoid bacteria (*Salmonella typhi*) infect turtles, leading one to suspect that Indians contracted the
disease from these animals when the two shared the same habitat or when Indians consumed turtle meat.[57] After infecting their host, the typhoid bacteria incubate for one to three weeks, after which time the germ causes a variety of
symptoms including headache, sustained fever, despondency, anorexia, slowness
of heartbeat, enlargement of the spleen, rose spots on the body, and bowel problems that involve constipation in some and diarrhea in others. Symptoms can
last for up to three weeks, during which time infected victims excrete millions of
the bacteria back into the environment through urination or defecation. In
modern times typhoid is a serious disease but not one of the deadliest, having a
case fatality rate among untreated victims of 10 percent. The disease is also widespread. For up to three months after symptoms disappear, 10 percent of typhoid
survivors harbor *Salmonella typhi,* and an even smaller percentage become permanent carriers, capable of spreading the disease great distances to unsuspecting
peoples far from the point of original infection.[58] But if typhoid was present in
the southeastern environment, incidents of the disease became common only after the horticultural transition. Only after indigenous peoples made the switch
to maize-intensive horticulture and established permanent settlements in floodplain environments did the proper ecological conditions emerge for the disease
to spread frequently from person to person.

Still, typhoid's presence in the Americas remains conjectural, leaving the possibility that Europeans and Africans introduced it. The germ does appear to be

an ancient scourge of humanity. Many newer, less evolved, diseases persist in the body for a relatively short time before either they kill their host or their host develops immunity, and thus they have a shorter window of opportunity to be passed to another victim. Typhoid has coevolved with humans for more than eleven thousand years, acquiring the ability to produce relatively mild symptoms and to remain in human hosts for a comparatively lengthy time.[59] Typhoid, though, possibly remained contained in tropical Africa until around six thousand years ago, after which time the development of irrigation and urbanization allowed the bacteria to become a commonly communicated disease in various parts of the Eastern Hemisphere. As a "crowd disease," typhoid would have come to the Americas only after 1492.

If typhoid was part of the Columbian Exchange, however, virginity does not explain the vulnerability of indigenous peoples. The absence of the disease did not necessarily give Europeans an advantage. Immunity to typhoid is relative.[60] After experiencing the disease once, a person can become infected again with large doses of the bacteria, and indeed Europeans who came to the Americas suffered miserably and repeatedly from the disease.[61] Indigenous peoples too were susceptible, but any predisposition to the disease depended not on their virginity but on the location of their settlements and their sanitation practices. Vulnerability was also largely a factor of their ability to protect their water supply from contamination, something that became difficult when they were faced with the presence of a European colonial regime.

Whether typhoid was aboriginal or new, indigenous peoples certainly had experience with a variety of other waterborne illnesses. One of these was most likely hepatitis A. This virus infects people and other primates usually through consumption of sewage-contaminated water or food. It results in relatively minor symptoms, including fever, nausea, and jaundice. Adults may experience a more difficult time than children, but the disease is rarely fatal. Hepatitis A remains an acute illness, wherein victims do not become permanent carriers, but compared to many other diseases, it has a better chance to persist in small-group societies. The virus incubates on average twenty-eight to thirty days and can be transmitted during the latter half of this period and for about a week after symptoms appear. This approximately three-week period in which the disease can be spread is substantially longer than with other acute illnesses, and in some instances an infected victim can excrete the virus for up to six months. Its ability to remain in the human body for a relatively long time makes the A virus a possible candidate to have accompanied hunter-gatherers across the Bering Strait, but as with typhoid, hepatitis may have had an aboriginal presence in the American environment. The virus has a widespread distribution today, with endemic focuses in many underdeveloped countries, leading one to suspect that the virus was ubiquitous in nature and plagued all peoples before modern methods of water treatment and sewage disposal curtailed its distribution.[62] Hepatitis A, if present in the Americas before 1492, certainly became even more problematic for indigenous peoples as they made the transition to horticulture.

In addition to waterborne illnesses, horticulture also presented potential infection from another broad category of pathogens: soil-borne germs. Repetitively working with the soil exposed indigenous peoples to a variety of fungi and worms that thrived in horticultural fields. Most of these pathogens caused minor ailments but one fungus in particular, *Blastomyces dermatitidis,* was indigenous to the Southeast and resulted in a serious disease for its Native victims. Inhaling this pathogen results in bronchopneumonia, and when it enters the bloodstream through the lungs, skin ulcers, bone degeneration, and genital disorders may appear. Left untreated, blastomycosis can cause death.[63] Of course, not all indigenous peoples suffered from this fungal disease, and for those who did, death was not certain. Blastomycosis, though, was another compromising factor in the health of horticulturalists. In the fourteenth century, for example, blastomycosis was endemic among the highly stressed Native communities of the Cumberland Valley and worked synergistically with bacterial infections and nutritional deficiencies to lower the level of individual immunity and to shorten life spans.[64]

Worm infestation was even more common than fungus. Formally known as helminths, worms are multicelled but tiny, often microscopic, organisms that have afflicted humans throughout our evolution and have plagued societies across the globe. Most helminths began as free-living parasites that became specifically adapted to humans, and several species of these types of worms were indeed present among pre-Columbian Native populations. The pinworm, *Enterobius vermicularis,* and the roundworm, *Ascaris lumbricoides,* have been identified in desiccated fecal remains in archaeological sites in the Southeast, while various species of the whipworm, *Trichuris,* are believed to have been widely distributed throughout North American populations.[65] Many scientists also include the hookworm species, *Ancylostoma duodenale,* among parasites indigenous to the Southeast.[66] Humans acquire the eggs or larvae of these various helminths by coming into close contact with material, especially soil and agricultural products, contaminated with the feces of infected individuals. The parasites mature in the human body, living off their hosts' nutrients and causing a number of different problems depending on the particular helminth. Generally, these worms produce mild symptoms, but heavy infestation can cause nutritional deficiencies, anemia, and growth retardation.[67]

With the exception of *Enterobius vermicularis,* helminths that infected indigenous peoples most likely originated from species native to the Americas. *Ascaris lumbricoides, Trichuris,* and *Ancylostoma duodenale* must usually complete part of their lifecycle in warm, moist soil before they become infective to humans, thus making it improbable that hunter-gatherer bands transmitted the pathogen to the Americas from Asia. The cold climate of the Bering Strait would have acted as a "cold screen," eliminating these soil-borne pathogens. Instead, Natives encountered these worms in the American environment, either as free-living organisms that they picked up from the soil or as parasites of other animals that found humans a better host. *Enterobius vermicularis,* on the other hand, possibly did survive the Bering Strait crossing. The eggs of this helminth can live up to two weeks outside a human host but do not undergo germination until passed to another host. Infection can occur immediately after defecation through a fecal-oral transmission, or indirectly through food, clothing, bedding, or other material harboring contaminated fecal matter. Since the parasite does not require germination in warm, moist soil, the artic cold screen was ineffective against it.

Worms and other soil- and waterborne pathogens were the most problematic for Native horticulturalists, but these germs have received little attention compared to two human-to-human diseases—syphilis and tuberculosis—whose suspected pre-Columbian presence has inspired intense scholarly debate. The characteristics of these two diseases allow for their survival in small-group societies, and they both show a high level of coexistence with human hosts. Syphilis and tuberculosis, indeed, are ancient diseases that have coevolved with *Homo sapiens* long before the Bering Strait crossing. Their presence in the pre-Columbian Americas, however, is not certain, and if they were in fact present, their impact on Native peoples is difficult to assess.

The bacteria that cause tuberculosis, *Mycobacterium tuberculosis,* probably evolved from an ancestral species that infected other mammals or that lived freely in the soil. Today *Mycobacterium* species remain endemic among some animal species and can still be found in dirt. Thousands of years ago, one of those species probably mutated into *M. tuberculosis* and became adapted specifically to humans; humans can transmit the disease only to other humans and not to other animals. Over time tuberculosis evolved into a chronic disease, capable of persisting within the human body for a lengthy period. After an individual inhales the bacteria, his or her body will respond by walling off the bacteria in the form of tubercles. While the victim remains healthy, tubercles will remain dormant in the lungs for the infected person's lifetime. But if the victim's immunity becomes weak, the walls around the tubercles will break down, symptoms will emerge, and infection of another person becomes possible. Active cases of the disease do not immediately result in death, although mortality does come quicker for the elderly, the malnourished, and victims fighting multiple infections. Most often tuberculosis works slowly on the body, destroying the lungs and eroding bone tissue, especially the lower (lumbar) vertebrae, giving its victims a hunchback appearance.[68] Paradoxically, the body's effective response to tuberculosis ensures the germ's long-term survival, even in small-group societies. By warehousing *M. tuberculosis* in the lungs, a lone person can harbor the pathogen for years, only later to suffer a sickness of long duration exposing other victims far away from the original point of infection.

Tuberculosis is a prime candidate for a pre-Columbian disease. Although typically associated with urban slums in the nineteenth century, tuberculosis's spread depended not necessarily on the number of people in a given society but on how those people lived. Cramped living conditions, whether in industrial cities, rural villages, or caves, facilitated the spread of germ-laden airborne droplets. It is conceivable that hunter-gather bands carried this chronic disease a great distance and passed the bacteria from person to person as they kept close quarters while roaming in cold environments and huddling together around campfires to keep warm. The skeletons of several pre-Columbian individuals further substantiate tuberculosis's presence. Since the body harbors the disease for an extensive period, the bacteria will erode bones, especially the vertebrae, causing severely angulated spines. Skeletons from several sites in the Americas display such skeletal evidence, with the sites associated with Southeastern horticulturalists providing a particularly large number of possible tuberculosis victims.[69] The desiccated remains of an Andean Native, though, give scholars the best evidence to substantiate tuberculosis's early presence. Scientists have extracted lung tissue from a Peruvian mummy that dates to AD 1000 and found a germ with the same DNA sequence as tuberculosis.[70]

Still, scholars are not in complete agreement about tuberculosis's preColumbian presence. Some confidently assert that tuberculosis is a crowd disease, becoming a problem for humanity only in recent times, when masses of poor, malnourished, and germ-ridden people became packed into the urban slums of industrializing nations. Critics of tuberculosis's pre-Columbian presence point out that degeneration as seen on ribs and the vertebrae of aboriginal skeletons are not necessarily specific to a particular disease. Bacterial infections as well as some fungal infections, including blastomycosis, can erode bone tissues in much the same manner as tuberculosis. The DNA analysis of the Peruvian mummy furthermore is problematic. Such analysis has not distinguished whether the germ responsible was *M. tuberculosis* or a related species, *M. bovine,* which commonly occurs in wild and domestic mammals.[71] Humans could have contracted this microbe through consuming the flesh of an infected animal, but such a victim would have been unable to transmit the disease to others.

Another argument against tuberculosis's pre-Columbian presence is based on the impact that the disease had on indigenous communities after contact. Plains Indian communities experienced high rates of infection and mortality in the late nineteenth and the early twentieth century, leading experts at the time to conclude that tuberculosis was a new disease to Native peoples. This view has received renewed support with the case of the Yanomami, who came into significant contact with people of European and African descent only in the twentieth century. This Amazonian tribe then suffered miserably from tuberculosis, with the number of those developing active cases exceeding the expected rate among non-Natives. The Yanomami also had unusual symptoms. After further investigation, scientists suggested that individual victims displayed an undeveloped immune response to the invading germ. Yanomami produced antibodies, which are helpless against tuberculosis, while non-Natives mobilized special white blood cells called T cells that attacked the bacteria much more effectively. For some scientists, this is evidence that natural selection had not been at work among the Amazonian tribes; their immune response to one of the most common diseases lagged behind that of other peoples.[72]

The severity of tuberculosis among the Yanomami and other Indians, however, cannot be attributed exclusively to their supposed virginity. The disease's tragic impact can just as easily be traced to the squalid living conditions, poor nutrition, and increased pathogen load of formerly mobile groups who had only recently become confined on reservations. Tuberculosis's infection and mortality rates, more so than most other common diseases, have varied considerably among populations across the globe depending on ecological conditions. The urban poor of nineteenth-century England, for example, had astronomically high death rates from tuberculosis, compared to better-fed and healthier Englishmen and women who occupied higher rungs of the socioeconomic ladder. If indeed the Yanomami or other indigenous peoples failed to attack tuberculosis with T cells, one should not automatically ascribe their weakened immune response to their gene pool. Instead poor health resulting from colonialism's dramatic reordering of the ecological conditions in which they lived adversely affected their ability to fight infection. In other words, Native virginity to tuberculosis was not as relevant as their compromised ability to control their own lives and environmental settings.

Syphilis's presence in the Americas also has substantial support, but its significance to the overall health of indigenous peoples remains uncertain. Europeans believed that syphilis was an American disease due to its appearance shortly after Columbus's fateful voyage. In 1494 the strange disease broke out in Europe, apparently following the travels of French soldiers as they disbanded after attacking Naples. Individuals had never seen such symptoms before, and the wretched disease continued to flare up in Europe and other areas of the Eastern Hemisphere through the early sixteenth century. Medical experts at the time linked the disease to the discovery of the Americas, and its American origin became fixed in the European mind, continuing to be an accepted fact among many scholars today.[73] Archaeologists and physical anthropologists have added further support for this view in their analyses of pre-Columbian skeletons. A significant number of these remains display cranial lesions, indicative of syphilis-causing bacteria, which reside in the body for extensive periods, eroding the bone structure of their victims. The Southeast in particular has provided a large sample of this evidence with rates of infection again increasing during the horticulture transition.[74]

Lately, however, scholars have questioned the occurrence of syphilis among the indigenous population, arguing instead that a related yet milder disease known as yaws prevailed. Both syphilis and yaws are caused by an infection of a spirochete bacterial species, *Treponema pallidum*. Treponematosis can be transmitted in different ways, resulting in symptoms so different that they appear to indicate two unique diseases. Yaws is passed through the open skin lesions that it creates on its victims. These lesions may be painful as they spread from the face to the extremities. After about a year, these symptoms abate, but the bacteria can remain disseminated throughout the body, causing bone degeneration and disfigurement. Yaws is rarely fatal. Syphilis, on the other hand, can be deadly. This disease results when *T. pallidum* passes from an infected victim to another through sexual intercourse. The germ will take permanent residence in the sex organs and is immediately contagious even during the first, four-to-six-week period before symptoms appear. The first signs of illness appear in the form of infectious lesions of the skin and mucous membranes, which may continue to erupt for up to a year. Thereafter, the disease enters a period of latency that may last several years, only to manifest itself later by invading the nervous and cardiovascular systems, causing severe illness and possibly death. In addition to sexual transmission, the disease can be passed congenitally, leading to complications such as abortion, stillbirth, and low natal weight.[75]

Ecological conditions suggest that yaws rather than syphilis prevailed among indigenous peoples. Historically, yaws has thrived among tribal populations in warm climates. Such people wear little clothing for a substantial portion of the year, thus giving *T. pallidum* ample opportunities to spread through skin-to-skin contact. Children, for example, would have come in frequent contact with the disease as their parents held them in their arms or as they played with other children. Early infection had an advantage. When infected as a young child, an individual's body became adapted to the disease and built immunity to future treponematosis exposure, including sexual transmission. Syphilis, thus, was rare among yaws-ridden groups, as most individuals became immune before reaching sexual maturity. On the other hand, syphilis has come to prevail among more thoroughly clothed people, who likely escaped infection at an early age and thus were susceptible to the more deadly sexual transmission later in life.

Overall, it appears that *T. pallidum* caused only minor health problems in the Native Southeast. Yaws likely prevailed among the majority of indigenous communities, which lived in ecological conditions favorable to the spread of the nonvenereal form of treponematosis. The bacteria do show increasing prevalence among Natives as they made the transition to horticulture, due in large part to the increasing number of human-to-human contacts that the growing population provided. Yaws may have also worked synergistically with other bacterial infections, including tuberculosis, and with nutritional deficiencies to contribute to the declining health of horticulturalists. But evidence of *T. pallidum* remains rare compared to other infectious diseases and to nutritional deficiencies, indicating that the indigenous population had become well accustomed to this ancient disease.

If syphilis was a problem for the indigenous population, it became more so after European colonization. In rare cases individuals living before the European invasion escaped a childhood exposure to *T. pallidum* and contracted the bacteria sexually later in life. But European colonization changed the ecological conditions in which many Native peoples lived, making it more likely for sexual transmission to occur. Woolen and cotton clothing were prominent trade items and became more commonly worn as indigenous peoples interacted with Europeans. Forced assimilation, especially among peoples associated with Christian missions, further changed Native fashion. European morality encouraged Natives to cover their bare skin, unintentionally curtailing yaws infection but leading to more people reaching sexual maturity without immunity to syphilis.

Chances of acquiring syphilis further increased for indigenous peoples as the frequency of sexual intercourse with non-Natives increased.

While syphilis has received much of the attention, another sexually transmitted disease, hepatitis B, has been largely overlooked as a possible pre-Columbian infection. This virus was probably widespread among the indigenous population.[76] Even more than the waterborne A virus, which is not transmitted sexually, the B virus is quite durable. It is able to survive boiling and drying and can remain active outside a human host for at least seven days, making it possible that an unlucky person may acquire the germ while walking barefoot and stepping on a sharp stone or thorn. More commonly, the virus is spread when people share bodily fluids. Sexual intercourse, piercing, tattooing, surgery, and acupuncture all provide an avenue into the human body for the opportunistic germ. Mothers can also pass the virus to their unborn children. Very few hepatitis B victims will experience an acute onset of symptoms, which include anorexia, nausea, vomiting, and jaundice. Rare individuals, especially those who have weakened immune systems, may experience liver failure and death shortly after infection. Instead of an acute illness, hepatitis B more often becomes chronic. Infected individuals, including 90 percent of infected children, display no symptoms but harbor the disease for several years, exposing countless others to the virus. These chronic carriers, though, are not free from the disease. Later in life, the virus may become acute, causing its host to suffer from liver cancer and premature death.[77]

Hepatitis B is believed to be an ancient disease and one that hunter-gatherers brought with them as they crossed the Bering Strait into the Americas. It is an infection that humans share with apes and monkeys today and one most likely inherited from primate ancestors. Its chronic and relatively mild characteristics indicate that it has coevolved over tens of thousands of years with humans and that it adapted to people while they remained hunter-gatherers. Today the virus is found worldwide, persisting even among relatively isolated indigenous bands in South America.[78] Indigenous peoples, however, possibly picked up the germ from the American environment. Scientists suspect that the pre-Columbian wildlife populations harbored hepatitis viruses. It is also possible for mosquitoes to transmit the disease, making it conceivable that Natives acquired hepatitis B from nature through an insect vector. Still, the virus most likely came with the first peoples to migrate to the Americas and continued to be passed from person to person through sexual intercourse or other activities in which bodily fluids were exchanged.

The extent to which hepatitis B bothered indigenous peoples of the Native Southeast is uncertain. The disease does not leave signature markings on the skeletal structure. Hepatitis B may have been as widespread among hunter-gatherers as it was among horticulturalists, but if so, it would have been more problematic for the latter group. The disease is known to work synergistically with other infections and nutritional deficiencies, leading to an earlier onset of acute cases among populations in poor health. There is good reason to suspect, then, that hepatitis B helped increase infant mortality rates and shorten life spans in some southeastern communities.

Another hepatitis germ, the delta agent, also deserves particular attention because of the severity of the disease it causes and its close association with the B virus. The delta agent is a viruslike particle transmitted through the sharing of bodily fluids, but it cannot harm a host by itself. It grows only in the presence of hepatitis B, which supplies a needed surface protein. When these two germs come together (coinfection) or when the delta agent is later introduced to a B carrier (superinfection), the consequences can be deadly. A modern outbreak among the Yucpa Indians of Venezuela illustrates this phenomenon well. Between 1979 and 1981, acute hepatitis erupted among 149 Yucpa, killing 34 and leaving 22 as chronic sufferers. The reasons for the thorough spread of hepatitis B are clear. One hundred percent of their children suffered from skin diseases that left open sores, while the common practice of pricking the skin with sharp objects to relieve pain or irritation increased susceptibility. Nevertheless, the ease with which blood-borne germs could be passed does not explain the high mortality rates. The Yucpa were neither grossly malnourished nor deficient in vital nutrients, and they were also free of debilitating diseases such as malaria. Evidence strongly indicates that a delta superinfection occurred among a people in which the B virus was already widespread.[79]

The origins of the delta agent are unclear. Scientists first identified this viruslike particle only in 1977, when they became aware of the germ as it afflicted vulnerable populations such as hemophiliacs and drug addicts in developed nations. Today the delta agent is known to be endemic in areas with a high proportion of hepatitis B carriers, including southern Italy, the Amazon Basin, parts of Africa, and the Middle East.[80] One wonders, though, whether the viruslike particle has had a longer history with humans. Perhaps it was a widespread and ancient infection that went through a period of remission in the twentieth century as an increase in sterilization techniques put the delta agent in retreat. The germ thus would have virtually disappeared in developed nations, while remaining isolated in underdeveloped nations. The delta agent's close association with the B virus and its ability to become a chronic disease do suggest a more ancient origin. It has even been suggested that it was part of the Columbian Exchange, resulting in a devastating outbreak among Natives of coastal New England from 1616 to 1619. The symptoms of the unfortunate victims of this epidemic closely resembled those that the Yucpa experienced in the twentieth century.[81] Given the lack of clinical detail and uncertainty about the delta agent's natural history, however, the germ's role in the Columbian Exchange remains conjectural. If the delta agent plagued humans long before its 1977 discovery, its presence in the Americas before 1492 cannot be ruled out.

The delta agent illustrates, although in an admittedly hypothetical way, the importance of disease ecology in shaping Native vulnerability. If the infectious particle was part of the Columbian Exchange, its impact was affected by preexisting factors. A likely endemic presence of the B virus would have allowed superinfection to occur, and ubiquitous practices of tattooing, acupuncture, and other skin-piercing techniques would have facilitated widespread and deadly outbreaks of hepatitis among the indigenous population. Of course, whether epidemic hepatitis was one of the biological consequences of 1492 remains unknowable, but what is certain is that preexisting pathogens and nutritional deficiencies that plagued Native bodies greatly shaped their vulnerability to newly introduced germs. When afflicted with multiple infections and deprived of essential nutrients, the human body experiences a suppression of its immune system, making it difficult at best to fight off a newly introduced germ. Also, chronic diseases that the body has managed to keep in check can become acute and even deadly when infection with a new pathogen occurs. Measles, in particular, has been known to suppress immunity and drive up mortality rates from common bacterial infections that human beings have experienced throughout our evolution.[82] Thus, indigenous peoples suffered high mortality rates not simply because they were a virgin population but because their bodies, like those of all human beings before modern medicine, hosted a variety of germs. Tragically, hunger acted synergistically with those germs to drive up mortality from new diseases once introduced by Europeans and Africans. In the colonial Southeast, this synergism was particularly severe when English-inspired slave raids disrupted subsistence routines, forcing war-wary and famine-stricken peoples to live in nucleated settlements and carry heavy pathogen loads.

Predisposition to New Zoonotic Diseases

As the discussion of typhoid and hepatitis illustrates, sorting out aboriginal diseases from those newly introduced to the Americas is not always easy. Nevertheless, scholars generally agree that some diseases were absent from the Americas before 1492. Among the most important of those were malaria, bubonic plague, yellow fever, typhus, smallpox, measles, influenza, diphtheria, and whooping cough. Each disease on this roster, however, had its own unique characteristics, leading it to pose either a greater or lesser danger to indigenous populations after 1492. Ecological factors indeed determined which Columbian Exchange diseases became the most serious. Several of the diseases that Europeans and Africans introduced to the Americas, for example, require animal vectors, meaning that epidemics would occur only if indigenous peoples lived in intimate contact with those pests responsible for infecting people. Zoonotic infections such as malaria, yellow fever, bubonic plague, and typhus all had the potential to make the transatlantic crossing, but there was no guarantee that any would proliferate among the indigenous population as they had among people in the Eastern Hemisphere. There human beings had come to live in close association with a variety of mosquitoes, fleas, lice, rats, and other animals responsible for harboring and spreading some of the world's deadliest illnesses. Similar ecological conditions had to exist in the Americas for the same zoonotic infections to occur.

Of the zoonoses, malaria most easily found a home in the Southeast. An ancient disease, malaria is caused by different species of protozoa belonging to the genus *Plasmodium*. The most severe but more limited species is *P. falciparum,* while the more common yet milder is *P. vivax*. General symptoms include a fever that slowly rises over several days, followed by intervals of shaking chills and rising temperatures, headaches, nausea, and profuse sweating. Relapses may occur weeks, months, or even up to two years later. The most severe cases may result in jaundice, blood-clotting defects, renal and liver failure, and excessive fluid build-up in the heart and brain, leading to coma and possibly death. Death rates vary considerably according to the level of the victim's health. In most cases malaria is a chronic and debilitating disease, causing death in less than 10 percent of untreated cases. Mortality occurs more frequently for individuals with preexisting health problems such as malnutrition or a heavy pathogen load.[83]

Plasmodia parasites have a long history with humanity. Malaria's only vector, mosquitoes belonging to the genus *Anopheles,* have passed the parasite among various primate species through the course of evolution, some six to ten million years, and even continue to do so today. By the time modern humans emerged, our bodies had long been hosts to plasmodia. Malaria's impact, however, remained limited until around eleven thousand years ago. Hunting and gathering bands did not serve as good host communities to the disease. Malaria-carrying mosquitoes generally have a short range, often less than one mile, meaning that humans and these insects had to share each other's habitat for an extended period in order for a continual chain of infection to occur. While mosquitoes did feast on the blood of hunter-gatherers, most malaria-carrying species had adapted to more abundant and permanent hosts within their habitats. Plasmodia, consequently, became adapted to these hosts as well and did not follow hunter-gatherers as they filled the globe.

With the advent of agriculture around eleven thousand years ago, human experience with malaria changed. Humans often found the habitat of anopheles, a ubiquitous pest found throughout the world, the best land to grow crops. Slow-moving waterways provided abundant fertile soil for the development of settled agriculture, but they also produced a patchwork of swamps, marshes, and other stagnant bodies of water that served as ideal breeding grounds for anopheles. Human alteration of the landscape also brought anopheles and people closer together. Clearing the land to plant fields resulted in the depletion of wild animals, forcing mosquitoes to feed on humans, whose permanent settlements provided a sufficient number of hosts to maintain a continual chain of infection. Irrigation canals served as yet another body of stagnant water to harbor disease-carrying insects.[84]

As agriculture developed in various places in the world, plasmodia parasites spread to wherever the combination of humans and anopheles came to live together. Of course, the disease stopped short of spreading to the Americas. It is often assumed that an arctic passage of hunter-gatherers acted as a cold filter, eliminating malaria. The frigid habitat did not include anopheles mosquitoes, giving plasmodia no chance to be passed along the way as people traveled from Asia to the Americas. It is doubtful as well that malaria was present among the ancestors of the Indians in the first place. The disease most likely did not spread out of Africa until some eleven thousand years ago, at the end of the Bering Strait crossing. Fatefully, two out of the three ecological conditions for the spread of malaria did exist in the Americas. The combination of anopheles mosquitoes and settled horticultural societies could be found in many temperate and tropical environments. The only element lacking was plasmodia parasites.

Those parasites arrived after 1492, and the Native Southeast proved particularly vulnerable. Since the disease is of a chronic nature, surviving in its human host for at least a year, it easily survived the transatlantic voyage. European sailors, even those in the early years of colonization, regularly picked up the disease on their journeys, which often involved stops in Africa, where malaria was endemic. The slave trade also served as a major vehicle for the spread of malaria, as enslaved Africans frequently carried the disease in their bodies. Once arriving in the Americas, plasmodia jumped from their European and African hosts to local anopheles populations, which then transmitted the parasites to indigenous peoples. Plasmodia, mosquitoes, and Natives thereafter became intimately linked into a chain of infection.

Indigenous peoples, however, were not uniformly vulnerable. In the Native Southeast, communities within broad river valleys and nestled amid swamps and oxbow lakes were predisposed to have major problems with malaria, once the germ arrived. On the eve of European invasion, the scene for malaria epidemics was already set, especially below the Fall Line, where the horticultural transition had led to compact human settlements within flood-prone environments and had consequently escalated human exposure to a variety of mosquito species, including anopheles. Dispersed settlement patterns, when possible, offered some protection by lessening the potential for mass infection. Location above the Fall Line, while not making communities invulnerable, nonetheless provided an environment with fewer stagnant bodies of water and consequently was to make malaria's impact patchier. For malaria, then, nothing had to change in the preexisting disease ecology, except for the introduction of the plasmodia parasite, in order for the disease to become fairly widespread across the Southeast. Malaria by itself, though, was not a massive killer. Some communities, especially those suffering high pathogen loads and nutritional deficiencies, were certainly vulnerable to high incidences of mortality, but in an otherwise healthy population, the disease has a chronic, debilitating effect, with a case fatality rate of less than 10 percent.

Population collapse of the magnitude of 50 percent or higher would require a disease more deadly than malaria. Other zoonoses in the Eastern Hemisphere—plague, yellow fever, and typhus—indeed had that potential. But while these were terribly lethal pathogens, the disease ecology of the Native Southeast posed substantial barriers that made it much more difficult for them to spread beyond the point of direct contact. Plague was the least likely zoonoses to become a problem for southeastern Natives. Caused by a bacterium, *Yersinia pestis* (formerly identified as *Pasteurella pestis*), plague was originally endemic among burrowing rodents in either central Africa or the Himalayan foothills between China and India. The germ had coevolved with these animals and was transmitted back and forth by fleas specifically adapted to the rodents. On what must have been rare occasions, hunter-gatherers stumbled into this habitat, became flea bitten, and found themselves infected by what was surely a fatal disease. In its bubonic form—an infection stemming directly from a flea's bite—plague acts quickly on the body. After incubating for two to six days, the bacteria cause high fevers, inflammation of the lymph nodes, septicemia, and shock. If a human host survives these symptoms, the bacteria will continue to work their way through the body, attacking the lungs and causing severe pneumonia. At this stage, it is possible for humans to transmit the disease through exhalation to another person, who will contract plague in its pneumonic form, which acts even more quickly on the body and brings death with an even greater certitude. Acquired immunity to the disease is relative. Individuals who suffered a prior infection can experience the disease again if exposed to a large dose of plague bacilli.[85]

Because of its deadly and fast-acting nature, plague remained a rare disease for early human beings and became problematic only in more recent history. The first appearance of *Yersinia pestis* in Europe most likely occurred in AD 542 with the famous Plague of Justinian. By that time, a viable transportation network had connected Mediterranean ports with India, whose native black rats began their own colonization of other parts of the world. This weedy species, traveling aboard ships and feeding off stores of grain, became widely circulated through the Mediterranean world. At some point, black rats picked up plague bacilli from one of the suspected endemic foci, thereby bringing the nasty germ to previously unexposed Europeans. Still, plague epidemics remained sporadic in Europe for the next couple of hundred years and even seemed to disappear until the infamous Black Death, which began in AD 1346.

By the fourteenth century, Europe had become ripe for the catastrophic spread of plague. Over the few hundred years before the Black Death, the population, especially in northern Europe, had grown to the point that few uninhabited lands were left, and resources, especially firewood, had become scarce. Especially during the cold season, Europeans huddled together in cramped, flea- and rat-infested dwellings. Along with this increased level of crowding, Europe had become more tightly integrated into a shipping network that connected Mediterranean and northern Atlantic ports. Improved shipping design and the opening of the Strait of Gibraltar allowed for greater communication between southern, western, and northern Europe. Tragically, *Yersinia pestis* entered into this network in 1346. By that time, the bacteria had become endemic along the Eurasian steppes, probably planted there by Mongol armies returning from war in the Himalayan foothills in the thirteenth century. These same armies carried the disease with them to the Crimea, where, after they abandoned a siege on the trading city of Caffa, the bacteria jumped aboard Mediterranean-bound ships. For four years plague ravaged Europe, killing approximately one-third of its population. The Black Death was followed by other outbreaks of the disease, which continued into the period of colonization.[86]

After 1492 the Americas were connected to a shipping network that carried plague. It remains debatable, however, whether *Yersinia pestis* made a transatlantic voyage. Some scholars argue that the Spanish carried plague into Mexico in the sixteenth century and that this scourge of Europe aided in the subjugation of Natives.[87] Other scholars are not convinced. The disease spreads and kills so quickly that it was likely to burn itself out among a ship's rat and human population before arriving in the Americas. For this reason, some scholars place plague's arrival in the Americas in the late nineteenth century, when an increase in human traffic and the speed of ocean-going vessels dramatically improved the bacteria's chances of surviving. At that point the disease did arrive, but instead of a transatlantic crossing from Europe, it came by way of a transpacific crossing from China, which supplied large numbers of immigrants coming from an area experiencing an epidemic. Plague bacilli, which are endemic today among burrowing rodents of the American West, thus arrived not by way of the Columbian Exchange but as a biological invasion from China, the ecological significance of which Eurocentric scholars have underappreciated.[88] Even if Europeans did carry plague to the Americas, it is doubtful that such a density-dependent disease had much if any impact on the Native Southeast. The deadly germ would have burned itself out quickly among those unfortunate Natives who came into direct contact with sick newcomers, and it would have found little opportunity to spread elsewhere among an indigenous population that was far from the saturation point that medieval Europe had reached.

Unlike plague, yellow fever's arrival in the Native Southeast is certain. But yellow fever became neither permanently rooted nor spread much beyond the point of direct contact between Europeans and indigenous peoples. The viruses that cause yellow fever belongs to the genus *Flavivirus* and are usually transmitted from host to host by various species of aedes mosquitoes. Originally, yellow fever was endemic among African monkeys, but it occasionally afflicted early hunter-gatherers who traveled through environments containing monkeys, aedes mosquitoes, and *Flavivirus*. People did not become a viable link in the chain of infection from this disease until the aedes mosquito became adapted to humans, and this occurred only after agriculture, when population size reached a level at which the insects could find sufficient numbers of peoples to feed on.

Even then yellow fever's geographic distribution remained limited. The virus remains in its human hosts for a short time, incubating for three to six days and then becoming communicable for three to five days. Severe mortality rates also inhibited its spread. The disease indeed is wretched, involving jaundice, high temperatures, bloody vomit and urine, and damage to the liver and kidneys; the mortality rate for untreated patients is as high as 40 percent.[89] More important, humans cannot transmit the disease directly to one another; instead it spreads only indirectly through specific species of mosquito, which in Africa means the *Aedes aegypti*. This insect has a restricted habitat, living year around in waterfront areas with temperatures that remain above 71°F. Until the fifteenth century, yellow fever remained endemic only in tropical Africa.[90]

After 1492 yellow fever broke out of Africa especially as Europeans escalated the transatlantic slave trade. Not only did European vessels carry captured Africans but they also transported *Flavivirus* and *Aedes* species, and whenever the two were deposited in coastal communities during the warm season, deadly epidemics erupted. The disease ultimately became endemic in the Amazon, where the resident monkey population provided a reservoir and native species of *Haemagogus* mosquitoes served as vectors. In the more temperate Southeast, however, yellow fever failed to find a permanent home. The region had neither a reservoir of monkeys nor suitable species of mosquitoes to spread the disease. Yellow fever, of course, visited the region when ships arrived at seaports during the warm season carrying both the disease and appropriate mosquito vectors. In such cases indigenous peoples who lived in close proximity to colonial towns, forts, or missions were most vulnerable, but given the complex ecological conditions in which yellow fever spread, the majority of Native southeasterners were to remain relatively safe from this disease throughout the colonial period. Instead, Europeans and Africans who inhabited coastal areas proved to be most vulnerable.[91]

More difficult to assess is whether typhus found the ecology of the Native Southeast favorable. Typhus is caused by *Rickettsia prowazeki* and is transmitted from human to human by lice. Once a louse contracts the disease, it is infective for two to six days, during which it can transmit the disease to a human by defecating on his or her skin. The human victim scratches the louse bite and rubs the rickettsial-filled feces into the abrasion. The pathogen incubates for one to two weeks, typically twelve days, after which an onset of symptoms including headache, chills, prostration, fever, and pain occurs. On the fifth or sixth day of illness, macular eruptions, which are nonelevated spots or lesions on the skin, spread from the trunk to all of the body except the face, palms, and soles. A fever may last up to two weeks. The infective period lasts for fourteen to seventeen days, during which time a louse can contract the disease by biting a victim. A louse remains infective for its lifetime, usually about a year. The disease can be serious, but likelihood of death varies substantially according to the level of health of the victim. In modern times, 10 to 40 percent of untreated patients die, with the elderly showing the highest levels of mortality. Survivors possess lifelong immunity to the disease.[92] By 1492 typhus had certainly become a problem for Europeans, and it became one of the diseases involved in the Columbian Exchange. The germ thrived among people living in crowded, impoverished, and filthy conditions—the very people who often manned transatlantic ships or came as indentured servants to the Americas. Typhus also struck European armies especially hard, as the mobilization of such large groups brought a large number of nonimmune people together and placed them in cramped, lice-ridden camps. The ships that carried these armies to the Americas proved to be especially notorious for typhus, a disease that received the alternative name "ship's fever."[93]

The question, then, is not whether typhus came to the Native Southeast but whether once it arrived to what extent did it spread. Was the Native Southeast a tinderbox ready for a conflagration of typhus? This is doubtful. Indigenous peoples lived in ecological conditions quite different from those that gave rise to typhus epidemics in Europe. The population density of the Native Southeast certainly paled in comparison to Europe and most likely never reached the level of crowding necessary for such a density-dependent disease. But typhus's spread was not an issue only of population density; it was also an issue of how those people lived. Frequent bathing as part of regular cleansing rituals, closely cropped hair, body paint that acted as a prophylactic, and the relative absence of clothing during much of the year kept Native bodies free of the pests that spread the disease.[94] On the other hand, Europeans, with their insistence on wearing clothing year around and their reluctance to bathe frequently, had bodies that provided ideal habitats for lice. When typhus-ridden ships arrived, then, the germ found the Native Southeast a dead end in the chain of infection. Typhus possibly struck some Natives who came into close contact with diseased newcomers, but the social landscape hardly resembled the crowded, pest-laden population that fostered epidemics in Europe.

For the major zoonoses of the Eastern Hemisphere, then, the Native Southeast was ripe only for malaria to become widespread. Only this mosquito-borne disease found a human population living in ideal ecological conditions for an epidemic. If bubonic plague survived a transatlantic crossing, which seems doubtful, it must have quickly burned itself out shortly after arriving. Yellow fever and typhus were certainly part of the Columbian Exchange; both survived the passage from Europe and Africa and circulated throughout the Atlantic world. The impact of both of these diseases, however, depended on a complex set of ecological variables. Yellow fever had some impact but only during the warm season among compactly settled coastal groups who lived near points of direct contact. The same groups were vulnerable to typhus but more so during the cold season, when the weather curtailed regular hygiene practices, forced individuals to wear more clothing, and encouraged tighter living arrangements.[95] Colonialism also played an especially important role in regard to typhus transmission. The susceptibility of Natives increased as they became drawn into colonial cities, forts, and missions, where they interacted with lousy Europeans.

Predisposition to New Human-to-Human Diseases

While the spread of malaria, bubonic plague, yellow fever, and typhus depended on indigenous peoples living in close relationship with specific animal vectors, the impact of other, more familiar diseases involved in the Columbian Exchange did not have such environmental limitations. Smallpox, measles, whooping cough, and influenza spread directly from one nonimmune person to another.[96] It might seem, then, that these diseases, once introduced, spread unabated through regions with virgin populations. One wonders, though, whether the Native Southeast was predisposed for a regionwide epidemic of these human-to-human diseases. As has been shown, it was fairly easy for suspected aboriginal diseases such as tuberculosis and treponematosis to spread from person to person. These chronic diseases could persist for years in their host's body, allowing for their survival in small-group societies and for their transportation over great distances. It was not as easy for other diseases that required only a human vector. Smallpox, measles, influenza, and whooping cough are considered acute infectious diseases, meaning the duration of each of these diseases is relatively quick. Once a person becomes infected, the germs that cause these diseases incubate for a brief time before symptoms appear and thereafter remain contagious for a short period until their victims either perish or acquire immunity. The spread of the Columbian Exchange's human-to-human diseases thus was not an automatic consequence of their introduction to a virgin population but depended on complex ecological conditions such as settlement patterns and economic activities that determined the degree to which human beings came into face-to-face contact with one another.

Of all human-to-human germs imported from the Atlantic world, the smallpox virus (*Variola major*) proved to be the most destructive to indigenous peoples. It depended less on the nonbiological aspects of colonialism to make Natives vulnerable to infection, and it had the best chance to spread beyond the point of direct contact to indigenous communities who had yet to see Europeans or Africans. Smallpox indeed is a truly horrific disease, capable of producing case fatality rates that exceeded 40 percent. On the first day the victim experiences headache, back pain, chills, fever, and malaise; this is followed by an even worse second day, which brings fever reaching as high as 104° F. along with delirium and possible coma. The third and fourth day may bring some abatement, but by the fifth day high fever returns and the characteristic pockmarks appear and spread. These lesions can be painful, especially around the mouth, throat, and eyes. Some pox sores will erupt and cause bleeding under the skin. If a host is fortunate enough to survive the high fevers and bleeding pox sores, the disease will have run its course within two weeks, although scabs may last up to a month after symptoms first appeared.[97] With such ghastly symptoms and with large numbers of Native people falling to the virus, it is no wonder that Europeans made frequent reference to smallpox in the colonial record.

The spread of smallpox exceeded all other highly lethal acute infectious diseases for two main reasons. First, smallpox has longer periods of incubation and communicability than most acute infectious diseases. Once a person inhales the smallpox virus, the pathogen incubates for a twelve to fourteen day period before symptoms appear. During these two weeks of symptoms, the disease is highly contagious. In contrast, influenza incubates one to two days, and its communicable period usually runs from three to five days.[98] Smallpox thus remains alive within a human host for a significant time, twenty-six to twenty-eight days, giving a victim a relatively lengthy period to carry the disease from place to place and infect other nonimmune people.[99] The unique ability of smallpox to survive outside a human host is the second reason that it could spread farther than other highly lethal diseases. Measles viruses (*Morbillivirus sp.*), in contrast, have an equivalent period of incubation and communicability but cannot live on their own and need to be passed directly from one person to another through exhalation and inhalation.[100] The bacteria that cause whooping cough (*Bordetella parapertussis* and *B. pertussis*) also persist in the body for about the same time that smallpox does, but their spread through indirect means is much more difficult. Persons who come into contact with mucus from a whooping cough victim can possibly contract the disease, but only shortly after discharge occurred.[101] Smallpox, on the other hand, can be transmitted much more effectively through indirect ways. After its two-week period of direct communicability expires, the virus can be transmitted for approximately two to four weeks longer to nonimmune persons who come into close contact with the scabs of a victim, even if they have fallen off the victim. Also, the virus can live for several months on cloth in a dry, cool environment and consequently can infect any nonimmune person who handles such contaminated material.[102] Transmission through inhalation and exhalation remain the most common mode of infection, of course, and the warm, humid climate of the Southeast presented a barrier to smallpox's spread. But among tightly packed households and villages, in which people shared the same bedding with people who had had an infection, the virus persisted when no one was actively sick, while other deadly acute infectious diseases disappeared relatively soon after an outbreak.

On the surface, then, it would seem then that political and economic developments during the transition to horticulture made the Native Southeast ripe for the spread of at least smallpox, if not other acute infectious diseases. Over the several hundred years before the European invasion, numerous chiefdoms emerged that integrated multiple communities into centralized polities that involved the flow of tribute from subordinate towns to paramount centers. Southeastern communities, whether in chiefdoms or not, also maintained long-distance exchange networks. An examination of aboriginal exchange, however, suggests that indigenous communities hardly constituted a regionwide network of intimate connections through which an acute infectious disease could easily spread. In other words, it is doubtful that aboriginal exchange by itself could have facilitated the significant spread of acute infectious diseases. Instead, such germs would need to have the help of other aspects of colonialism to become deadly on a regionwide scale.

A critical look at the precontact Native Southeast indeed reveals that significant economic changes had to occur before a regionwide epidemic could take place. The flow of tribute within the precontact southeastern chiefdoms has often been misconstrued and inflated. Much of our scholarly understanding of chiefdoms is based on examples from ancient Polynesia, an area much different from the Southeast.[103] In Polynesia, where environments change abruptly across small distances, towns occupied different ecological niches, consequently giving some communities privileged access to resources that others did not have. Communities became economically specialized, and paramount leaders came to control the flow of vital resources throughout an economically integrated polity. In the Southeast, on the other hand, single polities lay within the same environmental zone. The chiefdoms that came to dot the social landscape consisted of a group of towns, arrayed in a linear fashion within the floodplain of a major river and stretching for a distance of no more than forty kilometers from one end to the other.[104] These towns, while perhaps varying in their settlement patterns, were similar in terms of their economic production. Each constituent town had equal access to fish and waterfowl near the river, oxbow lakes, and swamps that lay near them; each had access to the soil in the floodplain; each had access to wild game in upland forests; and each had access to lithic resources, firewood, salt, and other essential nonfood items. Southeastern communities, as a whole, were in fact rather economically redundant and self-sufficient. While varying in degrees to which they practiced a particular activity, each southeastern community maintained diversified subsistence routines involving horticulture, hunting, gathering, and fishing, making intercommunity exchange unnecessary for day-to-day survival. Nearly all the food that an individual consumed, the clothes that an individual wore, and the tools that an individual used were derived from the labors of his or her own community members and from resources a short distance from that person's home.[105]

Exchange within southeastern polities, therefore, was both qualitatively and quantitatively different from theoretical models based on Polynesian chiefdoms.[106] Low-ranking towns in the Native Southeast provisioned elite leaders with a variety of items, including choice cuts of meat, maize, and animal hides. This surplus could be used to feed work crews, war parties, and the small group of religious leaders not involved in subsistence production. It could also be redistributed to the needy in times of scarcity.[107] The collection and redistribution of surpluses, though, occurred during periodic ceremonial occasions rather than on an everyday basis. Ordinary people, moreover, felt very little coercion. Belonging to a chiefdom brought a degree of protection both from famine and from common enemies, but such came with very little cost. Communities had the ability to refuse to offer tribute because of the economic independence they enjoyed. Without specialization of production in vital resources, communities could easily vote with their feet if the demands of their paramount leaders became too great. Indeed, that is what seemed to happen many times during the horticultural transition as chiefdoms went through cycles of evolution and devolution. The flow of tribute from peripheries to central towns thus remained contested and inconstant.[108]

Scholars should also be cautious in using evidence of long-distance exchange to assume that newly imported germs would become easily and widely spread.[109] To be sure, southeastern communities acquired nonlocal raw materials and finished goods from faraway places. None of these items came from Mesoamerica, but interior groups did accumulate marine shell from the Atlantic and Gulf coasts and copper from the Great Lakes region, while sending mica, deerskins, turkey feathers, and other things out to relatively distant places.[110] Such long-distance exchange, though, should not be inflated. Archaeologists have found that an overwhelming majority of grave goods in sites across the Southeast were made from local materials.[111] Nonlocal items, on the other hand, remain uncommon components of archaeological sites and were rarely transformed into utilitarian objects. Instead, exotic materials were made into status or ceremonial items, which often came to symbolize the power of leading individuals and families. Gorgets made of marine shell, headdresses adorned with images cut from sheet copper, and copper plates decorated with powerful cosmological symbols, for example, were included in several elite graves. These prestige goods represented the elite's assumed connection with mysterious outside forces and their power in war and diplomacy, through which they came to acquire exotic items. This power, of course, waxed and waned as geopolitical circumstances disrupted aboriginal exchange. In some chiefdoms leaders lost their status when rivals emerged who blocked their access to exotic materials. With the trickle of prestige goods ceasing, the elite lost the allegiance of subordinate towns and saw their chiefdoms collapse.[112] But even at the height of the power of particular southeastern chiefdoms, the exchange of exotic goods and materials occurred at a low volume and at irregular intervals.[113]

What made aboriginal exchange an even more unlikely avenue through which acute infectious diseases could have spread was the impact that warfare had on the social landscape. Southeastern polities, in fact, were more likely to fight than to trade with one another. Scholars propose a variety of reasons why indigenous peoples warred with one another: communities used military action to acquire territory and control resources; young warriors depended on success in battle to gain status; families sought vengeance for the loss of their kinsmen; and leaders exercised force to defeat and humiliate their rivals as well as to gain tribute from subordinate towns. Whatever the cause of such conflict, years of endemic warfare created contested spaces or buffer zones between rival polities, where humans could not live, hunt, or travel safely. Buffer zones were particularly common in upland areas between rival polities inhabiting parallel river valleys. Such contested areas could also be found within river valleys themselves as polities often found themselves warring with others either up- or downriver from them. At times conflict became so intense that vast areas of some river valleys, which held great horticultural potential, lay vacant. Wherever buffer zones existed, they demonstrated the ecological impact of warfare. These areas or buffer zones served as a sanctuary for wild game, which multiplied more rapidly in the relative absence of human predators.[114] Until English-inspired trading in indigenous captives dramatically altered the Native Southeast, buffer zones served as a barrier to the spread of acute infectious diseases.

Sixteenth-century European accounts describe a social landscape that had yet to be transformed by disease or colonialism but that consisted of a maze of buffer zones isolating rival polities from one another. Contested areas especially impeded travel through Florida. Groups such as the Calusas dominated the coasts and the swampy southern half of the peninsula.[115] They jealously guarded the territory from which they procured wild plant foods, fish, and game. Further up the peninsula, a large contested area likely existed between the Calusas and the more sedentary groups. The former protected their domination of marine resources, while the latter strove to check the advance of rival hunters into river valleys that supported terrestrial fauna, especially deer. Frenchmen who sought to establish a colony near the mouth of the St. John's River in 1564 stepped into a typical conflict between coastal and interior enemies. The headman of a coastal tribe solicited French aid in the conflict with their inland rivals the Timucuas.[116] The Timucuas themselves battled groups even further north. The French found that warring chiefdoms and tribes blocked the path to the Apalachees of the Florida panhandle.[117] Earlier, Spanish explorers found other challengers to the Apalachees, who certainly guarded the resource-rich area that they dominated from rivals to the west.[118] The area between the Ochlockonee and Apalachicola rivers was uninhabited in the sixteenth century.[119]

Buffer zones existed deeper in the interior. When Hernando de Soto advanced into the Georgia Piedmont, he encountered the small chiefdom of Ocute, lying near the fall line of the Oconee River. It was there that the Spaniards heard of a powerful leader, the "Lady of Cofitachequi," who headed an extensive polity. As the expedition set out to find Cofitachequi, they found themselves in what they described as a "desert." For 130 leagues, they found neither people nor villages, only pine groves and large rivers.[120] The area was the valley of the Savannah River, which stood vacant due to warfare between Ocute and Cofitachequi. A century earlier the "desert" had been the home of many people, but before Soto came, Natives had withdrawn to safer locations, creating a large buffer zone in the process.[121]

Rivalry among indigenous polities created even more buffer zones in the interior. The palisaded villages that Soto encountered among towns on the Little Tennessee and Coosa, for example, most likely indicated warfare with rivals living in the narrow valleys of the southern Appalachian highlands. In northern Mississippi, the Spanish traveled into the second largest buffer zone they encountered. There, land remained vacant between rival groups respectively occupying the Tombigbee and Mississippi valleys. Indigenous peoples on the Mississippi, moreover, appeared surprised at Soto's arrival, indicating that years of enmity with peoples to the east had stifled communications across the area.[122] In the Mississippi Valley itself, Soto found heavily palisaded communities and intense warfare between rivals, warfare that continued to characterize aboriginal societies into the late seventeenth century. One Frenchman, writing in 1682 but commenting on long-standing conflict between upriver and downriver groups, noted that members of several chiefdoms feared traveling into the delta region, claiming that Native tribes there would "eat" any intruders.[123] Another Frenchmen reported that indigenous peoples of the valley used a red post as a boundary marker between rivals who competed for scarce resources. The Bayagoulas and the Houmas, he wrote, "were so jealous of the hunting in their territories that they would shoot at any of their neighbors whom they caught hunting beyond the limits marked by the red post." This same Frenchman also claimed that European colonization brought an end to this rivalry. Mutual alliance with the French led the former rivals to abandon their animosity and essentially erase the buffer zone that had once separated them. "They hunt everywhere," the Frenchman claimed, "the ones with the others, and are good friends."[124]

Colonialism dramatically transformed the social landscape of the Native Southeast. Aboriginal exchange was reoriented to the Atlantic world, and a dramatically increased volume of goods flowed across the region. Old buffer zones were erased, and a new group of peoples—European traders—traveled through the region, linking even remote villages to extensive networks that connected them to disease-ridden European settlements. Compared to circumstances that emerged after colonization, though, aboriginal exchange failed to knit indigenous communities into a web of intimate connections capable of passing acute infectious diseases through the region. Native susceptibility to those germs, thus, was a factor of more than the biological aspects of colonialism. Virginity certainly made Native peoples vulnerable, but one cannot assume that diseases spread simply because they arrived on the shores of the Southeast. For the region's population as a whole, the economic aspects of colonialism had to change the Native disease ecology, making indigenous peoples even more vulnerable to newly imported germs. The most notorious of the diseases involved in the Columbian Exchange—smallpox—as we will see more clearly in chapter 3, arrived in most Native villages only after the Atlantic market economy had transformed the indigenous world.

The Issue of Genetics

Virginity indeed proves to be a misleading metaphor because it obscures the complex factors necessary for newly introduced diseases to affect indigenous peoples. The metaphor also has an even greater danger. Virginity has often been interpreted as meaning that indigenous peoples lacked genetic immunity. But Native bodies, when initially contracting new germs, responded no differently than those of Europeans infected for the first time. For first-time victims in both populations, white blood cells detected the presence of foreign pathogens and produced antibodies specifically designed to render the germs harmless, and for all first-time victims, such a response was ineffective. Regardless of race or geographical location, disease victims became sick because their production of antibodies was too slow to keep the viruses from replicating and interfering with the body's normal functions. Fortunately, individuals who survived their initial infection were spared future suffering. Antibodies, left in the bloodstreams of all people lucky enough to survive, were immediately ready to attack and destroy the viruses when they returned. Sometimes infants are born with a degree of acquired immunity due to antibodies they receive from their mother while in the womb or from their mother's breast milk. Such immunity does not last, and children eventually become susceptible to diseases from which their mother's antibodies originally protected them.

Of course, in 1492 no indigenous person possessed antibodies to fight smallpox and other diseases that Europeans and Africans would bring to the Americas. This was an accident of history, not a result of their genetic make-up. These diseases simply had been absent from the Americas, giving no one the opportunity to acquire immunity. Indigenous peoples were no less biologically equipped to deal with infectious disease than other peoples living in 1492. Their immune systems were composed of the same complex array of mechanisms that humankind had developed over the course of evolution. Their skin, mucus, tears, and saliva acted as a barrier to germs that awaited an opportunity to invade more vulnerable organs; stomach acids dissolved numerous pathogens that they consumed; and a variety of biochemicals in their bloodstreams attacked, killed, or redirected invading microbes to prevent or at least to limit sickness. Their bodies had become quite effective in dealing with germs, especially those that had plagued humanity since its beginnings some 500,000 years ago. Indigenous peoples of the Americas, as did other humans across the globe, even reached a level of coexistence with a variety of germs that resided in their bodies doing little harm and even helping stave off disease caused by more dangerous microbes.

Genetic immunity to infectious diseases is rare. It refers to specific inherited traits that give an individual a better chance to avoid a disease or suffer less than an individual who lacks those inherited traits. Such an advantage only develops after tens of thousands of years of natural selection and involves only a relative few diseases that are among the oldest known to humans. The case of the Yanomami, as previously discussed, suggests but does not prove that the absence of tuberculosis prevented natural selection from operating within that population for thousands of years and that their immune system lagged behind that of people of European and African descent.[125] Still, no true gene exists among any human population that provides resistance to tuberculosis.[126] Such a gene does exist in the case of malaria. Individuals with the sickle-cell trait fight off malarial infection much more effectively than those who lack the trait. This genetic "advantage" has led to high rates of sickle-cell carriers among populations that have had a long history with malaria, especially among Africans and their descendants. The increased number of sickle-cell carriers, however, comes with its own problems. Individuals who inherit the genes for this disease from both of their parents develop the irregularly shaped red blood cells that inhibit blood flow, cause anemia, and result in a number of other problems, including stroke at an early age.

No evidence confirms that genetic immunity exists for those diseases that caused the greatest catastrophes among American Indians. Again one can return to the Yanomami for evidence. When exposed to measles for the first time in the 1960s, members of this group suffered a case fatality rate no more severe than that found among peoples of European and African descent. Scientists furthermore propose that social and ecological conditions rather than genetics explained the deaths that did occur. Those conditions included social breakdown, inadequate care, respiratory infections, dehydration, and unavailability of breast milk for children over three years of age.[127] Measles has not been around long enough for natural selection to produce any genetic advantages. Similarly, indigenous peoples had no genetic disadvantages when confronted with smallpox. While it would seem that long exposure to smallpox offered Europeans ample opportunity to pass on stronger genes to their offspring, the virus afflicted no more than two hundred generations, a small blip in the entire trajectory of human evolution.[128] As late as the eighteenth century, European children were still dying at alarming rates. One study even claims that 80 percent of London's children under five years of age who became infected with smallpox during the eighteenth century did not survive the disease.[129] European colonists in America were also highly susceptible to the disease, especially Creoles who, like indigenous peoples, were essentially virgin populations. A modern study does suggest that smallpox mortality was greater among individuals with A-type blood, suggesting that other blood types offer a degree of protection from the disease. But the issue of blood-type advantage is still unresolved, and in fact it is a nonissue with regard to indigenous peoples of the Americas, who are almost universally O type.[130]

While genetic immunity did not play a role in favoring European colonizers over indigenous peoples, genetic homogeneity among the Native population may have figured in increasing their mortality rates. Scientists have found that RNA viruses can rapidly alter their genetic structure in response to the human immune system. Such an adaptation is an attempt by germs to escape destruction. When passed to a genetically similar victim, the virus is "preadapted," and the host's immune response will be slow and weak. DNA viruses, bacteria, and protozoa also have the ability to alter their genetic sequence to fool the human immune system but do so to a lesser extent than RNA viruses. Diseases, therefore, will become more severe as they are passed from one family member to another, making small-scale and isolated communities that have high rates of intragroup marriage most vulnerable. Some scientists argue that genetic homogeneity led to higher mortality rates among indigenous peoples than among Europeans.[131] Whether Native communities possessed a high degree of genetic homogeneity, however, is not certain. Among the entire indigenous population a considerable degree of genetic variation existed. This stemmed from several distinct waves of migrants coming across the Bering Strait at different times. By the time Europeans and Africans arrived with their diseases, Native peoples with different origins had had ample opportunity to mix together, producing communities with what one scholar calls "surprisingly extensive" genetic variability.[132] Still, catastrophically high death tolls indicate that genetic homogeneity within particular communities played a role in increasing the virulence of infectious diseases.

While genetic homogeneity likely factored in exacerbating the effect of virgin-soil epidemics, it can no longer be assumed that Natives possessed weaker genes than European invaders. Of all the diseases involved in the Columbian Exchange, malaria was the only disease to which genetic immunity clearly existed, and the immunity was found not among Europeans but among a small percentage of Africans. Indigenous peoples may have had a weaker immune response to tuberculosis, but if this was indeed the case, which is still highly debatable, genetics was only one factor among many that affected mortality from this disease. Smallpox, measles, and other infectious diseases that evolved after the Bering Strait crossing did not have sufficient time for natural selection to produce genetic advantages. Indeed, in our ability to fight most infectious diseases, humans today are not significantly different in their genetic make-up from the hunter-gatherers who composed the world's population eleven thousand years ago.[133] The genes of indigenous peoples of the Americas, therefore, did not make them any more or less vulnerable to epidemic diseases than were Europeans.

Rather than genetics, ecology provides a better approach to assess Native vulnerability. Such an approach proves especially valuable in discerning not only why catastrophic mortality rates occurred but also why virgin-soil epidemics had a differential impact on the Native population. In the Native Southeast, the preexisting disease ecology produced dynamic and varied health patterns. Some communities clearly enjoyed better health than others, while the well-being of individual communities changed over time. The interconnected factors of warfare, settlement patterns, nutrition, and disease provided for a fluid situation. Indigenous peoples when faced with endemic warfare sought safety behind the palisade walls of fortified towns, and in doing so they increased their exposure to infectious diseases. One cannot know fully what all of these diseases were; the jury is still out on tuberculosis, for example. But the archaeological record makes it clear that some communities experienced relatively high pathogen loads. The record also makes it clear that some communities had come to rely too much on maize and experienced nutritional deficiencies that worked synergistically with infectious diseases to increase infant mortality rates and to decrease life expectancies. Conversely, communities that enjoyed relative peace were able to maintain dispersed settlements and to continue to harvest a sufficient supply of wild game, consequently allowing them to enjoy a greater degree of health and well-being. Tragically, European colonialism made it even more difficult for Native peoples to control the conditions that affected their health and made Natives more vulnerable to infection and the resulting mortality from new diseases imported from the Atlantic world. Ultimately European colonialism and its germs caused massive population collapse that forever changed the social landscape of the region. Whether Spanish exploration and colonization of Florida in the sixteenth and seventeenth centuries bore responsibility for such a catastrophe is the subject of the next chapter.

Chapter Two

The Protohistoric Puzzle
1492–1659

"But again, it as other times pleased Almighty God to send unusual Sicknesses amongst [the Indians], as the Smallpox, . . . to lessen their numbers; so that the English in Comparison to the *Spaniard,* have but little *Indian* Blood to answer for," John Archdale, the governor of South Carolina, remarked after witnessing a horrific epidemic in the late 1690s.[1] Archdale, as did many English officials, sought to distinguish himself and his fellow colonists from the legendarily cruel Spanish. While the Spanish had acquired their empire through violent conquest, "the Hand of God" was at work graciously "thinning the Indians, to make room for the English."[2] The governor, however, obscured the fact that the noxious English practice of buying indigenous slaves did more than any other aspect of colonialism to destroy Natives. Beginning in 1659 Native raiders armed with English weapons appeared near the Savannah River, began taking captives from indigenous groups, including those within the Spanish mission system, and caused a myriad of population movements that radically changed the social landscape. Eventually smallpox and other diseases followed the course of the Native slave trade and caused massive depopulation. The English indeed bore primary responsibility for creating the conditions for newly introduced germs to do their most destructive damage to the Native Southeast.[3]

Like Governor Archdale, many scholars hold the Spanish, albeit their germs rather than their physical brutality, responsible for the destruction of the Southeast's indigenous peoples. Some scholars have claimed that the Spanish ignited regionwide epidemics that caused massive devastation during what is commonly referred to as the protohistoric period—the time between Columbus's first voyage and the arrival of English colonialism in the mid-seventeenth century.[4] Proponents of a protohistoric population collapse cite many possibilities for the spread of epidemic diseases. Perhaps outbreaks originating shortly after Columbus's inaugural voyage spread from Spanish colonies into the Native Southeast by way of aboriginal exchange networks or undocumented European visitors. If not by that way, then perhaps one or more Spanish expeditions introduced new germs when they explored the region. Juan Ponce de León (1513), Lucas Vázquez de Ayllón (1526), Pánfilo de Narváez (1528), Hernando de Soto (1539–43), Tristán de Luna y Arellano (1559–61), and Juan Pardo (1566–68) led parties of hundreds of men and livestock onto southeastern shores and to varying extents interacted with Native peoples in the land they called La Florida. If the Columbian Exchange did not derive from these early encounters, then perhaps it came after the Spanish established a more permanent presence in the region. In 1565 the Spanish founded St. Augustine—the first permanent European settlement in what would become the United States—and over the course of the next several decades, they extended a series of Catholic missions along the coast of Georgia and west across northern Florida. Perhaps by this presence on the periphery, deadly epidemics spread into the interior, devastating the indigenous population well before English colonialism arrived.

This chapter takes a closer look at the protohistoric period, however, and reveals that epidemiological events in the Native Southeast have been misunderstood and exaggerated. Malaria, a relatively mild chronic disease, likely became widespread, and early explorers certainly contaminated Native villages with germs associated with poor sanitation that were already present in the American environment. But the deadliest microbes circulating through the Atlantic world were not likely to accompany early explorers. Smallpox and other acute infectious diseases involved in the Columbian Exchange did arrive on southeastern shores after 1565 with the founding of St. Augustine, but given the limited extent of Spanish colonialism, these newly introduced germs did not spread outside the Catholic mission system. Indigenous peoples outside Florida at most experienced minor population loss and demographic changes due to malaria, non-Columbian Exchange diseases, and other traumas associated with Spanish exploration.

The Epidemiology of Early Encounters

Demographic changes fill the protohistoric archaeological record. Indigenous communities appear to have declined in number and size in some river valleys, and in some places entire populations disappear from geographic locations where they had lived for generations. When one begins with archaeology, then, it is tempting to conclude that newly introduced diseases had a catastrophic impact on the Southeast's social landscape at a very early date. Instead of beginning with the archaeological record, though, and instead of assuming that deadly germs must have spread through the region because Europeans visited it, let us, at least for now, put those germs at the center of the analysis and ask what diseases could have spread by way of early encounters between indigenous peoples and Europeans. In doing so, it must not be taken as fact that epidemics occurred as an inevitable and immediate result of the Spanish colonization in the Caribbean and Mexico or as an automatic consequence of Europeans setting foot onto southeastern soil.

The Columbian Exchange certainly began in Spanish colonies shortly after 1492. As early as 1493, Columbus's ships introduced some kind of germ that made the Natives of Hispaniola terribly ill. Malaria was the most likely culprit since the plasmodia parasite could have easily survived in the bloodstreams of European sailors as they made the long ocean crossing.[5] Eventually, the volume of traffic across the Atlantic increased to the extent that more deadly acute infectious diseases arrived as well. Smallpox, measles, influenza, typhus, and other major killers arrived in Latin America in the sixteenth century and became a potent aspect of European colonialism.[6] Smallpox in particular became a deadly consequence of Spanish conquest. In 1518 the lethal virus arrived aboard Spanish ships and struck indigenous peoples in Hispaniola and Puerto Rico. Once smallpox appeared there, it spread along Caribbean shipping routes and struck other island colonies, including Cuba in 1519. From there the virus followed the course of conquest to Mexico, where some individuals involved with Cortez's invasion arrived infected with the disease. Smallpox erupted with a fury when it was transmitted to the large and densely settled indigenous population of central Mexico. Aztec resistance crumbled in the virus's wake, and for the next two years, the dreaded disease wreaked havoc among Mexico's Native peoples. Credible evidence suggests that the virus spread even farther, traveling south through Central America and into South America and arriving among the Incas well before the Spanish did in the 1530s, making the smallpox pandemic that began in 1518 and continued into the 1520s one of the worst episodes of disease in world history.[7]

While aboriginal exchange networks probably facilitated the spread of smallpox through the densely settled populations of Mesoamerica, the same cannot be said of a northern spread of the virus or other acute infectious diseases that Europeans introduced into Latin America. Malaria certainly stood a chance of spreading gradually through the Americas, especially along the swampy rim of the Gulf Coast, where Natives fished and collected aquatic resources as part of their usual subsistence routines. Such a passage of smallpox or even less viable germs such as measles, influenza, and plague, though, was fraught with geographic and social obstacles. Deadly microbes, with relatively short life spans, found many dead ends among indigenous populations separated by formidable buffer zones. For acute infectious diseases to have spread from Mexico, one would have to find the existence of thriving trade networks that linked Native groups living great distances from one another. As of yet, no credible evidence of direct links between the Native Southeast and Mexico exists, and no goods of Mesoamerican origin have been found at southeastern archaeological sites.[8] Perhaps a more plausible route for new diseases to travel was from Cuba to Florida.[9] Members of the Calusa tribe who resided in the Everglades traveled to Cuba by way of canoes and traded with Natives there. For disease transmission to occur, though, such traders, who certainly arrived neither in great numbers nor on a daily basis, had to reach the island at the time in which a Columbian Exchange disease was present, contract the new germs, survive the ocean crossing back to Florida, and then transmit the germs to other Calusas. Once on the mainland, the foreign microbes would have had to travel hundreds of miles north through a variety of communities and the buffer zones that separated them before reaching more densely settled horticultural peoples in northern Florida.[10] Such a scenario could explain how malaria was introduced into the Southeast, but for deadlier germs such as smallpox, too many variables would have had to fall into place.[11] It is more likely that aboriginal exchange practices, which involved a low volume of items and were frequently impeded by buffer zones, were ineffective in spreading acute infectious diseases over the great distances that separated the Southeast from both Mexico and the Caribbean.

If acute infectious diseases appeared in the Southeast during the protohistoric period, one would expect them to come by way of direct rather than indirect transmission. Within the first few decades of the European invasion, Spanish navigators explored southeastern coasts, as did unofficial visitors such as slave raiders, pirates, traders, fishermen, and victims of shipwrecks. Could it be that any of these unrecorded or sparsely documented coastal forays spread the deadly diseases that ravaged Latin America's indigenous populations? One can never say with certainty whether smallpox or other highly lethal germs arrived on southeastern shores through such means, but four factors diminished the importance of these episodes in facilitating the Columbian Exchange. First, such visits involved only small parties. Second, it is a safe assumption that adult males, unlikely carriers of a childhood disease such as smallpox, composed the parties. Third, these small parties spent their stay near the coast and rarely, if ever, ventured into the interior to visit larger horticultural communities. And last, such visitors did not stay long.[12] Consequently, the ephemeral nature of any interaction between indigenous peoples and these small groups of predominately adult males greatly lessened the potential to spread an acute infectious disease. The Atlantic world's worst germs would have to wait until Europeans sent larger, more organized expeditions to the region before they had a chance to destroy Natives.

Juan Ponce de León led the first major European attempt to settle in the Southeast. In 1513 his three ships left Puerto Rico, sailed north through the Bahamas, and eventually arrived at what Ponce de León thought was a large island, which he called La Florida. Ponce de León then turned his ships southward, rounded the cape, and sailed as far north as Charlotte Harbor. The Spanish exploration lasted for nearly two months, during which time Ponce de León's men remained in sight of the coast and occasionally went ashore for firewood and fresh water. During such times, the Spanish found a hostile reception, perhaps because indigenous peoples had earlier experience with European slavers. Ponce de León, though, returned, and this time he planned on staying. In 1521 the Spanish adventurer assembled three ships with at least two hundred men and an untold number of women, children, and slaves that was not estimated in the various chronicles of the expedition. The Spanish landed again near Port Charlotte and quickly began to build houses, but such colonizing efforts were short-lived. The Calusas attacked the Spanish, wounding Ponce de León himself. The Spanish leader decided to give up the colonizing effort and sailed his ships and survivors back to Puerto Rico, where he died of his wounds.[13]

Despite leading a significant effort to colonize the Southeast, Ponce de León's visits to Florida stood little chance to spread acute infectious diseases. Malaria certainly could have accompanied his men in either of his expeditions. The plasmodia parasite had become endemic among Caribbean populations soon after 1492, and any sailors who had spent time on these islands stood a good chance of carrying malaria with them to faraway places. But acute infectious diseases were a different story. Ponce de León's first voyage occurred five years prior to smallpox's known arrival in the Americas, and the encounters between his men and Natives were sporadic, brief, and hostile. The second voyage did occur during a time in which smallpox was circulating through Latin America, but again the expedition's interaction with Natives was violent and short. Calusas would have little to do with the Spanish and drove the invaders away. Also, Ponce de León's second expedition was not particularly large and did not involve significant numbers of children. One sick adult male and a few nonimmune people of course could have constituted a chain of infection during the relatively short voyage from Puerto Rico to Florida, but one cannot assume that these hypothetically infected individuals then transmitted the disease to indigenous peoples, who were generally unreceptive of the newcomers. The available documents, which admittedly are scarce and vague, provide no evidence of disease transmission occurring. None of the chronicles of Ponce de León's expeditions mentions any of the Spanish being actively ill. If individuals involved in either of the expeditions had been infected with smallpox, one would expect to find mention of sickness shortly after the departure from Puerto Rico. One might also expect that Ponce de León would not have continued either of his missions with ships full of gravely ill crewmen. A lack of documentary evidence alone certainly does not rule out the possibility of a transmission of acute infectious diseases, but such evidence, combined with the demographic characteristics of individuals involved in Ponce de León's expeditions and the nature of contact between Natives and newcomers, strongly suggests that smallpox and other highly lethal diseases did not arrive on Florida's shores with the first major effort at colonization.

In the same year as Ponce de León's second expedition, another would-be conquistador set his sights on the Southeast as a potential area of Spanish conquest, thus providing another opportunity for smallpox to arrive in the region. As Ponce de León was being expelled from Florida, Lucas Vázquez de Ayllón sent Spanish ships led by Francisco Gordillo up the Atlantic Coast on a slave-raiding mission. Off the coast of South Carolina, Gordillo tricked at least sixty Natives into coming aboard his ships and promptly enslaved them.[14] Vázquez de Ayllón wanted more than slaves, though. He learned from the captives that the land they came from was known as Chicora, which he imagined as being rich with gold, silver, and more slaves. After receiving permission from the Spanish Crown, the Spanish adventurer set out to colonize Chicora. In mid-July 1526, Vázquez de Ayllón sailed from Hispaniola to South Carolina with six ships carrying approximately six hundred people, most of whom were Spanish men but including some women, children, and African slaves. Instead of the riches that he imagined, Vázquez de Ayllón found only disaster. One of his ships sank along the way, ruining many of the supplies that he would need. The remaining fleet landed near Winyah Bay and the Santee River on August 9, 1526. Trouble continued. After arriving, members of the expedition became desperately ill, and the barren and largely deserted coastal environment provided little food. Over the three month period in which the Spaniards attempted to establish a colony, exposure, famine, and sickness took their toll. Finally, in November the 150 survivors departed, abandoning their dead, including Vázquez de Ayllón, who perished in the land he thought would bring him great prosperity.[15]

Something certainly made Vázquez de Ayllón and the members of his expedition sick. But was it smallpox? If so, did it spread among indigenous peoples, causing widespread devastation? Tantalizing evidence suggests an affirmative answer to those two questions. In 1540 the Hernando de Soto expedition made its way into the Carolina Piedmont, just a short distance from the coastal location of Vázquez de Ayllón's failed colony. At the Native community of Cofitachequi, Soto and his men found a metal dagger, rosary beads, and steel axes, indicating an earlier Spanish presence in the vicinity.[16] The Spanish also learned of a recent disaster that had struck the area. One of Soto's chroniclers reported, "About the town [of Cofitachequi] within the compass of a league and a half league were large uninhabited towns, choked with vegetation, which looked as though no people had inhabited them for some time." Indigenous peoples informed the Spaniards that "two years ago there had been a plague in that land and they had moved to other towns."[17] A later and less reliable account of the Soto expedition called the disaster both a "pestilence" and a "plague" and mentioned four houses stacked with corpses.[18] It seems that another visitor, perhaps a deadly disease of European or African origin introduced during Vázquez de Ayllón's 1526 foray, had come to the Carolina Piedmont and its Native inhabitants before Soto arrived.

It is indeed tempting to conclude that the "plague of Cofitachequi" was a virgin-soil epidemic. Colonial documents are full of horrid accounts of indigenous peoples experiencing European germs for the first time, and contemporary scholars have heightened our awareness of the significant role disease played in facilitating European conquest. But scholars should be cautious in blaming newly introduced pathogens for Cofitachequi's fate. Soto's men did not directly observe the event; rather they learned of it from a Native interpreter, whose translation of the story into Spanish was certainly far from perfect and void of details. Europeans often used the terms "plague" and "pestilence" in generic ways to describe great sickness, and it is possible that the Spaniards misinterpreted the event as a plague when it was really a famine, an unfortunate but not uncommon phenomenon for southeastern horticulturalists. Floods, droughts, insect invasions, or a number of other problems could have destroyed harvests, resulting in widespread hunger and sickness due to indigenous diseases. Also, the houses with piles of corpses need not be seen as evidence of catastrophic mortality from novel germs. Southeastern Natives commonly kept the bones of their ancestors in mortuary temples for veneration.[19] Soto's men, furthermore, may have been inclined to interpret the plague from perspectives shaped by earlier Spanish experiences. Many of them had participated in the conquests of the Aztecs, read about it, or heard about it, and consequently knew about the devastation that smallpox had caused among Natives in Mexico in 1520 and 1521.

Assuming that the plague of Cofitachequi was a virgin-soil epidemic originating with the Vázquez de Ayllón expedition, however, can the identity of the germ culprit be determined? Absolute certainty is impossible, but some factors can help us eliminate smallpox. First, the Vázquez de Ayllón expedition was rather large and probably did include some children, whose presence the various chroniclers felt no need to mention, but the illness in question does not appear to be a childhood disease. Of the 500 adult males, 450 died, indicating that something other than a childhood illness was involved. Second, members of the Vázquez de Ayllón expedition did not become sick until after their nearly one-month long journey to South Carolina, a fact that would rule out acute infectious diseases, whose symptoms would be expected to appear shortly after departure. If some of Vázquez de Ayllón's sailors, for example, contracted smallpox on the day they left Hispaniola, then symptoms of the dreaded disease would have appeared within the virus's fourteen-day incubation period, well before the Spanish stepped ashore and long before sickness actually appeared among the ill-fated crew. Vázquez de Ayllón himself died on October 18, a month and nine days after first coming ashore. Third, and finally, the plague of Cofitachequi, according to Soto's chroniclers, occurred in 1538, twelve years after Vázquez de Ayllón arrived, a period much too long to suspect that an acute infectious disease had spread from the Atlantic Coast to the Piedmont. Smallpox would have spread much quicker, if it spread at all, before burning itself out. Something other than smallpox made Vázquez de Ayllón's party sick.

Exposure, famine, and dehydration may have caused many of the deaths, but the high mortality rate indicates that the Spaniards probably suffered from one or more diseases. Unfortunately, the available documentary evidence leaves no specific clues as to what those diseases might have been. Vázquez de Ayllón's party likely suffered food poisoning and other infections that any group camped in unsanitary conditions would, including dysentery, typhoid, and other waterborne illnesses. Common bacterial infections also took their toll. One man in particularly appeared to have a case of gangrene. Vázquez de Ayllón's chroniclers reported that after this gravely ill man took off his pants, "all the flesh came away from both legs from the knees downwards, leaving his bones bare." But of course, such common bacterial infections were not new to indigenous peoples and would not have been responsible for the plague of Cofitachequi some twelve years later. Hungry, tired, and depleted, Vázquez de Ayllón's men could have perished due to pathogens commonly found throughout the world and suffered high mortality due to unfavorable ecological conditions that weakened their immunity to those pathogens.

Nevertheless, Vázquez de Ayllón's short-lived expedition may have had epidemiological consequences for the Native Southeast. The evidence points to a transmission of malaria. Vázquez de Ayllón and his men had departed from a malaria-ridden area and arrived on the coast of Carolina at a favorable time of the year to spread the disease. The Spanish set up camp on August 18, still within the warm season, when anopheles mosquitoes were active. They camped for at least a month at a place historically known for its poor drainage and abundant insect life, giving anopheles enough time to contract plasmodia from carriers and then transmit the parasite to noncarriers among the expedition. One would expect that these newly infected individuals would begin to show symptoms within a period of twenty to forty-nine days, which is in fact what happened. Vázquez de Ayllón himself perished forty-one days after arriving.[20] Of course, the high mortality rate weighs against a diagnosis of malaria exclusively. But combined with famine, dehydration, bacterial infections, and other maladies, malaria can be devastating. Mortality rates, which today are around 10 percent for untreated yet otherwise healthy victims, certainly escalated among groups who lived amid ecological conditions conducive to poor health.

That malaria became permanently planted in the Southeast is a more difficult conclusion to make. Anopheles mosquitoes are rather localized animals, remaining within one mile of their breeding grounds during their relatively short life span of one year. Plasmodia, consequently, depend more on their mammal hosts to spread great distances. Vázquez de Ayllón, however, did not have much interaction with Native peoples, and his chroniclers made no reference to any indigenous community in close proximity to his expedition's campsite. For malaria to take root, then, Native travelers had to visit the location where the Spanish camped, contract the plasmodia germ, transport it back to their home town, and infect local anopheles populations that lived in intimate contact with their fellow community members. This scenario does not seem too far fetched, assuming that curious Natives investigated the scene of Vázquez de Ayllón's arrival, but the window of opportunity was not long either. Plasmodia would have disappeared from the mosquito population as infected pests came to the end of their short life cycle.

Still, malaria's ability to persist within a human host for a fairly lengthy time and the Southeast's predisposition to harbor the disease suggest that the disease took root in the Southeast at some early time, if not with Vázquez de Ayllón's expedition then with another. Malaria also would spread slowly and gradually through the region. It may have indeed taken twelve years for the pathogen to travel from the coastal area to the Piedmont. The plague of Cofitachequi, moreover, fits a description of malaria. The culprit disease was unevenly distributed, indicating that those people living in villages near swamps or stagnant bodies of waters where anopheles predominated became infected. The main town of Cofitachequi and other villages remained occupied and served as receptacles for people whose communities suffered. Also, the fact that famine accompanied the illness indicates malaria. The illness often flares up during the growing season, incapacitating workers needed to plant, maintain, and harvest crops.[21]

Connecting the plague of Cofitachequi with the Vázquez de Ayllón expedition remains conjectural at best, but examining that possibility illustrates the complexity involved in introducing new germs into the southeastern environment. One may be prepared to read the plague of Cofitachequi as proof of catastrophic virgin-soil epidemics, but a closer look at the evidence suggests that acute infectious diseases were an improbable cause; if any new disease was involved, it was likely to be malaria.

Examining other episodes of Spanish exploration of the Southeast yields further support for the conclusion that malaria and not smallpox became widespread during the protohistoric period. Pánfilo de Narváez's expedition, for example, had a similar epidemiological potential as that of Vázquez de Ayllón. Sometime after February 20, 1528, Narváez with a force of four hundred men, a few women, and some slaves left Cuba and sailed for Florida. On April 14, 1528, they landed near present-day Tampa Bay.[22] For over a month after arrival, the expedition remained healthy while they journeyed north seeking food to steal from Native peoples. The Spaniards eventually arrived at the town of Aute, whose Apalachee inhabitants had abandoned in advance of the newcomers' arrival. Arriving there during the summer and several months since departing Cuba, the Narváez expedition suffered from a serious illness. Alvar Núñez Cabeza de Vaca, one of the members of the expedition, later wrote that "there were not horses enough to carry the sick, who went on increasing in numbers day by day, and [they] knew no cure . . . the people were unable to move forward, the greater part being ill."[23] There had been sufficient food before sickness erupted, but with everyone coming down with the malady, few remained healthy enough to obtain sustenance. Casualties from disease and hunger, however, were not as severe as among members of the Vázquez de Ayllón expedition. Only forty of Narváez's men died.[24] The expedition nonetheless fell apart. Without food the expeditionary force stole from Native villages and invaded oyster-gathering sites, provoking reprisals and causing many Spanish deaths. Dissension broke out, and the Spaniards decided to build boats, abandon the sick and injured, and travel to Mexico. On September 22, 1528, Narváez's crew departed from the Florida pan-

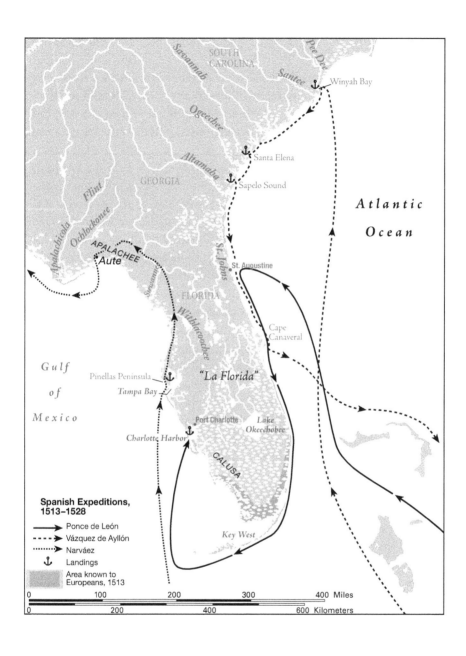

SOUTH
CAROLINA

Pee Dee

Santee

⚓ Winyah Bay

Savannah

Ogeechee

Altamaha

⚓ Santa Elena

GEORGIA

⚓ Sapelo Sound

Atlantic

Ocean

Flint

Ochlockonee

Apalachicola

APALACHEE
Aute

Suwannee

St. Johns

St. Augustine

FLORIDA

Withlacoochee

Cape
Canaveral

Gulf

of

Mexico

Pinellas Peninsula ⚓

Tampa Bay

"La Florida"

Port Charlotte

Lake
Okeechobee

Charlotte Harbor

CALUSA

**Spanish Expeditions,
1513–1528**

Key West

→ Ponce de León

- - → Vázquez de Ayllón

····→ Narváez

⚓ Landings

Area known to
Europeans, 1513

| 0 | 100 | 200 | 300 | 400 Miles |

| 0 | 200 | 400 | 600 Kilometers |

handle, and after traveling thirty days most of them became lost and perished somewhere off the coast of Texas. A group of eighty eventually made it ashore, camped that winter among local Natives, and in the spring began to travel overland. Only four of these men survived. Remarkably, Cabeza de Vaca and three others straggled into a Spanish settlement in northern Mexico after six years of wandering through what are today the states of Texas, New Mexico, and Arizona.[25]

As with the Vázquez de Ayllón expedition, Narváez's party did not bring acute infectious diseases with them to the Southeast. Again, one would expect that symptoms from the deadliest illness would have appeared shortly after Narváez's predominately male crew departed from Cuba, but sickness did not erupt until months after their arrival. Malaria was a possible culprit for what ailed the Spaniards, and indeed the intruders could have spread the plasmodia parasite wherever they traveled. But the Spaniards could have also become sick by contracting any one of several diseases that were already present in Florida. Sickness erupted only after Narváez reached Aute and only afflicted those who remained in the Native village, while sparing a scouting party that explored the coast. At Aute the Spanish remained tightly camped, since the Apalachees had surrounded their occupied town. Diseases associated with poor sanitation—food poisoning and illnesses related to contaminated water—could have easily become a problem. Typhoid, dysentery, and other illnesses could have erupted among the over four hundred Spanish, who contaminated their food and water with feces and urine. Similarly, the horses and swine that accompanied the Spanish expedition posed another health problem. These animals had to be kept in close quarters to prevent indigenous peoples from destroying them, but the bacteria-filled wastes of such animals made the Spanish violently ill. Whether carrying new diseases or those that all human beings have had to face, Spanish expeditions involved incredible filth that contaminated Native villages ill equipped to deal with hundreds of people and livestock. The Spanish experienced the health consequences of their own making by taking up temporary residence in the compact village of Aute. Indigenous peoples who had the unfortunate experience of having their villages invaded may have also been victims of diseases caused by poor sanitation—diseases that they had certainly experienced before but to which they were more vulnerable when unwelcome guests made sewers out of their villages.

An event that occurred during Cabeza de Vaca's journey to Mexico further suggests that a dysentery-type disease had plagued the Spanish expedition. A little over thirty days after departing from Florida, eighty survivors of the Narváez expedition arrived on the Texas coast. The Spaniards, desperately ill and hungry, began to die rapidly, with the survivors consuming the flesh of the dead for sustenance. Shortly thereafter local Natives, whom Cabeza de Vaca described as poor people living off shellfish and aquatic roots, began to suffer from the Spanish presence. "After this," Cabeza de Vaca reported, "the natives were visited by a disease of the bowels, of which half their number died." Indigenous peoples thought that the Spaniards, probably by using witchcraft, were responsible for their deaths. Cabeza de Vaca, though, convinced the Indians that if they had such power to make others ill, they would not have made their own people die. After all, only fifteen of the eighty who arrived on the Texas shore survived.[26] The "disease of the bowels" to which Cabeza de Vaca referred may have resulted from some form of dysentery-causing bacteria or intestinal parasites native to the Gulf Coast, but the Spaniards themselves could have been responsible for the sickness. Once ashore, the newcomers possibly deposited the same germs that made them sick at Aute by defecating and urinating near local drinking water or in aquatic areas where indigenous peoples gathered clams or oysters, food sources that often harbor dysentery-causing pathogens.

The illness that erupted among Natives of the Texas coast again illustrates how Europeans disrupted Native communities and heightened their vulnerability to those diseases already present in the American environment. Whenever large parties of Europeans and their livestock intruded, their filth and wastes presented a health problem for indigenous towns. In the case of the Narváez expedition, poor sanitation probably caused the suffering of the Spanish themselves. Fortunately, though, indigenous peoples had little direct contact with the Narváez expedition as well as with those that preceded it—those of Lucas Vázquez de Ayllón and Juan Ponce de León. Until Hernando de Soto's expedition, the majority of indigenous communities remained out of the purview of the Spanish. If anything of epidemiological significance happened, it was the introduction of malaria, which could have become rooted in the region and gradually spread among horticultural towns where anopheles and humans already constituted a viable chain of infection. None of these early Spanish expeditions, however, carried the most notorious germ of the Columbian Exchange, smallpox.

Smallpox was similarly absent even among the most successful Spanish expedition during the protohistoric period, Hernando de Soto's. In April 1538 600 to 650 men left the Iberian Peninsula with Soto. Several slaves and women not included in the official count also accompanied the expedition, bringing the total up to an estimated 1,000 individuals. Making the expedition more onerous,

Soto assembled over two hundred horses and even more swine for his planned conquest. In less than two months, Soto's ships arrived at Cuba, a trip that included a fifteen-day stop on the Canary Islands. The expedition remained in Cuba for nearly a year, gathering supplies for the journey to Florida. No reference to sickness was made while Soto's party made their transatlantic voyage or while the Spaniards prepared in Cuba, but one chronicler reported that Soto's party, while on the Caribbean island, "suffered much annoyance from mosquitoes, especially in a swamp."[27] Certainly, by 1538 malaria had become endemic in Cuba, making the Soto expedition likely candidates to spread the disease to the Southeast. On May 18, 1539, the expedition departed Havana; they arrived off the coast of Florida near present-day Tampa Bay thirteen days later.[28]

Soto's short voyage from Cuba was certainly enough time for someone with an active case of smallpox to carry the virus to Florida. But the evidence shows that no such transmission occurred. Spanish chroniclers made no reference to sickness either during the voyage or during the first several months that the expedition traveled from their landing at Tampa Bay to their winter camp near the Apalachicola River. There, several months after a smallpox outbreak would have run its course, Native slaves did become desperately ill, and most perished during the winter of 1539–40. Many of these individuals had been captured shortly after the Spanish arrived in Florida and were forced to serve the expedition as it made its way north.[29] Kept naked and in chains, these Natives certainly suffered from exposure, dehydration, malnourishment, and demoralization. Camped among Soto's large army of people, horses, and pigs, Native slaves also suffered from diseases associated with poor sanitation. The Spanish did not need to introduce smallpox or any other diseases from the Atlantic world; given the ecological conditions in which they were forced to live, Native slaves had very little chance to survive the germs that have plagued all humans throughout their evolutionary history. Still, one wonders if the Natives had been infected with malaria, either introduced by earlier expeditions or by Soto's party.

The Spanish themselves remained healthy during the first year of the journey, further weakening the case that they played a major role in bringing Columbian Exchange diseases. It was not until May 1540 that any Spaniard showed up ill in the various chronicles of the Soto expedition. After departing the Apalachicola River in March 1540 and advancing through the Piedmont of Georgia and into South Carolina, the expedition turned west and headed into the Appalachian highlands. Near the Native town of Xualla, many men reportedly became "sick and lame." Later one of Soto's horsemen traveling between the Native towns of Xualla and Guaxule, somewhere in the Appalachian Mountains, became "sick with fever" and wandered from the trail.[30] The number of ill increased as the expedition went farther. After passing over the Appalachian summit and halting on the French Broad at the town of Chiaha, some men became too sick to continue the journey.[31] The expedition members may have suffered from heat, dehydration, and malnourishment, but malaria also likely prevailed. Camping for an extended period of time in the Carolina Piedmont allowed carriers of plasmodia to infect mosquitoes and allowed the insects to transmit the pathogen to those still uninfected. The expedition may have even passed through areas made malarial by Vázquez de Ayllón's previous invasion. Weeks prior to the first report of illness, the expedition reached Cofitachequi, where they stayed for nine to ten days. Soto's men could have contracted the malady there and transported it deeper into the interior. Whatever the cause of the illness, casualties remained modest in comparison to earlier Spanish invasions. From May until September 1540, Soto and his men advanced from the Tennessee through the Coosa Valley and arrived on the Alabama River. By the fall of 1540, Soto had lost 102 of his men due to illness and violence.[32]

For nearly two more years, Soto and his men continued their journey without experiencing serious illness. The Spanish, despite being hungry and wounded from conflict with indigenous peoples, remained relatively healthy as they made their way north and west from Alabama across Mississippi and into Arkansas. When they returned to the Mississippi River, though, members of the expedition became sick. Soto himself became particularly ill, and after being "badly racked by fever," the famed explorer died on May 21, 1542. One chronicler described the famed explorer's death as an illness that began with "a slight fever" that was "slow on the first day and extremely severe on the third." The fever continued to increase until the seventh day, when Soto died.[33] Of course, one can never know what specific disease caused Soto's death, but one can be sure that it was not smallpox. There is absolutely no evidence the expedition harbored the virus, and even if they did, it would not have persisted among the Spanish army for almost three years. Soto's symptoms also did not resemble those of smallpox. Pustules would have formed within two to four days after he became feverish. Malaria is an intriguing possibility. The Spanish could have maintained a continual chain of infection throughout the journey. Some members of the expedition could have carried the germ with them to Florida and then passed it on to other members of their party when they camped for a period long enough for local anopheles to pick up the disease and then transmit it back to Spaniards who previously had not been exposed. Malaria would have remained to infect indigenous peoples wherever the Spaniards camped and would also have spread with the invaders, reaching as far west as the Mississippi Valley, where compact human settlements nestled amid numerous swamps and oxbow lakes comprised a disease ecology particularly predisposed to harbor the pestilence. But Soto's death, which admittedly is described by the least reliable of his chroniclers, does not indicate malaria. His temperature steadily increased rather than going through a cycle of fever and chills. A waterborne illness, food intoxication, or a variety of other common bacterial or parasitical infections likely afflicted the famed Spanish explorer. These diseases were problematic for the entire expedition as they made their trip across the Southeast. Malaria, while not being primarily responsible for Soto's death, still may have infected him, weakening his health and making him more vulnerable to several pathogens already common in the southeastern environment.

Although Soto's men themselves did not introduce acute infectious diseases into the Southeast, the possibility that their hogs may have transmitted influenza must be considered. It has been commonly believed that human influenza viruses move freely between people and pigs. In other words, the same germ that makes a person sick could then be passed on to a hog, making that animal come down with the same disease. Influenza follows a similar course in swine as in humans. The virus incubates for about two days, and thereafter its swine host sheds the virus for three to seven days and infects other pigs and humans who come into contact with its respiratory excretions. Hogs do not become permanent carriers of influenza but can serve as amplifiers in human influenza epidemics. By inflating the pool of susceptible victims, they can help spread the disease farther and sustain an epidemic longer than it would otherwise last if only humans were available to infect. Lately, however, scientific studies have cast doubt on such ease of movement and suggest that an influenza virus must undergo significant genetic adaptation before crossing from humans to swine. Hogs do not always become infected when they come into contact with human influenza but do so only on rare occasions when the virus undergoes an appropriate mutation necessary to pass the species barrier.[34]

What is even more certain is that influenza viruses that are specifically adapted to swine should not be considered a major cause of Native depopulation. Pigs have their own strains of influenza that circulate within herd populations. Handlers of infected hogs are known to come down with cases of swine flu, but to date none of these viruses has been found to have the properties necessary to be then transmitted from human to human.[35] To be sure, pigs are believed to have played an important role in sparking influenza pandemics that have swept the human population. It has been hypothesized that hogs serve as

"mixing vessels" in which strains of influenza from different species undergo genetic reassortment. Pigs can become infected with avian as well as human influenza viruses. It is believed that when such simultaneous infection occurs, human strains pick up genetic material from avian strains and thereby evolve into a
form to which no human has immunity.[36] Again, though, one should not assume that pigs always served as a vector for influenza when transported to the
Americas during colonization. Pigs have played a role in sparking pandemics,
but such events have historically originated in China, Southeast Asia, and Russia, where a high concentration of humans, pigs, and domestic fowl have provided the ideal ecological conditions for the emergence of new influenza viruses.
Once these emergent viruses crossed the species barrier, moreover, they depended on human beings for their global spread.[37]

It thus must be seen as highly improbable that Soto's hogs triggered an influenza epidemic within the Native Southeast. At most hogs may be suspected
of serving as an amplifier for a human strain, but there is no evidence that influenza was in circulation in Cuba when Soto's ships departed in 1539. If the
virus was in circulation and in the unlikely event that it had been transmitted to
Soto's hogs, the Spaniards themselves were the people most likely to become infected as they made their way to Florida aboard cramped ships. Such transmission would have occurred during transit, and symptoms of influenza would have
been apparent around the time Soto's expedition landed in Florida. It must be
remembered, though, that the Soto chronicles give no indication that the invaders carried an acute infectious disease with them. It might have been possible
for a human influenza virus to have circulated among Soto's swine herd without
infecting any Spaniards and then be transmitted to Natives through a stray pig
that wandered off from the Spaniards, but such a transmission had to occur relatively soon after arrival due to influenza's relatively short period of incubation
and communicability. The infected pig also had to come into close enough contact for a Native to contract the virus through respiratory excretions. (One cannot catch influenza through fecal matter or blood.) It makes for an incredible
story that an infected hog strayed from Soto's herd and wandered into an indigenous village, where curious Natives came into close enough contact with the
strange animal to contract one of the Atlantic world's nastiest germs. Such a
story remains a highly speculative one at best. Within the larger Columbian Exchange experience, humans rather than animals were more likely to transmit influenza to indigenous peoples, and in the case of early European exploration of
the Native Southeast, even humans stood little chance of sparking an epidemic
of that dreaded disease.

The epidemiological significance of Soto's expedition, thus, rests not on the new germs they introduced to the Native Southeast but on how their presence made indigenous peoples more vulnerable to pathogens already well known in the Americas. Those germs certainly included the syphilis- and yaws-causing treponemal bacteria. A number of Soto's men were widely traveled individuals who likely contracted treponematosis at some point in their lives as they visited different parts of the world, including European and African countries, the Caribbean Islands, Mexico, and Peru. Soto himself participated in Pizarro's conquest of the Incas. When in the Southeast, the Spaniards undoubtedly exposed Native women to syphilis. In every town they invaded, Soto's men demanded women to serve the expedition as slaves and concubines. According to one chronicler, the Spaniards "wanted the women . . . to make use of them, and for [the Spaniard's] lewdness and lust, and that they baptized them more for their carnal intercourse than to instruct them in the faith."[38] Captivity and rape were undoubtedly traumatic enough, but such crimes also made some female Natives lifelong syphilis victims, a condition that interfered with fertility and childbirth, increased vulnerability to common bacterial infections, and shortened life spans.

Soto's army imposed a great burden on the health of those Natives who stood in their way as they created a swath of destruction across the region. The Spanish planned to advance their search for wealth by invading indigenous communities, stealing their food, and enslaving people to serve as beasts of burden. Soto's men also hunted Natives, using dogs, which was an undoubtedly horrifying experience. "To set the dogs on [an indigenous person]," one Spanish chronicler claimed, "is to make the dogs eat them or kill them, tearing the Indian to pieces."[39] Many Natives fled the Spanish as they approached, abandoning their fields and leaving them for Soto's men to pillage.[40] Other communities saw the Spanish take their leaders captive and were asked to pay a substantial ransom in food and servants to free them.[41] At Cofitachequi the Spaniards, looking for gold, silver, and gems, robbed the graves of Native peoples. They did not stay too long, however, as there was no food, "except a very limited amount for the Indians to eat, and [the Spanish], with the horses and the people, used it up very quickly."[42] At the town of Chiaha, Soto put the community leader and fifteen others in chains, demanding a supply of burderners for ransom.[43] After getting their demand, the Spaniards destroyed Chiaha's entire supply of crops.[44] At the town of Coosa, Soto and his men took the leader hostage, rested twenty-five days, and consumed the surplus of this important ceremonial center. The invaders also acquired fresh burdeners. They "seized many Indians, men and

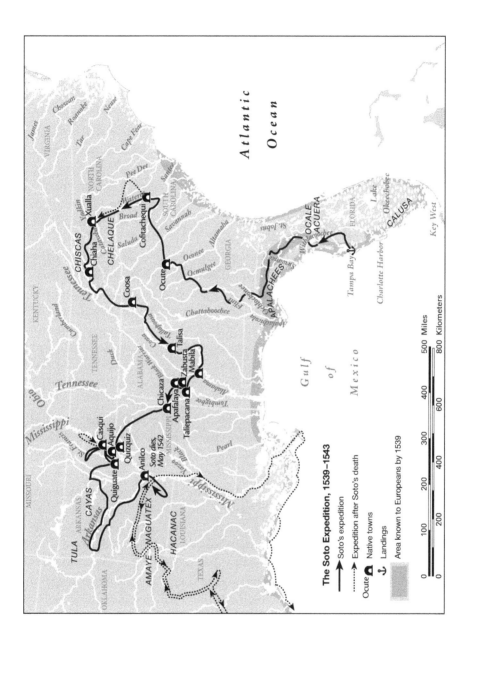

The Soto Expedition, 1539–1543

→ Soto's expedition
⤑ Expedition after Soto's death
⤑ Expedition after Soto's death
Ocute ⚓ Native towns
⚓ Landings
Area known to Europeans by 1539

women who were put in chains." Each Spanish man "took away as slaves those he had in chains, without allowing them to go to their lands."[45] After Soto left the main town of Coosa, he found several villages whose people had fled the marauding Europeans, leaving their fields at the mercy of the invaders.

Soto's men were no less ruthless as they moved farther west. The Spanish occupied the palisaded town of Mabila and in doing so, courted an attack from its Native residents. Several Spaniards were wounded, but by using their horses, metal armor, and superior weaponry, Soto's men counterattacked and inflicted major casualties. Spanish chroniclers reported the number of Natives killed at twenty-five hundred, probably an inflated figure but nonetheless indicative of serious losses. To make matters worse, Mabila was burned to the ground, and its surrounding fields and homes were pillaged of all food.[46] When Soto reached the Mississippi Valley, the Spanish were delighted to see some of the largest towns and maize fields of the region and continued to pillage as they had before. At Quizquiz, they took over three hundred women hostages, then returned them in exchange for food.[47] After an unproductive foray into Arkansas, the expedition came back to the Mississippi, seeking sustenance from the productive villages along the mighty river. To accomplish their purpose, the Spaniards allied with one Native group and attacked the village of Anilco. The Spanish captain commanded that all men should be executed, resulting in as many as one hundred deaths. Eighty surviving women and children were enslaved.[48]

Obviously, each episode of Soto's interaction with Native communities had devastating health consequences. Many villages saw their entire season's harvest stolen or destroyed; Native women faced rape and possible syphilis infection; and towns essentially became sewers filled with the wastes of the Spanish and their livestock. Also, malaria was most likely left in the environment and continued to debilitate Native peoples for generations after Soto departed. The Spanish did not need smallpox to inflict great harm; invaded communities were left with empty larders, contaminated water supplies, and grave illnesses. It is no wonder that indigenous peoples abandoned some of the towns that Soto had occupied. Nevertheless, the devastation that the Spanish brought was confined to those unfortunate towns they visited. Malaria may have spread beyond communities that the Spanish directly contacted, but without smallpox Soto's expedition can hardly be seen as a major episode in the transmission of Columbian Exchange germs. The Soto expedition, with its hundreds of people and livestock, simply did not carry any of the diseases capable of igniting a regionwide epidemiological nightmare.

The potential for the introduction of new diseases into the Southeast continued after Hernando de Soto's failed expedition. With a force of five hundred men, one thousand serving people, and 240 horses, Tristán de Luna y Arellano sailed from San Juan de Ulúa, Mexico, to Florida in an attempt to establish a string of missions that would extend from the Gulf to the Appalachian Mountains. The expedition left on June 11, 1559, and on July 17 reached Mobile Bay, where the Spanish obtained water as well as wood. The main body of the expedition finally came ashore at Pensacola on August 15. Luna's voyage apparently went well; no deaths or illness among the passengers were reported.[49] Soon thereafter, the Spaniards' good fortune disappeared. On September 19, Luna reported that a "hurricane" destroyed three of his ships that lay anchored off the coast. Most supplies went down with the fleet, and the rains ruined what food the Spaniards had managed to bring ashore.[50] Luna sent a letter asking Spanish officials to send more supplies, but only one ship arrived from Cuba.[51]

Desperate, the Spaniards sought food from Natives. The expedition moved further inland to an indigenous community called Nanipacana, most likely located on the lower Alabama River.[52] Natives, enlightened about the nature of Spanish conquest by the preceding Soto expedition, refused to aid Luna's party. One survivor reported that indigenous peoples "have gone from their houses, and have cut down and burned and pulled up all the fields, as we who have passed through them have seen."[53] By May 1560 the expedition experienced extreme hunger. The married soldiers who had brought their families along and native Mexicans pressed into service demanded that Luna allow them to return home.[54] Members of the Luna expedition received some supplies from Cuba and Mexico during the summer of 1560, but these were not enough as famine reduced Luna's men to eating grass and leather.[55] By spring 1561 the Spanish were ready to abandon attempts to settle the Gulf Coast and instead turned their attention to the Atlantic. Spanish officials relieved Luna of his command and sent Ángel de Villafañe to retrieve the survivors of the expedition. In April Villafañe arrived at Pensacola, where he collected most of the survivors, leaving only sixty to seventy soldiers to garrison a fort; these soldiers disappeared from the records.[56]

While Luna's men suffered greatly, nothing in the available evidence suggests they carried smallpox or other acute infectious diseases. One argument in particular holds that Luna's men inevitably carried influenza with them, since an epidemic of that disease was occurring in Latin America at the time of the expedition's departure. The report of influenza, however, was from Nueva Granada, or present-day Colombia, far distant from where Luna set sail.[57] Even if they had been carrying the disease, sickness would have been apparent during the voyage or shortly after landing at Pensacola. It was nearly ten months after arriving that members of the expedition reported illness, well past the time in which influenza or for that matter any other acute infectious disease would have run its course. Spanish suffering, moreover, was clearly associated with famine. Of course, Luna's expedition could have carried malaria, although it may have already been well established in the southeastern environment before they arrived, and they may have spread diseases commonly associated with poor sanitation. But unlike the Soto expedition, Luna's had less direct contact with indigenous peoples. Most Natives in the path of the Spanish fled and took their food with them, and when Luna reached the more densely settled Coosa Valley, he kept his party and horses camped outside indigenous towns, hoping not to alienate Natives whose help he desperately needed. This latter Spanish expedition, thus, neither carried the deadliest germs with them nor had the opportunity to infect indigenous peoples.

The Luna expedition, while having little if any epidemiological impact, does shed light on demographic changes in the protohistoric period. The Spanish expedition journeyed to the Coosa River, thus providing clues about the consequences of Soto's prior visit for the Coosa chiefdom and its communities. The evidence is mixed. On the one hand, some Spaniards claimed the Alabama and Coosa valleys remained well peopled, being much more densely populated than the coast. The military leader Mateo del Sauz, for example, reported that they had traveled through "a thickly populated country."[58] A missionary priest, Fray Domingo de la Anunciación, wrote back to Luna, "[The] people of this land are more numerous than in [the Gulf Coast], for the towns from fifteen or sixteen leagues back of where we now are and from here to Coosa are, according to the what the Indians say, near to each other." The priest went on to claim that the towns lacked the population of Nanipacana but judging from the fields and roads that he saw the land was well populated.[59] On the other hand, one Spanish chronicler portrayed the Coosa Valley as less populated than it had been earlier. Fray Agustín Davíla Padilla, writing some thirty years after the fact and receiving his information second hand from Anunciación, wrote the most detailed account of the Luna expedition. Padilla described the chiefdom as "poor and the villages few and small."[60] The chronicler furthermore cited some men who accompanied both Soto and Luna as authorities. These men, according to Padilla, "declared that they must have been bewitched when this country seemed to them so rich and populated [in 1540]."[61]

As with the plague of Cofitachequi, Padilla's account should not be read as proof of massive depopulation due to introduced diseases. Even assuming Padilla's account to be accurate, it does not correlate with the characteristics of virgin-soil epidemics. The Spanish chronicler reported that the town of Coosa itself experienced population loss, but at the same time its nearby rivals on the Tennessee River, the Napochies, increased, a fact that negates the occurrence of a regionwide epidemic. To be sure, Soto's expedition disrupted the Coosa chiefdom by occupying its towns and planting malaria among a horticultural population already predisposed to sustain the infection. Nevertheless, warfare can also account for the demographic imbalance. The Napochies' increase likely came from their ability to take captives from their nearby rivals. Not surprisingly, Coosa sought to retaliate, and with the help of the Spanish they defeated the Napochies. The people of Coosa, it seemed, were not so devastated that they gave up hope for holding their territory and avenging earlier losses. The history of the Coosa chiefdom, which has figured prominently in the literature on the protohistoric Southeast, does not provide proof, therefore, that Spanish exploration ignited massive epidemics.

Another Spanish expedition into the interior presents a picture of the limited effect of prior European invasions. In December 1566 Juan Pardo led a party of little more than one hundred men from the recently established Spanish outpost of Santa Elena through the Carolina Piedmont and into the southern Appalachians. Pardo's goals were ambitious: he planned on carving an overland route to Zacetecas, Mexico, and planting a series of missions along the way. The Spanish commander reached the foothills of the Blue Ridge, where he left a small detachment before returning to the coast in March 1567. On September 1, 1567, Pardo set out again along the same course and reached the soldiers who had remained. He continued over the Appalachians, marching along the western slope of the mountains and arriving at indigenous communities along the Little Tennessee River. Pardo, though, realized that his plans were impossible, and he returned to the Carolina coast by March 2, 1568. Five small Spanish garrisons remained in the interior, but Native peoples quickly destroyed these outposts, probably because they grew tired of Spanish demands for food.[62]

As with the Luna expedition, Pardo's epidemiological significance lay not in what germs the expedition brought to the region but in their observations of an area that Hernando de Soto had previously visited. Pardo's expedition, composed of adult males sailing for three months directly from Spain, remained healthy throughout the trip and presented no signs of sickness among their small number or among the indigenous peoples they encountered. Pardo, moreover, encountered many of the same indigenous communities that Soto had seen over twenty years earlier, and his chroniclers reported no evidence of massive

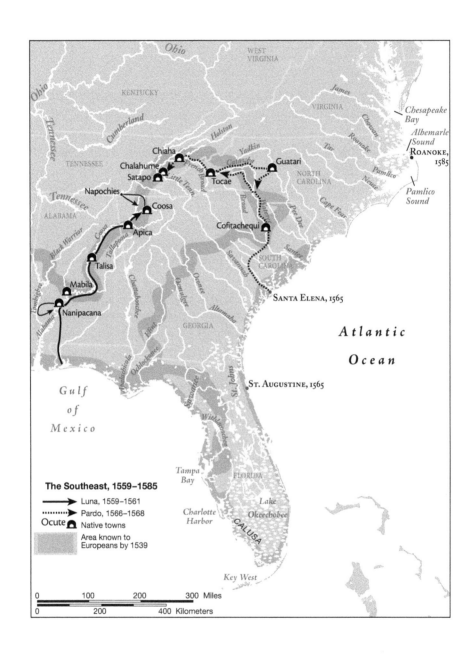

The Southeast, 1559–1585

→	Luna, 1559–1561
·····►	Pardo, 1566–1568
Ocute 🏠	Native towns
	Area known to Europeans by 1539

0   100   200   300 Miles
0   200   400 Kilometers

population loss from epidemic disease. The Spanish party advanced from one community to another without encountering deserted areas or abandoned towns. Pardo described the Carolina Piedmont, the home of Cofitachequi, as having "a great number of caciques and Indians."[63] Another Spaniard claimed that the area was "a rich land" that retained the features of a diverse social landscape that one could see before contact. "Good houses and humble, round huts, as well as very large and very good [huts] are [to be found] in all the settlements," he reported.[64] Malaria likely had become established in South Carolina, but if it had infected indigenous communities, they had made accommodations to this new disease, recovered lost numbers, and approached their precontact population sizes.

As Pardo advanced into the upper Piedmont and beyond, he found more Native communities bearing no apparent scars from previous episodes of European invasion. Some of the peoples that Pardo encountered included ancestors of tribal groups that would dominate the historical record of the eighteenth century. He met Siouan speakers whom he called "Cataba," "Ysaa," and "Uchiri."[65] These undoubtedly were ancestral groups of the eighteenth-century Catawba peoples. Pardo visited the town of "Tocae," most likely related to the eighteenth-century Cherokee village of Toqua. There he greeted leaders from other familiar Cherokee villages, including "Neguase," "Estate," "Tacoru," "Utaca," and "Quetua."[66] These corresponded with the eighteenth-century middle and lower Cherokee villages of Nequasse, Estatoe, Tugaloo, Watauga, and Kituwa. Members of the Pardo expedition also ventured into eastern Tennessee and came upon the town of Chiaha, a community that Soto had occupied over twenty years earlier. The Spanish found the town heavily fortified and estimated that over three thousand warriors hid behind its palisades, certainly an exaggeration but indicative of a fairly large indigenous community. Women and children were apparently absent, having fled from the Spanish, whom they understandably had learned to distrust.[67] Pardo visited other towns in the Little Tennessee Valley, including "Chalahume" and "Satapo," which he claimed had "many Indians." The documentary evidence from the Pardo expedition thus counters claims that new diseases had a catastrophic impact as a result of the Soto expedition.

To be sure, there are some indications that Native communities in eastern Tennessee and northern Georgia had suffered some disruption from their prior experience with the Spanish. It is not clear whether any of Pardo's men actually went beyond the Little Tennessee, but they did gain information about inhabitants of the Coosa Valley, which both Soto and Luna had earlier visited. The information again is mixed. On the one hand, Native informants told Pardo's men that the town of Coosa itself remained "a large town, the largest" there was, with 150 householders.[68] If householders meant adult males and if there were 3.5 women and children per adult male, then the population of Coosa numbered around 525 individuals, on the upper end of community size in the Native Southeast.[69] The Spaniards further learned that the chief of Coosa was "the grand cacique" of the region, and they came to believe that he was conspiring with other towns in the area to ambush and destroy the expedition.[70] On the other hand, they learned that the area between the towns of Coosa and Satapo was "lightly inhabited," while Soto's chroniclers portrayed the same area as well populated. Also, the town of "Olitifar" had indeed been abandoned sometime between 1540 and 1566.[71] Such evidence of disruption, however, need not be attributed to epidemic disease. Endemic malaria could have weakened some communities and encouraged them to move to healthier locations, but most likely warfare made living in the area hazardous. Luna found Coosa suffering from conflict with enemies to the west, while Pardo walked into heated conflict with towns to the east. A growing and expanding indigenous population in the southern Appalachians especially pressed upon their neighbors in the Ridge and Valley province, forcing them to strike a defensive posture and to move to safer locations.[72]

Juan Pardo's departure marked the end of European penetration into the interior, and those places and people that figured so prominently in sixteenth-century Spanish accounts would disappear from the documentary record, at least until Europeans arrived in the late seventeenth century. By the time Pardo departed, Columbian Exchange diseases had had little impact on the Native Southeast. Indigenous communities that had the unfortunate experience of being occupied by the Hernando de Soto expedition undoubtedly suffered from the common, ordinary germs that his men and animals carried. Malaria also became prevalent in areas of the Southeast, causing some communities to move to safer and healthier locations. Widespread and catastrophic depopulation did not occur. Smallpox and the Atlantic world's other lethal germs had little chance to arrive during the early encounter period. Acute infectious diseases stood little chance of traveling from places of direct European contact by way of aboriginal exchange, and they were unlikely to hitch a ride with any undocumented coastal visitors. The documented expeditions provide even further support for an absence of the Columbian Exchange in the early encounter period. With the exception of the plague of Cofitachequi, information from Soto's chroniclers described the Native Southeast as heavily populated and full of thriving Native polities instead of a region burned over by pandemics that hypothetically spread from Latin America and led to hemispheric catastrophe. Also, Soto and other would-be conquistadors failed to bring the Atlantic world's most notorious germs with them. Nothing in the surviving documents indicates that these groups of mostly adult men arrived with active infections of acute diseases. When they did become sick, it was weeks or months after arriving, indicating that the germs they suffered from were the ones fairly typical in any environment or at worst malaria. Fortunately, the vast majority of indigenous peoples in the Native Southeast escaped catastrophic epidemics during their early experience with the European invasion.

Pestilence on the Periphery

While Pardo's departure marked a reprieve for Natives of the interior, the protohistoric Southeast remained a potential target for introduced diseases as European activity on the Atlantic Coast continued. The French, the Spanish, and the English all attempted to establish coastal colonies, and with these attempts deadly new germs eventually arrived on the periphery of the Southeast. These early colonial projects, though, did little to alter the disease ecology of Natives outside direct contact, and as with previous European exploring expeditions, they cannot be blamed for a supposed regionwide population collapse.

St. Augustine, of course, was the first permanent European settlement in the Southeast, but the impetus for the founding of this Spanish outpost came with the entrance of the French into the imperial competition for Florida. On February 18, 1562, Jean Ribault commanded two ships that sailed directly from France for the destination of Florida. The expedition was nearly stillborn. Immediately after departure, sickness erupted among the crew of 150 men, forcing the French commander to expel the majority of his sailors before venturing across the Atlantic. Ribault pushed on, making the ocean crossing in less than two months and arriving at Port Royal Sound, in present-day South Carolina. Apparently, the sickness that earlier plagued the expedition had run its course before the French landed. Ribault reported that none of his men were ill and that the land was healthy. The French left twenty-six men in South Carolina, occupying a small colony that they named Charlesfort.[73] The French colony, however, failed. In 1564 the Spanish sent a ship to locate Ribault's party, but they found only one survivor, who reported that his party had antagonized local Natives and could not acquire enough food to sustain themselves. The lone survivor was left behind by his compatriots who decided to build boats and sail into the Atlantic, where an English ship eventually captured them. The abandoned

Frenchman gave no indication that either his party or the Natives had suffered from disease, which is not surprising because the French had expelled their sick before their two-month crossing of the Atlantic and because only twenty-six men were involved in the effort to build Charlesfort.[74] Ribault's expedition can hardly be seen as having significant epidemiological consequences.

A later French expedition to Florida illustrates well the muted epidemiological possibilities of European intrusion into the Native Southeast during the protohistoric period. On April 22, 1564, three ships set sail across the Atlantic and arrived three months later in Florida, near the mouth of the St. John's River, where the French established Fort Caroline. The trip involved brief stops in the Canaries and Dominica, which by that time had become thoroughly integrated into the shipping networks that circulated people and germs throughout the Atlantic world. Still, there is no evidence that the French contracted smallpox or other acute infectious diseases. The French arrived in a healthy state and experienced sickness only after living in Florida for two months, eliminating the possibility that they carried the deadliest germs that colonialism had to offer. Also, the disease that they did contract proved to be rather mild since everyone who had it recovered. Contaminated water or food poisoning certainly could have been to blame, but malaria deserves special consideration. According to one French account, a fire and a drought left many fish dead, causing a "putrefaction in the air," hardly a diagnosis strongly suggesting one disease or another but fairly typical of European explanations for the cycles of chills and fevers also known by the Italian words for bad air, *mal aria*.[75] The following August the French reported that another round of fever had struck their fledgling colony.[76] Some of the French could have picked up malaria during their trip to the Southeast and transmitted plasmodia to the local anopheles, which then infected the remainder of the party. The disease, moreover, could have been acquired in the Southeast. By 1564 malaria had likely become endemic in Florida from previous European invasions.

Regardless of which particular sickness plagued them, the French were in no shape to defend themselves against a Spanish force that arrived in 1565. Under Pedro Menéndez, a Spanish force of some eight hundred men destroyed the struggling French colony and in the process built the fort that became St. Augustine.[77] From this outpost in their far-flung empire, the Spanish hoped to integrate the region's Natives into a Catholic mission system and save the world from Protestantism. In doing so, they would permanently integrate the south Atlantic Coast into shipping networks that facilitated the flow of people, Christianity, and germs throughout the Atlantic world. It would be just a matter of time, then, before disease-ridden ships, carrying the most deadly pathogens involved in the Columbian Exchange, made an appearance in the Native Southeast.

Indeed, shortly after the founding of St. Augustine, indigenous peoples along the Atlantic Coast, which the Spanish identified as Guales, suffered from a mysterious illness. In 1570 two Jesuit missionaries arrived at Spain's northern most garrison, Santa Elena, on what is today Parris Island, off the coast of South Carolina. The missionaries hoped to convert the Guales but found these coastal peoples reeling from sickness. The Jesuits reported that many died, but used only the generic terms *una enfermedad* and *pestilentia* to describe the outbreak, giving no indications how far the disease had spread or what the illness was.[78] Another source reports that the missionaries themselves became sick, and while the two Jesuits did not die, they never fully recovered and had to travel back to Cuba.[79] Whatever caused such sickness, relations between Natives and newcomers became tense. The Guales refused baptism and became reluctant to supply the Spanish with food during such trying times, forcing the Jesuits to abandon their efforts in 1572. At the same time, Jesuits traveled farther north and found a difficult time among hard-pressed Natives of the Chesapeake Bay. In 1570 Catholic priests returned to the bay, which they had discovered on a brief trip four years earlier. An Algonquian captive named Don Luis guided the missionaries back to the area from which he was captured and found his people in a deplorable state. According to one missionary,

> We find the land of Don Luis in quite another condition than expected, not because he was at fault in his description of it, but because Our Lord has chastised it with six years of famine and death, which has brought it about that there is much less population than usual. Since many have died and many also have moved to other regions to ease their hunger there remain but few of the tribe whose leaders say that they wish to die where their fathers have died, although they have no maize, and have not found wild fruit, which they are accustomed to eat. Neither roots nor anything else can be had, save for a small amount obtained with great labor from the soil, which is very parched.[80]

Natives were in no mood to host the rude Spanish. Three Jesuits experienced martyrdom, bringing the Catholic missionary effort in Virginia to a quick end.[81]

Was there a connection between what the Guales and the Natives of the Chesapeake experienced in 1570? Were these two episodes linked as part of one larger epidemic from an introduced disease? An affirmative answer to both questions seems plausible. Between the years 1565 and 1570, Spanish ships continually visited the Atlantic coasts, bringing settlers, priests, and soldiers to occupy a serious of garrisons from St. Augustine to Santa Elena. Such traffic certainly increased the chances of an acute infectious disease arriving, and the reports of many Natives dying seem to indicate something very serious arrived. Smallpox was most likely not a culprit, because one would expect the Jesuits to list this easily identifiable disease by name instead of using the generic labels of *una enfermedad* or *pestilencia*.[82] Besides, the priests themselves became sick and had a lingering condition, suggesting something other than an acute infectious disease. For the same reason measles seems unlikely, although sixteenth-century observers would likely not identify the disease specifically, leaving the intriguing possibility that the 1570 outbreak was the Native Southeast's first experience with the deadly disease. Yellow fever is another intriguing possibility, but given the time that the outbreak occurred, one must be skeptical that this aedes mosquito–borne, warm-weather disease erupted sometime just before the March arrival of the two Jesuits. Typhus, perhaps, is the strongest possibility. This deadly disease certainly circulated around the Atlantic world among European ships in which filthy sailors and soldiers kept close quarters. Natives who visited Spanish garrisons, especially during the winter, put themselves at risk of contracting this louse-borne disease.

Still, the 1570 outbreak must be put into a larger ecological context. The influx of Spanish traffic to the Atlantic Coast certainly continued the spread of malaria to the southeastern environment, especially to those peoples who relied heavily on swampy estuaries to gather clams, oysters, and other aquatic food sources necessary during times of famine. Such people were also particularly vulnerable to common waterborne pathogens, which the Spanish and their animals continued to deposit in the Natives' water supplies and fishing areas. The Spanish did not need Columbian Exchange diseases to make indigenous peoples sick. The germs that commonly accompany human beings and livestock could make communities ill, gravely ill during times of widespread hunger and trauma. Coastal Natives would be particularly vulnerable. In the late winter and early spring—a time when game animals grew scarce and fish had yet to spawn—indigenous peoples of the Atlantic Coast experienced a seasonal period of deprivation, one in which Native bodies were already in a weakened state.[83] In comparison interior communities, whose heavily forested homelands sustained higher populations of game animals and whose soils produced larger horticultural surpluses, faced less severe periods of seasonal want.

Whatever the reasons for the deaths that indigenous peoples of the Atlantic Coast suffered, massive depopulation did not occur.[84] For the remainder of the sixteenth century, the Spanish faced continual hostility from a strong and vibrant Native population. The soldiers who remained at Santa Elena courted the ill will of local indigenous peoples, who rebuked demands that they obey the Spanish. In 1579 the Spanish mustered enough strength to force compliance by burning twenty Native towns and destroying their food supplies. Hostilities continued, though, and in 1587, the Spanish abandoned Santa Elena, giving up what was a tenuous hold on South Carolina. One would think that the introduction of smallpox, measles, or yellow fever would have allowed the Spanish to remain on the island outpost and perhaps have more success proselytizing Natives, but they received little help from diseases in reaching their imperialistic goals. At most a combination of typhus, malaria, and common waterborne illness made indigenous peoples sick, but not to the extent that they became receptive to Catholicism and willing to submit to Spanish rule.

At the same time the Spanish were losing their hold on Santa Elena, the English entered the imperial competition for the Southeast and in doing so opened another opportunity for the spread of new diseases to indigenous peoples. In 1584 the English conducted a reconnaissance mission to find a suitable spot to plant their planned colony of Virginia. The small party landed on the island of Roanoke off the coast of North Carolina, and not surprisingly, they reported that they had found a fertile land with friendly Natives who would welcome an English return. The following year, over 600 men set sail for Roanoke aboard five ships that traveled along what had become a familiar route in the transatlantic shipping network. The crew stopped at the Canary Islands and then traveled to the West Indies, where they lurked for about a month, refreshing themselves and restocking their vessels with invaluable goods, livestock, and captives pillaged from the Spanish. Eventually, the English arrived at their destination, where they left a company of 107 men to maintain the infant colony while the larger party returned to the mother country. Few in this small group, though, relished the opportunity to colonize a new land. All but 15 men eagerly departed Roanoke when Sir Francis Drake's fleet arrived in 1586, and those 15 who remained had disappeared by the time another English party arrived in 1587. This latter group also faced a difficult time. Of the 92 men, 17 women, and 9 children, as well as the 2 children born in the colony, none was to be found when English ships arrived in 1590. The Roanoke colony had been lost, and the English colonizing effort was to be stalled until the founding of Jamestown in 1607.[85]

While the English colony at Roanoke was fleeting, it appears to have had epidemiological significance. The English, as did their Spanish predecessors, likely continued the process of spreading malaria along the transatlantic shipping routes that linked Europe, Africa, the Caribbean, and the North American mainland. The Roanoke area could have easily been made malarial with even cursory English encounters. But something even more substantial may have happened. Thomas Harriot, who accompanied the 1585 expedition and was one of the survivors that Francis Drake picked up in 1586, wrote a narrative of his experience among indigenous peoples that included direct reference to what appears to be a virgin-soil epidemic:

> Within a few days after our departure from every Towne, the people began to die very fast, and many in short space, in some Townes about twentie, in some fortie, and in one six score, which in trueth was very many in respect of their numbers. This happened in no place that we could learne, but where we had bin, where they used some practices against us, & after such time . . . . The disease also was so strange that they neither knewe what it was nor how to cure it, the like by report of the oldest men in the Countrey never happened before, time out of minde.[86]

Ralph Lane, another Englishmen at Roanoke during the 1585–86 stay, produced another narrative of the English experience that provided some clues to back up Harriot's account of disease. Lane claimed that Native hostility resulted when indigenous peoples blamed the English for shooting them with invisible arrows that inflicted them with sickness and caused some to die. Lane, however, did not include the grim mortality statistics that Harriot did.[87]

Again, caution should be used when interpreting the Roanoke encounter as evidence of the Columbian Exchange. Harriot was writing to encourage his countrymen to support colonization and probably exaggerated the number of Native deaths. One would expect that Lane's account would have also reported massive casualties among Natives if they indeed occurred. It may be the case that Harriot, who had been familiar with reports of virgin-soil epidemics in Spanish chronicles, borrowed from these sources to promote English imperialism. Epidemics became an especially useful trope to incorporate into promotional discourse because such events led readers to believe indigenous peoples would fall before them, opening up land that would be easy to take.[88] Harriot's account can also be questioned from an epidemiological perspective. Both he and Lane commented that the English remained in good health during their visit to Roanoke, essentially ruling out the occurrence of an acute infectious disease. Had smallpox or another highly lethal disease introduced from the larger Atlantic world been involved, the English would have had active cases among them and experienced some deaths. During Harriot's stay, only four individuals died, and three of those were "feeble, weake, and sickly persons before ever they came thither."[89]

Although Harriot's narrative may have been fabricated, it is also possibly an exaggerated account of what was a familiar scene whenever large groups of Europeans and their livestock occupied indigenous towns. Just as Soto and his army invaded and contaminated Native communities, so did the English. The 107 men left at Roanoke placed a great health burden on indigenous communities, a burden made even greater with the addition of livestock. Typhoid, dysentery, hepatitis A, and other common waterborne infections would be left in the wake of such visits, and to make matters worse, Natives undoubtedly suffered from hunger as the English pillaged indigenous communities for food. It is no wonder that relations between the English and Natives became hostile and that Natives blamed the newcomers for making them sick. The germ culprits, however, were those fairly common within any early-modern human population, and such germs did not cause massive depopulation across a wide region. As if to underscore their continued vitality, indigenous peoples, in fact, mounted considerable resistance to the English throughout 1585 and 1586, forcing Harriot and Lane's party to flee when Sir Francis Drake arrived.

Rather than the Roanoke colonists, Drake's fleet may have been the culprit if the English introduced deadly diseases during the protohistoric period. Some scholars suggest that this famed privateer's fleet played a major role in the Columbian Exchange as it pillaged its way through the Spanish American Empire in 1585 and 1586. There is some evidence for this. Leaving England on September 12, 1585, Drake's forces consisted of over twenty-three hundred men aboard twenty-five ships. The large fleet stopped at Santiago in the Cape Verde Islands on November 16 and stayed for fourteen days. After it left, a severe outbreak occurred. One of Drake's chroniclers reported:

> From hence putting ouer to the West Indies, we were not many dayes at sea, but there beganne amongst our people such mortalitie, as in few days there were dead aboue two or three hundred men. And until some seven or eight dayes after our coming from S. Iago, there had not died any one man of sicknesse in all the Fleete: the sicknesses hewed not his infection wherewith so many were stroken, until we were departed thense, and then seazed our people with extreme hote burning and continuall ague, whereof some very few escaped with life, and yet those for the most part not with our great alteration and decay of their wittes and strength for a long time after. In some that died were plainly shewed the small spottes, which are often found upon those that be infected with the plague.[90]

Sickness continued to afflict the English fleet as it made its way into the Caribbean. Eighteen days after leaving sight of Santiago, Drake's ships arrived at the island of Dominica, where the English traded with local Natives. Drake's men did not stay there long enough to observe whether indigenous peoples suffered from any of the English germs, but not long after their departure, Drake's fleet anchored off the unoccupied island of St. Christopher, where they spent Christmas "refreshing their sick" and airing out their ships.

Pathogenic microbes continued to weaken the English. On New Year's day, Drake's armed forces began their attack on Hispaniola, and after completing their work, they sailed on to Cartagena, where illness continued to afflict them during their six-week stay. "The sicknesse with mortalitie before spoken off still continuing among us," one Englishman later recounted, "though not with the same fury as the first, and such as were touched with the said sickness, escaping death, very few or almost none could recouer their strength, yea many of them were much decayed in their memorie." The chronicler described the ailment as a "very burning and pestilent ague," and from the Spanish he learned that such a disease struck newcomers who exposed themselves to the "first night air."[91] Another account put the death toll at Cartagena at one hundred men. Already suffering heavy losses from their transatlantic crossing, the English were in no shape to attack Panama, as Drake had intended, but instead set a course for Roanoke, where the English hoped to unload some slaves and goods they had captured in the Spanish colonies.

Did the germs that made Drake's men sick travel along with them to the Southeast? Again, there is some evidence that the English fleet played a role in spreading diseases through the Atlantic world. From the end of March until mid-May, the English fleet lurked in the Caribbean, repairing damaged ships and acquiring fresh water and supplies for their homeward journey. No further references to sickness were made, but while occupying St. Augustine from May 28 until June 2, one of Drake's chroniclers referred to what on the surface has been taken as evidence of a virgin-soil epidemic. The Englishman reported, "[T]he wilde people at first comminge of our men died verie fast and saide amongst themselves, It was the Inglisshe God that made them die so faste."[92] If a Columbian Exchange disease was involved, it is possible that the English transmitted it even further north. On June 9 Drake's fleet arrived at Roanoke, where for nine days they negotiated with the stranded colonists the terms of their passage back to England.

Drake's crewmen certainly began their transatlantic crossing carrying a nasty germ that was possibly among the worst that colonialism had to offer. While typhoid, malaria, and other diseases could have afflicted the English, their high death toll and the graphic description of the epidemic indicates something more severe. Yellow fever has been cited as a culprit, and some have argued that Drake introduced the disease to the Americas for the first time.[93] This disease's characteristics—its black vomit and jaundice—do not appear in the English description of the outbreak, however, and some scholars doubt the virus made its debut in the Americas until 1647, when the African slave trade had provided the population numbers necessary to transmit the short-lived virus across the Atlantic and to sustain a major epidemic once it arrived.[94] With symptoms that include small spots, a diagnosis of smallpox is more likely than yellow fever, but the fact that this discernable disease was not mentioned by name and that so many grown men succumbed to the infection suggest another disease. The symptoms of typhus most closely resemble those the English described. This louse-borne germ indeed produces a cycle of chills and fevers followed by small macular eruptions, and of course, the disease, popularly known as "ship's fever," thrives among filthy individuals living in cramped quarters. Whatever the disease's identity, it undoubtedly survived the eighteen-day Atlantic crossing and continued to afflict the English while they rested on St. Christopher's Island on Christmas Day. One wonders, though, whether this original disease was the same one that afflicted them in Cartagena. The English observed that the sickness was not as severe, suggesting that Drake's crewmen were suffering from malaria, a disease that had become endemic in that part of the world and one to which the local indigenous population had become accustomed.

While Drake's men likely transported a highly lethal germ across the Atlantic, their importance in bringing it to the Southeast should not be exaggerated. When the fleet anchored off the Florida coast, it had been over five months since its encounter with deadly disease began. An acute infectious disease would have certainly run its course long before the English arrived at St. Augustine. If the culprit in Cartagena was a different germ, it too appeared to have run its course. During the forty-eight days between leaving Cartagena and landing in Florida, the English reported no active cases of sickness. Moreover, the English did not stay long at St. Augustine either; they occupied the area for six days, a time too short for the invaders to observe an outbreak of typhus, smallpox, measles, or other diseases whose incubation periods were typically longer. Influenza and yellow fever usually incubate for fewer than six days, but they also have very short communication periods, making their survival from even Cartagena extraordinary, especially when the fleet appeared to have no active cases. The introduction of new diseases thus was not an automatic consequence of Sir Francis Drake's voyage to the Southeast.

The context for the episode in which "wild people" died "very fast" upon the

English arrival, in fact, supports a nonepidemiological explanation. Drake's forces overwhelmed the undermanned Spanish and Native defenders of St. Augustine and used violence to intimidate indigenous peoples. For several days the English ransacked the area, stealing food and killing numerous Native peoples, including a "king" whom Drake's men believed to have "determined to murther all the Inglishmen. . . . Soe wee gave the kinge that for his paines which hee woulde have geeven us." To be sure, the large English force probably contaminated the water supply with typhoid and other nasty microbes and carried plasmodia to local anopheles mosquitoes, but mortality from these diseases would have been experienced after the departure of the English, whose arms rather than germs led to the great loss of Native lives recorded in the written account of their stay at St. Augustine. If Florida's Natives did not experience novel germs as a result of Drake's visit, indigenous peoples in and near Roanoke certainly did not either. Twenty-three of Drake's ships arrived off the coast of North Carolina shortly after departing Florida, but not all his men disembarked. Small parties were sent out to look for the stranded colonists, and after retrieving them, Drake's ships quickly departed on June 19, without significant interaction with Native peoples.[95]

Although Sir Francis Drake's voyage did not introduce the most lethal diseases to the Native Southeast, it nonetheless demonstrates how the region was becoming connected to the larger Atlantic world. European traffic to Florida certainly increased as imperial rivalry escalated in the late sixteenth and early seventeenth century. Of course, Spain remained the dominant player in the region, regularly sending ships to resupply its northern colony. It was just a matter of time before one of these ships carried smallpox and other acute infectious diseases from its more populous Caribbean colonies to Florida. For indigenous peoples, though, infection was not an automatic consequence of disease-laden ships arriving at St. Augustine. A means for germs to spread from nonnative carriers to indigenous communities had to be established. Tragically, such a means came with that most prominent aspect of Spanish colonialism in the Native Southeast, the Catholic mission system.

After the failure of the Jesuits in the 1570s, Franciscan priests took up the effort to proselytize indigenous peoples. In 1577 they began working among the Timucua communities that surrounded St. Augustine; in 1595 they reestablished a Catholic presence among the Guales and maintained missions among them for the next hundred years; and by 1639 Franciscans had extended their reach all the way to the Apalachicola River, bringing several Apalachee communities under Catholic influence. While the primary function of these missions was to convert indigenous peoples, Native communities also became units of production in the larger Spanish Empire. Spanish officials demanded tribute in the form of corn and other foodstuffs and required Native men to supply the labor necessary to transport such items to St. Augustine. Cattle were introduced, especially to the Apalachees, and by the mid-seventeenth century Florida began to export cowhides to Atlantic markets.[96] Spanish colonialism did not go without contest; the Guales in 1597, the Apalachees in 1647, and the Timucuas in 1656 revolted and forced the Spanish to make accommodations to their Native hosts, including tolerance of some Native religious practices and less harsh labor demands. Nevertheless, Spanish influence among indigenous peoples grew during the seventeenth century.[97]

As that influence grew, the Spanish brought the most lethal diseases of the Columbian Exchange to Florida's Native population. The Spanish mentioned some specific episodes of disease in the documentary record. In 1617 Franciscans reported that "great plagues [*pestes*] and contagious sicknesses" had struck their mission communities during the past four years, killing over half of their Timucua and Guale converts.[98] Another unidentified "plague" struck St. Augustine in 1649, while the Spanish specifically listed smallpox as afflicting their colony in 1655.[99] By 1657 virgin-soil epidemics had devastated indigenous peoples. A visiting Spanish official recorded that there were "very few Indians" in the Guale, Timucua, and Apalachee missions because "they [had] been wiped out with the sickness of the plague [*pestes*] and smallpox which [had] overtaken them in the past years."[100] Even if these references had not survived, it would be reasonable to conclude that Florida's Native population suffered severely from virgin-soil epidemics in the seventeenth century.[101] The mission system steadily grew, and St. Augustine was regularly visited by ships that had traveled from European nations and their various American colonies. As Native communities became links in a chain of supplies traveling to and from St. Augustine, they became increasingly vulnerable to the diseases circulating throughout the Atlantic world.[102] By 1680 the most heavily proselytized tribe, the Timucuas, had lost 90 percent of their population, while the Guales and the Apalachees suffered less but nonetheless saw their numbers dramatically decline.[103] Part of this depopulation resulted from their flight away from cultural oppression found in Catholic missions, but epidemics undoubtedly played a devastating role.

Smallpox certainly struck the most damaging blow to indigenous communities, but its impact should be assessed within a larger context of Spanish colonialism. The virus spread beyond St. Augustine because Natives received Catholic missionaries and become active participants in the flow of supplies

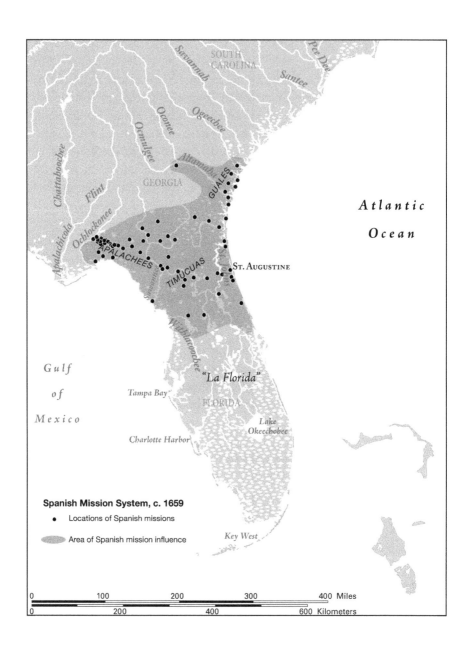

SOUTH
CAROLINA

Pee Dee

Santee

Savannah

Ogeechee

Oconee

Ocmulgee

Chattahoochee

Flint

GEORGIA

Altamaha

GUALES

Atlantic
Ocean

Apalachicola

Ochlockonee

APALACHEES

TIMUCUAS

ST. AUGUSTINE

Withlacoochee

Gulf

of

Mexico

"La Florida"

Tampa Bay

FLORIDA

*Lake
Okeechobee*

Charlotte Harbor

Spanish Mission System, c. 1659

•   Locations of Spanish missions

      Area of Spanish mission influence

Key West

| 0 | 100 | 200 | 300 | 400 Miles |
| 0 | 200 | 400 | 600 Kilometers |

throughout the Spanish Empire. To be sure, the Spanish did not initiate a trading system that compared either qualitatively or quantitatively to what the English were to create in the latter half of the seventeenth century, but they did reorient tribal economies to depend on outside items. Nails, metal utensils, woolen cloth, livestock, glass beads, and other goods flowed from St. Augustine to Native communities, and in return indigenous peoples sent maize and animal hides. Native men, moreover, often served as labor in transporting goods. Perhaps most significantly, Spanish colonialism erased buffer zones that had previously separated the Timucuas, the Apalachees, and the Guales. Aside from periods of rebellion when the Spanish pressured their Native converts to assist in putting down revolts, the colonizers served as mediators, building peace among traditional rivals. Spanish officials and Catholic missionaries traveled from community to community, often in the company of several Native companions, traversing formerly contested areas rather safely. Peace, though, had tragic implications. As people traveled more freely and more often from place to place, so too did the deadly germs recently imported from Europe. The Columbian Exchange, in other words, was not a product of biological inevitability but depended on the religious and economic aspects of the larger Spanish colonial project.

While Spanish sources refer specifically only to smallpox, other Columbian Exchange diseases certainly struck Spanish Florida. Some scholars have taken European reference to the plague, or *pestes,* at face value, claiming that that specific disease in either its bubonic or pneumonic form made a deadly appearance, but the weight of scholarly opinion cautions us from accepting such an early arrival of this difficult-to-spread disease.[104] Mention of plagues most likely refers to high fever–causing diseases such as measles or yellow fever. Typhus, which one would not normally suspect as afflicting small Native communities living in warmer climates, also could have become problematic. The disease especially would have thrived with the cultural changes that Catholicism induced. Prohibitions against nudity, less frequent bathing, and confinement in and near missions made Native peoples more vulnerable to the louse-borne disease. And of course, Native communities had long had experience with malaria, a disease that certainly debilitated indigenous peoples and made them more vulnerable to the more lethal germs that Europeans brought. Florida's indigenous population undoubtedly suffered from multiple new diseases that arrived as Spanish colonialism expanded during the seventeenth century.

Not only did the mission system heighten the chances of Natives becoming exposed to new diseases, but it also deteriorated their overall health and diminished their abilities to fight off infection. Catholic priests discouraged settlement dispersion, wishing to keep their converts close at hand to ensure regular attendance at mass and to foster routine religious instruction. This increased pathogen loads that Native bodies carried. Indigenous diets also became poorer. On the surface it might appear that Spanish colonialism had a positive impact on Native consumption practices. Beef, pork, and mutton were added to the Native diet, as were newly introduced fruits such as peaches and watermelons. Native diets, however, also became less diverse, less nutritious, and less abundant. Indigenous converts relied more on the primary staple of maize as they became increasingly sedentary, while the newly introduced foodstuffs failed to compensate for the loss of wild game, fish, vegetables, and fruits. Rates of iron-deficiency anemia in fact escalated through the seventeenth century and greatly surpassed that of nonmissionized communities in the interior.[105] In one telling example of this nutritional crisis, a Spanish official heard indigenous converts complain that they lacked food because missionaries expropriated their crops, while others charged that labor tribute prevented them from pursuing normal subsistence routines.[106] Catholic priests offered their Native converts salvation in the afterlife, and by becoming enmeshed in indigenous communities, they tragically shortened the time their converts had to wait to see if such promises came true.

By the time English colonialism came to influence the Native Southeast, then, the Timucua, Guale, and Apalachee populations had plummeted due to the introduction of new and deadly diseases, a process that necessarily depended on the larger context of European imperialism. Whether Spanish colonization had an epidemiological impact on other indigenous groups in the Native Southeast, however, remains doubtful. Ancestral peoples of the Lower Creeks who lived along the Apalachicola and Chattahoochee rivers may have received some new germs, because they hosted Spanish visitors as early as 1639 and sporadically traded with both Apalachees and Spaniards. But two interrelated factors caution against such a conclusion. First, hostility characterized the relations between Apalachicola communities and the Spanish and their Apalachee allies. Periods of peace interrupted what was a nearly continual state of conflict. Only after English-inspired slave raids did the Lower Creeks agree to have a Catholic mission established among them. Second, exchange practices that extended beyond the Spanish mission system remained limited. Catholic officials declared such trade illegal, and while it still occurred clandestinely, Spanish traders found Apalachee men unwilling to serve as porters and guides into what was certainly hostile territory to the North.[107] Even if they could convince their Native allies to assist them, the Spanish had a dismally small supply of goods at their disposal to initiate a significant increase in commercial traffic across the Native South-east. The few goods that do show up in the archaeological record of faraway sites, moreover, likely came from low-volume and down-the-line trading or from sporadic raids on mission communities rather than a high volume of sustained trading. The Spanish, in other words, did essentially nothing to reorient interior communities to the larger Atlantic world. Natives did not come to depend on the Spanish for everyday items—guns, ammunition, metal utensils, cloth, and other goods—that ultimately flooded their communities after the English arrived on the scene.[108] Consequently, the most lethal diseases circulating through the Atlantic world found it difficult to travel into the interior until colonialism radically altered exchange patterns and buffer zones across the entire region.

Assessing Protohistoric Demographic Change

Although Spanish colonialism did not transmit the Atlantic world's most lethal diseases into the interior, some archaeological and documentary evidence might seem to indicate otherwise. Abandoned towns, population dispersals, and va-cated river valleys in the archaeological record suggests a regionwide population collapse. Furthermore, the Soto chronicles describe several areas as well peopled, but those same areas were vacant by the time the English or the French arrived on the scene. Such alterations in the social landscape, however, do not prove a protohistoric occurrence of massive depopulation. There are explanations for demographic change that are more plausible than the introduction of the Atlantic world's deadliest microbes. Also, the entire social landscape did not change. Several indigenous communities experienced little if any disruption during the protohistoric period. An assessment of examples of change and sta-bility makes clear that colonialism and its germs created fewer changes to the Southeast's social landscape before 1659 than they did afterward.

For alternative explanations for protohistoric demographic change, the ar-chaeological record of the precontact eastern woodlands is a good place to start looking. The fate of the Cahokia polity illustrates that dramatic alterations in the social landscape could occur without virgin-soil epidemics. Cahokia, just east of what is today St. Louis, was once the largest ceremonial center north of Mexico, containing 120 mounds arrayed over sixteen hundred hectares. The largest of these, Monk's Mound, stood at over thirty meters high. At its height in the twelfth century, Cahokia stood at the top of a thriving polity with multiple communities located in the highly fertile American Bottom region. By the time of the European invasion, though, indigenous peoples had scattered, Cahokia's mounds had fallen out of use, and the entire American Bottom area lay vacant. Such a striking transformation has tempted some to assert that postcontact epidemics must have destroyed Cahokia, but archaeologists rule out newly introduced diseases by placing the American Bottom's abandonment in the fourteenth century.[109] The Soto chronicles lend support for a pre-Columbian collapse. When the Spanish reached the Mississippi Valley, the indigenous peoples described the land to the north as lightly peopled and full of buffalo.[110] Had Cahokia been at its height in the 1540s, one would think that Soto would have traveled there, thinking that the area and its peoples held the great wealth that he sought, but he evidently did not find it worth his time.[111] Why Cahokia was no longer in existence remains a mystery. Scholars cite a variety of explanations, including climate change, ecological disaster, warfare, and political instability, but whichever was to blame, Cahokia's demise epitomizes on a grand scale how the social landscape could radically change without the intervention of Europe's most lethal germs.[112]

Another area abandoned prior to 1492 further illustrates how demographic changes occurred without the European invasion being involved. The fall line of the Savannah River had been home to several large towns during the transition to horticulture, but sometime during the fifteenth century, these towns vanished. When Soto traversed the Savannah in 1540, he and his hungry men in fact found it a "desert." Archaeologists are not sure where the people who once inhabited these impressive communities moved, but they suspect that they went north and west into the Savannah's tributaries, eventually to emerge in the historical record as the Lower Cherokees. Such demographic changes appear to have resulted from a variety of related factors. Severe drought characterized the area from 1407 to 1476, leading to crop failures and famines. Indigenous peoples therefore relied even more on hunting and gathering, but this brought on increased conflict with communities in adjacent river valleys. The Cofitachequi chiefdom to the east on the Wateree River and the Ocute chiefdom to the west on the Oconee in particular placed great pressure on Savannah Valley peoples. Eventually, drought-stricken and war-ridden towns could not hold on to the Savannah and left for safer locations, leaving a valuable and fertile river valley essentially depopulated.[113]

Could these same nonepidemiological variables that created a dynamic social landscape prior to contact have produced the demographic changes often thought to be due to protohistoric epidemics? Let us explore that possibility by looking at an area that seems to be the scene of massive disease-induced depopulation, the central Mississippi Valley, especially the St. Francis Basin in what is today northeastern Arkansas. This area contained some of the most densely settled human communities in all the areas that Soto explored. There, the Soto expedition found several compact and fortified towns—Quizquiz on the east bank of the Mississippi and Pacaha and Aquijo on the west; Casqui on the Tyronza and Quiguate on the St. Francis.[114] When Marquette "rediscovered" the area in 1673, however, he made no mention of these towns. As the French missionary traveled between the Ohio and the Arkansas rivers, he encountered only an unidentified Native village on the east bank of the Mississippi and a Mitchigamea village at the mouth of the St. Francis.[115] Accounts of La Salle's exploration in 1682 reiterated what Marquette found. La Salle encountered some Chickasaws on the east bank but did not find Native villages along the Mississippi until he reached the Arkansas.[116] The archaeological record lends support to an evacuation of the St. Francis Basin prior to 1673. Archaeologists make a strong case that the location and description of Casqui and Pacaha as found in the Soto chronicles match the Parkin and Nodena sites, respectively. Excavations also have failed to certify the presence of French or English trade items at these sites, suggesting that abandonment occurred prior to the late seventeenth century. It may be tempting, therefore, to conclude that the discrepancy between what the Spanish found in the sixteenth century and what the French found in the seventeenth century can only be explained by catastrophic depopulation in the wake of germs that Soto's army supposedly carried.[117]

But such a conclusion is misleading. Soto reached the central Mississippi Valley nearly three years after arriving in the Southeast, a period far too long for his expedition to have transmitted acute infectious disease to the river's indigenous inhabitants. The Spanish also stayed in the area long enough to observe any outbreak that they might have caused, but no such observations are found in the Soto chronicles. Furthermore, archaeologists have found no mass graves or changes in mortuary practices that would suggest virgin-soil epidemics among the central Mississippi's Native population. Other archaeologists dispute the use of trade goods to time the area's evacuation and argue that human occupation of the St. Francis continued into the seventeenth century. Sites in the St. Francis Basin have long been subject to looting, and closer study of the few European artifacts that have been found may reveal that they actually came from the French rather than sixteenth-century Spaniards.[118] Last, the sparse documentary records left by members of the Marquette and La Salle expeditions are not as forthcoming with information as one would like. These later French adventurers may have had little to say about the inhabitants of the St. Francis Basin be-cause they did not seek them out as did Soto. Spanish invasion, thus, is not the obvious culprit that it appears to be.

Even if Native peoples had disappeared from the central Mississippi Valley by 1673, massive disease-induced mortality need not be the only explanation. Other scenarios that explain protohistoric demographic change are more realis-tic. First, the introduction of malaria may be responsible. Soto's expedition cer-tainly could have introduced the plasmodia parasite throughout their journey across the Southeast, and of all peoples who encountered the Spanish, residents of the St. Francis Basin were perfectly situated to suffer from malaria. A series of swamps and bayous lay between the St. Francis and the Mississippi River, and Native communities constructed defensive moats around their compact towns. Anopheles mosquitoes thrived in the area and enjoyed feeding on a densely set-tled human population, whose members hunted, fished, and farmed amid the numerous bodies of standing water. Once the plasmodia parasite was intro-duced, malaria likely became endemic and made almost everyone suffer from seasonal bouts of chills and fevers, thus taxing the health of individuals whose la-bor was needed to plant and harvest crops. Malaria also could have driven down birthrates, increased already high levels of iron-deficiency anemia, and height-ened mortality rates from indigenous diseases. The disease by itself would not have wiped out the entire population of the St. Francis Basin, but it certainly could have led communities to relocate to healthier locations, thus leading to an archaeological record that suggests massive population loss.

It was probably not malaria alone that led to the depopulation of the St. Fran-cis Basin. Soto's visit destabilized communities that had already existed under in-credible stress. In June 1541 Soto found the town of Casqui and its affiliates along the St. Francis and Tyronza rivers hungry due to drought and crop failure, while conflict with their neighbors had forced them to live behind palisades in compact villages.[119] The leader of Casqui begged Soto for help, hoping that the Spanish leader had a connection with the spiritual world and could make it rain. Soto replied that he had no such power, but the Spanish explorer did prove eager to help with Casqui's other problem—its rivals, the town of Pacaha and its affil-iates along the western and eastern banks of the Mississippi. With Casqui's war-riors in the rear, the Spanish invaded Pacaha, causing its residents to flee and to leave their fields and food open for the taking. Casqui's warriors sought vengeance; they desecrated the remains of their enemy's ancestors, destroyed re-ligious objects, and replaced the skulls of their own people, which had been im-paled on posts in the town, with the heads of Pacaha's own residents who had failed to escape the combined Spanish-Casqui onslaught. Although Soto managed to broker a temporary peace between the two rivals before the Spanish left, warfare undoubtedly continued to characterize the St. Francis Basin in the years that followed. Pacaha's warriors certainly took revenge on Casqui, inflaming the cycle of violence that plagued the area. To make matters worse, the drought became even more severe. Between 1544 and 1577 the St. Francis Basin experienced its worst dry period in 450 years, suggesting that violence became even more severe as Natives competed for scarcer food resources. Not surprisingly, survivors of Casqui, Pacaha, and other communities abandoned their towns in northeastern Arkansas. They did not die en masse from novel germs, but they instead found their residential situation intolerable and moved to safer and healthier locations elsewhere, as had residents of the Savannah and the American Bottom many years before the European invasion. Linguistic evidence supports this view. According to one theory, the Quapaws, whom the French located on the Arkansas River in the late seventeenth century, were the descendants of those communities the Spanish found in the St. Francis Basin. They are also believed to have been speakers of a Dhegiha Siouan language, closely related to the historic Omahas and Poncas, who lived in the Missouri Valley near the present-day boundary between Missouri, Iowa, and Nebraska, as well as to the Osages, who lived along the lower Missouri River and its tributaries. How all these related groups ended up so far apart remains a mystery, but it is possible that they all resided in the central Mississippi in the sixteenth century and then left in different directions to find better homelands sometime after Soto departed.[120]

Soto, however, may not have had anything to do with the abandonment of the St. Francis Basin. Pinpointing the timing of protohistoric events is difficult, and there are reasons to believe that demographic changes resulted from circumstances occurring much later than the Spanish invasion. An absence of French and English goods in archaeological sites does not mean that indigenous peoples left in the sixteenth century; it only means that they abandoned their towns before those goods arrived in quantities significant enough to show up in archaeological contexts, which would be sometime in the latter half of the seventeenth century. The window of time in which residents of the St. Francis Basin vacated their towns, thus, remains large—the 132-year period between Soto's and Marquette's visits. Alterations in the social landscape may have in fact occurred during the latter part of this period, when European expansion led to heightened intertribal warfare throughout the eastern woodlands.

For the source of these later protohistoric changes, one has to look far from the Southeast to what is today upstate New York, ancestral home of the Iroquois Confederacy. Throughout the seventeenth century, Iroquois warriors placed incredible pressure on Native communities in the Ohio Valley and Great Lakes region. The Iroquois wanted to expand their hunting territories in order to supply their Dutch and later English partners with beaver pelts; they also sought captives to replace kinsmen who had died from wars and disease. Beginning in the 1630s, Natives of the northeastern interior suffered from smallpox and other diseases as they became integrated into the fur-trade networks involving the Dutch, the French, and the English. The Iroquois believed that the spirit of their lost kinsmen would be doomed to roam the earth and not reach the afterlife if a captive was not taken in their place. These "mourning wars" sent shock waves through the trans-Appalachian West, sending thousands of Algonquian and Siouan speakers fleeing from gun-wielding Iroquois.[121]

Members of both the Marquette and the La Salle expedition, in fact, commented on the long-distance impact of the Iroquois wars. Marquette's narrative referred to the Ohio River as coming from the land of the Shawnees, who had thirty-eight villages, some of which were probably located in the Cumberland Valley. The French, who along with their Native allies had been trying to exterminate the Iroquois since the early 1600s, characterized the Shawnees as "innocent" people who allowed "themselves to be taken and carried off like sheep."[122] The Shawnees, of course, ultimately fled their homelands and became scattered throughout the eastern woodlands. The Illinois also faced incredible pressure but managed to retain their power by escalating their own raiding activities. "They are warlike and formidable to distant nations in the South and West," one of Marquette's chroniclers reported, "where they go to carry off slaves whom they make an article of trade selling them at a high price to other nations for goods."[123] The residents of the St. Francis Basin would have been easy targets for the aggressive Illinois, who easily could have reached these settled horticultural communities by canoe and then transported captives back to the multiple communities in the Ohio country, which sought to replenish their numbers lost during the Iroquois wars. By the time La Salle traveled into the Mississippi Valley, the Illinois were suffering even more severely from Iroquois attacks and had to venture even farther for captives. The central Mississippi in the area of its junction with the Ohio, according to the members of the La Salle expedition, was a "large burned-out land" as a result of the Iroquois driving peoples away. In one attack, the Illinois lost nine hundred individuals as they fled to the west side of the Mississippi River, where they hoped to find safety.[124] Spurred by such losses, the Illinois ventured far into the Missouri Valley and captured a large number of Pawnees to replace their lost loved ones.[125] Had the St. Francis Basin been populated at the time, the Illinois would likely have raided communities there, too, but they had probably driven Native peoples from that area some ten years earlier.

If the Illinois were not responsible for forcing the evacuation of the central Mississippi Valley, another tribe that faced Iroquois attacks may have. According to another theory of the Quapaws' origins, the Dhegiha Sioux were not the original occupants of the St. Francis Basin, but instead they inhabited the upper Ohio as late as the mid-seventeenth century. As did many other tribes, the Dhegiha Sioux faced Iroquois attacks and moved a considerable distance. Eventually they ended up on the Mississippi, where they split into the four groups, going their separate ways and ultimately appearing in the historical record by their more familiar names.[126] Quapaw intrusion south to the Arkansas River and Osage intrusion into central and southern Missouri, both of which happened sometime before 1673, may have forced the St. Francis Basin's evacuation. While the origins of the Quapaws remain mysterious, it is not too far fetched to believe that desperate refugees from the Iroquois wars flooded into the area looking for fertile land, hunting territories, and captives to replace their lost kinsmen, thus displacing indigenous groups previously believed to have been victims of epidemics. It may also be the case that the Dhegiha Sioux communities themselves became victims of Illinois raids and coalesced with other refugee tribes in the lower Arkansas Valley. Wherever the Quapaws came from, there are many plausible explanations for population movements and coalescence in the protohistoric Mississippi Valley that do not directly involve newly introduced diseases.

Of course, one will never know with a large degree of certainty which scenario actually took place in the protohistoric Mississippi Valley. But what should be acknowledged is that no solid evidence exists for massive mortality due to the Atlantic world's most lethal diseases. The documentary and archaeological record in fact suggests that while the central Mississippi experienced depopulation, the lower valley remained well peopled into the early colonial period. When La Salle's party descended the mighty river in 1682, they discovered that the Yazoo Basin was "densely populated with many different nations."[127] Another member of the expedition placed the number of villages in the Basin at forty, while thirty-four villages stood on the opposite side of the Mississippi near the mouth of the Arkansas.[128] These villages may have been recent arrivals, but their refugee status does not mean they suffered from newly introduced disease. Violence, in fact, gave indigenous communities more incentive than disease to pick up and move far away. Survivors of virgin-soil epidemics often did flee their locations because of the horror that they had just witnessed and relocated among other remnants to rebuild viable communities, but they did not necessarily have to travel great distances to do this. La Salle, in fact, encountered a rather crowded Lower Mississippi Valley, where numerous Native groups competed fiercely with one another for valuable hunting grounds.[129]

Another area that the Spanish visited, the upper Coosa Valley, epitomizes how scholars are often too quick to attribute protohistoric demographic change to European germs, when a more critical approach leads to other explanations. The upper Coosa and its tributaries had been home to a powerful chiefdom and a densely settled population when Hernando de Soto pillaged his way through the area in 1540 and when Luna returned in 1561, but by the eighteenth century the chiefdom had collapsed and its population had shifted downriver. As archaeologist Marvin Smith has shown, many communities disappeared from the archaeological record, while the former paramount town of Coosa itself had been relocated farther south, where it appeared in European accounts as one of several roughly equal and independent towns belonging to the Upper Creeks. Smith's sophisticated analysis of artifacts from the upper Coosa sites, moreover, suggests that such movements must have occurred before 1630, thus fueling speculation that Spanish germs wiped out the population during the protohistoric period.[130]

Nevertheless, blaming epidemics for the Coosa chiefdom's demise remains problematic. Soto's and Luna's occupation certainly took a toll on Native communities and put the chiefdom on a course of declension, but such damage stemmed from destruction of food, contamination of water supplies, and violence. There is little evidence that any germs more serious than malaria could have been introduced into the Coosa Valley during the protohistoric period. It must also be remembered that Native polities had a history of evolution and devolution due to indigenous causes that could easily explain Coosa's demise. In Coosa's case warfare must be seen as more plausible than disease for archaeologically observable demographic changes. Coosa's inhabitants were indeed hard pressed by enemies to the north—the Cherokees in the Appalachian highlands—and enemies to the west—the Napochies, who were most likely Alabama speakers living along the Tennessee River. After Luna's departure in 1561, the Napochies certainly took vengeance on Coosa's inhabitants, who were left without the Spanish assistance they had earlier relied on to inflict a stinging attack on their rivals. The Spanish, in other words, inflamed the cycle of violence that had kept residents of the Coosa and Tennessee valleys at war with one another for generations. The Cherokees also came into play, as these numerous peoples generally moved south and west during the protohistoric and certainly looked to the nearby Coosa watershed as valuable hunting grounds. The dispersal of the upper Coosa's inhabitants, therefore, should not be taken as evidence of massive mortality due to newly introduced diseases. Epidemics, in fact, did not in themselves provide nearly the incentive for flight as did the risk of being killed or captured by an enemy.[131]

The Mississippi and Coosa valleys featured altered social landscapes that are tempting to read as evidence of a regionwide population collapse due to Spanish germs. But during the protohistoric period no solid proof for massive disease-induced mortality exists, and concluding that virgin-soil epidemics occurred rests on problematic assumptions. Instead, the protohistoric period should be studied with a more critical approach. The Native Southeast would not have remained static in the absence of Europeans and their germs, and the changes observed in the archaeological record could well have derived from nonepidemiological causes. Highly lethal diseases, moreover, neither arrived as a routine consequence of every European visit to the region nor spread automatically beyond the Catholic mission system once they were introduced into Florida. The most likely scenario is that the only new disease to spread outside Spanish Florida was malaria, which added a new variable to what was already a dynamic situation in which warfare and drought played the major role in producing alterations in the social landscape of the region.

While protohistoric demographic changes hint at the occurrence of epidemics, many examples of protohistoric demographic stability exist as well. Such examples suggest that indigenous peoples did not experience the Atlantic world's deadliest diseases. The town of Cofitachequi, while suffering from some unknown cause prior to Soto's arrival, remained occupied and largely unchanged until its abandonment in 1672, at which time gun-wielding slave raiders made the area hazardous.[132] The Carolina Piedmont as a whole, in fact, displays no decline in the size or frequency of settlements in its protohistoric archaeological record.[133] The peoples of the Appalachian highlands went through a general transition as population moved south and west and as settlement patterns changed from compact to dispersed, but the narrow river valleys remained well peopled into the eighteenth century by Cherokees who had called the mountainous area their ancient homeland.[134] One would expect the peoples of the remote and difficult to access Appalachian highlands to be the most protected from newly introduced diseases, but given the continuity in the archaeological record of other locations, there were no serious germs to be protected from in the first place.

Indigenous settlements in several valleys in what is today Alabama also indicate continuity through the entire protohistoric period. Several Muskogean towns near the junction of the Tallapoosa, Coosa, and Alabama rivers, whose origins date to the precontact period, remained continuously occupied during the protohistoric. Apica on the Coosa River and Talisa on the Tallapoosa River display no severe disruption in their archaeological record, despite being on the path of both the Soto and the Luna expedition.[135] The Black Warrior River valley's protohistoric record remains more contentious; some scholars cite its original inhabitants as being decimated by European-introduced diseases while others place the river's abandonment in the late seventeenth and early eighteenth centuries. There is more evidence for the latter view. The Black Warrior was the location of the eastern woodlands' second most impressive ceremonial center, now known as Moundville. At one time Moundville's residents utilized at least twenty-six earthen pyramids for civic and religious activities and lived behind palisade walls enclosing three hundred acres. The ceremonial center likely integrated numerous smaller communities in and around the Black Warrior into a chiefdom that dominated central Alabama. Sometime before Soto's visit, a power shift occurred in the Black Warrior River valley, Moundville lost its prestige, its chiefdom collapsed, and some of its affiliated communities resettled to the west in the Tombigbee River valley. Soto's expedition probably visited the formerly impressive ceremonial center, calling it by its Native name Zabusta, but by the time they got there, Moundville had already devolved. Its ceremonial structures had fallen out of use and were overgrown with trees, and its stature had been eclipsed by two nearby towns, Taliepacana to the south and Apafayala to the north.[136] After Soto's departure, Moundville continued its apparent decline and was probably abandoned in the sixteenth century, but the Black Warrior River valley as a whole remained inhabited into the late seventeenth century. Archaeologists note more scattered settlements and higher rates of iron-deficiency anemia, which suggest the prevalence of malaria, but indigenous peoples continued to reside in the valley into the late seventeenth century.[137] Although the particular circumstances remain unclear, some of the Black Warrior River valley's inhabitants may have been among those who fled English-inspired slave raiders in the late seventeenth century and coalesced with others to form the Choctaw Confederacy. The French learned that two of the constituent Choctaw groups, the Chickasawhays and the Conchas, had formerly inhabited a prairie region and moved west at time when "the English caused a cruel war to be made upon them by their allies to whom they furnished firearms while the Chickasawhays and Conchas had only bows and arrows."[138] Like residents elsewhere in Alabama, inhabitants of the Black Warrior River valley suffered little from European colonialism until the Native slave trade radically transformed the region.

A similarly strong case for continuity can be made in the Tombigbee watershed in eastern Mississippi. There Hernando de Soto arrived in December 1540 and found a well-peopled landscape but one in which scattered settlements prevailed.[139] Of course, his arrival coincided with the approach of winter, when one would expect indigenous peoples to disperse from their compact settlements within floodplain environments and scatter themselves in upcountry areas for hunting. But dispersed settlements appeared to be the year-around rule for these peoples. Before the Spanish arrived, a permanent shift from the bottom lands of the Tombigbee to upland areas of the Black Prairie had occurred, with indigenous peoples locating their homesteads on the tops of ridges and bluffs overlooking small tributary streams. Natives still farmed, but they also enjoyed better access to deer, which thrived year around in cedar glades near their homes.[140] Natives continued to do so for many years after Soto's departure. These people were the Chicaza that Soto met and an ancestral group of the Chickasaws, who remained dominant in the region into the historic period. Archaeologists have found no evidence of depopulation during the protohistoric period and conclude that the area was continuously occupied up until the time English goods showed up within its archaeological record. Interestingly, the Chickasaws' scattered settlements away from the floodplains made them less vulnerable to the one new disease that the Spanish did introduce to the Southeast, malaria. It is not surprising, then, that Chickasaw settlement patterns display continuity, while communities in more malaria-prone locations showed some signs of disruption. To be sure, once the Chickasaws became active partners with English traders in the late seventeenth century, their scattered settlements no longer isolated them from Europe's most notorious germs. But until the expansion of English influence into the interior, the Chickasaws, like the vast majority of indigenous groups in the Native Southeast, remained unaffected by the Atlantic world's worst diseases.

Conclusion

The protohistoric period will always puzzle anyone who attempts to understand what actually happened during this mysterious time. One wishes the archaeological and documentary record could speak to us more clearly about the epidemiological consequences of Spanish colonialism. Scholars will undoubtedly continue to study the available evidence and continue to debate the causes and timing of demographic transformations. It is hoped, however, that further research will not begin with the assumption that the mere presence of Europeans on southeastern soil in the sixteenth century precipitated an epidemiological holocaust, or that the establishment of Spanish Florida automatically facilitated the transmission of the Atlantic world's most deadly microbes into the interior. Instead, a more critical approach leads to the conclusion that the protohistoric period was the false dawn of colonialism's biological nightmare.

Early European encounters have been overrated in their ability to facilitate the spread of new germs. Neither undocumented visitors nor officially sanctioned expeditions introduced acute infectious diseases. Composed mostly of adult males, early exploring parties were unlikely carriers of smallpox and other childhood bugs, and when members of these parties did become sick, the characteristics of their illnesses did not resemble such diseases. One would expect to see symptoms of acute infectious diseases within days after explorers' ships left their last harbor, but instead sickness erupted weeks or months after Europeans arrived in the Southeast, indicating a variety of possibilities except those acute infectious diseases that later proved to be most problematic for indigenous peoples. If any new disease became a problem due to early exploration, it was malaria, a scourge whose case-fatality rates were minimal compared to the Atlantic world's more serious diseases. The plasmodia parasite likely became planted among horticultural communities already predisposed to harbor the disease and could account for some of the population movements observed in the archaeological and documentary record. But malaria alone cannot be held responsible for massive depopulation. At worst malaria killed individuals whose immune systems were already compromised, drove up rates of infant mortality, and lowered life expectancies. One should be careful, though, in assigning blame to novel diseases. Early exploring expeditions were composed of filthy, germ-ridden men and livestock who contaminated Native villages with those typical pathogens that afflicted all human societies. Native peoples certainly suffered from a variety of nasty infections when hundreds of unwelcome guests and their livestock occupied their compact towns built for a few hundred people. Nevertheless, epidemiological damage due to European exploration, whether as a result of typical germs or malaria, remained limited, a fact borne out by an archaeological record that displays several examples of demographic stability.

Spanish colonialism further illustrates how the biological aspects of conquest are necessarily dependent on the larger political and economic context. The Atlantic world's most lethal germs did not arrive on southeastern shores until the establishment of St. Augustine in 1565; prior to then, the Native Southeast had remained on the periphery of conquest. But after the colony's founding, the region had regular contact with the outside world as ships carrying peoples, goods, and germs arrived in St. Augustine's harbor. As the Spanish colony's influence grew, indigenous peoples inhabiting a string of Catholic missions along the coast of Georgia and northern Florida became vulnerable to those germs that had earlier destroyed Native populations elsewhere in Latin America. Compelled to pay tribute in the form of labor, forced to carry goods back and forth from St. Augustine, and no longer protected by the buffer zones that had formerly stifled communication between rival communities, Florida's Natives suffered severely. Smallpox certainly spread along the newly established exchange nexus that connected indigenous peoples to St. Augustine, Havana, Seville, and other pestilential ports on the Atlantic Rim. Catholic missions not only exposed Native peoples to deadly germs, but they also made indigenous bodies more vulnerable in other ways. Prohibitions against nudity, curtailment of ritualized cleansing ceremonies, and confinement in compact towns led to higher pathogen loads and a susceptibility to louse-born typhus, while expropriation of surplus food and interference with traditional subsistence activities led to malnutrition. Natives living in missions suffered from calorie deprivation, protein deficiency, and anemia. The Columbian Exchange thus became a nightmare for them, and estimates of population declines of 80 to 90 percent are not without merit. It must be emphasized, however, that such a calamity occurred not because of the independent behavior of invisible microorganisms, but because Spanish colonialism had forced dramatic changes in the disease ecology of its converted Native communities. Missions tied indigenous peoples to the communication networks that facilitated the spread of acute infectious diseases, and mission life weakened the ability of Native converts to survive infection.

The worst impact of epidemics thus followed rather than preceded the spread of European influence, which leads to a final conclusion about the protohistoric period. The germs that devastated Florida's Native population did not spread throughout the entire southeastern region. The Spanish had induced great changes in the lives of the Guales, the Timucuas, and the Apalachees and made them vulnerable to infection, but the same cannot be said for all of the Native Southeast, whose indigenous inhabitants remained on the outside of European colonialism until the first English-inspired slave raids began to take place around 1659. The Spanish did trade with indigenous peoples, but direct contact

reached only as far as the Apalachicola River, and Spanish goods never circulated at the level that English goods were to by the late seventeenth century. Exchange remained rather limited in the Southeast, and buffer zones continued to
impede communication across the region. All of that, of course, would change as
the Native slave trade infiltrated the region.

Chapter Three

Slave Raids and Smallpox

1659–1700

When Nicholas Carteret and his party of settlers first approached the shores of South Carolina in 1670, they found indigenous peoples welcoming. As the party sailed near Port Royal, Carteret reported, Natives "ran up to the middle in mire and watter to carry us a shoare, . . . and brought deare skins, some raw, some drest, to trade with us, for which we gave them knives, beads and tobacco, and glad they were of the market."[1] Of course, Natives did not see that they were making a straight economic exchange. Obviously, they valued knives for their utility, beads for their aesthetic qualities, and tobacco for its narcotic affects, but more than that, coastal peoples sought an alliance with someone who could help them against the Westos, a tribe that arrived in the Savannah Valley in 1659 and that had been receiving munitions from Virginia in return for deerskins and captives. By giving gifts to the Carolinians and by the Carolinians reciprocating, Natives thought that they had established kinship bonds with a people who held great sacred power and who could protect them from their enemies. Now with European kinsmen, coastal Natives hoped they could acquire munitions and turn them against their enemies, who would no longer have a monopoly on trade items. Englishmen, however, would not act as proper kinsmen. They saw the land and its people through an economic gaze, one in which deer could be slaughtered for their hides and humans hunted as a source of slaves to supply the Atlantic world's insatiable demand for labor.[2] In the short term indigenous peoples may have been "glad they were of the market," but in the long run trading with the English escalated the level of violence, heightened dependency, and facilitated the spread of colonialism's worst germs.

With their inclusion within the Atlantic market economy, Natives outside the Spanish mission system became more vulnerable to smallpox and other acute infectious diseases than they had ever been before. Beginning around 1650 Virginia's traders ventured into the Carolina Piedmont, and by 1659 their commercial links extended as far south as the Savannah River. Virginia's goods, if not

Virginians themselves, also reached as far west as the Appalachian highlands, if not farther. After 1670 Carolinians expanded English influence to an even greater extent, sending traders from their newly established colony to the deep interior. By 1696 a thriving exchange network linked English colonies and Native communities from the James to the Savannah and from the Atlantic to the Mississippi. Many indigenous peoples took advantage of what European colonialism had to offer, acquiring a variety of new, useful, and mystical manufactured goods in return for deerskins and the human captives they took from their enemies. Other Natives became the victims of these new circumstances, serving as potential slaves for aggressive, gun-wielding raiders and fleeing great distances for safety. As English commercial expansion occurred over the last half of the seventeenth century, the Atlantic market economy, for the first time, became an indelible factor in the lives of indigenous peoples throughout the Southeast.

English trade dramatically changed the social landscape and disease ecology of the region. The flow of guns into the Southeast and aggressive raids of English allies led to numerous population movements, the cause of which archaeologists have been too quick to blame on virgin-soil epidemics. Before a regionwide smallpox outbreak occurred, English commerce flooded the Southeast with an unprecedented amount of goods and connected formerly self-sufficient communities to the larger Atlantic world. A quest for deerskins, of course, led English traders to venture far from colonial settlements, but more than anything their desire to purchase indigenous captives increased Native vulnerability to newly introduced germs. The Native slave trade dramatically increased the volume of human traffic, as traders, raiders, slaves, and refugees crisscrossed the region, even surmounting older buffer zones that had previously isolated rivals from each other. Also, the intense violence associated with slave raids forced numerous indigenous peoples to go hungry and to resort to the unhealthiest settlement patterns. Thousands of Natives huddled in fortified, compact, and unsanitary towns, where the fear of being captured kept them from going out to hunt game or harvest crops. It was into this new social landscape—one dramatically altered by nonepidemiological aspects of colonialism—that smallpox did the most damage it would ever do to the region and its people.

Native Articulation with the Atlantic Market

"No imployment pleases the Chicasaws so well as slave Catching," the South Carolinian Thomas Nairne remarked. "A lucky hitt at that besides the Honor procures them a whole estate at once, one slave brings a Gun, ammunition, horse, hatchet, and a suit of Cloathes."[3] Nairne, although observing the impact of English trade several decades after its first development, reported what must have been a common occurrence whenever his countrymen introduced their goods. Much more than the Spanish, the English carried new items to Natives, who came to use them on an everyday basis. Indigenous peoples in return supplied the English with commodities that the Atlantic market demanded. Deerskins in particular fetched a nice price back in England, where craftsmen transformed the soft leather into book bindings, gloves, boots, and other products. The Atlantic market also had an insatiable demand for labor. Native captives ended up on plantations in Virginia or Carolina, while others were shipped to the West Indies, where disease-ridden and deadly sugar plantations rapidly consumed their own labor force.[4] Indigenous peoples, except those who ended up enslaved and exported, did not understand why Englishmen wanted so many of their captives, but they certainly knew that only Europeans could provide such an impressive variety of valuable and irresistible manufactured goods. The seductive powers of those goods induced Natives into the pernicious activity of supplying the Atlantic world's labor demands, an activity that would lead to thousands of indigenous prisoners being exported from their homelands and one that would facilitate the spread of colonialism's deadliest germs.

The English built the Native slave trade on aboriginal practices of captive taking. By returning to their communities with enemies taken alive, male warriors gained considerable status.[5] Their captives could be ritually tortured and killed to avenge the loss of kinsmen—kinsmen whose spirits would be doomed to roam the earth instead of enjoying an afterlife among their ancestors unless their deaths were avenged.[6] Such ceremonies allowed an entire community to participate in humiliating their enemies and perhaps enact the worst of all punishments: if a Native captive pled for his life or cried out in pain, his tormentors captured his spirit, thus denying his entrance into the afterlife. Not all captives experienced such fates. Some were chosen to be adopted, a decision usually made by female elders.[7] Native captors particularly spared the lives of women of reproductive age and children, who could replace lost kinsmen and add valuable members to clans whose numbers had declined.[8] Some of these adopted members—both male and female—played important roles; if they retained knowledge of their original language, they could serve as interpreters who helped their adopted community build diplomatic relations with outsiders.[9] Some captives remained alive but yet were not adopted, remaining outside a community's clan system and having an ambiguous status. Natives of the Carolina Piedmont, for example, disfigured some of their unadopted prisoners and kept them at work in

their fields. Captors called such an unfortunate individual by a word synony-
mous with dog or cat.[10] Some of these slaves likely were men who showed cow-
ardice when being tortured and suffered the consequence of being made to do
women's work. The French, in fact, found Mississippi Valley tribes having "her-
maphrodites," male captives who not only performed female duties but also were
made to dress as women as a form of humiliation.[11] Similar individuals existed
among the Choctaws.[12] The Cherokees also had among them unadopted captives known as *atsi nahsa'i,* meaning "one who is owned." These individuals assisted women by dressing deerskins and clearing fields.[13]

When the English flooded Native villages with goods, indigenous peoples did
not completely abandon their traditional ways in which they dealt with prisoners, but the lure of such goods was great, leading to an escalation of warfare and
a high number of captives falling into the possession of Europeans.[14] The preponderance of women and children taken as captives also increased. English
masters especially wanted to buy young boys and girls as well as older females.
Native men proved especially troublesome slaves, since they came from societies
in which they did not perform agricultural field work. Male captives who remained enslaved on plantations in Virginia and Carolina also had high rates of
flight.[15] Even more insidious, the acquisition of Native women equalized sex ratios and increased reproductive rates among the slave population on English
plantations, which had a preponderance of males among captives coming from
Africa.[16] As this chapter will later show, Native slave raiders acquiesced to the
demands of their English partners by purposely attacking their enemies to gain
particular types of captives. Of course, this in part reflects Native desires as well,
since they wanted to keep male warriors for ritual torture to fulfill their cultural
obligations to their deceased kinsmen. Nevertheless, the desire for English trade
goods led indigenous raiders to seize females and children in far greater numbers
than they had before contact.

Native captors found immense rewards for the fruits of their labors. Woolen
clothing, which remained relatively soft even after becoming wet and drying,
offered more comfort than buckskins, which when dried-out became stiff,
cracked, and irritating to the wearer; metal pots did not break when dropped
and could be reshaped into sheet brass and cut into arrowheads; iron hatchets
spared Native artisans the difficult task of chipping hard stones to form tools
needed on an everyday basis; and horses expedited overland travel and relieved
Native hunters of carrying bundles of deerskins themselves. Natives also came to
desire another trade item, alcohol, which had no material value but was quickly
consumed and created a desire for more. European colonial authorities fre-

quently attempted to regulate the distribution of rum, brandy, and other intoxicating beverages, but alcohol flowed into indigenous communities despite official prohibitions. At times liquor came sporadically, and at other times, when officials relaxed regulations or even actively encouraged its distribution, it flooded into Native communities, leading to more warring, slaving, and hunting to supply the English with the goods they so eagerly sought.[17]

The commodity that had the most profound impact on indigenous peoples, however, was the gun. As with alcohol, firearms created the need for further trade. A gun in itself was useless without a constant supply of powder and shot, and its adoption as a weapon of choice required continuous relations with European suppliers. As early as 1670, for example, Piedmont communities had become inundated by a variety of European goods, but Natives, according to the German traveler John Lederer, would most "greedily barter for" guns, powder, and shot.[18] One may wonder why indigenous peoples committed themselves to the use of firearms when they brought such dependency. Documentary evidence makes it clear that Natives quickly developed a desire for guns and came to believe they could not live without them, but it is not entirely clear why they turned from aboriginal to European weapons.

A common argument as to why indigenous peoples so readily turned to guns revolves around the technological advantage that such weapons had over bows and arrows. Even early trade muskets, which were of shoddy quality, had greater accuracy and killing power, as they delivered deadly and invisible bullets that could travel through thick underbrush in forested areas and could easily penetrate an animal's hide or the leather and wooden armor of a human enemy. Arrows, when fired from a long distance, could be seen coming and could be thrown off course by limbs and branches that dangled between the warrior and his victim. According to John Stewart, a Scottish trader living in South Carolina since the 1680s, Natives could "get more hydes and furs in one moon than formerly with bow and arrow in 12 moons."[19] Related to such technological advantages, firearms offered indigenous peoples a labor-saving device. Production of arrows took a long time; Native artisans had to select durable wood and whittle it into straight shafts, and they had to chip and sharpen hard stones into triangular projectile points. Trade with Europeans, on the other hand, offered the opportunity for the Native hunter to acquire a greater supply of ammunition in return for a smaller amount of labor; one deerskin obtained in a day's hunting could purchase dozens of musket balls and enough powder to fire them, whereas it would take much more time and effort for an artisan to produce the same amount of arrows.[20]

Such materialist explanations, however, should not obscure the psychological reasons why indigenous peoples turned to guns. Being new and strange weapons that made a thunderous sound, emitted smoke, and killed with an invisible object, firearms terrorized Natives, especially in the hands of a determined enemy. A member of La Salle's expedition, for example, reported that when the French used their guns to intimidate a tribe on the lower Mississippi who had never before seen such weapons it "terrified" them. "They call it thunder not understanding how a wooden stick could vomit fire, and kill people so far off without touching them," remarked one Frenchman.[21] John Stewart made a similar observation. "The guns roar with powder like the claps of thunder frightening their enemies into flight and the enemies think they are wounded from the clouds," Stewart claimed.[22] The appearance of armed, aggressive slave raiders certainly sent communities fleeing, horrified by the mysterious new power that their enemies had harnessed. And, of course, when the victims received their chance to acquire weapons, they did so eagerly, hoping to turn the tables on those who had earlier attacked them. Whether Natives valued guns for their technological or psychological advantage, or both, obtaining munitions became necessary for survival in a region marred by massive slave raiding.

The desire for guns and other manufactured items pulled indigenous peoples into trade relations with Europeans, but such involvement did not destroy their conceptions of exchange. Natives certainly interpreted trade with Europeans as part of traditional gift giving. By giving captives and other items, indigenous peoples were extending an offer of kinship to the English, who would thereafter be treated with hospitality, permitted to travel freely through a community and its hunting territories, and allowed to intermarry. Natives also thought that the English by giving gifts had accepted the corresponding responsibilities. Traders were expected to share their food; they were to go to war to avenge the deaths of their new kinsmen; they were to participate in community councils; and they were to respect their elders. In other words, indigenous peoples did not look at their interaction with English traders in strictly materialist terms. They were gaining kinsmen, and in the case of the English, powerful kinsmen, who brought them a decided advantage over their neighbors. Of course, Englishmen, not fully understanding their kinship duties, often violated their obligations, leading Natives to become suspicious. Disagreements often resulted when traders refused to supply goods to their indigenous partners, who had yet to pay for goods that they had previously received. For the English this was an issue of debt, but for Natives it was a violation of kinship to refuse to supply their partners who were in need. Kinship obligations, moreover, were not subject to economic rationality. At times the goods that indigenous peoples desired were in short supply, leading Natives to wonder why the English were turning their backs on their kinsmen. Indeed, in Native societies peoples who did not exchange gifts were considered nonkinsmen and enemies.[23] John Stewart became well aware of this in 1690. "I was never less without fear," he remarked in his typically cryptic letters, "only the Indians troubled me to think on, for they were made believe that . . . selling them no powder was a design to cut of[f] all the neighboring nations."[24] The most skilled traders, thus, were those who understood Native ways and concerns, forgave debts when necessary, substituted goods in abundant supply for those in short supply, and continually visited, talked, and lived among their new kinsmen.[25]

While Native involvement in the Atlantic market economy was conducted according to the cultural values of gift-giving and kinship, it also revolved around indigenous conceptions of the sacred world and spiritual power. English traders were not just ordinary kinsmen. The goods they brought were viewed as exotics derived from a mysterious and spiritually powerful source, giving the possessors of them a connection with the supernatural world.[26] This connection was transferred to the Native men who obtained those goods through their hunting, warring, and raiding activities. At times ordinary male warriors became a threat to religious leaders in their community who garnered their spiritual powers through nonmilitary activities, including fertility and mortuary rites. In the more hierarchically organized chiefdoms in the precontact period, hereditary elites, sometimes assumed to descend from the spirit world, monopolized religious knowledge and symbolized their power with the few exotic items that found their way into their polities.[27] English trade, though, opened up the possibility for a wider array of people to acquire exotic goods and spiritual power and consequently weakened chiefly authority. Again Thomas Nairne provides a vivid example of how the slave trade affected the social structure of Native societies. When visiting the Chickasaws, he learned that Chief Fattalamee, civil leader of Hallachehoe, the mother town of his nation, had once had influence over several other towns, but that he lost his influence with the advent of English trade. Previously his job was devoted to peace. He demanded that Chickasaw warriors "keep firme to the Treaties of Peace with their Friends and Neighbours" and that Chickasaw women keep "to their Duty of making plenty of Corn." But "finding that the warriors had the best time of it, that slave Catching was much more profitable than formall haranguing, he then turned Warrior too, and proved as good a man hunter as the best of them." By turning his back on the duties he had been formally consecrated to perform and by engaging in warfare and shedding blood, Fattalamee had given up his claim to spiritual power through nonmilitary rites and saw his authority "dwindled away to nothing." Power became more evenly distributed, according to Nairne, among the head military officers, who undoubtedly were seen as spiritually powerful people for the quantity of exotic goods they brought into their communities.[28]

In trading their captives and deerskins for goods, warriors not only elevated their status over civil leaders but also altered power relations between men and women within their communities. Englishmen, coming from patriarchal cultures, preferred to deal with male partners, and by acquiring captives directly from war chiefs and warriors, traders diminished the power of Native women. Females had traditionally determined the fate of captives, but with the arrival of trade goods, male warriors found it more lucrative to unload their captives on the English. Women, moreover, valued those trade items and came to rely on men more than they ever had prior to European colonization. To be sure, female power within indigenous towns did not collapse; some captives remained in the possession of Native villages, and women continued to determine their fate. Women also maintained their traditional access to power. Menstruation and giving birth gave them a connection to the sacred world that men lacked, while their control of agricultural production secured their key roles in communal religious ceremonies.[29] Nevertheless, the growing desire for European trade items both for material comfort and as a means for men to gain status shifted power toward males, and as individual men competed for that power, they became even more enmeshed in the Atlantic market economy, a force that unbeknown to indigenous peoples was to facilitate biological catastrophe.

Virginia's Native Slave Trade

Both the Atlantic market economy and smallpox began their penetrations into the Native Southeast from Virginia. Over the last half of the seventeenth century, traders from Virginia, or the Old Dominion, as England's eldest colony became known, dispersed over a large geographic region, integrating numerous indigenous communities to the south and the west into a commerce that involved, among other items, captives. This trade network eventually overlapped with that of South Carolina, which, of course, conducted an even more voluminous and expansive commerce, but Virginia's impact on the Native Southeast should not be underestimated. Commerce in firearms and slaves between indigenous peoples and the Old Dominion created dramatic ripples through the region's social landscape, resulting in population movements from several areas that appear to have been abandoned in the archaeological record. Even more significant, it was through Virginia's trade network that the smallpox virus spread down into the Carolinas, where it exploded into an epidemiological nightmare in the 1690s.

Virginia's trade with indigenous peoples who lived far beyond the Tidewater plantations began to escalate around the middle of the seventeenth century. Virginia had been a colony since 1607, but an array of Algonquian speaking communities blocked its way to the south and the west. From 1644 to 1646, however, Virginians reduced neighboring Algonquian tribes to tributary status and extended their settlements to the Fall Line, where they confronted Siouan and Iroquoian speakers, some of whom had already acquired firearms by trading with the Dutch and the Swedes to the north. Ostensibly to protect its settlers from these tribes, Virginia established a series of forts on its frontier, but the men in charge of these forts saw new opportunities for economic expansion. In 1646 Abraham Wood built Fort Henry at the falls of the Appomattox River, and from there, English trade ultimately reached deep into the Southeast. Wood, in fact, represented a vanguard of Virginians, including Cadwallader Jones and Thomas Stegge, who sought profits from something other than tobacco cultivation and looked to the Native trade to make their fortunes. That most famous of Virginia's leading families, the Byrds, also accumulated a great deal of their wealth from such commerce. William Byrd I had joined his uncle Thomas Stegge in his business endeavors by 1670, inherited his wealth, and continued a thriving exchange with indigenous peoples until his death in 1704.[30]

While these great men reaped most of the profits, a variety of less-known and more-numerous individuals actually conducted the trade. Servants and employees of leading Virginians loaded imported European goods onto teams of packhorses, led these caravans to distant indigenous partners, and then trucked Native products back to their employers, who then used them to pay off their creditors in England. Leading Virginians also acted as creditors, supplying freemen goods on the promise they would return with enough Native-supplied items to clear their debts.[31] And, of course, almost always accompanying English traders were parties of indigenous peoples. Pamunkeys and other tributary groups often served as guides, protectors, and translators. Abraham Wood, for example, depended on the Appomattox, a small tribe that lived adjacent to Fort Henry.[32] It was this combination of servants, employees, freemen, and Natives, whose voices and actions rarely show up in the historical record, who extended the Atlantic market's reach deep into the Southeast. It was this motley crew who carried manufactured goods to distant Native communities and transported deerskins, beaver pelts, and that most insidious commodity—indigenous captives—back to the Old Dominion.

Much of the actual face-to-face interactions between Englishmen and Natives went unrecorded, but Virginia's laws shed some light on the trade between its colonists and indigenous peoples, particularly revealing how a high volume of munitions flowed into Native communities. The colonial government had long had regulatory acts on the books restricting the trade to a few licensed men, but by 1656 colonial leaders realized that such laws were being openly defied, and to match law with reality, the assembly passed an act making it legal for any freeman to trade with Natives.[33] In 1659 the assembly went even further. It removed the prohibition on supplying indigenous peoples with guns, powder, and shot, recognizing that Englishmen and "foreigners"—a reference to the Dutch and the Swedes to the north—had in fact been trading in these dangerous items already and to ban them would ruin any competitive advantage for Virginia.[34] For the next five years, a rather unrestricted trade flowed between Virginians and Natives, causing many English to worry about the growing number of firearms among indigenous peoples on Virginia's frontiers. In 1665 the assembly ordered another prohibition on guns, powder, and shot, but again traders defied the law, and commerce in weapons continued unabated until Bacon's Rebellion in 1676.[35]

Bacon's Rebellion brought only a temporary halt to the Native trade. What began as a disagreement between Virginia's settlers and the Doeg tribe in Maryland over ownership of some hogs escalated into a full-scale race war in which Virginia's settlers attacked all Natives, friend and foe alike. The conflict also spiraled into a social upheaval in which Nathaniel Bacon and his followers took over the colony, in defiance of Governor Berkeley's administration, which had declared Bacon an outlaw for engaging in war without the assembly's approval. In the end Bacon's rule crumbled and Berkeley's regime regained control, but not before numerous Algonquian and Siouan peoples fled their homes, leaving only four small tributary communities within the Virginia colony and thus making vast areas of land available for further English expansion.[36] During the social upheavals in the colony, the assembly outlawed commerce with indigenous peoples altogether and enacted the death penalty for anyone who sold munitions to Natives.[37] The funneling of weapons to Native communities, the wealth that some of Virginia's leading men accumulated from such trade, and the reluctance of the colonial government to open up western land, in fact, fueled the discontent of Bacon and his men. With Native resistance crushed and no longer appearing to be a threat, Virginia reopened the trade. In October 1677 the assembly passed a law regulating the renewed commerce with indigenous peoples. Trading was to be done at annual marts in various counties only for forty-day periods and at times determined by county officials or stipulated by the assembly.[38] Such regulations did not hold, and in June 1680 the Virginia government repealed all trade regulations and declared "a free and open trade for all persons att all tymes and places with [their] friendly Indians."[39] Finally, in 1691 the assembly even eliminated the word "friendly" from the law establishing a free trade, essentially allowing Virginians to trade whatever they wanted with whomever they wanted, something that they had been doing anyway since the 1650s.[40]

Virginia's laws make it clear that its traders had been taking munitions and other items into Native communities throughout the last half of the seventeenth century. The Old Dominion's statutes also reveal that a flow of slaves came into its settlements from the Native trade. By 1662 Virginia's subjects were bringing in captives they had purchased from their indigenous partners and then reselling them as slaves, forcing the assembly to react to what was essentially an illegal practice. Such captives were not taken directly by Englishmen in a just war, and so the colonial legislature nullified their enslavement and instead declared them indentured servants. "What Englishman, trader, or other shall bring in any Indians as servants and shall assigne them over to any other," the assembly ruled, "shall not sell them for slaves nor for any longer time than English of the like ages should serve by act of assembly." Furthermore, English planters who employed such Native servants had to take out a license to do so.[41] Nevertheless, a general confusion reigned in Virginia concerning the status of indigenous captives, and Natives continued to be sold into slavery. In October 1670 the assembly again reacted to a practice that it could not control. This time it made concessions to those involved in the captive trade but stopped short of converting all indigenous prisoners into slaves. "Whereas some dispute have arisen whither Indians taken in warr by any other nation, and by that nation that taketh them sold to the English, are servants for life or terme of yeares," the assembly ruled, "that all servants not being Christians imported into this colony by shipping shalbe slaves for their lives; but what shall come by land shall serve, if boyes or girles, until thirty yeares of age, if men or women twelve and no longer."[42] The legal status of Natives held by Virginians, thus, lay somewhere between that of white indentured servants and that of imported Africans. But in all practicality, indigenous captives were slaves for life. If taken as a child and put to work on a Chesapeake plantation, a Native had only a minimal chance of surviving to thirty, while adults also were likely to perish before their twelve years of service ended.

Bacon's Rebellion sent the colony even farther down the road of legalizing what was already in reality the enslavement of indigenous peoples. As a result of their attacks on Natives in and near their colony, Bacon's followers wound up with large numbers of captives. The men who benefited from this additional land and labor wanted a stronger guarantee that their prisoners would be considered property. Under Bacon, the assembly ruled that "all Indians taken in war be held and accounted slaves during their life."[43] In February 1677 the assembly, facing continual conflict with Natives, encouraged mobilization of Virginia's settlers by promising them the right to keep the spoils of war, including captives, who would be permanently bound.[44] In April 1679 the colonial legislature declared that soldiers could buy and sell the slaves among themselves.[45] In 1682 Virginia's laws went even further: the colonial legislature repealed its act of 1670 and determined that "all Indians," including those sold to Englishmen by Native allies, were slaves and that conversion to Christianity did not free them from bondage.[46] For the remainder of the seventeenth century, white masters were legally free to do what they had been doing since the 1650s. They could buy indigenous captives and keep them as slaves for life, whether they converted to their masters' religion or not.

The Virginia assembly's laws were clearly reactions to the practices of English subjects, who were inspiring Native slave raids by the early 1660s. In fact, the assembly's 1662 law clarifying the status of captives purchased from friendly tribes may have stemmed from the recent activities of Englishmen and their most notorious allies, the Westos. The Westos were an Iroquoian-speaking people who originally lived along Lake Erie and had received guns through their relatives the Susquehannas, who had direct relations with Englishmen downriver in Maryland. After suffering defeat by the Dutch-allied Five Nations in 1655, the Westos moved into Virginia, where they established trading relations with the English, before relocating even farther to the south.[47] By 1659 they had settled near the Savannah River, and according to the Spanish governor of Florida, they arrived with firearms and had among them some Europeans, suspected to be from Jacán, the name the Spanish had given to the Jamestown settlement. The English and the Chichumecos, as the Spanish called the Westos, furthermore, were "laying waste to the land."[48] In 1661 the Spanish and their Native converts themselves suffered from the arrival of these aggressive newcomers. In that year "a nation of a great number of Indians who said they were Chichumecos" and "some Englishmen with firearms" attacked the Guale province. The attacking force was large, with Spanish estimates ranging from five hundred to two thousand warriors.[49] The Westos and their English allies destroyed the Mission de Santo

Domingo de Talaje, a Christian Guale community near the mouth of the Altamaha River. Some of the attackers then pursued the Guale refugees from the mainland to Sapelo Island but did not have much success. The current took the Westos out to sea, where their canoes capsized, causing all seventy men to drown in eyesight of those whom they pursued. When the main body of the raiders retreated toward their homes near the Savannah River, Spanish soldiers and their Native allies went in pursuit and killed several.[50]

The Westo attack on Talaje was not that successful since apparently few slaves were taken and the raiders lost many of their warriors in the effort, but it nonetheless signified the dramatic arrival of English colonialism in the Southeast. Indeed, since their arrival in 1659, armed Westos traumatized countless Native communities across a broad area who had yet to acquire European firearms and who fled great distances to escape capture. In fact, such raids began the process of pushing Hitchiti speakers out of the Oconee and Ocmulgee valleys, an area the Spanish called La Tama. Some of these Hitchitis fled to Catholic missions, where they were generally identified as Yamasees, while others fled to the Apalachicola River, where they joined other Hitchiti and some Muskogee communities who were coalescing into the peoples the English would later call Lower Creeks. These peoples, in what the Spanish called the Apalachicola province, had resisted Spanish influence for several years, but facing Westo attacks they agreed to the construction of two Catholic missions, probably hoping that the Spanish soldiers who often accompanied such institutions would help defend against their new enemies.[51] It is also likely that slave raids, largely conducted by the Westos, struck residents of the Coosa and Tallapoosa valleys, leading to the further coalescence of various Muskogean communities to form the peoples that the English would later call Upper Creeks.[52]

When Englishmen showed up on the Atlantic Coast in 1670 to establish the colony of Carolina, they found that Virginia's violent commerce in firearms and slaves had preceded them. Nicholas Carteret, for example, discovered that the Westos had just recently stuck the indigenous inhabitants of Santa Elena Island. "The Westoes, a rangeing sort of people reputed to be the man eaters, had ruinated that place, killed sev'all of those Indians, destroyed and burnt their habitations," Carteret learned from Native survivors.[53] Another Carolinian, William Owen, observed the coastal Cusabos living in great fear. "Ye Westoes are behind them a mortall enemie of theirs whom they say are ye man eaters of them they are more afraid then ye little children are of ye bull beggers in England," he commented.[54] Another Carolinian, Stephen Bull, made it even clearer that the Westos were conducting slave raids. He found that the Westos had guns, powder, and shot and warred against "all Indians." They particularly struck around harvest time, because they could steal not only their enemy's corn but also their children, whose work in the fields left them vulnerable to capture.[55] The destination of those captured children was undoubtedly Virginia. In 1674 Henry Woodward traveled to the Savannah River and found the Westos at their fortified town of Hickahaugua and engaged in continual wars with groups in the interior. They were also well supplied with guns, ammunition, cloth, and other trade items that they acquired "from the northward for which they truck drest deare skins, furrs, and young Indian slaves."[56]

The Westos were not alone in conducting raids when Carolinians arrived on the scene. Other major players in Virginia's trade network included the Tuscaroras, another Iroquoian-speaking tribe whose villages were originally located near the fall line of the several rivers that flowed out of the Carolina Piedmont. As early as 1650, English traders were working among the Tuscaroras, who used their newly acquired firearms to expand their hunting territories at the expense of coastal Algonquians.[57] By 1670 one Tuscarora town had developed into what the German traveler John Lederer called a "place of great Indian trade and commerce." The town's leader at that time furthermore was described as a "haughty Emperour," who had demanded that Lederer surrender his gun and ammunition.[58] Such description suggests that Tuscarora towns may have been the "northward" location to which the Westos shipped their pelts, deerskins, and slaves. Tuscarora warriors may have also been among those Chichumecos or Westos who raided coastal and mission communities to the south. Regardless of any connection with the Westos, the North Carolina tribe came to play a major middleman role in Virginia's growing trade network. For the remainder of the seventeenth century, Tuscaroras accumulated a surplus of English goods, including kegs of rum that they transported hundreds of miles away.[59] Tuscaroran traders, moreover, refused to conduct business in any language other than their own and could find a few individuals who spoke it in nearly every community in the Piedmont.[60] Not surprisingly captives were among the Native items that Tuscaroras offered to their English suppliers. In the 1680s, when Englishmen began settling around Albemarle Sound, Tuscaroras came to their new neighbors to sell them captives.[61]

Virginia's leading traders, however, had little patience with the Tuscaroras and other Native middlemen who blocked their way to more lucrative opportunities among communities beyond the Blue Ridge. Virginians especially complained about of the Ocaneechis, a Siouan-speaking community on the fall line of the Roanoke River near the present-day Virginia–North Carolina border. Since the

1650s Englishmen had traveled southwest on the Ocaneechi Path to meet a variety of Natives coming from multiple locations. The Westos were certainly among those, and probably like many other indigenous peoples, they ran into problems with their Native rivals. In 1670 the Ocaneechis murdered four Westos, adding to the bad reputation of the former and to the problems of the latter getting their items to their Virginian partners.[62] Three years later Abraham Wood organized a trading party to circumvent the Ocaneechis, a people he described as "soe insolent for they are but a handful of people, besides what vagabonds repaire to them it being a receptackle for rogues."[63] The trading party consisted of a freeman named James Needham, an indentured servant named Gabriel Arthur, and eight Appomattox guides. On their way past the Ocaneechis, they met a party of fifty-one "Tomahitans" who were on their way to trade, something they had likely been doing regularly for many years. Having met Wood's men, the Tomahitans welcomed the opportunity to circumvent the Ocaneechis. Eleven of them traveled onward to Virginia, where they met with Abraham Wood, while the rest of their party escorted Needham, Arthur, and an Appomattox man on a twenty-four-day southwestern journey to their town. The trip was an arduous one, involving crossing the Appalachian Divide before the party arrived at the Tomahitans' heavily fortified town on a westward flowing river. Early scholars believed the destination to be the Little Tennessee, while the most recent and most thorough reconstruction of the route places the Tomahitans on the Coosa, near present-day Rome, Georgia.[64] After a short stay, Needham and his Appomattox companion escorted twelve Tomahitans back to Wood's plantation, while Arthur remained with the Tomahitans for over a year. Eventually, Arthur returned home and provided his master with the details of his experience. Wood then used that information, along with the knowledge he gained from those Tomahitans who had earlier visited him, to write an interesting account that illustrated how guns and slave raids were remaking the Native Southeast.

Undoubtedly, the Tomahitans were among those armed Chichumecos whom the Spanish claimed were "laying waste to the land." When Wood interviewed his Tomahitan visitors, he learned that they had sixty guns, which were described as different from the ones coming from his traders. Wood stated that his visitors' weapons did not have "such locks as [his and his traders'] bee, the steeles are long and channelld where ye flints strike."[65] This does not rule out that the guns came from the Old Dominion, since other Virginians such as William Byrd may have marketed a different style and the Tomahitans had by 1673 had trading relations with Native middlemen. But Wood likely would have recog-

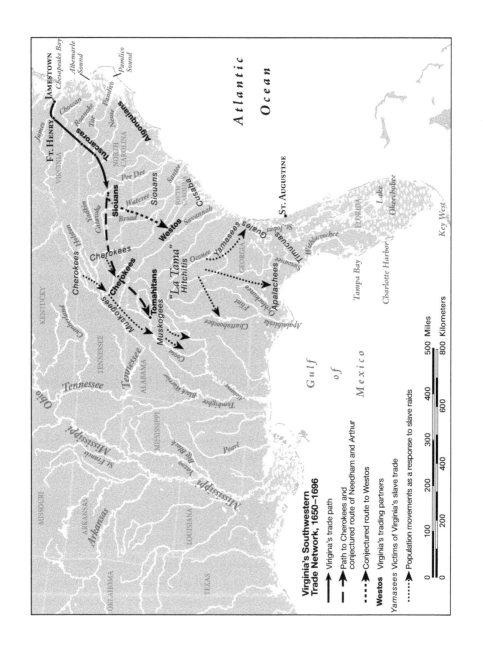

Virginia's Southwestern
Trade Network, 1650–1696

→ Viriginia's trade path

→ Path to Cherokees and
  conjectured route of Needham and Arthur

⇢ Conjectured route to Westos

Westos Virginia's trading partners

Yamasees Victims of Virginia's slave trade

⋯⋯▸ Population movements as a response to slave raids

nized his competitors' guns. The weapons may have come from either raiding or trading with the Spanish, but such claims remain doubtful given the fact that the Spanish prohibited trading in firearms and that acquisition of sixty guns from raids on what were poorly armed missions would have been an amazing feat.[66] Instead, the weapons probably came from the same source from which the Westos originally acquired theirs: Native middlemen connected to the Dutch on the Hudson, the Swedes on the Delaware, or the Marylanders on the Susquehanna. The Tomahitans indeed were allies of the Monetons, who lived ten days due north on what was probably a tributary of the upper Ohio, an area inundated with firearms since the 1640s. Although unverified, the Tomahitans themselves may have had been from the North and related to the Monetons. As did the Westos, the Tomahitans may have fled their original location during the Beaver Wars and taken their guns with them, while maintaining their relationship with their Moneton relatives who remained in the upper Ohio. When relocated in the South, they sought out trading relations with Virginians to keep themselves supplied with powder and shot. Regardless of their origins, armed Tomahitans raided their neighbors and forced multiple population movements. In the eighteenth century the Cherokees recalled that the Yamasees had been part of the Lower Cherokees before the Tomahitans had driven them out of the upper Savannah. Those Lower Cherokee refugees fled south, melded with other refugee groups, and eventually came to speak a non-Cherokee language.[67] The Tomahitans also could have been responsible for the Muskogee communities that had been part of the Coosa chiefdom fleeing further downriver, where they ultimately became part of the Upper Creeks. Wood learned that the Tomahitans maintained twelve-foot palisades and fought "many nations of Indians" who lived downriver from them.[68]

Not only did the Tomahitans attack interior groups, but they also conducted raids on Spanish missions and non-Christian Native communities along the Atlantic Coast. One Tomahitan who visited Wood claimed that he had escaped from a European people who had captured him. This man was among a party of twenty who left their village and descended another river, probably the Chattahoochee, laden with beaver pelts they intended to give to a "hairy people." The hairy people, though, killed ten and put the other ten in chains. That these captors were Spanish seems certain by the escapee's description of them to Wood. Describing what was clearly a Catholic mission, the Tomahitan told Wood, "Ye white people have a bell which is six foot over which they ring morning and evening and att that time a great number of people congregate together and talkes he knowes not what." The Tomahitan added that many blacks lived among the white people, who lived in brick buildings and kept herds of cattle and swine.[69] Why the Spanish would imprison the Tomahitans is not all that surprising; they were in no hospitable mood with Natives descending from the mountains after Chichumecos had struck them and their indigenous converts. If the Tomahitans had not taken part in earlier Chichumeco attacks, Spanish brutality guaranteed that they would exact vengeance. Wood reported that the Tomahitans captured several prisoners, executing all the whites and blacks they took and sparing the lives of two mulatto women. Gabriel Arthur's experience confirmed an acrimonious relationship with the Spanish. The young servant participated in a Tomahitan raid into Florida. Arthur and his hosts traveled eight days to the southwest before coming upon a "great carte path" that ran between a settlement of "blacks" and a Spanish town. There they killed two people, taking their personal effects back to their village. Arthur also became involved in a Tomahitan raid on coastal Natives. The young servant's host insisted that he participate in a raid against the newly founded Carolinian settlement. Arthur at first refused, but the chief promised him that no Englishmen would be harmed. When they arrived near Port Royal in December 1673, the Tomahitans "made a very great slaughter upon the Indians" and plundered the English of their goods.[70] Interestingly, Carolinians were at war with the Westos in late 1673 and into early 1674. The Tomahitans, then, were responsible for some of the attacks that the Carolinians blamed on the Westos.

The similarity between the Tomahitans' and Westos' raiding activities suggests the two groups were in league with each other in trafficking slaves to Virginia. The Tomahitans had to travel through the Westos' territory to conduct raids on common enemies who lived along the Atlantic Coast, thus suggesting that the two groups were allies rather than enemies. Direct evidence of the Tomahitans sending their slaves northward as did the Westos is absent, but the Tomahitans did hold several Siouan children at the time of Arthur's visit. Wood claimed to believe that the Tomahitans deliberately captured boys so that they could be raised into warriors, but when the Tomahitans escorted Arthur back to Virginia in 1674, they presented Wood with a "Spanish Indian boy" as a gift.[71] The Tomahitans, some of whom Wood described as "great lovers" of the Ocaneechis, probably had prior experience sending young captives northward, and with direct relations with Virginians after 1674, they likely continued the practice.[72]

Whether trafficking in slaves or not, the Tomahitans' use of firearms and their raiding activities played an important role in shaping the social landscape of the Native Southeast, but unfortunately little else is known about them. Scholars wonder, for example, if they became part of the Creek or the Cherokee Confederacy. On the one hand, the eighteenth-century trader James Adair identified the "Ta-me-tah" people as a refugee group originally from the north that lived among the Creeks.[73] On the other hand, the Tomahitans were enemies of Muskogee towns downriver, mirroring the long-standing enmity between Iroquoian speakers in the highlands and those Muskogee communities that had been part of the Coosa chiefdom. Also, the word "Tomahitan" bears more than a superficial resemblance to the name of an eighteenth-century Cherokee town, "Tomatly." The Tomahitans' alliance with the Monetons further suggests an Iroquoian connection. The Monetons certainly spoke an Iroquoian language; they derived the name of their town from their word for water, *money*, and *ton*, which meant great.[74] Both terms correspond closely with the contemporary Cherokee words *ama* and *utana*, which respectively mean "water" and "great." It is possible that the Tomahitans and the Monetons were more than just friends and were, in fact, part of the Iroquoian-speaking population that ultimately coalesced in the southern end of the Appalachians as the Cherokees.

While the Tomahitans' ethnic affiliation and ultimate destiny remain ambiguous at best, it is clear that the introduction of firearms played an important role in the formation of the Cherokees. Archaeologists have long argued that at least some of the Cherokees' ancestors lived northeast of where the nation was located in the eighteenth century.[75] Cherokee oral history supports such an argument and sheds light on when this shift occurred and what caused it. Two Cherokees, speaking separately in the early nineteenth century, claimed that their people lived in an area that is drained by the Holston, Clinch, and Powell rivers, which encompasses what is today southwestern Virginia, northeastern Tennessee, and eastern Kentucky.[76] One of these men related a story of how the Five Nations had forced them to abandon the area during a time when the northern Iroquoians had guns but the Cherokees did not, which places the Cherokees' movements south sometime after the 1640s.[77] Part of this population shift also resulted from conflict with Siouan speakers to the east, who when armed with guns from Virginia preyed on their mountain-dwelling neighbors as a source of slaves. Both Cherokee and Catawba oral history suggests just that. The Cherokees claimed that at one time they had lived and hunted among the tributaries of the Catawba River and that they had only loaned the area to the Catawbas. The Catawbas, though, recalled that they conquered the area when they enjoyed the advantage of firearms. They forced the gunless Cherokees to retreat to the west and to agree that the upper Broad River would serve as a boundary between the two peoples.[78] Armed tribes to the north and the east, thus, appear to have forced Iroquoian-speaking communities to coalesce in the southern Appalachians, a process responsible for the formation of the historic Cherokees.

By the mid-1670s the relationship between the Old Dominion and Appalachian highland communities changed. Virginians established more direct routes into the mountains due in part to Bacon's Rebellion. As a consequence of the intense racial violence, not only did Virginia's laws change even further to legalize the Native slave trade but access to the numerous and powerful communities in the mountains became more open. In 1676 Siouan-speaking groups became targets for Bacon and his men, with the Ocaneechis especially suffering. Siouans were driven south of the present-day Virginia–North Carolina border, and their middleman status became even weaker. Formerly victims of firearms, the Cherokees now gained the advantage of guns themselves. Following the lead of Abraham Wood's traders, if not preceding them, William Byrd's men trooped into the Appalachian highlands. William Byrd II, writing in the 1730s at the time Georgia was attempting to monopolize the Cherokee trade, bragged, "[W]e had carry'd on this Trade 80 years before that Colony was thought of."[79] Such words, of course, were boastful; they put Virginia's traders among the Cherokees in the 1640s or 1650s. Nonetheless, they reflected an early, long-distance trade between Virginians and the Cherokees' ancestors. Cadwallader Jones was not too far behind his competitors. By 1682 his traders were leading packhorse caravans over four hundred miles to the southwest. Their destination was likely the Appalachian highlands, since he was at that time eagerly seeking marine shell beads, a product that would have been in high demand among mountainous communities hundreds of miles from the coast.[80]

The actual conduct of trade between Cherokees and Virginians remains obscure. Had Wood, Byrd, or Jones simply called their distant trading partners "Cherokees," they would have left little doubt that Virginians were trading with highland communities. There is no reason, however, why Virginians would have used the name "Cherokee" until it entered English discourse through the Carolinians. As do many tribal names, "Cherokee" has an origin foreign to the people to which it applies. It comes from the Muskogee language, whose speakers frequently used *chalaque* as a generic term to denote "people of a different speech," which included the Iroquoian-speaking ancestors of the Cherokees as well as their Siouan and Algonquian neighbors. Unacquainted with Muskogean peoples, the Virginians did not hear the word "Cherokee" until Carolinians made its use more common among the English. It was not until 1698 that Virginians recorded a name bearing resemblance to "Cherokees," when Cadwallader Jones included the "Chericos" on a crude map that he drew of the eastern woodlands.[81]

The Cherokees' involvement with Virginians, though, had a profound impact on the social landscape of the southern Appalachian highlands. Specifically, Virginia's commerce in guns and slaves allowed the Cherokees to push residents out of eastern Tennessee and into central Alabama and Georgia. The Tennessee River valley and the valleys of its tributaries the Hiwassee and the Little Tennessee had been home to several communities whose members likely spoke a Muskogean language. These communities had composed the northern half of the Coosa chiefdom, which the Spanish encountered in the sixteenth century. Tucked in the Ridge and Valley province, these Muskogean towns enjoyed broad river valleys to grow crops and close access to the game-rich Cumberland Plateau, but they also faced nearly continuous conflict with Iroquoian speakers in the highlands, who themselves were being pushed by enemies to the north and the east. By the early eighteenth century, the original Muskogeans had been displaced by Iroquoian speakers, who became known as the Overhill division of the Cherokee Nation, a process that an abrupt cultural transition in the archaeological record makes clear.[82]

Documentary sources demonstrate that English-allied Cherokees were responsible for the cultural transition in eastern Tennessee's archaeological record. Spaniards, unlike Virginians, did communicate with Muskogean speakers and used the name "Chalaque" to identify the numerous Iroquoian-speakers in the Appalachian highlands. In 1681, for example, Spanish officials identified the "Chalaques" along with the Chichumecos as English-allied enemies roaming on Florida's frontiers.[83] In 1686, just four years after Virginia had legalized the Native slave trade, the Spanish discovered an even deeper involvement of the Cherokees with the English. Then the Spanish official Marcus Delgado journeyed to the Coosa-Tallapoosa confluence and found recently arrived refugees that he called the "Qusate" people, certainly a reference to the Koasatis, an ethnic group affiliated with the eighteenth-century Upper Creeks. The Spanish official claimed that they "came from the north because of persecution from the English, and Chichumecos and another nation called chalaque, which obliged them to flee from their lands in search of a place to settle, finally arriving at the margins of the river of Mobila."[84] Delgado's reference to the Chichumecos is more puzzling than his mention of the Cherokees. The former group may have been Westos, who after being driven from the Savannah by Carolinians and their allied tribes in 1680 took refuge with the Cherokees and become part of the Overhills. They may have also been one of any number of English-allied slave raiders that Delgado's Muskogee informants could not specifically identify. Whether with Westo aid or not, the Cherokees continued to displace Muskogee speakers from eastern Tennessee into the 1690s. In 1693 South Carolinians learned that "some Northerne Indians" were coming to settle near Muskogean speakers who had recently relocated to the Ocmulgee, Oconee, and Ogeechee river valleys.[85] One of the host groups, the Tusquiquis, were recent refugees from the north as well, having moved from the Little Tennessee, where the Spanish located them in the sixteenth century. Some Tusquiquis remained in their original homeland, becoming surrounded by the Overhill Cherokees, whose oral history regarded the Tusquiquis as a foreign people who spoke a different language.[86] But many found living next to the expansive Cherokee peoples unbearable and moved to live near friendlier Muskogean-speaking communities coalescing to the south.

Cherokee oral history, in fact, reinforces the documentary and archaeological record. Cherokees told their literate kinsmen Major John Norton in the early nineteenth century that "when they came from the North East, they drove the Creeks, or Muscogee, from the country bordering on the Tennessee." Those dispersed Creek villages included one at the junction of the Hiwassee and Ocoee rivers, where "mounds" and "ancient corn fields" still stood. Norton's Cherokee informants further claimed that Creeks once lived on the Duck River, a western tributary of the Tennessee, but they too were driven away. Norton checked this story with "Old Traders," who said the people were not Creeks but "Alibamons," another Muskogean-speaking group closely related to the Koasatis who fled south, locating themselves on the river that came to bear their name.[87] Another Cherokee, Charles Hicks, recorded in 1826 that firearms first reached his ancestors 155 years earlier, making their arrival in 1671 remarkably close to when Needham and Arthur found the armed Tomahitans. Hicks also reported that conflict between the Cherokees and the Creeks erupted about the same time that his ancestors became involved in English trade.[88] A variety of evidence, then, supports the notion that the Cherokees incorporation into Virginia's trade network in the 1670s altered the social landscape of the southern Appalachians by allowing Cherokees to expand into eastern Tennessee and push Muskogean-speaking peoples farther south into the historic home of the Upper and Lower Creeks.

While Cherokee expansion represents a major ripple effect of Virginia's commercial expansion to the west, tantalizing clues suggest that goods and perhaps even people from the Old Dominion reached the Mississippi River before the French and the Carolinians did. In 1673 the Marquette and Joliet expedition discovered an unidentified Native group between the mouths of the Ohio and Arkansas rivers that had beads, hoes, axes, knives, and guns.[89] At least one scholar claims that the mysterious group was the Muskogean-speaking Chickasaws, who by that time hosted traders from Virginia.[90] In the late seventeenth century, the Chickasaws had several villages located along streams that flowed into the upper Tombigbee and on the lower Tennessee and its tributaries.[91] It is not inconceivable that Virginians had by 1673 used their connections with the Cherokees to negotiate their way across the Appalachians, to the Tennessee, and from there proceed to Chickasaw villages downriver.[92] Marquette's chroniclers again offer suggestive comments that Virginia had lured the Chickasaws into their slave-trade network. The French learned from the Quapaws that armed Natives had "cut off their passage to the sea, and prevented their making acquaintance of the Europeans, or having any commerce with them." Since their enemies were "armed and used to war," the French decided they "could not, without evident danger, advance on that river which they constantly occupy," thus suggesting that whoever these gun-wielding Natives were, they were permanent residents of the area.[93]

Other evidence, though, suggests that they were not the Chickasaws but perhaps another displaced Iroquois-speaking group. One French missionary reported that the Natives had acquired the items from "Europeans on the eastern side [of the Mississippi]; that those Europeans had rosaries and pictures, that they played on instruments; that some were like [him], who received them well."[94] Such a description points to a Catholic colonial regime, likely the French in the Great Lakes region. Marquette's chronicler claimed that the Native men marked their bodies in the "Iroquois fashion" and the women wore "the headdress and clothing" of Hurons. Last, the Chickasaws themselves remembered a time before they had guns when armed Iroquois "made great Havock of them" and drove them out of their towns.[95] Of course, the people whom the Chickasaws remembered may have been not actual members of the Five Nations but one of any number of Iroquoian-speaking communities that like the Westos fled great a distance during the Beaver Wars.

Whatever the identity of those armed Natives who met Marquette in 1673, they did not appear to have had a major impact on the Mississippi Valley. La Salle's expedition nine years later gives only mixed evidence of guns and slave raids. On the one hand, La Salle discovered a horrifying site at a Tongibao village just below the mouth of the Red River that could have been a possible slave raid. "On approaching," one Frenchmen claimed, "we saw only carcasses of men and women, ruined huts, and others full of dead bodies, a coating of blood on the ground and all their canoes broken and cut up with axes."[96] Later La Salle's party asked an indigenous woman who was responsible for the massacre; she responded, "Auma, Auma, Chicquilousa."[97] She undoubtedly was referring to the Houmas, a tribe on the east side of the Mississippi, and to the Chickasaws, who had an important town known as Chicquilousa. On the other hand, La Salle's chroniclers made no reference to an escalation of firearms in the Mississippi Valley. They mentioned finding only the Taensas, a powerful chiefdom near the mouth of the Arkansas, in possession of European weapons, and these were "three old guns and a Spanish sword" kept guarded in a cabinet of the chiefdom's temple.[98] Other Natives of the valley had reportedly never seen firearms and were intimidated when the French used such terrifying weapons.[99] If armed slave raiders had reached the Mississippi Valley in 1682, they had yet to transform its social landscape.

Marquette's and La Salle's accounts give only a vague impression that Virginia's Native slave trade may have extended much farther to the West than previously thought. What is certain, though, is that English-inspired slave raids did eventually have a devastating impact in the Mississippi Valley. By the 1690s English traders had established themselves among the Chickasaws and other peoples, whose slave raids led to countless indigenous captives being sent back to the East. Virginians may have been among those Englishmen, but Carolina's trade network had come to dominate the noxious commerce in human property. It is likely that if some of the Old Dominion's freemen had been living in or near the Tennessee River and had intermarried into indigenous communities, they fell into Carolina's trade network, finding the southern colony the easiest destination to reach and the best market for their human cargo. It is noteworthy that when the French arrived in 1699 to establish Louisiana, the governor of Virginia received the information by way of Carolinians, suggesting that the elder colony's communication with the Chickasaws was weak at best.[100] English colonialism stemming from Carolina, thus, ultimately affected Native residents of the Mississippi Valley to a much greater extent than that from Virginia.

Nevertheless, the significance of Virginia's Native slave trade should not be underrated. The Old Dominion's demand for indigenous captives had three important consequences. First, substantial numbers of indigenous peoples wound up as slaves on Chesapeake plantations. A reliable estimate of how many Native captives Virginians bought, of course, is impossible to calculate. Until 1682 keeping Natives as slaves was illegal, and such activity went largely unreported. Even later, most purchases of indigenous captives went unrecorded. Unlike the purchase of Africans, who came in advertised ships carrying large numbers, Na-

tive slaves arrived often as individuals or small groups coming from the back
country through myriad transactions involving multiple peoples. Anecdotal evidence, though, suggests that on any given Virginia plantation African slaves
were likely to be found working side by side with indigenous peoples. English
masters, for example, continually complained about Native runaways and listed
indigenous slaves as property in their wills.[101] The complete story of Native slavery in Virginia has yet to be written, but the leading scholar of the topic has concluded that Chesapeake planters bought "many more Indians than has usually
been recognized."[102] Unfortunately, scholars of slavery have largely ignored Native captives, whose presence certainly played an important role in the development of African American culture on Chesapeake plantations.

The second significant aspect of Virginia's Native slave trade involves its devastating impact on the social landscape of the Southeast. Before Carolinians arrived, Virginia's commerce in human captives had ignited a series of population
movements, which began the coalescence of diverse peoples into the Cherokee
and Creek confederacies. By trading guns to their Siouan- and Iroquoian-speaking allies, the English inspired raids that reached into Georgia and Florida and
resulted in major sections of the Oconee, Okmulgee, Chattahoochee, Coosa,
and Tallapoosa watersheds becoming vacant. Hitchitis and Muskogees were especially victimized by such raids, which led to further coalescence of these peoples who would compose the Lower and Upper Creeks. The southern Appalachian highlands also underwent considerable change as the Cherokees at
first faced armed raiders and shifted their settlements farther to the southwest.
In the 1670s the Cherokees became incorporated into Virginia's trade network
and used their newly found power to push their Muskogean-speaking enemies
out of eastern Tennessee. Although less certain, Virginia's commerce may have
had a ripple affect that reached the Mississippi Valley. By the time Carolinians
arrived, at least one resident community had received European trade items,
possibly through direct trade with Virginians or through their Native allies.
Even if Mississippi Valley tribes were not connected to the Old Dominion's
trade network, English commercial influence had a dramatic effect on a large
portion of the Southeast's indigenous population, affecting them in a disastrous
way even before the arrival of the Atlantic world's deadliest germs.

Third and most significantly, Virginia's commerce in firearms and slaves integrated Natives into a thriving trade network capable of spreading acute infectious diseases. By 1696 Virginia's trade saturated the Carolina Piedmont. John
Lawson, for example, toured North Carolina in 1701 and everywhere found evidence of long-standing trade. The snobbish visitor frequently commented on

the intermarriage of his countrymen with Native women, lamenting the fact that the offspring of these relationships were deprived a proper English upbringing because they remained with their mother's community.[103] Lawson did not mention if one of these men he met on his journey, John Stewart—not the Scottish trader from South Carolina but another man with the same name who hailed from James River—had a Native wife, but he did add that the Virginian had traded with Carolina's indigenous peoples for many years and that he just recently had unloaded seven horse loads of cargo. This was much less than another caravan that Lawson encountered, which included thirty horses and four or five men—a substantial trading caravan that was perhaps even modest by comparison to what had come from Virginia before smallpox and competition with Carolina had lessened the trade. William Byrd II, writing in 1723 but reflecting on the trade that his father's men had once conducted, claimed that "[f]ormerly, a Hundred Horses have been employ'd in one of these Indian Caravans, under the Conduct of 15 or 16 persons."[104] Byrd may have exaggerated the size of individual teams of packhorses, but his characterization of a once-flourishing trade corresponds with other evidence of how Virginians had flooded the Southeast with a high volume of goods and incorporated numerous Natives into the Atlantic market economy over the last half of the seventeenth century.

Carolina's Native Slave Trade

At the time of Carolina's founding in 1670, then, a broad array of Natives were already engaged with the English in trading. Carolinians eagerly became involved in such commerce themselves, especially the slave trade. Carolina's traders rapidly moved across the interior and ultimately reached the Mississippi Valley, leaving few indigenous communities in the region untouched by English colonialism. Indeed, by 1696 Carolina's Native slave trade had made the indigenous population extremely vulnerable to becoming infected by smallpox and dying from the disease once it arrived from Virginia.

Unlike the Old Dominion, Carolina was founded with race-based slavery securely in place. In 1663 King Charles II gave eight of his loyal followers a patent to establish the new colony of Carolina. These Lords Proprietors gained exclusive rights to govern and declared in the colony's Fundamental Constitution in 1669 that a master had absolute power over his "negro" slaves' religious lives and that conversion to Christianity did not free slaves from their bondage.[105] The Lords Proprietors took it for granted that Carolina's settlers would import enslaved Africans, who would labor on the colony's plantations; they did not envision their colony as a depot through which indigenous captives were to be exported from their homeland for sale on the Atlantic market. They realized that bartering goods for deerskins and pelts would be part of Carolina's economy, but they worried that the purchase of captives would lead to conflict and potential destruction of the infant colony. Shortly after settlers arrived in the new colony, the Proprietors instructed them that "Noe Indian upon any occasion or pretense whatsoever is to be made a Slave, or without his owne consent be carried out of [their] Country."[106] As in Virginia, though, colonists defied the law and engaged in an activity that was too lucrative to pass up. Carolinians, many of them coming directly from Barbados, had an intimate familiarity with race-based slavery and an eagerness to cash in on the West Indian sugar industry's insatiable demand for labor. They were an aggressive profit-seeking group that ignored proprietary restrictions on dealing in Native slaves and expanded English commerce far to the west.[107]

The Savannah River served as a crucial link in Carolina's trade network. After receiving gifts from Henry Woodward in 1674, the Westos fell out of Virginia's trading orbit and into Carolina's. The raiding tribe promised Woodward that in exchange for goods they would provide deerskins, furs, and "young slaves."[108] Indeed, for the next few years the Westos' Savannah villages became the market center for Carolina's growing slave trade, leading the Spanish to become alarmed for the safety of their colony and its missions. Spanish officials learned from a Native woman in 1675 that the Carolinians were "united and in league with a hostile tribe of Indians who are called Chichimecos for the purpose of making war upon the natives [then] converted to the Catholic religion." The English, furthermore, "were teaching them to use firearms with the purpose in view of coming to attack [St. Augustine]."[109] Many Westos, of course, had previous experience with guns, and neither the Natives nor the Carolinians at that time had plans as ambitious as attacking the heavily fortified capital of La Florida. The level of violence certainly increased, though. Dwelling closer to a munitions supplier, the Westos continued their raids on the many enemies they had made over the years, inspiring even more population movements to the lower Chattahoochee and to Florida's Catholic missions. The Spanish in fact had established two new missions on the Apalachicola River by the end of 1675, probably in response to Native requests for assistance against English-allied tribes.[110] Also, Yamasees continued to flee La Tama and became a majority of the population in the Guale province.[111]

The Westos' days as Carolina's main ally were short-lived, however. In 1677 the proprietors had grown concerned about the number of unauthorized traders doing business on the Savannah and places even farther west. They thus ordered that such long-distance trade should cease and that the Westos and other groups should come to one of two Carolina plantations, where they would trade with selected individuals who represented the proprietors' trade monopoly. The proprietors, furthermore, reiterated their opposition to buying and exporting indigenous captives.[112] Such restrictions chafed independent traders and the proprietors' own appointed officials, who knew this would cut into the profits they had made through the slave trade. In 1679 these disaffected men concocted a scheme to keep commerce open and expansive. They instigated a war on the Westos. Enlisting the aid of some Shawnees who had just recently moved into the Southeast, the Carolinians and their new allies obliterated the Westos, captured all they could, drove the survivors away from the Savannah, and reduced their population to an estimated fifty people. The men responsible for such actions later claimed that they were retaliating for Westo raids against coastal groups that allegedly had harmed Englishmen. The proprietors criticized their colonists for failing to protect friendly Natives, but ultimately they could not stop the slaving activities of Carolina's leading men.[113]

By 1680 Carolina's major partner had become those Shawnees who had helped them defeat the Westos. Originally, the Shawnees consisted of several communities that spoke similar dialects of an Algonquian language and at one time lived near one another in the upper Ohio Valley. By the mid-seventeenth century they began to face raids of armed Iroquois from the North, and through the remainder of the century they scattered throughout the eastern woodlands. Carolinians had a particularly difficult time speaking and writing the name of this wandering tribe, who called themselves "Chawonoch," and rendered it into the similarly sounding English word "Savannah."[114] It was on the river that came to bear their corrupted name that Carolinians first met Shawnees. During his visit to the Savannah, Woodward greeted two Shawnee men, whose language neither he nor the Westos understood. But through "signs" the Shawnees indicated that they had traveled for twenty-days from a southwestern location, which would have put their point of departure near the Chattahoochee-Apalachicola junction and near the Muskogee town of Cussita. Ostensibly they came to warn the Westos of an attack by the Cussitas and two other groups who were also known to have hosted Shawnee refugees in the seventeenth century, the Chickasaws and the "Chiokees." (The latter group was probably not the Cherokees but an Illinois group, the Cahokias, who lived just north of the Chickasaws.) Such a warning, though, may have been a bluff in order to investigate the possibility of securing an English trade themselves. While the Westos repaired their palisades, the Shawnees presented Woodward with some Spanish beads and other presents, telling him that "they had comerce with white people like unto [him], whom were not good."[115] The Westos treated the Shawnees civilly but dismissed them before Woodward departed, perhaps wanting to stifle their efforts at establishing commerce with the English. Nevertheless, the meeting had a lasting impact. Not only did the Shawnees assist the Carolinians in defeating the Westos, but for the next decade their raids helped extend the English slave-trade network that ensnared even more Natives into a deadly cycle.

The Shawnees' alliance with Carolina's slave dealers grew despite proprietary impediments. In 1680 the Lords Proprietors declared that any slaves exported from their colony had to come from communities at least two hundred miles away from the limits of English settlement.[116] This may have motivated some traders to seek allies farther to the west, but Carolina's slave dealers defied such restrictions. Soon after dispatching the Westos, the Shawnees fell upon the Waniahs, a people who lived along the coast near the present day border of South and North Carolina. A Carolinian then purchased the Waniah captives and exported them to Antigua, provoking a sharp rebuke from the proprietors. The colonists responded that they were sparing the Waniah captives from certain torture and death. The proprietors did not buy such a contrived excuse but could only chastise the colonists for their hypocrisy:

> By buying Indians of ye Sevanahs you induce them through Covetousness of your guns Powder & Shott & other Europian Comodities to make war upon their neighbours to ravish the wife from the Husband Kill the father to get ye Child & to burne & Destroy ye habitations of these poore people into whose Country wee are charefully Rec[eived] by them, Cherished & supplied when wee were weake or least never have done us hurt & after wee have set them on worke to doe all these horrid wicked things to get slaves to sell ye dealers in Indians call it humanity to buy them & thereby keep them from being murdered.[117]

Despite such admonitions, for the remainder of the seventeenth century Carolina's Native slave trade grew virtually free of proprietary restriction and provided one of the best ways for opportunistic men to acquire wealth and climb to the top of an emerging colonial social order.

The Guale missions were especially vulnerable to slave raids. In 1680 three hundred warriors including some Englishmen destroyed the Guale mission on Santa Catalina Island. The Spanish, of course, blamed the Chichumecos, but this was because they had only a vague notion of events that had happened on the Savannah River during the prior year. In October 1679 an Irish servant who had escaped from his English master made his way to the Guale province and told the Spanish that the English had armed those Chichumecos who had been involved in earlier attacks on the Spanish missions. But he added that "about seven months ago another Indian troop of a different nation, probably the Chiscas, came and fought the ones supposed to be Chichimecos."[118] Such news alarmed the Spanish, but they did not realize that the Westos had been displaced, and they continued to apply the Chichumeco label to Carolina's dominant trading partner, the Shawnees. The Spanish did, however, specifically mention two other groups as being involved, the "Chiliques" and "Uchises." The former probably were not the Cherokees, for they appear as "Chalaques" in another Spanish account that includes reference to the "Chiliques" as a different people.[119] The "Uchises" were probably the Yuchis, a people whose villages originally lay in the Hiwassee Valley in eastern Tennessee. By 1680 they had been pressed upon by the Cherokees to the north and the Westos to the south. With the Westos defeated, they took the opportunity to secure an alliance with the English, and some of their people relocated to the Savannah Valley. The Yuchis' participation in the 1680 raid on Santa Catalina, indeed, reflects a new colonial order that Carolina brought to the Native Southeast. Carolinians relied on a heterogeneous population of Natives accumulating on or near the Savannah to expand the volume of slaves that they exported through their colony.

The Spanish mission system remained a target of this eclectic group of slave raiders. Following the 1680 attack, the Spanish attempted to get the Guales to move back to Santa Catalina. They refused, claiming that if forced to go they would commit mass suicide.[120] Years of English-inspired raids had made life in the Guale provinces dangerous, and by 1683 the missions had been reduced to a relative few that had been removed entirely to the Sea Islands. Such a location, however, left them exposed to sea attacks, which came in 1683 and 1684. In those years French and English pirates, who had left from Charles Town, conducted several raids on the Guales and forced survivors to flee to St. Augustine. By 1685 the Spanish would no longer have a presence on the coast of Georgia. Also, their Timucua missions were to come under attack from an unsuspected source. As early as 1683 the Yamasees began to repopulate the no man's land on the Atlantic Coast between Charles Town and the northernmost Guale missions. The defeat of the Westos and their friendship with the Shawnees most likely lured these former refugees to leave northern Florida and the Chattahoochee. They also received hospitable treatment from Scotch settlers at Port Royal, who established the short-lived Stuart's Town there in 1684. Late in that year the Scots supplied a Native leader, "the Altamaha King", with twenty-three muskets and a supply of powder and shot. His fifty warriors reciprocated by later returning with twenty-two Timucua captives.[121] Inspired by such success, the Scots recruited more indigenous peoples to settle near them. In February 1685 one Scotsman bragged that a thousand or more Natives were coming to Stuart's Town every day. This was no doubt an exaggeration, but throughout 1685 the Yamasees attracted a heterogeneous collection of Natives, even some Guales and other deserters from Spanish missions, to settle among them around Port Royal.[122] The Spanish were not pleased with this development and made efforts to stop it. In August 1686 they sent a small fleet of their ships up the Atlantic Coast and destroyed an abandoned Stuart's Town, whose residents had been forewarned by their Yamasee allies. From there the Spanish set sail for Charles Town. On their way they burned the governor's plantation on Edisto Island before running into a hurricane that forced them to return to St. Augustine. Later in the year an armed force of about three hundred Timucuas, Apalachees, and Guales followed up the earlier attack by striking the Yamasees and forcing them to retreat north of the Savannah River. The Yamasees would stay there for the next twenty years and Stuart's Town would not be rebuilt, but both Englishmen and Scotsmen continued an active trade with the Yamasees, who would continue to supply slaves taken from the Spanish mission system and other locations.[123]

The Yamasees' relocation marked a significant transition in the Carolina slave trade. Gone from the Savannah Valley were the Westos, and in their place stood a remarkable polyglot of Native communities. These included Shawnees, Yamasees, Yuchis, and other groups, which had largely been victims of slave raids before 1679, but after that they became agents of Carolina's growing commercial empire. The losers in this new arrangement were the Cherokees.

The Cherokees indeed appear in Carolinian records as a source for slaves rather than as a supplier. In 1674 Henry Woodward located the "Chorakees" on one of the branches of the Savannah River and claimed the Westos had been at continual wars with them. Later, though, the Spanish claimed that the Chichumecos and the Cherokees were in league with each other, suggesting that after being defeated by the Shawnees the Westos had fled into the Appalachian highlands for sanctuary among a people who spoke a language similar to theirs. Whether due to the continuing persistence of the Westos in the mountains or to long-standing animosity toward the Cherokees, the Shawnees conducted slave raids into the Appalachians. In 1681 Carolina exported several "Seraquii" slaves, who were possibly Cherokees that the Shawnees and perhaps their Yuchi allies had captured.[124] Until 1690 the Cherokees were absent from English documentary records. Savannahs and Yuchis impeded access into the Appalachians because they did not want their enemies to gain access to Carolinian goods. In 1690 the Cherokees reappeared in English records. James Moore, a notorious slave dealer, made two trips into the Appalachian Mountains, hoping to find gold, silver, and other precious metals that he thought the Cherokees' homeland possessed.[125] Moore did not find the mineral wealth he sought, and on his second trip he inflamed the already-hostile relations between Carolinians and Cherokees. Moore claimed that his adventure west was halted in the mountains by what he claimed to be "a difference about Trade . . . between those Indians" and him.[126] Later the Lords Proprietors learned that Moore and his men "without any war first proclaimed" had "fallen upon the Cherokee Indians in a hostile manner and murdered several of them." They further warned that such action "may be of very dangerous consequence not only of ye peace of [their] province but alsoe to Virginia and other of his Majesty's colonys."[127] It is unclear whether Moore netted any slaves from his venture, but the South Carolina Council punished him by requiring him to first receive permission from the governor and council before traveling out of the settlements and trading with remote tribes again.[128]

The council did little else to halt violence against the Cherokees. In 1693 the Commons House of Assembly learned that "the Savanna Indians had been at one of the Charrekeys Townes and meeting only with ye old men there (the young men being absent) killed them and Carryed away the women and children and Sold some of them for slaves to the English Traders who had brought them to this settlement and sold them for slaves." Neither the proprietors nor the colonial government made an effort to punish the Carolinians involved in such actions.[129] Later in the year twenty Cherokee leaders protested the enslavement of their people and tried to regain individuals whom they had lost. They visited Carolina's governor and complained that the Esaws, the Congarees (two Siouan-speaking groups), and the Savannahs had sold their people into slavery. The governor told the Cherokees there was nothing he could do since the captives had already been exported.[130] Not until 1698 do the Cherokees and Carolinians appear to have had any friendly intercourse. Then a Virginian appealed to the government of South Carolina that one of his Native slaves had wound up in the hands of Joseph Cooper. Cooper had bought the runaway from the Cherokees.[131] It was also in that year that the Virginian Cadwallader Jones listed thirty Cherokee towns as being in South Carolina's trade orbit.[132] Before then the Cherokees had been on the other end of Carolina's colonial stick.

While the Cherokees remained largely outside Carolina's trade network until the end of the seventeenth century, Native residents of the Chattahoochee Valley became inextricably involved. This major river was originally home to numerous Hitchiti-speaking communities. In the 1660s and 1670s Yamasees and other groups took refuge among the Hitchitis after fleeing from the east to escape Westo raids. Two Muskogee communities, Cussita and Coweta, also relocated to the Chattahoochee around the same time. Cussita was located on the lower Coosa in the sixteenth century, but in 1662 the Spanish placed this town near the fall line of the Chattahoochee River, on the northern end of the province they called Apalachicola. Sometime after that, Coweta had emerged on the opposite side of the river from Cussita. Whether Coweta had been an independent town that followed Cussita or whether it emerged as an offshoot after the Muskogee migration to the Chattahoochee is not entirely certain.[133] Why these two towns moved is also not clear. They may have been fleeing armed raiders from the north, particularly the Tomahitans, but ecological factors also may have played a role. According to the Cussitas' migration legend, in their previous location they had no corn and subsisted on only roots and fish, suggesting that a major drought had forced them to look for food and fertile soil elsewhere.[134]

Whatever the origins of these Muskogee towns, they proved receptive to the English in the 1670s. In 1674 Henry Woodward gained a vague notion of the two towns. He placed the "Cowatoe" on one of the western branches of the Savannah River (probably mistakenly), and from the Shawnees he learned that the "Cussetaws" were preparing to fight the Westos. It was probably through those Shawnees, who likely had been living on or near the Chattahoochee, that Woodward or his fellow Carolinians made inroads into the west. One year after Woodward first met the Shawnees, English traders had reportedly reached Native communities within five days travel of the Apalachee missions.[135] By 1677 Carolinians were trading with the Cussitas, although it is not certain whether such commerce occurred in their main town on the Chattahoochee River, in satellite villages that lay somewhere between there and the Savannah, or through Native middlemen.[136] Two years later indigenous middlemen certainly extended English influence into the Chattahoochee Valley. Then the Spanish learned that the Chichumecos had been in communication with the Cowetas, whose leader had forced recently arrived Catholic missionaries to leave the Hitchiti town of Apalachicola.[137] Whether these Chichumecos were Westos, Shawnees, Yuchis, or combinations of various English-allied groups is not certain, but what is certain is that the English slave trade was on its way to affecting Natives living far to the west of the Carolina colony.

The Westo War had a mixed impact on the nascent relationship between the English and the Muskogees. On the one hand, in the aftermath of the conflict some Chichumecos came to live at Coweta, indicating that some Westo survivors possibly took refuge among the Muskogees. Also, the Spanish received a message through the Hitchiti town of Sabacola in the fall of 1680 that Coweta would welcome Spanish soldiers and missionaries to live among them, suggesting that Westo refugees had persuaded the Cowetas of the English's bad intentions. On the other hand, two Native Christians were killed in the Apalachee province in the summer of 1681, and their deaths were attributed to bandits and fugitives under the leadership of the Coweta chief. The Spanish investigated further and learned that Chichumecos with firearms were among the Cowetas, indicating that whoever these newcomers were, they continued to have access to English goods and that their presence made Coweta the most feared town on the Chattahoochee.[138] In any event, a direct English presence in the Chattahoochee Valley did not appear until 1685. The Chattahoochee Valley's residents likely received Native middlemen from the Savannah, but from 1681 to 1685 Hitchiti and Muskogee communities, including Coweta, made regular trips to St. Augustine to pledge their loyalty to the Spanish.[139]

In 1685 Carolina's traders developed a more direct and sustained relationship with Muskogees and Hitchitis in the interior. Then, Scots settlers received word that the Cowetas and the Cussitas wanted to trade with them. Such communication most likely happened through the Yamasees, who were intimately familiar with residents of the Chattahoochee Valley and with the paths that led to this important river. Scots traders eagerly planned an expedition, but before they could get organized, Henry Woodward, who was also familiar with the Yamasees, beat them to the Chattahoochee. In the summer of 1685 Woodward arrived at Coweta along with seven or eight English traders and a group of fifty Yamasee companions.[140] The chief of Coweta welcomed Woodward, accepted his gifts, and even extended his niece to the Englishman as a bride to solidify kinship bonds. Woodward immediately sought to establish a permanent English presence. He ordered the building of two fortifications—one near the town of Coweta and the other just above Tasquiqui, the northernmost town, which was inhabited by refugees from eastern Tennessee. Hearing that Woodward and his traders had arrived, the Spanish took draconian measures. In 1685-86 Lieutenant Antonio Matheos led a force of Spanish and Apalachee soldiers up the Chattahoochee and burned Coweta, Cussita, Colone, and Tasquiqui, the four newest towns in the valley. The eight Hitchiti towns lower down on the Chattahoochee avoided destruction by pleading ignorance of the English presence, although they certainly had known about Woodward and welcomed the opportunity to trade. Despite Spanish efforts the English continued to trade. In August 1686 Woodward and 150 Native burdeners carried guns, powder, shot, and other merchandise to the Hitchitis, who had recently lost a dozen of their warriors in a conflict with the Spanish-allied Chiscas. Knowing that they had not received such supplies from the Spanish, indigenous inhabitants of the Chattahoochee Valley turned to the English, the very people whose arms and slave raids had earlier made victims of them.[141]

Spanish pushing and English pulling led to another major episode of population movements. Following Matheos's invasion, many residents of the four burned towns fled. These refugees would be joined by another wave of out-migration in 1690, when the Spanish constructed a fort on the river and manned it with Apalachee soldiers. The act must have appeared hostile to the Chattahoochee's Native residents, who abandoned the valley and would not return there to live for another two and a half decades. Many joined Muskogee towns near the junction of the Coosa and Tallapoosa rivers, where refugee groups escaping Cherokee raids from the north were also coalescing. Others fled east, dispersing themselves out among the several creeks and tributaries that flowed into the Ocmulgee, the Oconee, and the Ogeechee, gaining the name "Creeks" from their English trading partners.[142] Carolinian traders indeed valued their Creek allies and welcomed their resettlement nearer their trading posts.[143] The Spanish, however, could do little to halt the expansion of the English colonial regime. By the end of 1690 the Spanish had abandoned their Chattahoochee fort, realizing that their plan to cow Natives into submission had backfired and that they should spend their resources and energies protecting their missions in Florida, which stood vulnerable to the heavily armed English allies.[144]

With the collapse of Muskogee and Hitchiti relations with the Spanish, Carolina expanded its commercial influence to the numerous communities coalescing near the Coosa-Tallapoosa confluence. Since many of the area's Native residents were related to peoples who had assembled nearer the Savannah, the English came to call them Creeks as well and eventually "Upper Creeks" to distinguish them from the "Lower Creeks," who lived closer to the English. It was likely through the guidance of those Lower Creeks that Henry Woodward made his way to their relatives on the Tallapoosa in 1685.[145] Whether or not Woodward deserved such credit, Carolinians steadily escalated their trading activities with the Upper Creeks through the remainder of the seventeenth century. Intimately familiar with being victimized, Natives near the Coosa-Tallapoosa confluence knew the security they could gain by having a steady supply of munitions and welcomed an English alliance. They also turned into powerful raiders to supply the Atlantic market's demands for labor. When the French arrived at Mobile Bay, they discovered Carolinian slave dealers entrenched among communities up the Alabama and its tributaries. One Frenchman commented:

> English were in those nations every day, and that they take pack horses burdened with clothing, guns, gunpowder, shot, and a quantity of other goods which are sold or traded to the savages for cured deer hides, for fresh deer hides with hair, and for the buffalo that are covered in a fine wool being gray in color like a mouse. But the greatest traffic between the English and the savages is the trade of slaves which the nations take from their neighbors whom they war with continuously, such that the men take the women and children away and sell them to the English, each person being traded for a gun.[146]

From 1685 on, regular and sustained commerce, indeed, characterized the relations between South Carolina and the Upper Creeks, who sent many of their captives back with English traders who traveled along the route that became known as the "Upper Path."

Such commerce victimized a variety of Native peoples, but it particularly affected an unarmed indigenous population to the west, who became known as the Choctaws. The Muskogees referred to their neighbors and enemies to the west as the "Chata," a word meaning "flat heads" used to identify those numerous peoples situated between the Tombigbee and the Mississippi who practiced cranial deformation. Such a practice involved strapping infants' heads to boards while young to flatten their skulls, a physical feature considered a sign of beauty in a variety of Native cultures. As late as 1686 the Choctaws were holding their own against their enemies, even driving some communities to the Upper Creeks. The same Marcus Delgado who found refugees who had fled from the Cherokees and other English-allied tribes also found refugees on the Tallapoosa who had fled from the Choctaws, but unlike in the former case, he made no mention of Europeans being involved with the Choctaws. Delgado identified refuges from Choctaw attacks as the "Pagna," "Aymamu," and "Qulasa," whose names correspond closely with "Taliepacana," "Alibamo," and "Caluza," which Hernando de Soto's expedition located just to the west of the Tallapoosa. Taliepacana (Muskogean for "town of the Pacanas") was a fortified community on the Black Warrior River, while the Alibamo consisted of at least one small village and a fortified town on one of the Tombigbee's western tributaries. The location of the Caluzas has not been determined, but they were a numerous people likely having several villages somewhere in what is today central Mississippi.[147] Conceivably, the descendants of the Taliepacanas, the Alibamos, and the Caluzas had remained in the same general location where Soto found them in 1540-41, only to be pushed to the east during the last half of the seventeenth century by an emerging Choctaw Confederacy and pulled likewise by the lure of English trade goods. The Black Warrior and portions of the Tombigbee river valleys, thus, appear to have been vacated sometime in the last half of the seventeenth century due to factors other than epidemic disease. These two rivers would remain a contested zone between the Creeks and the Choctaws for the remainder of the colonial period.

The Upper Creeks' participation in Carolina's Native slave trade was instrumental in the development of the Choctaw Confederacy. In the late seventeenth century, the Choctaw homeland attracted many victims of Creek raids. Within the remote watersheds of the Pearl, Leaf, Chickasaway, and Tombigee rivers, refugees could find a degree of safety. Some of these refugees came from Mobile Bay communities, whose leaders appealed to the Spanish for help in 1687, but who received little aid as the Spanish were struggling to protect their mission system.[148] When the French arrived in the late 1690s, they found Natives along the Gulf Coast from the Mississippi River to Pensacola Bay huddled in fortified villages and fearful of performing ordinary subsistence activities due to the threat of being captured. Had the French arrived earlier, they would have found even more peoples in the area. But shortly before they arrived, slave raids had forced a large number of survivors to flee into central Mississippi and coalesce with others in the emergent Choctaw Confederacy. To be sure, the process of Choctaw genesis was not complete by the time the Great Southeastern Smallpox Epidemic struck; other groups would coalesce with them throughout the eighteenth century.[149] But Carolina's commerce in guns and slaves in the late 1680s and 1690s certainly played a major role in creating population movements and mergers that laid the basis for the formation of this powerful Native confederacy.[150]

Not long after Carolinians began to trade directly with the Upper Creeks, they incorporated the Chickasaws into their network as well. If these strategically located peoples did not have their first experience with English goods through Virginians, they certainly did through Carolinians. To reach the Chickasaws, most English traders took an extension of the Upper Path from the Coosa-Tallapoosa confluence to the upper Tombigbee. Henry Woodward's men were believed to have been the first Carolinians to reach the Chickasaws and open trade with them in 1686.[151] They certainly did not find their way there on their own. The Upper Creeks, who were at that time allied with the Chickasaws, guided Woodward's men and would thereafter assist the English in maintaining a regular and sustained trade with the distant Natives. Throughout the 1690s, in fact, English traffic to the west steadily increased. By the end of the decade, Carolinians had reportedly "had many journeys through the Country Westward to above 1000 or 1200 miles distance."[152] Such reports were undoubtedly exaggerated but not by much, since by then Carolinian traders had reached the Mississippi, a river some 650 miles distant from Charles Town on a direct path. One of those men to make the trip was Thomas Welch, who in 1698 mapped the well-worn Upper Path and went even farther than most Englishmen by going onto the Mississippi and descending it to the mouth of the Arkansas.[153]

A second route to the Chickasaws was more circuitous, involving mostly a water passage by way of the Tennessee River. If Virginia traders had been visiting the Chickasaws, they almost certainly came by way of this river, whose tributaries ran from the Appalachian homeland of their Cherokee allies. The first Carolinian to follow this path is unknown, but Scots traders may have followed this route shortly after their English rivals under Woodward opened the Upper Path. In 1690 John Stewart and his partners planned to lead three caravans of trade goods across the mountains to the Chickasaws. In 1693 the Scotsman bragged, "[I] travel'd by water and land o-w-tward bond from my departure 930 myle and wes 240 myle further than evr doctor Woodward went."[154] Stewart may have exaggerated his estimated mileage, but not by much if he had traveled up the Savannah, crossed the mountains, picked up either the Hiwassee or the Little Tennessee River, followed one of these tributaries into the Tennessee, and then sailed to Chickasaw villages that lay very near the Mississippi. Stewart further boasted that he was the first white man to reach such distant Natives and that he personally opened the "large trade" between the Chickasaws and Carolina. Stewart's claim should, of course, be taken with a grain of salt; Soto, Marquette, and La Salle had certainly preceded him, and Virginia's traders may have been there before him as well. Also, Stewart may have outdistanced his fellow Carolinians, but he certainly did not proceed much farther than the Carolinians who had gone before him. On his way west he encountered numerous other Europeans along his route who had become enmeshed with Native communities. Stewart exclaimed to his patrician commercial partner, "[B]lest be god, I return'd frie from that Epidemick vice, too accustomary to Indian traders to cohabit-e with ther women, a thing I abhor'd to think of."[155] Despite his boasting, however, Stewart did represent something very significant. He was an ambitious man driven by his colony's aggressive search for slaves, a search that would lead him and others to find more expedient routes to the Mississippi Valley, where a numerous array of unarmed and highly populated Native towns stood vulnerable to the raids of English-allied tribes.

When the French arrived in 1699, they indeed discovered that the Tennessee was being used for English commerce. They also found that such trade involved unexpected participants, renegade French coureurs de bois. Following La Salle's 1682 voyage down the Mississippi, French traffic down that river became more regular, leading to the establishment of an outpost at the mouth of the Arkansas in 1687. These Frenchmen were far removed from their sources of supply, and many turned to trading with the English. One Frenchman, Jean Couture, deserted his post on the Arkansas and traveled through the Southeast before ending up in Charles Town. There he bragged about his knowledge of the West and told the English that there were silver deposits beyond the Appalachian Mountains.[156] Nothing significant ever came of the English plans to go into the mining business, but Couture made himself useful to Carolinians engaged in what for them was already a gold mine, the commerce in indigenous captives. By 1700 Couture had made his way back to the Mississippi, where Pierre Le Moyne, sieur d'Iberville, the French commander in charge of establishing the Louisiana colony, learned that his renegade countryman had guided several Englishmen to the mouth of the Arkansas. Couture and his party had given the Quapaws thirty guns along with powder, shot, and other goods and encouraged them to go to war against the Chackhiumas, a people then living in the Yazoo Basin.[157] Couture was certainly not the only Frenchman to become involved with the English. In 1700 the Catholic priest Paul du Ru celebrated mass for a large number of Europeans who literally came out of the woods to receive communion. "There are all sorts of people here, voyageurs, soldiers, French Canadians, sailors, filibusters, and others like them," du Ru commented.[158] At the same time, the French commander of Fort Biloxi learned that three coureurs de bois had been to visit the governor of South Carolina, traveling by way of what must have been the Tennessee. The renegade Frenchmen reported that on one end of the river were the Chickasaws, while on the other end were the Cherokees, who lived near the river of the "Chavanons," certainly a reference to the Savannah River. Along their way they found the "Calés," among whom was "an Englishman established to trade in slaves, as they [were] among numerous other nations."[159] By the late seventeenth century, then, the Tennessee River had become an avenue of South Carolina's aggressive search for slaves.

Whether traveling by way of the Tennessee or the Upper Path, Carolina's traders succeeded in transporting countless captives back to their colony to be sold as slaves. In 1698, for example, the Chickasaws, along with some Shawnees who had come to live among them, surprised a division of the Illinois then living along the Mississippi, killing just ten men but taking nearly one hundred captives, including women and children.[160] Undoubtedly many of these Illinois prisoners wound up in the hands of the English. In 1699 d'Iberville found several Englishman living among the Chickasaws and doing an "extensive" business in Native slaves.[161] At least one of these Englishmen directly participated in slave raids. D'Iberville commented, "[F]or several years this Englishman has been among the Chicachas where he does a business in Indian slaves, putting himself at the head of Chicacha war parties to make raids on their enemies and friends and forcing them to take prisoners, whom he buys and sends to the islands to be sold."[162] Among those to suffer such raids were the Choctaws. In 1699 the French first took note of the Choctaws, learning from indigenous informants that they were "very numerous," having forty-five villages. They also learned that the English bought Choctaws that the Chickasaws and other Natives had captured.[163] This infuriated the Choctaws and fueled a war that would continue through much of the eighteenth century.[164] In 1702 d'Iberville tried to forge peace between the two warring groups and bring them into an alliance with France. The French governor claimed that raids were futile, arguing that while the Chickasaws had taken five hundred Choctaw slaves and killed another eighteen hundred over the last eight to ten years, they had lost eight hundred people themselves. Only the English profited from such violence, d'Iberville maintained, by selling the captives at slave markets in Charles Town and the Caribbean islands.[165] Before smallpox ever struck the area, then, English commerce in Native captives had had a dramatic impact as far west as the Mississippi. Faced with Chickasaws to the north and Creeks to the east, many unarmed indigenous peoples coalesced into the Choctaw Confederacy, a defensive alliance that allowed constituent communities to confront the harsh realities that English colonialism presented.[166]

The formation of the Choctaw Confederacy was just one of many consequences resulting from English commerce in guns and captives. South Carolina's and Virginia's Native slave trade caused countless communities to move great distances either to flee slave raids or to be closer to European allies. It was amid this heightened violence and population movement that historically known confederacies began to coalesce. Virginia's Native allies in particular forced Iroquoian-speaking peoples to become concentrated in the southern Appalachians, and when these Cherokees acquired guns from the Old Dominion, they in turn put pressure on Muskogean speakers in eastern Tennessee, who fled south to join a variety of Muskogee and Hitchiti communities that were coalescing along the

Chattahoochee and the Coosa-Tallapoosa. By the mid-1680s these Lower and Upper Creeks became armed themselves and facilitated the expansion of Carolina's trade network to their allies the Chickasaws. Together the Chickasaws and the Creeks forced various communities to coalesce in central Mississippi, where they would become known as the Choctaws. Between 1659 and 1696 the social landscape of the region took on a new look. Several river valleys became vacant, and the well-known and historically important Native polities of the interior Southeast began to take shape.

Smallpox and population decline also played an important role in the emergence of the Cherokees, the Creeks, the Choctaws, and the Chickasaws, but the later arrival of the Atlantic world's most lethal germs should not obscure how devastating the captive and gun trade was for indigenous peoples. Before 1696 slave raids rather than epidemics proved to be the aspect of European colonialism most hazardous to the health and safety of the region's Natives. Scholars will likely never know with certainty how many indigenous persons wound up as slaves, but historian Alan Gallay offers some sound estimates. He calculates that South Carolinians acquired between 30,000 and 50,000 captives from 1670 to 1715.[167] Based on Gallay's numbers, the yearly average of Native slaves taken was between 667 and 1,111 individuals, making the total number of Natives enslaved during the twenty-six years before smallpox was known to have spread across the region to be between 17,342 and 28,886. Include with those numbers the slaves that Virginians took, and the demographic impact becomes even larger. Aside from the sheer numbers taken, the slave trade added to indigenous population loss by selectively removing women and children from their communities, thereby lessening reproductive rates and making it difficult to recover lost population. Warfare certainly took a toll on raiding groups as well, and by exchanging female and young captives to the English, Native suppliers deprived themselves of individuals who otherwise would have been adopted. Demographic losses were even more severe due to the violence and chaos associated with slaving activities. Countless men lost their lives trying to protect their communities from armed raiders. Hunger and aboriginal diseases only compounded the situation. Heightened warfare forced communities to maintain compact settlements in which common germs took their toll on individual bodies, while fear of enslavement led Natives to leave their fields unplanted or their crops unharvested. Men also were more likely to stay at home to protect their communities rather than venture out into well-stocked yet dangerous hunting grounds. For many groups the only solution was to seek out European trading partners, leading them to become incorporated into the Atlantic market economy. Tragi-

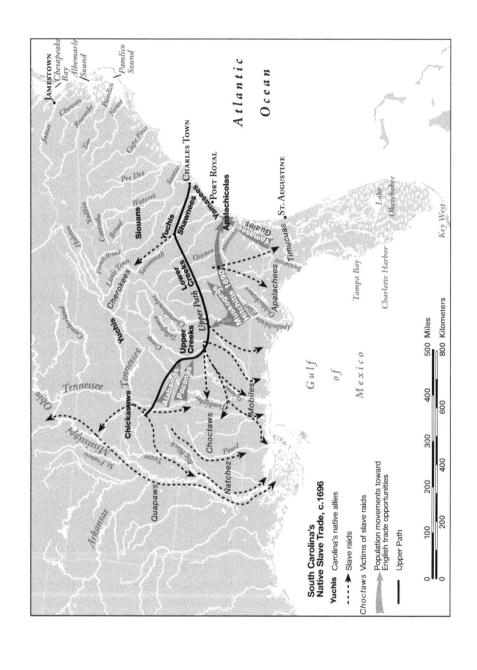

**South Carolina's
Native Slave Trade, c. 1696**

Yuchis Carolina's native allies

- - -> Slave raids

➤ Slave raids

Choctaws Victims of slave raids

➤ Population movements toward
English trade opportunities

━━━ Upper Path

Scale bars:
0 — 100 — 200 — 300 — 400 — 500 Miles
0 — 200 — 400 — 600 — 800 Kilometers

Labels on map:

JAMESTOWN
Chesapeake Bay
Albemarle Sound
Pamlico Sound
Chowan
Roanoke
Neuse
Pamlico
James
Tar
Cape Fear
Pee Dee
Wateree
Yadkin
Catawba
Broad
Hiwassee
Santee
Little Tenn.
French Broad
CHARLES TOWN
PORT ROYAL
Siouans
Yuchis
Shawnees
Yamasees
Apalachicolas
ST. AUGUSTINE
Guales
Yamasees
Timucuas
Lake Okeechobee
Key West
Atlantic Ocean
Cherokees
Savannah
Oconee
Lower Creeks
Upper Path
Apalachees
Oconee
Ocmulgee
Ochisees
Tampa Bay
Charlotte Harbor
Yuchis
Tennessee
Tennessee
Coosa
Tallapoosa
Chattahoochee
Upper Creeks
Muskogees 1690
Alabamas
Pacanas
Apalachicola River
Mobiles
Gulf of Mexico
Cumberland
Chickasaws
Ohio
Mississippi
St. Franc.
Tombigbee
Choctaws
Pearl
Big Black
Yazoo
Natchez
Quapaws
Arkansas

cally, indigenous peoples were trapped in this highly vulnerable state of warfare, slaving, resettlement, and malnourishment when smallpox spread through the region in the last four years of the seventeenth century.

The Great Southeastern Smallpox Epidemic

In 1696 English colonialism connected Native communities with each other and with the larger Atlantic world as they had never been before. Traders were contacting groups from the Atlantic Coast to the Mississippi. English commerce was affecting indigenous peoples living even in the remote southern Appalachians and as far away as the mouth of the Arkansas. A high volume of people— traders, Native middlemen, raiders, captives, and runaways—was passing along an extensive trade network. Multiple population movements and mergers were occurring, and new confederacies were forming. Once introduced into this environment of people on the move—trading, warring, escaping, and coalescing— the smallpox virus made its deadly way throughout the entire region.

The Great Southeastern Smallpox Epidemic began where the Native slave trade started. In 1696 the virus spread through Virginia and forced the assembly to recess.[168] Smallpox probably arrived in the Old Dominion by way of ships loaded with African slaves. Such vessels proved notorious for spreading disease as they cramped together hundreds of young captives gathered from African societies and then transported them to various slave markets in the Atlantic world.[169] After Bacon's Rebellion Virginia increasingly became a destination for such human cargo, importing more slaves from 1695 to 1700 than it had over the previous twenty years combined.[170] Concurrent with this influx of Africans, Virginia's European population had grown particularly vulnerable to acute infectious diseases. The early Chesapeake settlers had been notoriously sickly due to malaria, typhoid, and other rather common maladies, allowing the colony's population to grow only by continual immigration. But by the late seventeenth century, life expectancies had increased, families had become more stable, and more children were being produced, leading to a Creole population that had not experienced the typical childhood diseases of Europe.[171] When introduced in 1696, smallpox found an English and African population ripe for a major epidemic and a population that had multiple connections to neighboring Natives. The Old Dominion's tributary Natives indeed fared poorly. Years of war against the English had already greatly reduced their numbers, and after the Great Southeastern Smallpox Epidemic, their population shrank even more. In 1697 Governor Edmond Andros claimed, "[T]he Indians in Virginia are so decreased as now hardly worth ye name of Nations." To make matters worse, the continual threat of Iroquois raids kept Virginia's tributary groups in concentrated communities near germ-ridden English settlements. The James River valley, for example, had once had dozens of indigenous towns with thousands of warriors, but in 1697 only four communities, which together could field only 160 men, were located on this river.[172] To be sure, Native communities persist in Virginia to this day, but such survival is quite remarkable given the conditions that they faced in the late 1690s.

Shortly after ravaging Virginia's English, African, and Native population, smallpox spread to indigenous peoples bordering their colony. South Carolina's governor, John Archdale, reported that in 1696 "a great Mortality" struck tribes living near the Pamlico River. The governor remarked, "[I]t seemed to me as if God had an Intention speedily to plant an English settlement thereabouts."[173] Rather than citing divine providence as responsible, Archdale should have attributed the cause of such a calamity to something that must have been more visible to him. English commerce played the more immediate role in spreading smallpox throughout the Piedmont and the Coastal Plain. While touring the Carolinas in 1701, John Lawson commented that smallpox had produced catastrophic results, destroying "many thousands of these natives" and "sweeping away whole towns." "Neither do I know any savages," he added, "that have traded with the English, but what have been great losers by this distemper."[174] Lawson appropriately made the connection between smallpox and English trade, pointing to rum as the most desired commodity. In the 1690s Natives in Virginia's trade network came to desire the addictive commodity and welcomed Tuscarora middlemen who trucked alcohol from community to community. Intoxication was not the only consequence of such trade. Mass infection by smallpox tragically resulted from the high level of human traffic associated with such commerce.[175]

The rum trade was just one of several linkages that spread smallpox from the Old Dominion into the Native Southeast. The slave trade was another. With the virus infecting such a wide array of peoples in colonial Virginia, it stood a high probability of accompanying the dozens of English freemen, servants, and indigenous auxiliaries who regularly led trade caravans hundreds of miles south of the James. The many Englishmen married to Native wives also maintained regular communication between their home colony and adopted communities, whose economies since the 1650s had become increasingly reoriented to the Atlantic market. Those slaves whom the market demanded added to the human traffic. After being sold to Europeans, Native captives often escaped and attempted to return to their homes. Such flight led to numerous complaints from European masters and to a 1699 proclamation from Governor Nicholson forbidding Virginians to harbor Natives.[176] Virginia's ruling race knew all too well the difficulties of keeping indigenous peoples bound in their own homeland, and tragically the desire of Natives for freedom served as yet another stream of human traffic that potentially spread the smallpox virus beyond the Old Dominion.[177]

Coming by way of multiple linkages between Virginia and indigenous peoples, the smallpox virus caused massive mortality and produced what historian James Merrell has called a "kaleidoscopic array" of population movements and mergers among the Piedmont Siouans.[178] John Lawson found this occurring during several legs of his 1701 journey. His travels took him up the Wateree and Catawba rivers, where Native communities were merging together to form the peoples that collectively became known as the Catawbas. He witnessed one of those constituent groups gather for a ceremony in which community members performed a song "in Remembrance of their former Greatness, and Numbers of their Nation."[179] Further to the north on the Yadkin River, he found the Tutelos and the Saponies, two tribes that had been driven south during Bacon's Rebellion, joining together with the Keyauwees. These three "small nations," Lawson said, "were going to live together, by which they thought they should strengthen themselves, and become formidable to their enemies." The enemies were the Senecas, a people who certainly would come back to retaliate against the Saponies for taking five captives from them earlier. The Tutelos persuaded the Saponies not to torture the captives but to send them back to their homes as a peace gesture to the more powerful member of the Five Nations. In the meantime, however, war was the rule, leading communities recently stricken with smallpox to continue to live in fortified villages, the least healthy settlement pattern.[180] Similarly, Lawson found Enos, Sugarees, and Usherees "mixt" together and living in a fortified town along a tributary of the Neuse River.[181] These formerly independent groups valued their distinctive identities, but given the severe population loss and restrictions from marrying first cousins and members of one's own clan, they had little alternative but to merge, especially amid the continuing violence of slave raids. "Although there is nothing more coveted amongst them, than to marry a Woman of their own Nation," Lawson claimed, "yet when the Nation consists of a very few People (as now adays it often happens) so that they are all of them related to another, then they look out for Husbands and Wives amongst Strangers."[182] Of course, some of these strangers were captives adopted into the community, but at other times such a process involved more peaceful forms of integration based on traditional practices. Lawson witnessed Natives from different nations coming together, engaging in mutual gift giving, singing, and dancing, and after which concluding that "their Sons and Daughters shall marry together, and the two Nations love one another, and become as one People."[183] Later episodes of disease and continuing warfare would force further conglomeration, but the Great Southeastern Smallpox Epidemic was an especially intensive period of coalescence among Carolina's Siouan-speaking population and a seminal event in the genesis of the Catawba people.

As smallpox ravaged the Piedmont, it entered into South Carolina's trade network and made its way into that colony's non-Native population. By February 1697 English settlers in the colony had become sick from the virus, leaving some representatives unable to attend meetings of the Commons House of Assembly because they, their families, or their servants were ill.[184] The disease continued to rage throughout the year. In March 1698 colonial officials reported back to Britain, "We have had ye Small Pox amongst us Nine or ten Months, which hath been very Infectious and mortall, we have lost by the Distemper 200 or 300 Persons."[185] To be sure, the documentary evidence does not reveal the exact point of entry of the virus into the colony, leaving the possibility that smallpox came to Charles Town through ships that had earlier visited Virginia or another port in which the disease was epidemic. But given two factors, it was highly likely that the virus made an overland journey from the Old Dominion to its sister colony to the south. First, South Carolina's and Virginia's trade networks overlapped in North Carolina, making it probable that Carolinians contracted the deadly germ somewhere on the trading path and carried it back in their own bloodstreams or in the bloodstreams of the indigenous captives whom they purchased. Second, an eight-month period elapsed between the first report of smallpox in Virginia (June 1696) and first evidence of the disease in South Carolina (February 1697), suggesting a steady spread through the myriad Native communities between the two colonies.

Once the smallpox virus entered South Carolina's trading network, it exploded into an even more massive epidemic for indigenous peoples. One Carolinian commented on what must have been a truly horrific site: "Smallpox . . . has been mortal to all sorts of the inhabitants and especially the Indians who tis said to have swept away a whole neighboring nation, all to 5 or 6 which ran away and left their dead unburied, lying upon the ground for the vultures to devouer."[186] For some Carolinians worried about the slave trade causing Natives to rebel, the epidemic was a blessing. Because so many indigenous peoples died, colonial officials expected that trade would diminish; as Governor Joseph Blake informed the Lords Proprietors, the Carolina settlers would have "no Reason to Expect any Mischeif from ye Indian Trade, the Small-pox hath killed so many of them that we have little Reason to believe they will be Capable of doing any Harm to us for severall Years to Come."[187] Indeed, the epidemic had a vast geographic spread involving numerous Native communities. By Blake's account, smallpox had "Swept off great Numbers of [indigenous peoples] 4 or 500 Miles Inland as well upon ye Sea Cost as in our Neighbourhood."[188] The governor's remarks, while certainly understated, revealed that he and his fellow colonists had just witnessed one of the worst demographic tragedies ever to happen in the Southeast.

Blake's comments in fact underestimated the geographic extent of the Great Southeastern Smallpox Epidemic. After arriving in South Carolina sometime before February 1697, the virus made an overland trip from South Carolina to the Mississippi Valley and the Gulf Coast, where the French found Natives reeling from the disease from 1698 through 1700. Smallpox undoubtedly arrived there by way of South Carolina's Upper Path trading allies. By the late 1690s regular trade caravans involving Englishmen, Africans, and Natives headed west from South Carolina, peddling a variety of manufactured goods to multiple villages along the way in exchange for deerskins and slaves. Those slave raids took Carolina's allies to the Gulf Coast and into the Mississippi Valley, where the virus that they carried ignited a tremendous outbreak. No firsthand accounts reveal in detail the Great Southeastern Smallpox Epidemic's impact on Upper Path communities, but Thomas Nairne's 1708 journal provides unambiguous evidence that the event had affected them. Nairne traveled the Upper Path and provided the most detailed observations of the southeastern interior since Hernando de Soto's expedition in the sixteenth century. The traveling Carolinian reported that the Creeks could remember a time when their communities grew too large and had to send out colonies, whose inhabitants deferentially referred to their parent as "grandfather." But in recent times the reverse had been the case. Upper Path communities had faced smallpox and were forced to unite their communities "for want of inhabitants." Since there had been no occurrence of smallpox between 1700 and 1708, the outbreak that forced them to do so must have been the Great Southeastern Smallpox Epidemic. Just as it had in the Carolina Piedmont, then, depopulation due to the virus caused multiple population mergers and led to the further coalescence of Native peoples into the fewer communities that composed the emerging Lower Creeks, Upper Creeks, and Chickasaws.[189]

Unlike its devastation among Upper Path communities, the Great Southeastern Smallpox Epidemic's impact on the victims of slave raids on the Gulf Coast shows up vividly in the documentary record, albeit of the French rather than of the English. In 1699, for example, d'Iberville and his men witnessed the results of the epidemic as they explored Mobile Bay. There they discovered, according to one Frenchman, "a prodigious number of human skeletons that they formed a mountain."[190] D'Iberville counted sixty men or women, whose remains had not yet rotted, and came to believe that they had died in a massacre; hence he named the island "Massacre Island."[191] The French later learned that the corpses were those of "a numerous nation who being pursued and having withdrawn to this region, had almost all died here of sickness."[192] Those pursuing these unfortunate people were certainly English-allied slave raiders, while the culprit that made them sick was smallpox. This deadly combination of germs and violence became obvious to the French as they visited other villages along the Gulf Coast. D'Iberville came upon the Mougoulachas and the Bayogoulas united in a single village and found a ghastly scene. "The smallpox, which they still had in the village," he reported, "had killed one-fourth of the people." The Natives placed these newly dead victims on scaffolds outside their village, making a wretched smell that made the French sick.[193] As did the inhabitants of Massacre Island, the Mougoulachas and the Bayogoulas lived in a highly vulnerable situation. The two nations had 200 to 250 warriors and relatively few women and children, suggesting that smallpox and slave raiding had taken a toll. A ten-foot-high palisade surrounded their community, offering some protection from slave raids but also providing an ideal situation for smallpox to spread thoroughly among people likely experiencing malnourishment and carrying a heavy pathogen load. D'Iberville noted that the residents obtained their drinking water from just one small creek that ran close to their village.[194] He did not stay long among the Bayogoulas and the Mougoulachas, but if he had, he likely would have seen the ongoing epidemic produce an even greater number of deaths. One of his lieutenants, in fact, later reported that the Mougoulachas merged with another disease-stricken group, the Quinipissas, whose chief became the leader of the newly amalgamated community.[195]

The French found even more examples of smallpox's wrath along the Gulf Coast, where massive depopulation caused yet another kaleidoscopic array of population mergers. In 1700 d'Iberville ascended the Pascagoula River four and a half leagues and found a deserted village that belonged to the "formerly quite numerous" Biloxis, who had been "destroyed two years ago by diseases." He found abandoned horticultural fields on both sides of the river and elaborate fortifications surrounding the vacant town. The palisades were made of posts eight feet high and eighteen inches thick. Rising above the town's walls were three ten feet by ten feet "lookout boxes" constructed of clay and grass, which had "several loopholes" for warriors to shoot their arrows through. "It was strong enough for them," d'Iberville judged, "to defend themselves against enemies that have nothing more than arrows."[196] Musket balls, of course, penetrated such defenses with more ease than arrows, but even more deadly to the peoples huddling behind such palisades was the smallpox virus, for once it got inside the town, no one escaped infection. Some Biloxis did survive, but the remnants of this community did what many other smallpox-stricken peoples had to do: they coalesced with others. Sixteen leagues up the Pascagoula River, the Pascagoulas, the Biloxis, and the Moctobis had combined but still remained small, having "altogether not twenty cabins."[197] English-inspired slave raids and its biological companion had indeed created an unprecedented catastrophe on the Gulf Coast.

Just as vulnerable as peoples on the Gulf Coast were indigenous communities farther up the Mississippi River. The Great Southeastern Smallpox Epidemic, in fact, produced a disaster like nothing that had ever happened to the river valley's inhabitants, including the upheavals associated with Hernando de Soto's visit some 150 years earlier. In December 1698 a French missionary party from Canada descended the Mississippi and discovered the ongoing epidemic.[198] At the mouth of the Arkansas, they found a Quapaw village and reported: "We were sensibly afflicted to see this nation once so numerous entirely destroyed by war and sickness. It is not a month since they got over the smallpox which carried off the greatest part of them. There was nothing to be seen in the village but graves."[199] They further commented that the stricken village had been two separate communities that had combined, but it still had a disproportionate number of adult males. "All the children and a great part of the women were dead," wrote one Catholic priest.[200] Such gender and age imbalance was not due to deaths from smallpox alone. English-inspired slave raids had certainly taken their toll on the Quapaws, whose Chickasaw enemies sought to supply the Atlantic market with the female and young captives it demanded. The demographic imbalance that slave raids produced only added to the Quapaws' epidemiological nightmare, making it difficult for their community to increase its birthrate and recover from disease-induced mortality. Not surprisingly, the Quapaws lived "in constant fear of their enemies" and did not send their men out during the hunting season, thus compounding their health problems by inducing a dearth of protein.[201] When d'Iberville ascended the Mississippi in 1700, he arrived at the end of the Great Southeastern Smallpox Epidemic and found a Native population whose numbers had been greatly reduced.[202]

Amid such devastation, the French found indigenous peoples somewhat receptive to the trappings of Christianity. By the late seventeenth century, Christian missionaries knew very well that epidemics provided a window of opportunity for them to convert Natives, and they took the opportunity that the Great Southeastern Smallpox Epidemic presented them. The Quapaws allowed the visiting Catholics to erect a cross in their village before they departed down the river to visit other communities. On their way back up the Mississippi, the priests found that the Quapaws had planted a cross on the river bank and awaited a permanent missionary with "great impatience."[203] The Tunicas, who lived on the east side of the Mississippi in the Yazoo Basin, also were susceptible to acculturation. In January 1699 the French missionary party arrived among them and found them reeling from disease. Probably believing the priests to have healing powers that their own medicine men lacked, the Tunicas allowed several of their sick children and even one of their leading chiefs to be baptized. Such deathbed conversions did not stop him or many other Tunicas from passing away during the Catholics' eight-day stay.[204] "They were dying in great numbers," one French priest reported bluntly.[205] The Tunicas permitted Father Anthony Davion to remain among them, but as was so often the case, such flirtation with Catholicism was only superficial. After Father Davion ordered the destruction of the Tunica's temple and its sacred objects, his hosts drove him from their community. By that time, however, the Tunicas saw their destiny tied to the French colonial regime. Reduced in numbers and pressed hard by the English-allied Chickasaws, the Tunicas, as did many other Mississippi Valley and Gulf Coast tribes hit by disease and slave raids, eventually relocated farther south and on the western side of the Mississippi, where they served as a client tribe, or *petite nation,* of French Louisiana.[206]

After ravaging the peoples of the Mississippi Valley, smallpox's four-year impact on the Native Southeast came to an end. By the end of 1700 active cases of the disease in the region ceased, likely because there were very few indigenous communities left untouched. The virus did spread north into the Illinois country, where it persisted for a few more years, but until 1711 smallpox would not cause another epidemic in the Southeast.[207] Still, neither the 1711 outbreak nor any other subsequent epidemic equaled the catastrophic impact of the Great Southeastern Smallpox Epidemic. Documentary evidence makes it clear that the virus spread over a vast area from 1696 to 1700, afflicting a wide array of people and causing high casualties among a population made especially vulnerable by the violent expansion of English trade in Native slaves. It is reasonable to conclude that with indigenous peoples suffering from smallpox over such an im-

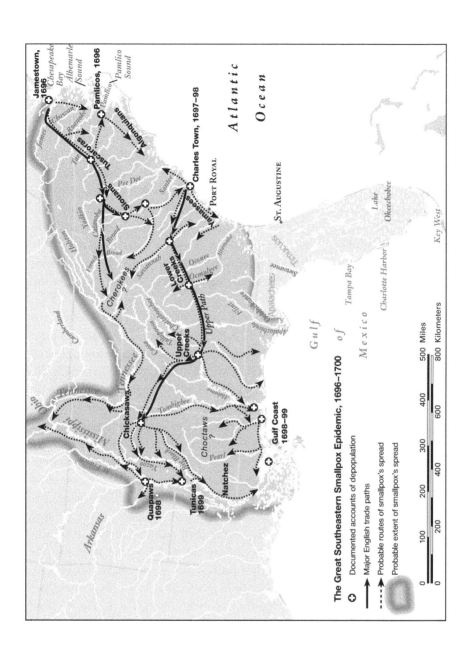

The Great Southeastern Smallpox Epidemic, 1696–1700

Jamestown, 1696

Pamlicos, 1696

Tuscaroras

Algonquians

Siouans

Charles Town, 1697–98

Cherokees

Lower Creeks

Upper Creeks

Chickasaws

Choctaws

Gulf Coast 1698–99

Quapaws 1698

Tunicas 1699

Natchez

Chesapeake Bay

Albemarle Sound

Pamlico Sound

Pamlico

James

Chowan

Roanoke

Tar

Neuse

Pee Dee

Catawba

Yadkin

Santee

Congaree

Broad

Broad

Cape Fear

Savannah

Oconee

Ocmulgee

Upper Path

Altamaha

Flint

Apalachees

Apalachicola

Suwanee

Timucuas

Tampa Bay

Charlotte Harbor

Lake Okeechobee

Key West

St. Augustine

Port Royal

Atlantic Ocean

Gulf of Mexico

Hiwassee

Tennessee

Holston

Cumberland

Tennessee

Ohio

Mississippi

Arkansas

Coosa

Tallapoosa

Chattahoochee

Tombigbee

Yazoo

Black

Pearl

Alabama

Mobile

The Great Southeastern Smallpox Epidemic, 1696–1700

Documented accounts of depopulation

Major English trade paths

Probable routes of smallpox's spread

Probable extent of smallpox's spread

0   100   200   300   400   500 Miles

0   200   400   600   800 Kilometers

mense territorial expanse and with English commerce permeating the entire region, many more communities experienced the outbreak than those whose tragedies were recorded in European records.

No documentary evidence confirms the occurrence of smallpox among the Cherokees, for example, but a variety of factors suggests that at least some of their villages experienced the virus in the late 1690s. Although not as vulnerable as Upper Path communities, the Cherokees were linked to the larger Atlantic world through itinerant traders, Native middlemen, slave raiders, and runaway captives who made their way into the mountains. Cherokee settlements on the upper Savannah, of course, would have been most susceptible given their relatively close location to Carolina's closest allies, who lived downriver and who were certainly infected. The most northerly Cherokee villages also stood a fairly good chance of becoming infected, given their location at the western terminus of Virginia's trade network, which had originally facilitated the spread of the deadly virus into the Southeast.

Indirect evidence indeed supports an argument for the Great Southeastern Smallpox Epidemic's impact on the Cherokees. Around 1711 Alexander Longe recorded a remarkable conversation he had with a Cherokee religious leader. The Native man related a tale of the enchanted town of Agustoghe, whose leader had persuaded almost the entire community to follow him to a paradise that lay underneath a river. All but sixteen to twenty individuals went into the river through a "great turn pool," and they were never seen again. According to Long's informant this happened "about 10 year before the English were amongst them."[208] Longe was, in fact, one of the first Englishmen to intermarry and live among the Middle Cherokees, having arrived in their territory sometime around 1710, thus dating Agustoghe's disappearance to the time of the Great Southeastern Smallpox Epidemic. To be sure, Agustoghe may not have been a Cherokee town. A map produced in 1722 located the town near the junction of the Hiwassee and Tennessee rivers, a place where the Yuchis were known to have lived.[209] Nevertheless, if the virus had reached that remote place, one wonders whether it could have traveled there without affecting Cherokees on the upper Savannah, who then carried it over the Appalachian Divide to peoples living in eastern Tennessee. If not by that route, then smallpox may have traveled down the Tennessee River by way of Cherokees who lived closer to Virginia. The same mapmaker that located Agustoghe on the Hiwassee included a caption north of the Little Tennessee that read "abandoned settlements." Those villages had certainly been devastated by slave raids, but perhaps smallpox delivered the finishing blow, forcing surviving Iroquoian speakers to move southwest and to merge with other peoples and in the process became the historic Overhill Cherokees of eastern Tennessee. An account recorded in the late nineteenth century by ethnologist James Mooney indeed supports the idea that disease played a role in the Cherokees abandonment of their northerly villages. According to Mooney's informant, the Cherokees "long ago" had settlements on the French Broad River. One of those towns, "Kǎna'sta," had become plagued by "wars and sickness," and its people went to live with mythical people who lived inside Pilot Knob Mountain, thus disappearing, never to be seen again.[210]

If smallpox did travel into the Appalachian Mountains, the Cherokees' experience with smallpox was not likely to be uniform. In the 1690s the Cherokees were not united into a coherent polity in which regular communication among the various divisions was maintained. Instead, independent clusters of communities could be found along a number of narrow rivers; some flowed to the east and others to the west, with mountains and difficult-to-traverse terrain in between. Some of these clusters were trading with Virginians; some were trading with Carolinians; and some may have had little experience, either directly or indirectly, with English commerce. Conceivably, smallpox entered some Cherokee towns in the late 1690s but spared others. The Great Southeastern Smallpox Epidemic thus probably struck some but not all Cherokee settlements.

One area that did not appear to be on the Great Southeastern Smallpox Epidemic's path was Florida. Florida's mission population, of course, had the earliest and most prolonged experience with the Atlantic world's deadliest diseases, including at least one experience with smallpox. Since that episode occurred in 1655, however, everyone but those Natives over forty-one years of age lacked acquired immunity to the disease in 1696, making the vast majority of Florida's mission population virgin soil. Nevertheless, no evidence that the Great Southeastern Smallpox Epidemic struck the Apalachees, the Timucuas, or the Guales can be found. Two factors suggest that this lack of evidence stems from smallpox's absence from Florida rather than the failure of the Spanish to record its presence. First, none of these groups was heavily involved in trading with the English, and second, a truce between the Lower Creeks and the Apalachees from 1698 to 1702 curtailed slave raids across the buffer zone that separated English-allied tribes from Spanish Florida. To be sure, some Apalachees took the opportunity of peace to travel to the Lower Creeks and trade with the English who lived there. Some Apalachees even took up residence there as the Spanish colonial regime became increasingly oppressive in the 1690s. By comparison the Lower Creeks had yet to face the encroachment of Europeans and their livestock as the Apalachees did; they also were not obligated to pay their European allies tribute in the form of labor and foodstuffs; and they received a wider variety and larger quantity of manufactured goods than the Spanish ever supplied to their Native allies. Still, Apalachee interaction with the Creeks and their English allies remained tenuous at best, keeping travel across the buffer zone between the Oc-mulgee River and northern Florida at minimal levels and curtailing the spread of smallpox. The good fortune of avoiding smallpox in the 1690s, though, made the approximately twelve thousand Natives within Florida's mission system a more attractive target for slave raiders after the Great Southeastern Smallpox Epidemic had destroyed many of their other potential sources of captives.[211]

The Choctaws, another group that the English looked to as a source of slaves after the Great Southeastern Smallpox Epidemic, may have avoided exposure to the virus in the 1690s as well. Assessing the epidemic's impact on the Choctaws, though, is very difficult. On one hand, among all the major southeastern groups, the Choctaws were the least involved in European trade, giving them a degree of protection. Their villages also sat along remote creeks and streams, thus remaining away from major axes of communication. Furthermore, the Choctaws emerged shortly after 1700 with the largest population in the eastern woodlands, suggesting that the deadly virus had somehow avoided their homeland in the 1690s. On the other hand, documented cases of smallpox occurred all around the Choctaw homeland among communities that were not partners with the English but victims of slave raids just as the Choctaws were. Conceivably, smallpox spread to the Choctaws through the same traffic of traders, slave raiders, runaway captives, and Native middlemen that appears to have infected Mississippi Valley and Gulf Coast tribes.

Choctaw oral history suggests just that. According to Nathaniel Folsom, a European American trader married to a Choctaw who gave an account in the 1820s, the Choctaws were the largest nation east of the Mississippi River before Europeans arrived, "but when the French came th[ey] brought the Small pocks and carried [the Choctaws] of[f] by thousands." Folsom, who had been among the Choctaws for sixty years, claimed that the epidemic happened long before his time and that he had learned the information from an elder named Ogha Humah, who died sometime before 1798 at the age of one hundred.[212] Ogha Humah's longevity can be doubted, but his placing the arrival of smallpox at the same time the French arrived supports the view that the Great Southeastern Smallpox Epidemic did strike his people and that the event was a factor in the further coalescence of diverse communities into a Choctaw Confederacy. Nevertheless, Choctaw oral history recorded in the nineteenth century should be seen as a composite of memories of several different communities having different geographic and ethnic origins. Rather than a unitary phenomenon for all his ancestors, Ogha Humah's story may have come from his ancestors who lived outside the homeland in the 1690s. Throughout the eighteenth century, the Choctaw Confederacy grew with the influx of remnant groups from places such as Mobile Bay and the Yazoo Basin, two places where the French found indigenous communities reeling from disease during the Great Southeastern Smallpox Epidemic.

While every location that the Great Southeastern Smallpox Epidemic struck cannot be determined with certainty, what is certain is that mortality rates from the disastrous event varied across the region. Smallpox did not exist in a disease vacuum; the presence of a variety of endemic germs inhibited the ability of some peoples to survive. Malaria had certainly already been introduced to the Southeast during the protohistoric period, but as English settlement grew, the plasmodia parasite became even more widespread. Clearing the land of timber to make room for agricultural fields created even more shallow pools of stagnant water, in which anopheles mosquitoes and malarial parasites thrived.[213] Also, the steady growth of English and African populations continually introduced typhoid and other fairly typical waterborne diseases into the slow-moving swamps, streams, and rivers that drained the Coastal Plain. Colonial Virginia, of course, went through this process early in its history, with appalling death rates among its early settlers, whose presence and economic activities produced an unhealthy environment. Virginia continued to produce such ecological changes throughout the seventeenth century as its settlements expanded to the Fall Line and down the coast into North Carolina. South Carolinians added another source of disruption. Just as Virginians had been doing since 1607, Carolinians changed the land such that malaria, typhoid, and other endemic illnesses thrived, making an even more poisonous environment in which their nearby Native neighbors had to live. With many of those neighbors living in compact villages to protect themselves from slave raids, pathogen loads must have been dangerously high.[214]

The explosive mortality rates from smallpox and endemic pathogens, indeed, led several groups below the Fall Line to dwindle to near invisibility. In 1701 John Lawson found a group of Sewees near the mouth of the Santee River struggling to survive and commented that they had "been formerly a large Nation, though now very much decreas'd, since the *English* hath seated their Land." He attributed their demise largely to smallpox but added that wherever Europeans settled indigenous peoples were "very apt to catch any Distemper they [were] afflicted withal."[215] The Sewees, of course, were not alone. By 1700 coastal Carolina's aboriginal population had shrunk, leaving Pee Dees, Cape Fears, Santees, Congarees, Winyaws, Cusabos, Etiwans, and a variety of other remnant groups to face a future of becoming "settlement Indians" or small communities surrounded by a larger non-Native population. Interestingly, Lawson blamed the fate of these groups in part on their own failings. He claimed that their high casualties from disease resulted from their "immoderate government" and supposedly dangerous healing methods, which included submersing fever-stricken victims in water. More than improper treatment, though, it was a combination of smallpox, malaria, bacterial infections, and nutritional deficiencies among the war-weary communities of coastal Carolina that accounted for the ghastly scenes of whole villages being destroyed. Native healers who led feverish patients into cool water offered some relief to their patients having dangerously high temperatures, a method that if performed during relatively warm weather would have been benign. Rather, factors outside indigenous control—the European invasion, the Native slave trade, economic dependency, and the transformation of their environment—made the Great Southeastern Smallpox so deadly.

Colonialism also caused Natives as far west as the Mississippi Valley to suffer from multiple germs. In February 1700 d'Iberville ascended the Mississippi and found that the Houmas had been suffering from diarrhea for the past five months and had lost half their people from the dreaded illness.[216] In March the French commander discovered a similar situation in the main village of the Natchez, whose leader lay dying of dysentery and whose people were grief stricken.[217] Any number of germs that have plagued humanity throughout its evolutionary history could have caused such an outbreak, but the European invasion certainly disrupted Native disease ecologies and led to higher rates of infection from those common dysentery-causing infections. Human traffic steadily increased through the Mississippi Valley in the last few years of the seventeenth century. French coureurs des bois, allied Natives, and Catholic missionaries from the north descended the river to greet d'Iberville's forces and to help in their colonial project. On his way up the Mississippi with d'Iberville in March 1700, Father Paul du Ru reported seeing fifteen to sixteen "vessels filled with Frenchmen going up and down the river."[218] On top of all this, Fort Biloxi contained a sickly contingent of men, who received supply ships sailing from the disease-ridden Caribbean.[219] The fort could have been the original source for a dysentery-causing pathogen such as typhoid, which became widespread through raiding and trading activities and deadly among compactly settled indigenous communities. The Houmas, for example, may have made themselves vulnerable to typhoid by capturing Bayagoulas, who had had contact with the French when they arrived in early 1699.[220] The threat of Chickasaw raids, however, gave Mississippi Valley tribes little opportunity to halt the epidemic, as population dispersal was not an option. The English slave trade and fairly typical germs, thus, combined to make the Great Southeastern Smallpox Epidemic a catastrophic epidemiological event for Gulf Coast and Mississippi Valley peoples.

Fortunately, the various communities then coalescing to form the emerging Cherokee, Creek, Chickasaw, and Choctaw confederacies suffered less-severe mortality rates because the European invasion had disrupted their disease ecologies to a lesser extent. Being farther removed from European settlements, they had less experience with malaria, typhoid, and other endemic diseases, which drove up the pathogen load of many unfortunate communities in coastal Carolina. The slave trade also affected them in a less detrimental way. With the exception of the Choctaws, the emerging interior confederacies played the role of raiders more than victims in the Native slave trade. As such, the Cherokees, the Creeks, and the Chickasaws could maintain diverse subsistence practices and avoid the nutritional deficiencies that plagued many war-weary communities during the 1690s. The position of the Cherokees, the Creeks, and the Chickasaws in the English trade network also gave them a higher degree of security than most Native groups in the Southeast, allowing them to live in dispersed settlement patterns. The Choctaws remained outside the English trade network, but their environment gave them a degree of protection that nearby victims of slave raids did not have. A few of their towns closest to their Chickasaw and Creek enemies had fortified and compact settlements, but the majority of Choctaws lived scattered along small creeks within impenetrable forests that made it very difficult for their enemies to find them. The Choctaws, thus, enjoyed a degree of protection from the dual hazard of germs and slave raids that devastated their more exposed neighbors to the south and the west. Many of those devastated groups would seek refuge in central Mississippi because of the advantages that the Choctaw's environment afforded.[221]

The Great Southeastern Smallpox Epidemic, indeed, was an event in which the nonbiological aspects of colonialism mediated the spread and impact of diseases and produced a differential pattern of depopulation. From 1696 to 1700 the smallpox virus traveled through a virgin population, afflicting all but the most secluded villages tucked in the Appalachian Mountains and in the dense forests of central Mississippi, but the explosiveness and devastation of the epidemic cannot be attributed simply to the biological consequence of a deadly virus being introduced to a previously unexposed population. Virginity obviously played a role, but smallpox arrived in so many indigenous communities be-

cause the Native slave trade had incorporated the Southeast into the larger Atlantic world. Smallpox spread so widely because a high volume of traders, Native
middlemen, slave raiders, and indigenous captives traveled across the region.
The slave trade also shaped death rates from the disease. Victims of raids were
the most vulnerable to mass infection, mortality, and depopulation. Before
smallpox arrived, English colonialism had greatly compromised their health,
and when exposed to the virus, they suffered the most appalling death tolls. Re-
covering from those tragic losses, moreover, was extremely difficult given the loss
of women and children to slave raiders. The health of English-allied tribes in the
interior—the Cherokees, the Creeks, and the Chickasaws—had been less compromised. Living above the Fall Line away from European settlements, the communities of these emerging confederacies had less experience with typhoid,
malaria, and other endemic illnesses.[222] As powerful and well-armed raiders in
the English trade network, they had a degree of security that permitted them to
maintain stable subsistence routines and that allowed large numbers of their
people to live in dispersed settlements. At the end of 1700, then, indigenous
power was concentrated in the interior, while Native communities within the
Coastal Plain, on the Gulf Coast, and in the Mississippi Valley were on their way
to becoming small enclaves within the larger European colonies that engulfed
them.

Conclusion

Although not all indigenous peoples suffered equally, diseases still had an intense impact on the Native Southeast from 1696 to 1700. The Great Southeastern Smallpox Epidemic had devastated a virgin population from the Atlantic
Coast to the Mississippi Valley. But the virginity metaphor alone does not explain why this event happened and why it was so devastating. Smallpox spread so
widely and produced such catastrophic mortality because nonbiological aspects
of colonialism had made indigenous peoples vulnerable. For several decades before the tragic event, the English slave trade had transformed the region and established the course through which smallpox would later spread. Beginning
with Virginia's traders in the 1650s, English commerce reoriented indigenous
economies to the larger Atlantic world as they became dependent on the munitions, cloth, rum, and other goods that only Europeans could supply. English
commerce became even more regular and sustained after the development of
South Carolina, a colony whose traders were doing business on the Mississippi
River perhaps as early as 1686 and certainly by 1696. By the latter year a high

volume of traffic including Carolinians, Virginians, Native middlemen, slave raiders, and runaway captives was crisscrossing the entire region. English, African, and indigenous peoples were linked into what would be a continual chain of infection that stretched from the James River to the Gulf Coast and from the Atlantic Ocean to the Mississippi Valley.

While English commerce facilitated the spread of an acute infectious disease, the commoditization of aboriginal practices of warfare and capture made Natives even more vulnerable. Once supplied with munitions, Virginia's and South Carolina's indigenous allies aggressively expanded their warfare activities to supply their partners with captives. By 1696 thousands of Natives had fled their villages and at times moved over a hundred miles away to escape violence. Smallpox, indeed, arrived at a time after many of the archaeologically observed population movements must have occurred. Moving, though, did not bring complete safety. Slave raids permeated the region in the 1690s, giving indigenous peoples little choice but to live in compact and fortified villages, where germs typically associated with poor sanitation took their toll on the health of whole communities. During such violence, victims of raids also suffered from lack of food. Traditional subsistence activities became hazardous as raiders lurked near the corn fields, hoping to capture women and children, the very individuals whom the English most valued as slaves. Male warriors were also not safe in their hunting territories and often abandoned the hunt to stay at home to protect their loved ones. When smallpox hit such communities, mortality was catastrophic, and population recovery was extremely difficult, especially when great numbers of women and children had been stolen. At the end of 1700 a great number of smallpox-stricken communities had merged together in order to have populations large enough to defend themselves and to provide young people an opportunity to find nonrelated marriage partners. The Great Southeastern Smallpox Epidemic was indeed a turning point in the history of the Native Southeast. An unparalleled and unprecedented population collapse occurred from which the indigenous population would not recover. To make matters worse, the biological nightmare continued into the eighteenth century, giving indigenous communities little reprieve from the suffering they had experienced in the 1690s.

Chapter Four

The Epidemiological Origins
of the Yamasee War

1700–1715

In September 1713 and again in September 1714, two successive hurricanes battered the Carolina coast. Amid the devastation an Anglican minister, Benjamin Dennis, came to believe that "if another happen[ed] [that] year the inhabitants [would] be obliged to desert the Country."[1] Many South Carolinians indeed had to desert their farms and plantations shortly after Dennis made his dire prediction, but instead of another hurricane, indigenous peoples led to their evacuation. On April 15, 1715, the Yamasees began a multitribal revolt against the South Carolinians that very nearly destroyed their colony. "God grant the Inhabitants of the Province may amend their ways," the Anglican minister Robert Maule exclaimed during the Yamasee War, "by several warnings they have had lately given them: we have been exercised with various Epedemicall Diseases with Inundations, Hurricanes and (which is no less dreadfull than any of the Rest) an Indian War."[2] Maule, like many early-modern Europeans, categorized the Yamasee War as a natural phenomenon that their god used to chastise his wayward children. In doing so he came closer than anyone to placing the conflict within the epidemiological context to which it rightfully belonged. Hurricanes, to be sure, played no discernible role in sowing the seeds of the Yamasee War, but epidemics shaped the origins of that conflict in powerful ways.

The Great Southeastern Smallpox Epidemic was just the beginning of a devastating nineteen-year period of the Native Southeast's experience with the Atlantic world's most lethal germs. Following the introduction of smallpox in 1696, other Columbian Exchange diseases came into English colonies, found their way into Native communities that had become irrevocably connected to the larger Atlantic world, and ignited a series of deadly aftershocks for peoples who could hardly afford any more depopulation. English records made note of several "pestilences," "plagues," "distempers," "grievous sicknesses," and other vaguely identified outbreaks in Virginia and the Carolinas. The particular diseases involved can only be identified with certainty in the 1699 and 1706 episodes of yellow fever and the 1711–12 occurrence of smallpox. Given the unusually high fatalities that resulted from them, those unidentifiable diseases surely included some of colonialism's more deadly microbes rather than simply being milder germs such as malaria, typhoid, and dysentery that were already endemic in many parts of the region. Measles, influenza, typhus, whooping cough, and diphtheria were all possibilities. Other European colonies served as entry ports for deadly pathogens too. Spanish Florida recorded two major outbreaks of unidentifiable diseases, one in 1703 and another in 1708, while French colonists carried a mysterious "plague" with them in 1699, imported another "plague" in 1704, and then suffered from a "general sickness" in 1706. Whatever the identity of the diseases that European colonization introduced, they achieved their most lethal potential because of the English commerce in indigenous slaves. The taking of infected captives and the dispersion of such individuals along trade routes spread germs more widely than they otherwise would have been. Also, violence associated with the Native slave trade continued to have the same impact as it had during the Great Southeastern Smallpox Epidemic. Victims of raids remained highly vulnerable to massive infection and exceedingly high mortality rates.

Eventually those germs that accompanied raiders, captives, traders, middlemen, guides, porters, and others involved in the slave trade caused the violent commerce in human beings to collapse. Between 1696 and 1715 germs and captive raids had worked synergistically to bring unprecedented and unparalleled depopulation in the Native Southeast. The lethal germs that accompanied the Atlantic world's most pernicious commerce put South Carolina on a collision course with its own indigenous allies and resulted in the Yamasee War, the conflict that brought the Native slave trade to its climactic finish.

Aftershocks between Virginia and South Carolina

With several other novel diseases arriving shortly after smallpox's introduction in 1696, many indigenous communities faced virgin-soil epidemics, as historian Alfred Crosby has characterized the Native experience in general. Multiple diseases struck nonimmune peoples in rapid succession, produced disastrous rates of infection and mortality, and drove indigenous groups to the point of extinction.[3] Because each of the multiple diseases involved had its own unique nature and because the nonbiological aspects of colonialism mediated the spread and impact of those diseases, however, not all Native communities had the same ex-

Table 1. Aftershock epidemics (see pp. 250–52 for notes)

Date	Location	Description	Cause
1698 July	Virginia	"great sickness and mortality"	influenza (conjectural)
1699 January–March	Gulf Coast	"plague"	typhus or influenza (conjectural)
1699 August–November	Charles Town	"Infectious, Pestilentiall & Mortal Distemper"	yellow fever
1703 [unknown]	Florida	170 Apalalchees perished at Mission San Luis	unknown
1704 July–September	Mobile	"plague"	typhus, influenza, or measles
1706 summer–fall	Charles Town and James River	"pestilential fever"	yellow fever
1706 [unknown]	Louisiana	"general sickness"	yellow fever (conjectural)
1708 September	Virginia	"severe and extraordinary fevers and other sicknesses"	multiple and unknown
1708 summer	Pensacola	"plague"	unknown
1709 February	South Carolina	"strange distempers" involving paralysis of arms and legs	unknown
1709 April	Virginia	"pestilential distemper"	unknown
1709–1710 winter	Virginia	"extraordinary sickness & Mortality"	unknown
1711 January	Virginia	"a Dangerous Epedemick Distemper"	unknown
1711 winter	South Carolina	"many spectacles of sickness and mortality"	unknown
1711 May–1712 March	South Carolina	several direct references to smallpox	smallpox
1711 summer	North Carolina	600 to 900 Palatine immigrants dying after arrival	yellow fever (conjectural)
1711 December	North Carolina	"pestilential distemper"	typhus (conjectural)
1711 fall–1712 winter	South Carolina	"Pestilential ffeavers" "Pleurisy" and "Malignant Feavers" "spotted fever"	yellow fever influenza (conjectural) measles or typhus (conjectural)

perience from aftershock epidemics. By revisiting the Great Southeastern Smallpox Epidemic's path between Virginia and South Carolina and examining what happened to that event's survivors between 1698 and 1715, one can, in fact, see how the nonbiological aspects of colonialism caused subsequent outbreaks to have a differential impact. By 1715 multiple germs and slave raids had drastically depopulated indigenous peoples in the Coastal Plain and the Piedmont, while the Cherokees in the Appalachian highlands emerged as the largest and most important Native polity between Virginia and South Carolina.

Among the first to experience the Great Southeastern Smallpox Epidemic were North Carolina's Tuscaroras and coastal Algonquians. They managed to remain in their homelands in the Pamlico and Neuse river valleys despite the ravages of smallpox, but they unfortunately could not withstand the wave of colonialism and its germs that followed. When the English traveler John Lawson finished his tour of Carolina in 1701, he crossed from the Neuse to the Pamlico River and found the area "very thick of *Indian* Towns and Plantations."[4] Such observation seems remarkable considering smallpox's arrival some five years earlier and the possibility that whatever had made the Old Dominion's settlers so sick during the summer of 1698 had spread south as well. Even yellow fever, which could have been responsible for the outbreak in Virginia and certainly devastated Charles Town in 1699, could have done some damage to at least coastal Algonquians. By the 1690s a handful of Englishmen had taken up residency along Albemarle Sound, thus making the area a regular stop for vessels coming from Virginia. Pirates also connected the Natives to the larger Atlantic world, as they frequently cruised into the sheltered harbors of the North Carolina coast.[5] It is not unreasonable to suggest that ships anchored near Algonquian villages introduced the yellow fever virus and its aedes mosquito carrier. Still, the Algonquians and the Tuscaroras persisted in numbers large enough to impress Lawson. This was in large part due to a mutually beneficial alliance that the two groups forged. Algonquians received protection from the militarily powerful Tuscaroras, who served as a buffer against raids by Cherokees, Siouans, and Five Nations Iroquois. The Tuscaroras in fact maintained good relations with their Iroquois kinsmen to the north, whose southern raids had gobbled up large numbers of other Natives from Virginia and the Carolinas. For their part Tuscaroras benefited from an alliance with Algonquians because of their declining fortunes in the Virginia trade network. Siouans and Cherokees kept the Tuscaroras out of the more lucrative western hunting grounds, thus forcing the Tuscaroras to hunt toward the coast or to acquire deerskins from tribes that lived there.[6]

In the first decade of the eighteenth century, colonialism bore down with increasing intensity on the Tuscaroras and their Algonquian allies. Following the Great Southeastern Smallpox Epidemic, Virginians settled around Pamlico Sound in increasing numbers and took up residence within Algonquian and Tuscarora hunting, gathering, and fishing territories.[7] New settlers and their livestock certainly saturated the environment even more with malaria, typhoid, and other endemic diseases that made living, traveling, and hunting in coastal Carolina more hazardous. Continuing trade and intercourse with the English made Tuscaroras and Algonquians vulnerable to the more serious diseases that swept the eastern seaboard. The yellow fever epidemic that struck both South Carolina and Virginia in 1706 might have had some impact on the North Carolina coast as well, although there is no record of it. More certainly, the deadly germ that struck Virginia in 1708 spread through coastal Carolina. The Tuscaroras certainly succumbed to the disease, to which their Algonquian allies were no less vulnerable.[8] One person who witnessed the declining fortunes of the Pamlico and Neuse river valleys' Native residents was John Lawson. After completing his 1701 journey, Lawson stayed in North Carolina and became that colony's surveyor general. Over the next several years, he observed Natives more carefully than most English settlers and compiled his observations in his 1709 book, *The History of Carolina*. Lawson wrote extensively about indigenous peoples trying to deal with a variety of sicknesses, and he concluded, "[O]n good grounds, I do believe, there is not the sixth Savage living within two hundred miles of all our Settlements, as there were fifty years ago." Lawson blamed smallpox and rum for doing the most damage but added, "These poor Creatures have so many Enemies to destroy them, that it's a wonder one of them is left alive near us."[9] In the context of Lawson's discussion, he clearly used "enemies" as a metaphor for disease and alcohol. Alcohol certainly proved a disruptive factor, but more detrimental were germs coming from continuing trade with the English and newcomers invading their homeland.

The situation for the Tuscaroras and the Algonquians deteriorated even further after Lawson published his book. The English continued to flood in from Virginia, whose governor made several complaints that his colony's "poorer sorts" constantly escaped their masters and creditors and fled into North Carolina.[10] The arrival of a group of German and Swiss settlers, known as the Palatines, in particular made Carolina's Algonquians vulnerable. In the winter of 1710 these refugees from Europe arrived in Virginia quite sickly, having come down with "ship's fever" or typhus on their voyage from England. They may have, in fact, sparked the 1710 epidemic in the Old Dominion. Palatines continued to die as they settled in North Carolina in the summer of 1710. They certainly suffered from fevers, agues, and fluxes during their seasoning process, but their mortality was extremely high. By July 1711 only three hundred of the original nine hundred Palatine settlers had survived.[11] And of those three hundred, many remained deathly ill into the fall of 1711.[12] Still, the Palatines persisted and composed a portion of the population of New Bern, a new settlement that stood at the junction of the Trent and Neuse rivers. The diseases that the Palatines brought were yet more aftershocks to North Carolina's Algonquians and Tuscaroras, whose own demographic decline fueled their discontent with the growing European presence.

Such discontent led to the Tuscarora War (1711–13). By 1711 the Algonquians had become more enmeshed with their Tuscarora allies. Both had lost members to disease; many Algonquians moved farther inland, taking up residence with the Tuscaroras; and intermarriages had occurred. By 1710 an anti-English Tuscarora headman, known as Hancock, had begun to draw a following of Tuscaroras and Algonquians. Before taking up arms against the English, though, Hancock's faction investigated the possibility of relocating to land claimed by the colony of Pennsylvania and becoming affiliated with the Five Nations Iroquois.[13] Not surprisingly, the messages they sent to their northern allies expressed fear of becoming enslaved. Seneca and Shawnee representatives sent wampum belts to Pennsylvania officials on behalf of Tuscarora children, requesting "that Room to sport & Play without danger of Slavery, might be allowed them." They also gave wampum belts on behalf of young Tuscarora men who wanted to hunt "without fear of Death or Slavery."[14] Indigenous peoples of the Southeast had been well aware of what happened to smaller communities that could not defend themselves from enemy attacks; they were gobbled up by more powerful groups trying to maintain their own numbers, or they were imprisoned and sold to English traders. The Tuscaroras had, of course, been involved in slave raids and the sale of captives to Virginians since the 1650s, but by the early 1700s, Native power had shifted southwestward into the hands of Siouans and Cherokees who occasionally took captives from coastal Carolina. To make matters worse, Algonquians had seen Englishmen kidnap and enslave some of their tribal members over several years before the outbreak of the conflict.[15] Despite the insecurities that came with their own demographic decline, the Tuscaroras and the Algonquians stayed in North Carolina into the summer of 1711, when tensions erupted into war.

On September 22, 1711, Tuscarora and Algonquian raiding parties descended on settlers who had come to live too uncomfortably close to them.

One-hundred twenty English, Swiss, and Palatine colonists were killed within a few hours, dozens of others were captured, and hundreds sought shelter behind the walls that guarded the towns of Bath and New Bern. Many survivors also fled south toward Cape Fear or north toward Virginia. Not all the Tuscaroras joined in such raids; a collection of villages closer to the Virginia border declared their neutrality. The majority of warriors who composed the initial raiding parties were in fact Algonquians, whose communities had suffered most severely from colonialism over the last ten years. By driving out the invading Europeans, they certainly hoped that they could reverse their misfortunes.[16] Tragically, however, the decision of Algonquians and Tuscaroras to fight had an effect opposite of preserving their people from colonialism's biological destruction.

North Carolina called on its wealthier and more powerful sister colonies for help. Virginia offered its Native allies, including neutral Tuscaroras, six blankets for every scalp from a male combatant and "the usual price of slaves for each woman and child delivered captives," but the Old Dominion refused to send its own men to fight North Carolina's battles.[17] Instead, South Carolina, with its heavy appetite for slaves, came to the rescue. In October 1711 the South Carolina Assembly authorized one of its leading men, the Port Royal planter John Barnwell, to assemble and lead an army of "warlike Indians" to fight against the Tuscaroras and the Algonquians. It took several months to amass that army, but by the end of January 1712, Barnwell and 32 other Englishmen stood alongside 495 indigenous warriors on the banks of the Neuse River. Carolina's allies consisted of Yamasees, Apalachees, and Yuchis from the Savannah Basin as well as Siouans from the Coastal Plain and the Piedmont.[18] The Tuscaroras and the Algonquians presented a vigorous defense against Barnwell's forces. They had no less than nine fortified towns, and even some of their women took up arms and fought to their deaths. On January 30, Barnwell's army took the first of their enemy's towns, but shortly after their victory the majority of Carolina's indigenous allies departed. Only one company of 148 Natives, mostly Yamasees, stuck with Barnwell. After retreating to the coast and regrouping through the remainder of February, Barnwell set out in early March, found Hancock's Town, and began to lay siege. The town had an impressive defensive structure with high walls and a surrounding trench. It also contained dozens of white and black prisoners, whom Tuscarora and Algonquian warriors had taken in earlier raids on English settlements and whom they threatened to kill if Barnwell did not retreat. The English commander agreed to back off on the condition that Tuscaroras and Algonquians appear at treaty negotiations within ten days, but when they did not show up within the allotted time, Barnwell's forces again descended on Han-cock's Town. From April 7 to 17, Barnwell's forces kept their enemies sur-rounded, eventually wore them down, and forced them to sign a punitive treaty in which they gave up their claim to much land around Pamlico Sound. The English commander wanted more for his efforts, however. The Tuscaroras and the Corees disagreed over the terms of the treaty, leading Barnwell to lament that he did not have enough provisions on hand to "oblige ye Tuscaroras to have delivered all the [Corees] for slaves."[19]

Enslavement was only one of the threats that the Tuscaroras and the Algo-nquians faced. Barnwell's invasion placed all indigenous participants in a highly vulnerable state with regard to infectious diseases. Multiple germs circulated among the North Carolina residents through the fall of 1711. In December 1711 a "pestilential distemper" that took "away great numbers" inhibited the North Carolina governor from assembling his council and prevented the assem-bly from meeting.[20] It was probably from captives taken from an infected settler population that Tuscaroras and Algonquians contracted a deadly disease. When Barnwell's forces entered Hancock's Fort in April, they found a ghastly sight. "There was a good number of sick and wounded and a very great mortality which with their nastiness produced such stink," Barnwell complained.[21] Barn-well and his men themselves became infected, possibly during their negotiations with the Tuscaroras in March. Barnwell reported that sometime before March 25 he and "several whites" became seriously ill as did "a great number" of his Na-tive troops "of whom 4 or 5 died."[22] What the disease was is not entirely clear. In his 1737 book, *The Natural History of North Carolina,* John Brickell claimed that smallpox had ravaged Natives during the Tuscarora War, and the virus was known to be in circulation in South Carolina at the time.[23] But one would think that Barnwell would have mentioned smallpox specifically if his enemies and al-lies had succumbed to that particular disease. At least one lethal disease and per-haps more were at work. Regardless of the identities of the germ or germs in-volved, the Tuscaroras and the Algonquians suffered the most. Huddled in their forts and forced to live amid unsanitary conditions, they were vulnerable to a va-riety of diseases including typhus, a scourge that would have proliferated among the Tuscaroras and the Algonquians if carried to them by infected European captives. Whatever the disease involved, famine only added to their problems. For those Natives there was no hunting during the 1711–12 season; hickory nuts had to serve as their main food source, but gathering these nuts put them at risk of being spotted by Barnwell's slave-hunting troops. The deadly synergism of germs and slave raids thus produced a tragic outcome for the residents of Han-

cock's Town as it had for many other indigenous communities in a region ravaged by English colonialism.

Barnwell's campaign did not end the Tuscarora War. Following the peace
agreement after the fall of Hancock's Town, the surviving Algonquians were still
being hunted down and either killed or enslaved. The governors of Virginia and
North Carolina blamed Barnwell's forces, claiming that they had taken nearly
two hundred Algonquian women and children on their departure.[24] The original leader of the Palatine settlers also charged Barnwell and his "tributary savages" for luring their victims to meet with them under a false pretense and then
enslaving them.[25] North Carolina settlers, though, were just as likely to commit
the deeds since they believed that the Natives had been insufficiently punished
for killing over 130 settlers.[26] Moreover, Governor Hyde of North Carolina
later bragged that his forces had killed or enslaved between three hundred and
four hundred of their enemies.[27] Regardless of who conducted the attack, such
actions inspired retaliation by the aggrieved peoples and their Tuscarora allies.
During the summer and fall of 1712, North Carolinians were embroiled in war
again. As during the previous year, they were hardly in a position to fight. Another round of fever afflicted the colony, leading to the death of Governor Hyde
in September. His successor, Thomas Pollock, complained that his colony was in
"great poverty" and "sickness" and again appealed to his neighbors for help.[28]
Lured by their sister colony's promise of three to four thousand slaves, South
Carolina once more answered the call for help.[29] This time Barnwell declined to
lead. He had been shot in the leg and probably doubted that his efforts would be
rewarded.[30] South Carolina called on James Moore Jr., the son of the notorious
slave trader by the same name, to lead the final assault on the Tuscaroras and the
Algonquians. By March 1713 Moore had assembled an army of 107 Englishmen
and approximately 760 indigenous warriors, which included 310 Cherokees and
650 individuals from several other tribes.[31] The Tuscaroras rebounded somewhat from their ordeal of the preceding year. They gained the support of some of
their formerly neutral brethren as well as some members of the Iroquois Confederacy. With the aid of artillery, though, Moore's army burned the fortified
town of Nohoroco, delivering a knockout punch that ended in approximately
900 individuals being killed or captured. Following their victory all but 180 of
Moore's Native allies departed, taking an untold number of captives with them.
Moore and his reduced force stuck around through the summer, helping to
round up refugees and bring an end to Native resistance.[32] Those Tuscaroras and
Algonquians who survived did so by joining the neutral Tuscaroras in Virginia
or heading north to join the Iroquois Confederacy. By the end of the year,

coastal Carolina had been depopulated of its original Tuscarora and Algonquian inhabitants. These remarkable peoples had somehow managed to persist in the area after the Great Southeastern Smallpox Epidemic, but they could not withstand the aftershocks. As the victims of colonialism and its germs, the Tuscaroras and the Algonquians decided to take action, but unfortunately English retaliation against them only intensified their experience with the Atlantic world's deadliest diseases.

As one examines what happened to other groups on the Great Southeastern Smallpox Epidemic's path, one continues to see peoples ravaged by that event's devastating aftershocks. The Tuscaroras' immediate neighbors to the southwest, the various Siouan-speaking peoples of the Carolina Piedmont, indeed faced even more destruction following their experience with smallpox. Again John Lawson's 1701 observations provide a starting point for assessing the damage. The English traveler found the greatest concentration of Siouans along the Wateree and Catawba rivers. Siouan communities had been there before the European invasion and then attracted other groups that had been shattered by slave raids and the Great Southeastern Smallpox Epidemic. The English would increasingly refer to them as Catawbas during the first decade of the eighteenth century, but Lawson instead listed the Catawbas as one group living among others including the Waterees, the Waxhaws, the Esaws, and the Sugerees. The English adventurer also located other allied Siouan groups—the Saponies, the Tutelos, and the Keyauwees—on the nearby forks of the Yadkin River. These various Siouan peoples could remember having greater numbers in the past. The Catawbas told the English trader James Adair in the mid-eighteenth century that their tribe alone could muster up to fifteen hundred fighting men when South Carolina was in its "infant state."[33] By 1701 the number of Catawbas and their neighbors had plummeted, forcing them to coalesce together to remain formidable to their enemies. Still, this coalesced society impressed John Lawson. The Esaws, the name with which he collectively referred to them, comprised "a very large nation containing many thousand People." The English traveler furthermore described them as "powerful" and as having a "thick" collection of towns.[34]

A comparison of Lawson's description with an official count that South Carolina officials made of the colony's Native allies in 1715 illuminates even more decline among Piedmont Siouans after 1701. John Barnwell compiled this census by perusing the journals of other South Carolina officials and correcting their figures based on his own knowledge. The census, of course, has its problems, which makes it a difficult piece of evidence to use. The accuracy of the numbers varied from group to group. South Carolinians gave what appear to be fairly accurate counts of their allies to the south—the Yamasees, the Apalachicolas, the Apalachees, the Shawnees, the Lower Creeks or Ochesees, and the Upper Creeks ("Abikaws," "Tallibooses," and "Alabamas")—whose numbers were exact and divided into the four categories of men, women, boys, and girls. On the other hand, the numbers for the Catawbas were rounded off and divided into only two categories, "men" and "women and children." Thus, South Carolinians had a vaguer conception of population dynamics among the Catawbas than they did for the groups that had a longer and more important role in their trading network. Nevertheless, Barnwell's estimate gives a glimpse of the Siouan population that stands in stark contrast to earlier assessments. Barnwell listed seven Catawba towns with 570 men and 900 women and children that South Carolinians had counted in 1715, indicating severe depopulation. The 570 warriors belonging to the polyglot assemblage of Catawbas, Esaws, Waterees, Sugarees, Tutelos, Keyauwees, and Saxapahaws who had moved to the Catawba Valley between 1701 and 1715 paled in comparison to the 1,500 warriors that the Catawbas alone could mobilize when South Carolina was in its "infant state."[35] A group numbering only 1,470 total individuals, moreover, did not match Lawson's depiction of a "powerful" people numbering "many thousand" and having a "thick" collection of towns, indicating that between 1701 and 1715 epidemiological aftershocks had a devastating impact on Piedmont Siouans as well.

The Catawbas and their affiliates were indeed highly vulnerable to infection and mortality from epidemics between 1701 and 1715. Their location within both Virginia's and South Carolina's trade networks made them susceptible to the variety of germs that circulated in those colonies. Virginians had dominated the trade with Piedmont groups up to 1707, when South Carolina's assembly passed an act declaring its jurisdiction over such trade. In that year Carolina officials confiscated over fifteen hundred deerskins that Virginia traders had stored among the Sugarees. Carolinians then rushed in to take over the Siouan trade. Virginians did not give up and continued to trade with Siouans and even persuaded the queen's Privy Council to declare Carolina's monopoly illegal. From 1708 to 1715 Virginians and Carolinians competed fiercely for the Siouan trade, bringing the Catawbas and their allies even more fully into the Atlantic world's swirl of goods and germs. It is not unreasonable to assume that at least one of the lethal pathogens that afflicted Virginia and South Carolina during this particularly deadly period made its way into the Catawba Valley, decimating Native communities. The pathogen responsible for the 1708 outbreak among the Tuscaroras, for example, should be suspected of spreading along with the

Table 2. A census of South Carolina's Native allies, 1715 (see p. 252 for notes)

Miles and direction from Charles Town		Villages	Men	Women	Boys	Girls	Total
Upper Path							
Yamasees	90 SW	10	413	345	234	228	1,220
Apalachicolas	130 SW	2	64	71	42	37	214
Apalachees	140 W	4	275	248	65	55	643
Shawnees	150 W	3	67	116	20	30	233
Yuchis	180 WNW	2	130	270 women and children			400
Ochesees	250 W&N	10	731	837	417	421	2,406
Abicas	440 W	15	502	578	366	327	1,773
Tallapoosas	390 WSW	13	636	710	511	486	2,343
Alabamas	430 WSW	4	214	276	161	119	770
Chickasaws	640 W	6	700	1,200 women and children			1,900
Cherokees							
Upper	450 NW	19	900	980	400	480	
Middle	390 NW	30	2,500	2,000	950	900	11,210
Lower	320 NW	11	600	620	400	480	
Catawbas (Piedmont Siouans)	200 NW	7	570	900 women and children			1,470
Coastal Plain groups							
Saras	170 N	1	140	370 women and children			510
Waccamaws	100 NE	4	210	400 women and children			610
Cape Fears	200 NE	5	76	130 women and children			206
Santees	70 N	2	43	60 women and children			125
Congerees	120 N	1	22				
Winyaws	80 NE	1	36	70 women and children			106
Sewees	60 NE	1		men, women, and children			57
Etiwans	mixed with English Settlements	1	80	160 women and children			240
Cusabos		5	95	200 women and children			295
Total							26,731

flow of trade goods into the Piedmont, while the plethora of diseases striking South Carolina in the summer and fall of 1711 should as well. In November 1711 the Anglican minister Gideon Johnston, in fact, exclaimed, "N[e]ver was there a more sickly or fatall Season than this." He added, "[T]he small Pox, Pestilential ffeavers, Pleurisies, and fflex's have destroyed great numbers here of all Sorts, both Whites, Blacks, and Indians, and these distempers still rage to an uncommon degree."[36] Johnston did not specify which "Indians" had come down with the assorted diseases, but given their growing importance in South Carolina's trade network, Piedmont Siouans certainly had a good chance to become infected.

Participation in the Tuscarora War also provided a dangerous opportunity for Siouans to suffer from epidemics. The assemblage of hundreds of men from various places carried a great potential to spread dangerous germs. Men from Piedmont villages joined up with Englishmen, Africans, and Natives from the germ-ridden Low Country. The slow pace of such mobilization, in fact, suggests that epidemics raging at the time inhibited Barnwell's efforts. The assembly authorized the mobilization of an army of its Native allies in October 1711, but it was not until sometime in January 1712 that Barnwell's forces crossed the Pee Dee into North Carolina. His army, moreover, disintegrated shortly after his campaign began. Before arriving on the Neuse River on January 28, Barnwell reported that a "great desertion" of his Native troops had occurred. After their initial assault on the Tuscaroras and the Algonquians, hundreds more departed by February 5, leaving Barnwell with only a company of some 158 warriors from the Savannah Valley. Barnwell did not disclose the reasons for such desertion, but with various diseases rampant in South Carolina, disease should be suspected. It is plausible that at least one deadly germ then in circulation in South Carolina made its way through the assembled forces and caused warriors to strike out for home rather than remain with their infected comrades. If Barnwell's troops did not carry serious diseases with them, they still had a good chance of contracting diseases from the Tuscarora and Algonquian prisoners they took. The Siouans who remained with Barnwell during his initial assault ended up with most of the slaves and carried them back with them to their home villages, where any subsequent outbreak went unrecorded. Barnwell and his Yamasee company after all did become gravely ill from a germ that they likely contracted from the Tuscaroras. The Tuscarora War, thus, was a recipe for epidemiological disaster for a wide array of Natives, including Piedmont Siouans, whose numbers in South Carolina's 1715 census were recorded much lower than what John Lawson's 1701 observations suggested.

Any experience the Siouans had with diseases was exacerbated by their continuing struggle against the Five Nations Iroquois. Lawson found Siouans living in fortified villages to protect themselves from their northern enemies. Unfortunately, this arrangement forced Siouans to carry higher pathogen loads and to confront novel germs in a weakened state. The intense state of war escalated even more after 1701. The Five Nations concluded a general peace with their long-standing French and indigenous enemies in Canada, upper Ohio, and the Great Lakes region. This allowed them to send more warriors to the south to find captives.[37] The situation grew more complex in 1707, when a group of Shawnees fled the Savannah River to seek protection with the Iroquois. South Carolina officials interpreted this as a revolt and enlisted the help of the Catawbas, who ended up killing or enslaving several Shawnees. Late in the year 130 Shawnees and Senecas conducted a devastating raid on the Sugarees, who lost 45 women and children.[38] Such raids did not abate, and some Siouans choose to flee. Some Saponies, Tutelos, and Keyauwees removed closer to Virginia; in 1708 thirty Saponie men and their families petitioned the government of that colony to become a tributary community.[39] Some, of course, remained and moved in with their Siouan kinsmen on the Catawba River, but in evacuating the Yadkin, the Catawbas no longer had a buffer against Iroquois raids. Such raids increased because of the Tuscarora War. The inclusion of Tuscarora and Algonquian refugees in the Iroquois Confederacy added a further motive for the now Six Nations to attack their southern enemies. Every Catawba woman and child taken by Iroquois raiders served as a devastating blow to a people trying to survive amid the ever-increasing influence of colonialism and its germs.

Amid such trauma even more coalescence occurred in the Catawba Valley. One group that fled to the Catawba was the Saxapahaws, whose story illustrates the plummeting fortunes of Siouans after the Great Southeastern Smallpox Epidemic. The Saxapahaws, along with their neighbors the Enos, the Shakoris, and the Ocaneechis, were part of a Siouan polyglot that had drifted around the Piedmont since the days of Bacon's Rebellion. By 1711 these once numerous peoples had dwindled into tiny communities living a precarious existence. The Tuscarora War undoubtedly confronted them with hard choices. The Tuscaroras had been their allies, trading rum and other Virginia goods to them and offering them protection from Iroquois raids. The Saxapahaws, however, rebuked Tuscarora efforts to enlist their support against the English, and as a result the Tuscaroras attacked and killed sixteen of them.[40] Not wanting to be seen as an enemy of the English and thus subject to enslavement, the remaining Siouans between the Catawbas and the Virginia border fled. Some went to the Old Dominion to become a tributary community, while others sought to avoid such a status and live a more independent existence among other Natives.[41] The Saxapahaws sought the latter option but did so in way that acknowledged their dependence on a European colonial power. In April 1712 leaders of the war-weary and diminished peoples appeared before South Carolina officials and requested permission to settle among the "northern Indians," a catchall phrase for Natives who lived north of Charles Town.[42] They received that permission and ultimately wound up on the Catawba River as a small village attached to the Sugarees.[43] Back in 1697 the Saxapahaws had had the audacity to refuse the South Carolina Commons House of Assembly's request to surrender its warriors who had participated in the murder of a prominent Carolinian, but after fifteen years of experience with colonialism and its deadly microbes, they had been reduced to such a level that they felt the need to ask the English where they could live.[44] With its violence and germs, the Tuscarora War thus accelerated the further concentration and amalgamation of Piedmont Siouans into the collective body that the English referred to as the Catawbas in their 1715 census.

Farther along on the Great Southeastern Smallpox Epidemic's path, the Catawbas' immediate neighbors to the west, the Cherokees, also suffered from aftershock epidemics. As with the Piedmont Siouans, the Cherokees directed the bulk of their trading activities toward Virginia at the time smallpox spread in the 1690s and then gradually became more involved with South Carolina in the first decade of the eighteenth century. In 1708 the governor of South Carolina, Nathaniel Johnson, characterized the Cherokees as a "numerous people but very lazy" and claimed to have inconsiderable trade with the mountaineers. He estimated the Cherokees to have sixty villages that could field five thousand men.[45] Cherokees, of course, were not lazy but instead went to war against tribes to the north and the west rather than engage in Carolina's organized slave raids against Spanish- and French-allied groups to the south. Carolinians, though, did recognize their strategic position. At the same time that the governor of South Carolina declared the Cherokees lazy, Thomas Nairne reported back to London that the Cherokees were "now Entirely Subjuect" to the English and were "Extreamly well scituate to keep of any Incursions which Either ye Illinois or any other french Indians may think of making into Carolina."[46] Thereafter, the Cherokees became more important within Carolina's trade network. By 1711 several Carolinian traders had taken up residence in the southern Appalachians, and in their many journeys back and forth from Charles Town, those traders employed parties of Cherokees to serve as porters, guards, hunters, and guides. Communications among the independent and disparate Cherokee towns, moreover, escalated as trading parties ventured from village to village carrying a high volume of goods in exchange for deerskins. By 1713 the Cherokees were certainly major players in the Southeast. Over three hundred of their warriors accompanied James Moore Jr. in his campaign against the Tuscaroras and the Algonquians.[47]

With the escalation of their involvement with South Carolina, the Cherokees' vulnerability to epidemics increased. As with smallpox in the 1690s, tracking aftershock epidemics into the Appalachian Mountains cannot be done with certainty, but some evidence suggests that the Cherokees paid an epidemiological price for their trade and intercourse with South Carolina. In the 1715 census John Barnwell downgraded his colony's 1708 estimate of the Cherokees by one thousand warriors. On the surface the change in numbers may appear to be simply the result of the English acquiring a more accurate knowledge of the mountaineers, but given the rampant spread of germs throughout the Carolinas during the Tuscarora War, Carolinians may have heard that the Cherokees had a recent experience with disease. Cherokee oral history supports such a view. In a narration of his people's conflicts with the Creeks, Charles Hicks referred to smallpox striking the Cherokees before the outbreak of the Yamasee War in 1715. "It must have been before this war," Hicks claimed, "that the small pox had been introduced in the nation by some of the visitant Cherokees from the seashore." Perhaps those "visitant" Cherokees were part of a trading party that visited Charles Town sometime between May 1711 and March 1712 when smallpox was rampant there. Or perhaps smallpox had lingered within the Native or newcomer population into 1713, when Cherokee participation in the Tuscarora War resulted in their warriors returning home with the virus either in their own bloodstreams or in those of their captives. John Brickell thought of the Cherokees as part of North Carolina's Native population; perhaps he was including them in his reference to smallpox being widespread during the Tuscarora War. Whatever the source of the virus, it hit all but two Cherokee towns and proved most destructive to the Valley settlements, which included villages along the rather remote Hiwassee River and its tributaries. There it destroyed "mostly whole towns" and in "some whole families falling victims."[48] Hicks's reference, of course, remains vague, but by indicating that the Valley towns suffered the most, his account suggests that some Cherokee divisions had prior exposure to the terrible virus and suffered fewer casualties. It is conceivable that in 1711 or 1712 smallpox found the few villages that had escaped its wrath in the 1690s and those villages were the most remote of the Cherokee Nation, whose more exposed communities—those closest to South Carolina and Virginia—had partially immunized populations from prior exposure.

Understanding the timing of the Cherokees' first experiences with smallpox presents a difficult problem, but epidemics affected the Cherokees in a much simpler way than they affected other groups. Living in the Appalachian highlands protected the Cherokees from the multiplicity of germs that circulated in European colonies between 1698 and 1712. Smallpox, of course, followed the course of trade and arrived in Cherokee villages, while measles, if responsible for one of the "distempers" or "plagues," also stood a chance of being introduced into the highlands. The Cherokees' experience, though, certainly did not compare to that of the Tuscaroras and the Algonquians, who faced not only a wide range of diseases but also the invasion of their land by settlers and livestock, a brutal war waged against them, and the capture and enslavement of thousands of their women and children. To be sure, Iroquois raids led communities on the northern frontier of the Cherokees' homeland to maintain fortified, compact settlements. Such arrangements led to an elevated pathogen load, but unlike Natives in the Coastal Plain, the Cherokees were not forced to live next to a newcomer population of settlers, slaves, and livestock, whose presence made the land even more saturated with malaria, typhoid, and other endemic diseases. That the Cherokees emerged as the most powerful group in Carolina's trade network by the second decade of the eighteenth century was not because they escaped the Columbian Exchange altogether—their trade and intercourse with Virginia and then South Carolina indeed put them in a vulnerable state. Instead, the Cherokees ascended because colonialism had not yet engulfed them and transformed their experience with the Atlantic world's most dangerous germs into the biological nightmare that plagued many others in the Southeast.

Aftershock epidemics, indeed, had a much more devastating impact as one retraces the Great Southeastern Smallpox Epidemic's path through the Carolina Low Country. With multiple outbreaks occurring on the heels of smallpox, Natives within the Coastal Plain from the Cape Fear River to Charles Town had an experience that closely resembled the model for virgin-soil epidemics that Alfred Crosby proposes. They were subject to the same epidemics that laid many of their European and African neighbors in their graves between 1698 and 1712. Unlike the colonial population, though, indigenous peoples could not replenish their lost numbers with replacements from distant continents. Warriors from the various Low Country tribes participated in Barnwell's campaign and likely returned home with prisoners, but such captives could not replace the number of people that diseases associated with the Tuscarora War killed. To make matters worse, Low Country Natives repeatedly saw their women and children kidnapped by interior raiders and English slave dealers, thus inhibiting their ability to recover. As they rapidly became a minority group in their own homeland, many Low Country Natives fled. In 1710 the Anglican missionary Francis Le Jau reported that "free Indians" near his prosperous Goose Creek parishioners no longer had any elders among them who could remember the meaning of their tribal ceremonies and that many had simply left their homeland to go "further up in the country."[49] Le Jau added that such flight came because of the ill treatment that traders had heaped upon them, but it is doubtful that indigenous peoples would have put up with such treatment had they not been weakened by colonialism and its germs. The Anglican missionary reported one year later that many of the nations listed on old maps still persisted, but "some [were] removed North of [the English] through discouragement, their Numbers decrease[d] very much."[50] Such a decision, of course, did not come lightly. Distinct languages and customs separated groups from one another as did a history of enmity, thus making it abhorrent for some to move to the territory of the Catawbas, the Cherokees, or the Creeks, where more powerful communities would threaten their independence and distinctive identity. Natives of the Low Country thus faced great anxiety as they chose between two unsatisfactory options. "As for our free Indians," Francis Le Jau wrote amid a devastating epidemic in February 1712, "they goe their own way and bring their Children like themselves with little conversation among us but when they want something from us, I generally P[er]ceive something Cloudy in their looks."[51] Le Jau could not offer a reason for such discontent, but at the time he and his parishioners were in mourning for the loss of many of their own people from the multiple epidemics that had recently afflicted them. Given the vulnerability of Carolina's "free Indians" to infection and mortality, Le Jau was likely observing a people in mourning from the deaths of many of their own and a people facing hard choices that disease and depopulation had forced them to make.

Native communities did persist in the Low Country despite the repeated aftershocks they faced and the flight of their peoples to the interior, but their numbers had fallen dramatically because of English colonialism. In 1715 the Low Country's original inhabitants included two groups of "settlement Indians": the Etiwans, whose one community had 240 individuals; and the Cusabos, whose five communities contained 295 individuals. Both groups were certainly heterogeneous collections of the once numerous peoples who inhabited the various sounds, inlets, and islands along the south Atlantic coast. Other groups indigenous to the Low Country were not listed yet as "settlement Indians" but faced the looming prospect of having such a classification. The Low Country population consisted of four towns of Waccamaws with a total population of

610 people; five towns of Cape Fears with a total of 206; three towns of Congarees and Santees with a total population of 125; one town of Winyaws with a total population of 106; and one town of Sewees with a total of 57. These 1,639 individuals, whose largely Siouan ancestors once inhabited the Coastal Plain from the Edisto to the Neuse River, represented the survivors of peoples who had been depopulated by as much as 90 percent. The settlement of some Siouans known as the Cheraws or Saras below the fall line of the Pee Dee did very little to reverse the demographic catastrophe that had happened in the wake of English colonialism. These refugees from the upheavals of the Tuscarora War added 510 people, keeping the 2,149 Native residents of the Coastal Plain north of Charles Town a minority facing a colonial population that had increased to 8,600 Africans and 5,600 Europeans.[52]

In summary, the series of epidemiological aftershocks that reverberated from South Carolina and Virginia achieved their deadliest potential among Native residents of the Coastal Plain. By 1715 a myriad of different disease-depleted communities had either fled the Coastal Plain, become small enclaves that the English referred to as "settlement Indians," or tragically disappeared. The Tuscaroras and the Algonquians especially suffered from the combined impact of colonialism and its germs and attempted to reverse their declining fortunes by ridding their land of the growing number of European newcomers. Their decision only made them more vulnerable to the diseases that those newcomers introduced into the region. Piedmont Siouans and Appalachian Cherokees too experienced aftershocks, especially as their trade and intercourse with South Carolina escalated during the first decade of the eighteenth century and culminated with their participation in the Tuscarora War. Infected from diseases coming from multiple directions, Piedmont Siouans became severely depopulated, leading to further population movements and mergers that resulted in the development of the Catawbas. Being located in the remote valleys of the Appalachian highlands, the Cherokees were vulnerable to smallpox yet protected from the multiple infections that plagued their Low Country neighbors. If any people had a virgin-soil experience with smallpox in 1711–12, it was those Cherokee villages that the virus had missed during the 1690s, but mortality rates, while severe, were not as great as other southeastern groups, whose bodies became increasingly unhealthy as English colonialism engulfed them. By 1715, then, the Great Southeastern Smallpox Epidemic and its aftershocks had dramatically transformed the social landscape between Virginia and South Carolina. Up to 90 percent of the Coastal Plain and the Piedmont's original indigenous population had been swept away by the germs and violence associated with English colonialism, while only the Cherokees had significantly large numbers.

Rebuilding the Upper Path

To the south along the Upper Path trade route from Charles Town to the Mississippi, Native communities also faced aftershocks that followed the Great Southeastern Smallpox Epidemic. Carolina's southern allies—those Savannah Basin groups (Yamasees, Shawnees, and Yuchis), Lower Creeks (Apalachicolas and Ocheses), Upper Creeks (Tallapoosas, Abeikas, and Alabamas), and Chickasaws—had suffered tremendous upheaval from smallpox in the 1690s. These Upper Path peoples lost numerous individuals, were forced to consolidate their villages, and then faced another wave of diseases soon after the Great Southeastern Smallpox Epidemic. Some of these diseases came from the opposite direction than smallpox did in the 1690s. By raiding Spanish- and French-allied tribes, South Carolina's Native partners made themselves vulnerable to infection from the outbreaks that struck the Gulf Coast in 1699, 1703, 1704, 1706, and 1708. Because those epidemics had an even more devastating impact on victims of slave raids, whose fates will be discussed in the next section, the volume of slaves sent across the Upper Path substantially declined, thus leading many of the colony's southern allies to fall deeply into debt. Disease-depleted Upper Path communities, moreover, added to the tensions between themselves and their Carolinian partners by incorporating remnant groups and adopting captives whom the English wanted to take as slaves.

On the eastern terminus of the Upper Path, the Yamasees had a disastrous experience with colonialism and its germs after the Great Southeastern Smallpox Epidemic. Since assembling in the Carolina Low Country between the Combahee and Savannah rivers in the 1680s, the Yamasees had been heavily involved in trading slaves with their English neighbors. Severe population loss in the late 1690s did not stop such trade. Yamasee raids into Florida continued and merged with the larger imperial goals of the English. During Queen Anne's War (1702–13), England faced both Spain and France, allowing South Carolinians to merge their desire for slaves with the goals of their mother country by organizing attacks on the Spanish mission system and on the French-allied Choctaws. In August 1702, for example, hundreds of Yamasees joined Governor James Moore Sr.'s invading force of five hundred whites, who attacked St. Augustine. Moore failed miserably in his attempt to take the impenetrable Castillo de San Marcos, which guarded Spanish Florida's capital, but his forces did manage to capture Native slaves.[53] The Yamasees were particularly helpful since they had once been allies of the Spanish and knew the best places to hunt for captives. The Yamasees returned with more slaves than their English allies, leading to disputes between the two over possession of the captives.[54] The Yamasees certainly wanted to sell many of their slaves, but they also kept a number of Native Floridians among them. They persuaded two Christian communities of Guales and Yoas to incorporate with them near the Savannah, a strategy that undoubtedly helped the already heterogeneous Yamasees regain a portion of the numbers they had lost from smallpox.[55]

Still, slave raids and intercourse with the English made the Yamasees vulnerable to Columbian Exchange diseases. John Stewart, for example, reported in a 1711 letter that he was among the Yamasees at an earlier time when they returned home from their enemy's country and suffered from a "raging pestilence." Stewart dates this episode in his cryptic fashion to twelve years after a Spanish invasion had burned Yamasee villages.[56] Since such an invasion occurred in 1686, the outbreak would have occurred in 1698, making it possible that the eccentric Scotsman was referring to smallpox, which was then ravaging the Carolina Low Country and spreading toward the Mississippi. But Stewart's choice of "raging pestilence" rather than smallpox and his vague identification of the epidemic's timing suggest that he was referring to one of the Great Southeastern Smallpox Epidemic's aftershocks rather than to that event itself. The raging pestilence could have been a result of the 1699, the 1703, or the 1704 epidemic that struck the Gulf Coast. It also could have been a result of the Yamasees participation in the defense of Charles Town during the summer of 1706. At that time yellow fever ravaged South Carolina's capital as the English fought off an attempted Spanish and French invasion. Carolina's enemies, in fact, learned of the epidemic and chose to attack when they did because they reasoned that rural dwellers would stay away from the pestilential port and leave it ripe for the taking. The English, though, held on to Charles Town with the help of its Native allies, and as a result, both suffered terrible casualties from the disease.[57] James Moore Sr. perished as did many other English inhabitants and their "friends."[58] Yamasee warriors were the colony's most dependable allies and likely were among those friends. Yellow fever may have also spread to Yamasee villages during that deadly summer. One English account claimed that the disease spread "throughout the whole province," suggesting that other coastal areas such as Port Royal, around which Yamasee villages were located, succumbed to the disease.[59] Whether infected during the 1699, the 1703, the 1704, or the 1706 epidemic or during more than one of those deadly episodes, the Yamasees paid a heavy epidemiological price for their alliance with the English.

That price became even more severe with the Yamasees participation in the Tuscarora War. They stuck with Barnwell's forces to the end of his campaign in the spring 1712, and it was from within their ranks that the four or five recorded deaths from disease occurred.[60] Surviving Yamasees, although having to travel a significantly longer distance than Carolina's Siouan allies, still had the potential to carry back nasty germs with them, either in their own bloodstreams or the bloodstreams of their Tuscarora and Algonquian prisoners. The speed with which the Yamasees returned to their homes was, in fact, expedited because many of them traveled by boat.[61] There is no way to determine whether Yamasee warriors transmitted whatever it was that had made them sick in North Carolina to their home villages, but about the same time that Barnwell's forces and captives returned to South Carolina, his fellow colonists grew alarmed about the threat of yet another epidemic to hit their disease-ravaged colony. South Carolina did not need another round with disease after facing four straight years of epidemics, and so on May 21, 1712, Thomas Nairne brought a bill before the Commons House of Assembly that eventually became "An Act for the More Effectual Preventing the Spreading of Contagious Distempers."[62] The Yamasees especially did not need another round of infectious diseases. In 1713 Francis Le Jau claimed that all of South Carolina's "allies and neighbors" had decreased and pointed especially to the Yamasees as a declining people. The Yamasees, Le Jau claimed, were "formerly very numerous but by degrees they are come to very little they could muster 800 fighting men and now they are hardly 400."[63] Barnwell's 1715 census reaffirmed Le Jau's estimations. The Port Royal planter counted 413 men among a total of 1,220 Yamasees.[64] Considering that the Yamasees adopted substantial number of captives and even incorporated two communities of Guales who fled from Florida in 1702, their losses were likely in excess of the 50 percent that Le Jau indicated. The Anglican missionary claimed that warfare was to blame for such losses, but he was only partly correct. Many Yamasee warriors who engaged in English campaigns did not come home because they died from disease, while many Yamasee women and children perished in their villages that lay near epidemic-ravaged Carolinian settlements.

Also, Yamasee fatality rates from any Columbian Exchange diseases must have steadily climbed as they faced increasing disruptions to their disease ecology. As late as 1707 English settlements around Port Royal were located on the Sea Islands, but in the following several years, the English expanded inland. From their African slaves Carolinians developed an expertise in rice cultivation and consequently realized their long-sought goal of reaping profits from staple commodity production.[65] Yamasee land was well suited for such production, and English planters embarked on an ambitious project of damming streams and flooding the land. The Yamasees understandably became wary of the English. They complained of livestock invading their crops and asked Carolina officials many times if they intended to take their land.[66] Adding to such anxiety were the epidemiological consequences of living in the changed environment. Not only did they face the same barrage of diseases that struck their English and African neighbors, but they were also forced to carry heavier pathogen loads from malaria, typhoid, and other endemic diseases. Much like the Tuscaroras and the Algonquians in 1711, the Yamasees reached a critical point in their history in 1715, when colonialism and its germs threatened to overwhelm them.

Following the course of the Great Southeastern Smallpox Epidemic from the Yamasees up the Savannah Valley, one recognizes that germs and slave raids produced a fluid situation in what was already a highly dynamic area of Native settlement. In 1704 another nonlocal people, Apalachees from northern Florida, moved into the former buffer zone and helped repeople the Upper Path, which the Great Southeastern Smallpox Epidemic had ravaged. Ironically, it was their escape from smallpox in the 1690s that heightened the vulnerability of the nearly eight thousand Apalachees to the raids that ultimately forced them from their homeland.[67] Smallpox had taken away vast numbers from smaller and unarmed groups, leaving the Apalachees as a more attractive target. Happily for the Carolinians, a series of events led to the breakdown of the truce that had existed between the Apalachees and the Lower Creeks since 1698. In August 1702 a Spanish official imprisoned and abused a visiting chief from the Hitchiti town of Apalachicola. In May of the following year, the Apalachicolas retaliated by raiding and desecrating a Catholic mission among the Timucuas, and on their retreat some Apalachees killed two of the invading warriors. A few months later, the Apalachicolas took vengeance for the loss of their kinsmen. They seized four Apalachees then on a mission to trade with them; three were ritually tortured and killed, while the fourth escaped. The Spanish, embarrassed by their inability to protect their mission population, mobilized an army of some eight hundred Native warriors to punish the Lower Creeks. In late 1702 and early 1703, the largely Apalachee force made its way up the Flint River, but a force of Creeks and some Englishmen who were then on their way to raid the Apalachees ambushed them. A reported six hundred "Spanish Indians" were either killed or captured.[68] Later in 1703 Carolina's allies struck with even more ferocity. Lower Creeks burned three Apalachee towns and returned with over five hundred captives. In 1704 slave-seeking Carolinians and their Native allies completed what the Apalachees' long experience with Spanish colonialism and its germs could not do. James Moore Sr., then governor of South Carolina, led a massive assault into northern Florida with a force that included dozens of Englishmen and over a thousand allied Natives. Moore's army defeated Apalachee and Spanish forces and destroyed five missions. Several months later, an independent Creek raid of six hundred warriors delivered the finishing blow, attacking the remaining Apalachee towns and forcing the survivors to flee from their ancient homeland. As a result of the 1703 and 1704 raids, the entire population of Apalachees was eliminated from northern Florida. Hundreds certainly ended up dead due to the violence, while several thousands were either sold to the English as slaves or adopted into Upper Path communities.[69] Some managed to avoid captivity. Approximately eight hundred individuals made their way to the French at Mobile, while a few hundred more wound up at St. Augustine.[70] Another thirteen hundred agreed to surrender to Moore's forces and were allowed to relocate near the fall line of the Savannah.[71] There the Apalachees fulfilled a vital role in South Carolina's Upper Path trade network. "These people are seated very advantageous for carrying our trade," Governor Nathaniel Johnson remarked in 1708. "Indians seated upwards of seven hundred miles off are supplied with goods by our white men that transport them from [the Savannah River] upon Indians' backs."[72] Such service kept the Apalachees in contact with kinsmen who lived among their adoptive communities.[73]

The Apalachees who made it to the Savannah arrived there amid an intense experience with slave raids and germs. After their disastrous defeat on the Flint early in 1703, the few Apalachee survivors retreated to their home villages, where life remained precarious. The threat of renewed enemy raids interfered with subsistence routines and kept them confined to their missions, where in such a weakened state they fell prey to germs. In 1703 an unknown disease ravaged Mission San Luis, which served as the central base for the Apalachee province. The epidemic appears to be the result of one of the Atlantic world's deadliest germs because it took the lives of 170 individuals in San Luis alone. It probably spread to outlying villages as well.[74] For those survivors who took up residence on the Savannah, hunger, demoralization, and diseases took a toll. From a population of some 1,300 individuals who relocated on the Upper Path in 1704, the Apalachees' number fell to 643 in 1715.[75] Disease-induced mortality was not solely to blame for the loss of so many Apalachees. Some, especially women and children, fell into the hands of English slave dealers, while others fled to Creek communities where many of their relatives lived. But one or more of the numerous epidemics that struck the region from 1704 to 1712 certainly accounted for a significant portion of the Apalachees' losses.

On the Great Southeastern Smallpox Epidemic's westward trek from the Savannah, aftershock epidemics had an impact on the Lower Creeks, the Upper Creeks, and the Chickasaws as well. In his 1708 journey, for example, Thomas Nairne not only found evidence that smallpox had preceded him but commented that "other European distempers" had too. Deaths from multiple diseases along with those from the use of firearms had forced the Creeks and the Chickasaws "to break up their Townships and unite them for want of inhabitants."[76] Unfortunately, neither Nairne's journal nor any other European source reveals what those "other European distempers" were, when exactly they struck, and from where they came. As part of Carolina's vast trade network, the Creeks and the Chickasaws were vulnerable to diseases introduced from the East, but as with the Yamasees, the Creeks and the Chickasaws were vulnerable to epidemics on the Gulf Coast in 1699, 1703, 1704, 1706, and 1708 through their captive raids. The 1703 epidemic in particular had a high likelihood of infecting Upper Path communities. In that year hundreds of Apalachee captives and refugees streamed north and were either adopted into Upper Path communities or traded on to South Carolina. Their germs likely accompanied them and became disseminated widely among Carolina's Native allies. Similarly, the 1704 epidemic had a great potential to spread into Upper Path communities because Carolina's indigenous allies were engaged against Mobile-area communities, which that year contracted the lethal "plague" that the French had imported.[77] The exchanges of slaves for manufactured goods had filled the Upper Path with a high volume of traffic in the 1690s and allowed for smallpox to spread north to south and east to west. In 1703 and 1704 the Upper Path again was a deadly avenue for the spread of newly introduced diseases, as infected captives ignited aftershocks that spread in the opposite direction.

Some evidence, although sparser than one would like, suggests that the Creeks and the Chickasaws declined by more than 68 percent due to the Great Southeastern Smallpox Epidemic and its aftershocks. In 1690 John Stewart asserted that the various Muskogee and Hitchiti towns that had fled from the Chattahoochee to be closer to South Carolina numbered some twenty-five hundred men.[78] These constituents of what became the Lower Creeks mostly settled on the Ocmulgee River and its tributaries, with some spilling over into the nearby Oconee and Ogeechee river valleys. During the tumultuous events of the 1690s and early 1700s, Lower Creek settlement remained fluid. People moved in and out of Muskogee and Hitchiti communities, and they changed the location of their villages at various times. Overall, though, the Lower Creeks attracted more people than they lost through these relocations. Large numbers of remnant groups and adopted captives were added to Muskogee and Hitchiti villages. Still, their population numbers plummeted and became increasingly concentrated in fewer towns just as Thomas Nairne indicated for Upper Path peoples in general. By 1715 the Lower Creeks had become concentrated along the Ocmulgee, with the exception of some Apalachicolas, who seemed to alternate locations between the lower Savannah and the lower Ogeechee River. Together residents of the Ocmulgee area and the Apalachicolas could field 795 warriors, a 68 percent decrease from the number of warriors that their ancestors could field just twenty-five years before. If the entire Lower Creek population declined by the same percentage as did their warriors alone, then they declined from 8,188 people in 1690 to 2,620 people in 1715. Because hundreds of those counted as Lower Creeks in 1715 were captives who had been adopted or who were from formerly independent groups that had been incorporated, the rate of depopulation was probably even greater than 68 percent. To be sure, the Lower Creeks, whose villages were located above the Fall Line and far away from European settlements, did not face the extreme rates of depopulation experienced among Low Country and Gulf Coast groups, whose numbers likely declined by as much as 90 percent or more. Aspects of colonialism other than germs, though, did play a role in depopulating the Lower Creeks. The Spanish burned several of their villages in 1686, forcing a stream of hungry refugees to flee the Chattahoochee and assemble to the east, where continual conflict with the Spanish and their Native allies took a toll. The English offered some help, but the guns and ammunition they gave in exchange for captives was accompanied by the Atlantic world's deadliest germs. The rate of Lower Creek depopulation consequently lies somewhere between 68 percent and 90 percent. A rate of decline of around 75 percent seems a more reasonable assumption, making the Lower Creek population around 10,500 before 1696.

One would suspect that the Upper Creeks and the Chickasaws declined by a somewhat lower percentage than the Lower Creeks. Not having to flee their homes and being farther removed from South Carolina, they experienced fewer traumas from colonialism and its germs. Nevertheless, some evidence in regard to the Chickasaws suggests that communities on the western half of the Upper Path declined by a similar percentage as did the Lower Creeks. The French reported that the Chickasaws could field as many as 2,000 warriors in 1692, whereas the English counted only 700 warriors in 1715, a 65 percent decline from what they could muster just twenty three years earlier.[79] Most of those losses occurred during the Great Southeastern Smallpox Epidemic, but after-shocks reduced the Chickasaws' number of villages from nine in 1701 to just six in 1715.[80] Warfare certainly played a role in the high death toll for Chickasaws. The French-allied Illinois and Choctaws engaged Chickasaw men in battle and sought out women and children captives to replace those that slave raids and disease had carried off. The Chickasaws' population, however, would not have declined as greatly had they not suffered repeated epidemics. If the rate of depopulation of the Chickasaws was indeed 65 percent, then the 1,900 Chickasaws that the English counted in their 1715 census represented the survivors from a population that numbered around 5,500 in the early 1690s. Since the Chickasaws too appeared to incorporate some of the remnant groups from the Yazoo Basin and certainly adopted at least a portion of their captives, their rate of depopulation likely exceeded 65 percent. The Upper Creeks too faced substantial military losses from French-allied Choctaws and their long-standing rivals the Cherokees, making their combined rate of depopulation from warfare and germs similar to that of the Chickasaws. The 4,886 Upper Creeks that the English counted in 1715 conceivably represented the survivors of a population that had declined by as much as 65 percent or, expressed in other terms, the remnant of a population that had numbered 13,960 before becoming incorporated into South Carolina's trading network. If people on the western half of the Upper Path declined by as much as the conjectured 75 percent that the Lower Creeks appeared to have declined, then one arrives at pre-1696 populations of 7,600 for the Chickasaws and 19,544 for the Upper Creeks. Regardless of the specific rate of decline for the Creeks and the Chickasaws, their populations suffered severely from the biological consequences of being incorporated into the larger Atlantic world and its flow of peoples, goods, and germs.

To make matters worse, Upper Path peoples found it increasingly difficult to acquire captives to adopt into their communities to augment their sagging numbers. The same diseases that afflicted them so terribly caused even worse casualties for those groups that had been the victims of their raids. By the end of 1706 South Carolina's allies had destroyed the Spanish mission system, leaving a mere three hundred refugees, whose small communities remained within sight of St. Augustine.[81] Carolina's Native allies traveled far to the south of St. Augustine and hunted members of the Tocabagas, the Calusas, and other tribes. In 1708, Thomas Nairne commented that South Carolina's Native allies were "now obliged to goe down as farr on the point of Florida as the firm land [would] permit" in search of slaves. He added, "[T]hey have drove the Floridians to the Islands of the Cape, have brought in and sold many hundreds of them, and Dayly now Continue that Trade so that in some few years they'le Reduce these Barbarians to a farr less number."[82] Fewer captives were also coming from the Gulf Coast and the Mississippi Valley. Germs and slave raids, as will be discussed in the next section, had taken a grave toll on France's Native allies, leaving the formidable Choctaws as the only indigenous group of significant size. Growing indebtedness to English traders was a consequence of their declining fortunes in acquiring captives. In 1711 South Carolina officials observed that it would take 100,000 deerskins for the Lower Creeks to pay English traders for the goods they had purchased on credit.[83] The Tuscarora War, to be sure, provided Carolinian slave dealers and their Native allies an opportunity to acquire slaves when supplies of potential captives had greatly diminished, but the epidemics that occurred during the conflict undoubtedly took away a large number of those captives. Also, the great bulk of prisoners went to Siouans and Cherokees rather than Upper Path peoples. Debt continued to plague the relationship between Carolinian traders and their Upper Path partners in the years leading up to the Yamasee War.

Deerskins, moreover, did little to revive the Upper Path trade. This becomes clear when one analyzes South Carolina's annual exports of deerskins to England. South Carolina officials tabulated the numbers of deerskins sent from their colony for every year from 1699 through 1715. Interestingly, the number of deerskins increased steadily between the Great Southeastern Smallpox Epidemic and the 1704 epidemic and then plummeted in 1705, when it reached its low mark of a mere 10,289. Such a drop off could be attributed to a number of factors, including disruption of shipping due to Queen Anne's War or a decline in demand from the mother country. But it is plausible that the 1704 epidemic persisted into the fall of that year and interfered with that hunting season, whose harvest of deerskins would have been collected by English traders in the spring of 1705 and then exported later that year. The deerskin trade rebounded and reached its high mark in 1707, when South Carolina sent 121,355 hides to England. But again exports plummeted to 31,939 the following year and never again came close to reaching its 1707 mark, suggesting that the series of diseases between 1708 and 1712 had interfered with the ability of Native communities to supply the number of deerskins that they once had.[84] One would think that the Creeks and the Chickasaws, having been spared the upheavals of the Tuscarora War, would have stepped into the breach. There is no evidence that deer had grown in short supply, and indeed Carolina's Native allies had essentially unlimited access to Florida, where an absence of human residents allowed wild game populations to explode.[85] But the Creeks and the Chickasaws did not step into the breach, or perhaps more accurately, their English trading partners would not let them. Dwindling supplies only drove the price of slaves higher, making Carolinians demand that their indebted Native clients return with what colonialism and its germs had made a very difficult commodity to find. Perhaps such pressure on the demand side led Francis Le Jau to remark in 1713, "I suspect there is no other Necessity for those [indigenous] Nations to Warr against their Neighbours but that of making slaves to pay for the goods the traders Sell them, for the Skins trade do's not flourish as formerly."[86] With fewer captives being traded and the deerskin trade being neglected, the economic basis for the relationship between South Carolina and its Upper Path allies was collapsing during the prelude to the Yamasee War.

In the backdrop of all of this collapse, of course, were the epidemics that hit Upper Path communities particularly hard between 1696 and 1715. The Upper Path underwent a great deal of change during those years, as communities along Carolina's trading network lost population in excess of 65 percent, if not more. The Yamasees, the Creeks, and the Chickasaws continued to trade captives to the English for manufactured goods, but germs and violence had brought the Native slave trade to the verge of collapse by the end of the first decade of the eighteenth century. The Tuscarora War propped up the noxious commerce for a brief period but did little to revive the Upper Path slave trade. Not only did the declining supply of captives undermine South Carolina's commerce with its southern allies, but the growing unwillingness of indigenous peoples to part with their captives did as well. The Yamasees, the Creeks, and the Chickasaws, having suffered catastrophic population losses themselves, depended heavily on the adoption of captives and the incorporation of remnant groups to keep themselves from dwindling into obscurity and becoming easy prey for their enemies. The composition of Upper Path communities, in fact, became even more heterogeneous during the first decade of the eighteenth century. Captives taken from the Spanish-allied Apalachees, Guales, and Timucuas as well as those taken from French-allied tribes on the Gulf Coast and in the Mississippi Valley gave a much-needed population boost to Upper Path communities but did not come close to bringing their numbers back to their former level.[87]

English Enslavement, French Germs, and Louisiana's Allies

It was indeed South Carolina's commerce in Native slaves that made epidemics so deadly on the Gulf Coast and in the Mississippi Valley. Slave raids forced a wave of population movements toward the newly established French outposts on the Gulf Coast, where refugees hoped the newest colonial regime in the

Southeast would offer them help against their more powerful English-allied enemies. Tragically, such flight made those refugees face the extreme biological consequences of the European invasion. Confined to malaria- and typhoid-ridden areas of the Gulf Coast and the lower Mississippi Valley, Louisiana's allies experienced aftershock epidemics in the worst possible situation. Hunger, violence, high pathogen loads, and the Atlantic world's deadliest diseases wiped some groups off the face of the map, while others dwindled into small dependent communities, or what the French called *les petite nations*. Some, of course, avoided the fate of becoming small appendages to the fledgling colony of Louisiana. The Choctaws, whose nearly hidden villages remained difficult but not impossible for newly introduced diseases and English-allied slave raiders to find, fared comparatively better and remained a populous and important Native polity. The English looked upon these French-allied Natives as fair game for conquest during Queen Anne's War, but their remote location, large numbers, and French-supplied guns made them an unattractive target for South Carolina's indigenous partners. By 1715 English colonialism in the West had hit a wall. French-supplied germs had utterly devastated myriad groups that English-allied raiders had put in such a vulnerable position, while French guns made Louisiana's one significantly large ally, the Choctaws, a formidable opponent whom South Carolina's much-weakened trading partners could not enslave.

After the Great Southeastern Smallpox Epidemic, indigenous residents in the Mobile Bay area and refugees who fled there continued to suffer a steep decline from the biological and nonbiological aspects of colonialism. Amid the mountains of skeletons and deserted villages, the French found two distinct groups of survivors, the Mobiles, who remained on the river named for them, and the Tohomes, whose villages stood on both sides of the junction of the Mobile and Tombigbee rivers. Estimates of their population varied. Bénard de La Harpe recorded that the two nations together could field 700 men in 1699, while d'Iberville believed that they could muster only 350 "able-bodied" men in 1702.[88] It is possible that they suffered substantial population loss from the mysterious "plague" that afflicted d'Iberville's crew as it sailed to the Gulf Coast, from the deadly strain of dysentery that the French found among Mississippi Valley groups in 1700, or from a combination of both. But it is also likely that d'Iberville underestimated the Mobiles' and the Tohomes' numbers. His brother and the future governor of Louisiana, Jean-Baptiste Le Moyne, sieur de Bienville, recalled in a later memoir, that the Tohomes alone could field 800 warriors when the French first arrived.[89] What is certain is that the numbers of the Tohomes and the Mobiles plummeted even lower after the French arrived.

Indeed, the French saw firsthand just how deadly their germs and English slave raids could be for indigenous peoples. Living in fear of South Carolina's Upper Creek allies and having no firearms among them, the Mobiles and the Tohomes eagerly welcomed the French much as Carolina's Natives had welcomed the English in the 1660s and 1670s. "I dare flatter myself that the savages will do blindly everything that we want," d'Iberville's second in command, M. de Sauvole de La Villantray, claimed, "although they are lazy; they have confidence in what we tell them."[90] It was not that Natives were docile creatures ready to obey European masters. The Tohomes and the Mobiles faced desperate circumstances and looked to the French as a way to protect themselves from their enemies to the north. Sauvole de La Villantray later found Tohome and Mobile leaders at his door begging for protection from the Koasatis and the Pacanas, two of the constituent groups of the emerging Upper Creeks, a confederation that the French would refer to as the Alabamas.[91] The French not only assisted their new allies with firearms; they also enflamed the already intense level of violence. Bienville, who took charge of Louisiana in his brother's absence and after Sauvole de La Villantray's death, offered Natives a reward of ten crowns—presumably paid in manufactured goods—for each Alabama scalp that they acquired.[92] In 1704 Bienville went one step further and organized an attack on the Upper Creeks. Not only were three to four Englishmen there trading for slaves but also the Alabamas had killed a Frenchman the year before. Bienville could strike against his mother country's enemy, intimidate the Alabamas, and prove to his Native allies that the French were brave warriors themselves. For three days in August over 220 of Louisiana's newest allies gathered on the Mobile River and prepared for war. The Mobiles, however, proved somewhat reluctant. Bienville led Tohomes, Pascagoulas, and Choctaws to the Alabama River, where they waited for three days before the Mobiles showed up. Finally, they arrived and the army set off on foot on a four-day search for the Alabamas' villages. Along the way tragedy struck. Sickness spread through Bienville's forces, among both French and Native, leading his indigenous allies to desert. Bienville carried on his planned attack with only Frenchmen, who stumbled upon a party of Upper Creeks and killed two but lost two themselves. Bienville mistakenly believed that the "terrified" Alabamas would cease their attacks on Louisiana's allies.[93]

More than the terror of French arms, a germ gave Louisiana's enemies and allies something to fear. The French ignited a deadly epidemic in 1704. In July a supply ship arrived, carrying soldiers and settlers infected with a "plague" that they had contracted at Havana. Twenty-three sailors died on the trip, another twenty men and two women perished after arrival, and then two-thirds of the existing French garrison fell ill.[94] The same deadly germ that put so many French in their graves was certainly responsible for the sickness that erupted among Bienville's forces as they marched toward the Alabamas. Bienville specifically mentioned the Tohomes becoming ill and returning home, and then he later recalled that the "plague" of 1704 "almost annihilated" their entire nation.[95] Scholars commonly assume that the disease involved was yellow fever, but that virus is contraindicated because sickness among Bienville's forces erupted six days after they had originally assembled; at least some cases of the yellow fever virus, which has an incubation period of three to six days, should have started appearing before then. Also, one French source reported the disease was "widespread," suggesting a germ that had fewer environmental restrictions than did yellow fever.[96] What exactly the disease was cannot be known, but the death toll among the Tohomes indicates that it was one of the more dangerous germs that colonization introduced. Since warriors belonging to the Mobiles, the Pascagoulas, and the Choctaws also became infected, they likely spread it back to their villages just as the Tohomes had done. And as mentioned previously, the mysterious pathogen likely made its way into the Upper Path through the bloodstreams of captives that South Carolina's allies took, despite Bienville's blustering comments to his superiors in Paris that he had humbled the Alabamas.

Louisiana's allies suffered the most. When Bienville estimated the Tohomes' population, he claimed that their number of warriors had fallen from eight hundred in 1699 to ninety in 1720s, a staggering 89 percent rate of depopulation.[97] The Mobiles' numbers likewise plummeted; they could mobilize only sixty men in the 1720s. Adding to the already tragic scene was the arrival of hundreds of Apalachee refugees at Mobile River. Some of these unfortunate people may have taken up refuge near the French as early as 1702, but the biggest wave arrived in the deadly summer of 1704, when the germ that had laid so many others in their graves took an equally terrible toll on their tired and hungry bodies.[98] Bienville claimed that the Apalachee refugees near Mobile could at one time field five hundred warriors but that "disease" had "made great ravages among them and [had] reduced them to one hundred men."[99] Later epidemics also bore some responsibility for the staggering decline of the Tohomes, the Mobiles, and the Apalachees, but the 1704 outbreak appears most vividly in the available documents, indicating its particular severity. Also, it struck the Mobile Bay area's Native residents at a time when they were especially vulnerable. They were struggling to escape the noose of English enslavement, putting them in a greatly weakened position to survive disease. The Tohomes, the Mobiles, and the Apalachees had a particularly intense experience during the 1704 epidemic, because

English-inspired slave raids confined them to an area notoriously rife with malaria and typhoid, disrupted their subsistence routines, and forced them to seek out help from the French, whose connections to the larger Atlantic world introduced a deadly "plague." By 1715, in fact, the majority of Natives living near Mobile Bay were not original inhabitants but remnant groups from Florida and the Mississippi Valley that had been shattered by slave raids and infected with the Atlantic world's most lethal germs.

Several tribes to the west of Mobile Bay attempted to escape the noose of English enslavement only to fall prey to French germs. The Biloxis, the Pascagoulas, and the Moctobis, for example, coalesced on the Pascagoula River amid slave raids and smallpox in the late 1690s. They could field somewhere between 130 and 200 warriors in 1699 and then collapsed even further during their interaction with the French colonial regime.[100] In 1704 they supplied some warriors to Bienville for his ill-fated mission against the Alabamas, which likely brought the plague of that year into their villages. Around that same time the Biloxis relocated near a French outpost on the Lower Mississippi, where they served as providers of food for the notoriously germ-ridden soldiers.[101] Sometime thereafter the Biloxis moved back toward the east, taking up residence on the lower Pearl River along with a group that the French identified as the "Pensacolas," a remnant group that had fled Spanish Florida between 1704 and 1706 amid the upheavals of English slave raids. Together the two peoples could field only 40 warriors in the 1720s. Meanwhile, the Pascagoulas and the Moctobis remained where the French had originally found them but fared little better. They could field only 40 warriors as well.[102]

Slave raids, germs, and depopulation characterized the experience of the Colapissas as well. In 1699 the Colapissas had at least three villages on the lower Pearl River. When the French encountered them, they had recently endured a brutal attack by the Chickasaws and two Englishmen, who had sacked two of their villages and enslaved fifty of their people. The survivors feared subsequent raids, refrained from hunting, and instead remained confined to their "great village," which was then surrounded by "a palisade of pointed stakes."[103] In the wake of such attacks, d'Iberville sent a threatening message to the Chickasaws by way of Henri de Tonty. Tonty was to inform the Chickasaws that the French "have settled on the Mississippi—friends of all nations nearby, with whom we are doing business in everything; that it rested entirely with them to do as much and become friends of ours by ceasing to make war." D'Iberville specifically mentioned the Natchez, the Colapissas, and the Choctaws as victims, and he wanted the Chickasaws to know that "if they did not make peace with them, [he] would arm those nations with guns like the ones they had, because of which they would be unable to hold out against so many Indians equipped to fight them."[104] The Chickasaws and South Carolina's other allies, of course, did not stop their attacks. The next time the French mentioned the Colapissas was in 1705, when they agreed to welcome a remnant group of Natchitoches from the Red River to live among them in a newly established village on the north shores of Lake Pontchartrain. Weakened by slave raids and disease, the formerly numerous Colapissas certainly needed to add numbers to their community. Their demographic decline became apparent with the drastic actions they took to keep the Natchitoches from leaving them. In 1712 the Natchitoches attempted to move back to the Red River, but according to one Frenchman, the Colapissas, upon seeing that "Nassitoches women, too, were leaving and were going away with their husbands, . . . fell upon the Nassitoches with blows of guns, arrows, and hatchets and killed seventeen quite close to [him] without [his] being able to stop them." Then, the Colapissas "seized more than fifty women or girls," whose departure would have directly threatened their survival.[105] As a heterogeneous community, the Colapissas did manage to persist as one of Louisiana's *les petite nations*. In 1718 they took up residence on the Mississippi just thirteen leagues above New Orleans but moved back to the north of Lake Pontchartrain, where Bienville located them in the 1720s. Bienville described them as "very brave" and "great hunters" who furnished New Orleans with fresh meat. At that time, though, they had just one hundred warriors, or 75 percent less than the four hundred warriors that they could field in 1699.[106]

To the west of the Colapissas on the Mississippi River, the French found in 1699 the Bayagoula people. Their single village also included Mougalouchas, who had just absorbed another people, the Quinipissas. Suffering at the time from smallpox and facing their Mobile enemies to the east and Houma enemies who lived just to the north at the junction of the Mississippi and Red rivers, the Bayagoulas and the Mougalouchas found some protection in coalescence, but such a strategy did not occur without problems. Neither people wanted to give up its separate identity. The Bayagoulas and the Mougalouchas both maintained their own temples in their one village, and both sent leaders to meet with d'Iberville when he visited in 1699.[107] In May 1700 those tensions exploded. Then the French learned that the Bayagoulas had killed all the Mougalouchas and invited other peoples to live among them, including the Colapissas and the Tioux, a tribe originally from the Yazoo Basin that had fled south amid Chickasaw slave raids.[108] The French did not indicate the immediate cause for the Bayagoulas' destruction of the Mougalouchas, but it could have resulted from

French interference in Native diplomacy. D'Iberville encouraged the Bayagoulas and the Mougalouchas to forge peace with the Houmas, but the Mougalouchas most likely did not want to take part in such a peace since they had suffered the most from Houma raids. With the Mougalouchas out of the way, the Bayagoula leaders could assume the dominant role in relations with the French. French colonialism, however, brought little help to the Bayagoulas. English-inspired slave raids caused a ripple affect of violence down the Mississippi. In 1706 the Bayagoulas welcomed the Taensas to live among them. The Taensas had been a rather large chiefdom, located along the western banks of the Mississippi between the Arkansas and Red rivers, but disease and Chickasaw slave raids ultimately forced them to abandon their villages.[109] The Taensas sought refuge among the Bayagoulas, who in 1706 existed, according to one Frenchman, as "remnants," living near a French outpost on the Mississippi.[110] As with the Mougalouchas, though, the Bayagoulas and the Taensas did not get along. This time the Taensas "massacred almost the entire [Bayagoula] nation."[111] The Taensas then took a number of slaves from the nearby Colapissas, Houmas, and other tribes and returned north, where they fought against myriad English- and French-allied enemies until they relocated to the Mobile River in 1715.[112] There they had only 70 warriors, whereas in 1699 they could mobilize as many as 250.[113] Meanwhile, the Bayagoulas once large village nearly disappeared. "It was very populous about 20 years since," the visiting Jesuit missionary Pierre Francois Xavier de Charlevoix remarked in 1722. "The smallpox has destroyed a part of its inhabitants, the rest are gone away and dispersed. They have not so much as even heard any news of them for several years, and it is a doubt whether there is a single family remaining."[114] Bienville, though, did include them among Louisiana's *les petite nations,* locating them not far from where they had been in 1699. With just 40 men—84 percent less than they had in 1699—it is no wonder that Charlevoix thought they had disappeared.[115]

The Tunicas were yet another Mississippi Valley tribe whose lives became shattered amid the germs and violence associated with the deadly intersection of English and French colonialism. By 1699 smallpox and slave raids had forced the Tunicas to coalesce in the Yazoo Basin with other similarly stricken peoples, which the French identified as the "Yazoos, Offogoulas, Coroas, Bitoupas, and Oussipez."[116] Farther up the Yazoo stood another nation known as the Chakchiumas, who were related to the Chickasaws but not yet united with them. In 1700 the peoples of the Yazoo faced English-inspired slave raids coming from two directions. The Chickasaws continued to seek them out as captives, while to the west the Quapaws began trading captives to an Englishman who had taken

up residence among them.[117] The Tunicas and their confederates at first welcomed the French; they even allowed a Catholic missionary to live and work
among them.[118] Neither the French god nor French arms could help the Natives
out of the bind that English colonialism put them in. Some residents of the Yazoo chose the path of least resistance and cultivated an alliance with the Chickasaws and the English. In 1702 the Koroas allegedly killed a Catholic priest and
three Frenchmen. Bienville instigated the Quapaws, who had abandoned their
relationship with the English, to fight them, resulting in an attack that the
French commander believed had "entirely destroyed" the Koroas.[119] In December 1704, though, the French learned that the Koroas had not disappeared but
had joined with the Yazoos and hosted "a few Englishmen" who were "carrying
on the slave trade." Bienville at first claimed he would drive the Englishmen
from the Yazoo Basin, but he changed his mind about a planned attack, perhaps
as a result of the devastating plague that hit his soldiers and his Native allies that
summer.[120]

The Tunicas bore the brunt of the attacks by English-allied tribes. Remaining
Louisiana's ally, the Tunicas captured an Englishman in 1706 and sent the pris-
oner to Mobile. Fearing that the Upper Creeks and the Chickasaws would over-
whelm them, they abandoned their villages and moved down the Mississippi
River to unite with the Houmas. For unclear reasons the Tunicas and the
Houmas did not get along. The Tunicas ended up killing over one-half of the
Houmas, who then fled south and west taking up residence on the Atchafalaya
River, where in the 1720s they could muster only 50 warriors from the original
400 they had in 1699.[121] The Tunicas would remain in their new location into
the 1720s, but years of slave raids and disease had taken a tremendous toll.
French records made no specific mention of the 1706 epidemic occurring
among the Tunicas, but it was during the latter outbreak that they moved south,
where they stood a higher chance of catching whatever germs the French imported from the larger Atlantic world. Living near what was certainly a malaria-
infested oxbow lake and resisting continual slave raids the best they could, the
Tunicas saw their population plummet. Bienville estimated that they had over
500 warriors in 1699 but in the 1720s they only had 120.[122]

The flight of the Tunicas must have sent a clear message to other Mississippi
Valley groups. They could either join the English trade network or move closer
to the French. Natchez leaders in particular must have been pondering their options in the early 1700s. Smallpox, dysentery, and Chickasaw raids had taken a
grave toll on them in the 1690s.[123] Still, their twelve hundred warriors and nine
villages made them the largest polity on the Mississippi itself and gave them

larger numbers than the Chickasaws. The Chickasaws and the English indeed tried to recruit the powerful Natchez into South Carolina's trade network. By 1707 English goods were flowing into the Yazoo Basin and even farther south to the Natchez, leading Bienville to order the Chakchiumas to stop the English from sending a trade convoy to those he considered Louisiana's allies.[124] The Chakchiumas plundered the caravan of its goods, but they were unwilling to kill the English or their Hitchiti escorts, because they were "a big nation," and the Chakchiumas certainly feared enslavement if they did.[125] It was the following year that Thomas Nairne arrived among the Chickasaws with a mission to convert Louisiana's two most powerful allies, the Natchez and the Choctaws, into slave raiders for the English. According to Bienville, who learned of Nairne's visit from some coureurs des bois, the Carolinian proposed to the Choctaws that they supply them with slaves taken from the *les petite nations,* including the Tohomes, the Apalachees, the Towassas, the Mobiles, the Taensas, the Pascagoulas, and the Pensacolas. The Choctaws reportedly refused the offer and told the English that they would oppose them and their allies from marching through the Choctaw homeland.[126] Nevertheless, the English did have some success with the Natchez.

The Natchez, the Yazoos, and the Chickasaws cooperated together in slave raids that continued up until the time of the Yamasee War. In 1713, for example, one French official found an Englishman in a Natchez village preparing to buy their captives. The captives came from the Towassas, a people who had settled near the French after South Carolina and their allies forced them out of Florida. In Louisiana they did not fare much better. A party of Natchez, Yazoos, and Chickasaws visited the Towassas "under the pretext of singing their calumet of peace," then killed their chief, and absconded with eleven prisoners.[127] By allying with the English, the Natchez avoided the destruction that so many of their neighbors had endured. They lost people from the Great Southeastern Smallpox Epidemic and its aftershocks, but their rate of depopulation was significantly less than that of others. Bienville's count of the Natchez in 1720s listed them as having six hundred warriors.[128] A 50 percent population decline certainly was staggering but still significantly less than the 80 percent rates that their neighbors had faced. It would not be until the late 1720s, when French settlers and slaves took up residence near the Natchez, that they arrived at a crisis point where they felt on the verge of becoming yet another of Louisiana's *les petite nations.*

The Natchez entered South Carolina's slave trade network when it was on the verge of collapse. Just as they were traveling increasingly greater distances to acquire captives in Florida, English-allied Natives were traveling farther to find captives at the western end of the Upper Path as well. In his 1708 visit, for example, Nairne reported that the Chickasaws went "a man hunting . . . down to the sea side along both sides of the great river, and 150 miles beyond it."[129] Hiding his colony's economic motives with an imperial cloak, Nairne applauded the destruction that such raids brought. "The good prices The English Traders give them for slaves," the Carolinian said of his Native partners, "Encourages them to this trade Extreamly and some men think that it both serves to Lessen numbers [of Louisiana's allies] before the french can arm them and it is a more Effectuall way of Civilizing and Instructing, then all the Efforts used by the french missionaries."[130] The English market for indigenous captives did in fact do what Nairne had hoped it would but not exactly in the way he desired. South Carolina benefited from thousands of captives taken from what was once the most densely populated area in the eastern woodlands, but slave raids brought smallpox in the 1690s, drove survivors into unhealthy environments, and made Louisiana's allies highly vulnerable to the deadly aftershocks that French germs ignited. Epidemics, made incredibly intense by South Carolina's commerce in human commodities, ensured that countless Natives died before they could work a day on an Englishman's plantation.

The Choctaws, though, managed to withstand the blistering assault of English colonialism and the Atlantic world's deadliest germs. In 1715 this emerging confederacy could mobilize more warriors than all the other groups on the Upper Path combined. Bienville estimated that in the 1720s they could field as many as eight thousand warriors, keeping them larger than the combined total of French and African settlers in Louisiana. Still, there are reasons to believe that the Choctaws experienced some population losses from the combined impact of slave raids and epidemics in the first decade of the eighteenth century. Bienville claimed that "a short while before the exploration of the country they were in a position to oppose twenty thousand men to their enemies."[131] Especially with the Choctaws, the French governor's numbers must be taken with a grain of salt. At the time of their arrival, the French had only a vague idea of who actually composed the Choctaw Confederacy, and through the years, population within central Mississippi remained fluid as new refugee groups moved there. In other words, the extent of Choctaw population decline cannot be assessed with any degree of certainty. Bienville's figures, although likely off in terms of total numbers, nonetheless suggest a reasonable rate of depopulation. It was entirely possible that the population within the Choctaw homeland shrank by as much as 60 percent from the Great Southeastern Smallpox Epidemic, its aftershocks, and slave raids. From the time the French arrived until the end of Queen Anne's War

in 1713, English-allied raiders continually ventured into the Choctaws homeland and took captives, while at the same time, the Choctaws steadily increased
their trade and intercourse with the French. Consequently, the Choctaws became increasingly vulnerable to the Atlantic world's deadliest diseases. A 60 percent population loss, though, was still significantly less than what many of their
neighbors faced. Their distance from French outposts gave them some protection from germs, especially yellow fever, while their relatively hidden locations
along remote creeks and dense forests of central Mississippi allowed them to
keep dispersed settlement patterns, even amid constant harassment by English-
allied raiders. Pathogen loads were certainly lower and nutrition was certainly
better among the Choctaws than it was among Louisiana's other allies, whose exposed locations, compact settlements, close contact with the French, and residence in germ-ridden lowland areas led to astronomically high depopulation.

The differential impact of epidemics along with French-supplied weapons
made South Carolinians and their Native allies painfully aware that the Choctaws presented no easy target for raiders. Since 1702 the French had kept the
Choctaws well supplied with firearms and ammunition, making them less intimidated by their English-allied enemies and even more aggressive in retaliating
against them. In 1705, for example, an English-led invasion of several thousand
warriors descended on the Choctaws. According to one source, the invaders had
as many as four thousand men, who absconded with 300 captives.[132] The English and their allies, however, did not have as much success as they wished. Bienville learned that the Choctaws' enemies "ravaged" their homes and fields and
then headed back to the Upper Path. On their retreat the Choctaws attacked
and killed several of the invaders. "[The Choctaws] returned to Louisiana very
proud of this feat, attributing this advantage to the guns that [Bienville] had
given them," one French source noted.[133] Despite such difficulties the English
and their allies struck the Choctaws again. Probably using tactics involving small
raiding parties, the Chickasaws obtained 150 captives in an attack on the Choctaws early in 1706.[134] Many of these captives probably wound up in the hands of
Thomas Welch, whom the South Carolina assembly reimbursed for powder and
shot that he had given to the Chickasaws to keep them in friendship with the
English and enmity with the French.[135] English traders and their Native companions traveling the Upper Path from the Coosa River to the Tombigbee,
though, faced constant harassment. "The Choctaws often beat up the[se] quarters and kill travelers in this path," remarked Thomas Nairne in 1708.[136] Hundreds of Chickasaws and Creeks lost their lives due to Choctaw retaliation. In
one particular case, for example, fifty Upper Creeks fell upon a Choctaw hunt-

ing party in 1709 but suffered the loss of thirty from the armed hunters.[137] Governor Bienville, moreover, frequently received gifts from his allies in the form of scalps and captives taken from English-allied tribes.[138] In 1711 the English planned another large scale assault in what they hoped would be a decisive blow to the Choctaws. The English trader Theophilus Hastings led a force of Native allies west that consisted of three hundred bowmen and one thousand gunmen, who each received from South Carolina one pound of shot and two pounds of powder. Hastings's army converged with Thomas Welch and a contingent of Chickasaws in the Choctaw homeland. As with the earlier invasion, the Choctaws mostly fled, leaving their homes and villages to be burned. The Choctaws did lose 130 captives to Hastings's forces and a like number to Welch's.[139] Despite losing hundreds of captives, though, the Choctaws withstood such blistering raids and did not suffer the same fate as did other victims of slave raids such as the Apalachees and the Tuscaroras.

The Choctaws indeed never became the source of slaves that the English envisioned. The failure of the English-inspired raids on the Choctaws became obvious on both ends of the Upper Path. "The English of Carolina are sparing nothing to have our Indians destroyed by theirs," Bienville complained in 1709. "They come continually against them in large bands which accomplish almost nothing."[140] Louisiana's governor, moreover, bragged that he sent his allies to avenge themselves, and he rewarded them for bringing him captives and scalps.[141] The English and their allies also concluded that raids on the Choctaws were futile. John Stewart, who may have participated in the campaigns against the Choctaws or learned about them from those who did, provided the best English account of the invasions into central Mississippi. On at least one of the raids, Stewart claimed, the English and their allies did not even see a single Choctaw. They had escaped from their scattered villages into the nearly impenetrable swamps and forests, where Choctaw warriors waited to pick off individuals from the retreating invaders. Stewart claimed that stealthy Choctaws used bows and arrows instead of guns so that they could not be seen or heard. And when the Choctaws captured one of the invaders alive, they executed him in an excruciating torture ritual. In Stewart's mind no nation was more "brutal" than the Choctaws. His Native friends confessed to him that they too feared going into the Choctaws' homeland. "Now our Indians are so discouraged that they will never more attack the Choctaws," Stewart reported in 1711.[142] "They cannot be destroyed or harryd but ar Invincible."[143] South Carolina's allies received little out of their efforts to acquire slaves from the Choctaws.

After Queen Anne's War the Choctaws' relative power made the English rethink their system of alliances in the West. Sometime before the Yamasee War, another English expedition ventured into the Choctaws' homeland. This time the intent was to lure the Choctaws into South Carolina's trade network rather than to enslave them. The three Englishmen with twelve hundred Native warriors, according to Bienville, came "to destroy the villages of that nation that would not declare themselves for them and abandon the French." Three villages apparently refused, and they later relocated to be near the French fort at Mobile.[144] If the Choctaws could not be enslaved, perhaps they could be a better supplier of captives, given their power and proximity to the small nations that still dotted the Gulf Coast and the Lower Mississippi Valley. That was what South Carolinians had tried to do in 1708 and what they appear to have been up to again.[145] The English indeed believed that they had won over the Choctaws until the French lured them back during the Yamasee War.[146] English intrigue with the Choctaws coincided with French efforts to forge peace with the Upper Creeks. Beginning in 1712 the Upper Creeks became more receptive to peace overtures from Louisiana, in large part because of their growing wariness of fighting the Choctaws. The French saw this as an opportunity to undermine the English, but peacemaking was a complicated process. The Creeks may have wanted peace with the Choctaws and welcomed French gifts, but they did not necessarily want to end warfare against all of Louisiana's allies. Nevertheless, in the three years leading up to the Yamasee War, the Upper Creeks and the French established friendlier relations.[147]

Germs undoubtedly played a role in the realignments that began to take shape on the eve of the Yamasee War. By 1715 the Great Southeastern Smallpox Epidemic and its aftershocks had depopulated most of the Mississippi Valley and the Gulf Coast, leaving a collection of *les petite nations* who had become tied irrevocably to the French. The French gave their new friends weapons and support against English-allied raiders, but their small numbers hardly sufficed to supply enough captives to satiate South Carolina's appetite for slaves. English-allied tribes could not bring in near the number of prisoners as they had formerly without raiding the Choctaws. The differential impact of epidemics and French-supplied firearms had tipped the balance of Native power in favor of the Choctaws, however. That the English stepped up efforts to court the Choctaws must have made the more heavily depopulated communities of the Upper Path increasingly suspicious of South Carolina, whose traders had demonstrated their willingness and abilities to use stronger Native groups to enslave the weaker. By 1715, then, South Carolina's demographically stressed allies were wondering if they too would find themselves captured and sold to English masters.

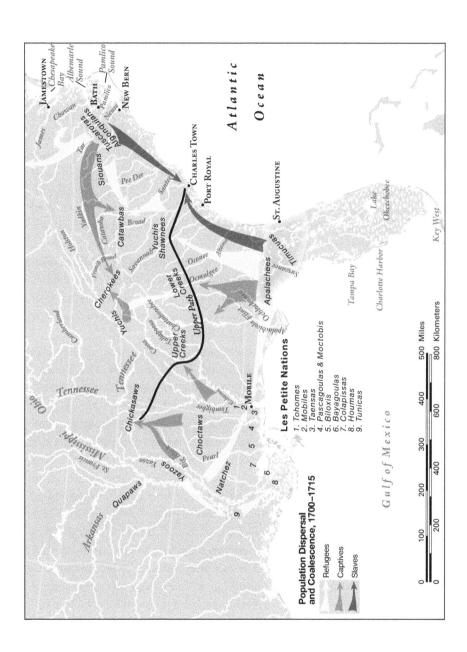

Population Dispersal and Coalescence, 1700–1715

Refugees
Captives
Slaves

Les Petite Nations

1. *Tohomes*
2. *Mobiles*
3. *Taensas*
4. *Pascagoulas & Moctobis*
5. *Biloxis*
6. *Bayagoulas*
7. *Colapissas*
8. *Houmas*
9. *Tunicas*

Atlantic Ocean

JAMESTOWN
Chesapeake Bay
Albemarle Sound
Pamlico Sound
NEW BERN
BATH
Chowan
Neuse
James
Tar
Tuscaroras
Algonquians
Siouans
Pee Dee
Catawbas
Broad
Catawba
Yadkin
Holston
French Broad
Cherokees
Yuchis
Tennessee
Coosa
Tallapoosa
Chattahoochee
Upper Creeks
Upper Path
Lower Creeks
Yuchis
Shawnees
Savannah
Oconee
Ocmulgee
Altamaha
Apalachicola/Flint
Apalachees
Timucuas
Suwannee
CHARLES TOWN
PORT ROYAL
ST. AUGUSTINE
Lake Okeechobee
Key West
Charlotte Harbor
Tampa Bay
Santee
Chickasaws
Cumberland
Tennessee
Ohio
Mississippi
St. Francis
Arkansas
Quapaws
Yazoo
Big Black
Natchez
Pearl
Choctaws
Tombigbee
Alabama
MOBILE
1
2
3
4
5
6
7
8
9

Gulf of Mexico

0   100   200   300   400   500 Miles
0   200   400   600   800 Kilometers

The Yamasee War

On April 15, 1715, the Yamasees began a revolt against their former English allies that quickly spiraled into a multitribal war against South Carolina. On that day they killed Carolina officials visiting them and several resident traders. Within a matter of days, Carolinian traders working among the Apalachees, the Yuchis, the Shawnees, and the Lower Creeks were killed as well. The Yamasees and warriors from other disgruntled groups then conducted raids against settlers around Port Royal, killing or capturing hundreds of English and Africans and causing the survivors to flee to Charles Town for safety. The revolt radiated west along the Upper Path, where traders working among the Upper Creeks, the Chickasaws, and the Choctaws wound up dead as well. By early May the Cherokees and the Siouans became involved in the conflict. They too killed Carolinian traders and even sent their warriors into outlying English settlements, coming very close to the prosperous Goose Creek plantations. Less than a month after the Yamasee War began, South Carolina's Native slave trade was in ruins and the colony itself appeared to be on the verge of destruction.[148]

The Yamasees took such drastic action because in their own words they were profoundly afraid that South Carolina intended to enslave them. One Yamasee leader, the Huspaw king, dictated a note to an English captive taken in the early stages of the war that was later found on a dead man's body. The Huspaw king informed his new enemies that John Wright, one of the Carolinians executed on the morning of the fifteenth, had "said that the white men would come and Ketch all the Yamasees in one night, and that they would hang four of their head men, and take all the rest of them for Slaves, and that he would send them all off the Country."[149] Later, Yamasee emissaries made their way to St. Augustine to appeal to the Spanish governor for help. They explained to the governor that Carolinian traders acted abusively in order to receive payments for debts. They claimed to have offered the English livestock, vegetables, and lard to pay off their debts, but such an offer was refused. In fact, they had come to believe that Carolinians had even executed a prominent Lower Creek man, who was the son of the powerful chief of the Cowetas, because he failed to pay off his debt. Carolinian traders, moreover, threatened their clients with enslavement if they did not supply slaves. The Yamasees told the Spanish governor that they feared losing their women and children, and they struck out against the people who had become so threatening to them. The fact that the English began to construct a fort at Port Royal only added to their fear. Indigenous peoples did not resort to fortifications when friends and allies surrounded them, so why would the English do so unless they were planning for war?[150] Years after the war some Yamasees claimed that they had taken up arms because the census of 1715 appeared to them as a preliminary step for their enslavement. Why else would Carolinians want to know the exact number of men, women, boys, and girls in each of the towns with whom they traded?[151] The Yamasees, of course, had specific grievances against South Carolina that did not involve enslavement. They had seen settlers and livestock increasingly encroach on their lands as well. "The reasons which the Indians give for their breach with Carolina," the governor of New York, Caleb Heathcote, learned from his Native allies in July 1715, "is the injustice which hath been done them by taking away their land without being fairly purchased and paid for." The fear of enslavement, though, accompanied the message that Heathcote received. The governor added that Carolina's former allies "also complain[ed] that their children, who were many of them bound out for a limited time to be taught and instructed by the Christians, were contrary to the intent of their agreement transported to other plantations and sold for slaves."[152]

Why, though, did the Yamasees become so fearful of enslavement? Why did such fears propel them to undertake such a dramatic course of action? And why did such a wide array of Native groups join the Yamasees against South Carolina? Any discussion of the origins of the Yamasee War should place the event within the epidemiological context in which it took place. The massive depopulation from the Great Southeastern Smallpox Epidemic and its aftershocks indeed sowed the seeds for future conflict between South Carolina and its allies. It did so in one way that this chapter has already discussed. The synergy of germs and slave raids wiped numerous groups off the map and reduced survivors to small appendages to European colonies, thus making it difficult for South Carolina's allies, especially those on the Upper Path, to find enough captives to supply English traders. Epidemics, in short, destroyed the economic basis of South Carolina's relationship with many of its indigenous clients. Disease also shaped the origins of the Yamasee War in two other important ways that need further elaboration. First, because they too had lost substantial numbers from diseases, South Carolina's allies increasingly valued their captives for their potential to be adopted rather than exchanged. Native peoples indeed saw the transformation of captives into kinsmen as necessary for their survival. Traders, though, operated according to market imperatives to reclaim the property of their debtors in order to pay off their own creditors and thus resorted to kidnapping individuals from the communities that claimed them. Tensions over possession of those scarce captives added an explosive element to the relationship between market-oriented Carolinians and their disease-depleted Native clients. Second, the differential impact of epidemics added to the insecurity felt by those Natives who played the greatest role in planning and executing the Yamasee War. By 1715 Native power had clearly shifted to the Cherokees and the Choctaws and away from the various communities of the Coastal Plain, the Piedmont, and the Upper Path. Given the increased English intercourse with the Cherokees and the Choctaws and the several examples in which the English used its more powerful friends to enslave weaker groups, a wide array of indigenous peoples had credible evidence to believe that South Carolina was preparing for their enslavement.[153]

English slave traders began to interfere with aboriginal practices of capture and adoption as soon as they showed up with their exotic goods. They encouraged a higher level of warfare, the capture of more women and children, and the disempowerment of women in determining the fate of those captives.[154] When the Native Southeast remained well populated with numerous unarmed and vulnerable communities, English interference posed little threat to their allies and many benefits. There were plenty of captives to go around. That changed after the Great Southeastern Smallpox Epidemic. Even when thousands of captives from Florida were being brought north during the early 1700s, South Carolinians and their allies had disputes about the status these conquered people would have. The Yamasees, for example, took several slaves during Governor Moore's 1702 invasion of St. Augustine. They complained that the governor did not give them liberty to dispose of their captives as they saw fit but instead insisted that they be sold to agents whom the South Carolina government had authorized, presumably Moore's selected men.[155] The sources do not clearly explain what the Yamasees wanted to do with these captives, but given their heavy losses from the Great Southeastern Smallpox Epidemic and its aftershocks, the Yamasees had a tremendous incentive to adopt as many captives as they could. It was during the 1702 invasion, one will recall, that the Yamasees convinced two Christianized communities to flee Florida and incorporate with them, suggesting that their participation in English invasions had the dual motive of acquiring captives to trade and to adopt. In any event, Moore's demands certainly undermined the Yamasees' prerogative in determining the fate of their own captives. Yamasee men expressed their people's complaints against Moore's demands, but they were likely relaying the concerns of their kinswomen, who had seen many of their loved ones laid in their graves by the mysterious and invisible actions of microbes. The resentment of women undoubtedly escalated as so many captives became English slaves rather than Yamasee kinsmen.

As the eighteenth century progressed, English sources revealed some startling episodes of traders taking people against the will of the communities to which they belonged. In December 1706, for example, charges against the trader John Musgrove came up for consideration in the Commons House of Assembly. He allegedly had enslaved twenty-two free people belonging to the Apalachees and another nine free people from the Lower Creeks. He had also taken another batch of captives and free people from the Apalachees because they had allegedly killed some of his cattle. Also, Musgrove had threatened the lives of a headman and another man belonging to the Tuckesaws, the people of a Lower Creek town, unless they gave him four captives. Musgrove claimed that he was due these slaves because the Tuckesaws had taken away his Native wife as well as the wife of another English trader, but the Natives claimed that the women in question left of their own accord—a female prerogative in the matrilineal societies of the Southeast. The Tuckesaws agreed to Musgrove's reduced demand of three slaves as compensation, but another trader had absconded with two of those captives, leaving Musgrove greatly disgruntled.[156] The assembly declined to arrest Musgrove and bring him to trial but did require him to remain in Charles Town. Within six months, though, he was again conducting his business among Natives.[157] Musgrove's actions demonstrated what were becoming common occurrences across the Upper Path. Englishmen laid claim to peoples that their Native clients did not want to see enslaved.

Such abuses continued unabated in the years leading up to the Yamasee War. In September 1710 the Commissioners of the Indian Trade, a body created by the South Carolina Commons House of Assembly to regulate trade with Natives, began to hold regular meetings in which they heard several cases involving the illegal enslavement of Natives and trader interference with indigenous practices of capture and adoption. From September 21, 1710, to August 1, 1711, the commissioners heard cases involving thirteen Natives that Englishmen allegedly had taken without the consent of the indigenous communities that claimed them.[158] Information regarding these cases is scant, but the few details suggest that some if not all of the abducted Natives had been adopted into indigenous communities. One case, for example, involved John Cochran's theft of "a free Indian Brother" who belonged to a Yamasee town.[159] Other cases involved Cornelius Macarty taking "the Wife and Child" of a Native man while he was off to war and George Wright stealing a "free Woman that had a Husband in Tomatly Town."[160] In one instance the board freed an Apalachee man name Massony, whom John Musgrove was holding as a slave. Interestingly, the board ordered Musgrove to prove that the headman of "Tomolla," either a Yamasee or an Apalachee town, had declared Massony a slave in order to reclaim him, thus tacitly acknowledging the prerogative of Native communities to determine the fate of their own captives, although mistakenly placing such power in the hands of a male rather than a female leader. It is not known whether Musgrove actually complied with the board's order.[161]

To deal with the incessant complaints about traders, the commissioners established new rules in August 1711. Such policy changes acknowledged that South Carolinians had been heavily involved in kidnapping adopted kinsmen. Traders could only acquire slaves within their Native client's town and only after their client had been home for three days with his captives. The commissioners reiterated proprietary limitations on buying only slaves taken in war and most importantly excluded *"those taken in War and made free by their respective Masters."* Such individuals should *"be deemed free Men and Denizens"* of their new community.[162] In other words, traders had to respect the wishes of the Native community in regard to the fate of its captives; they were to wait until a community had a chance to decide what to do with incoming captives; and they could not touch those captives who had been adopted. Traders may have thought that they were taking property owed them by their indebted clients, but instead they were taking kinsmen who were vital to the population recovery of their adopted communities.

When Carolina's allies returned from the Tuscarora War, however, traders broke the new regulations and did not wait for their clients to get back to their home villages. In April 1712, for example, charges were brought against Samuel Hilden for buying multiple slaves before they had been brought to their captor's towns. An Apalachicola man named Wenoya verified the charges. Wenoya, one of the relatively few Lower Creeks who participated in Barnwell's 1712 campaign against the Tuscaroras, informed the commissioners that Hilden had stopped him and forced him to surrender one slave for goods valued at 160 deerskins. Later Hilden appeared before the commissioners and confessed to buying six slaves from Apalachicolas but pleaded ignorance that his actions were against trade regulations.[163] Hilden was not the only one involved in such practices. Three other traders were charged with forcibly taking captives from their Native captors the first day they brought them into the Yamasee town of Pocataligo.[164] Carolinians continued to interfere with the captives of warriors when they returned home from James Moore Jr.'s 1713 campaign. In May 1714, the "Coosata King," presumably the headman of the Lower Creek town of Cussita who participated in Moore's expedition, complained that Theophilus Hastings had persuaded him to send seven of his prisoners from North Carolina with Colonel Alexander Macky to be left at the plantation of John Stanyarn, another leading South Carolinian involved in the slave trade. The "Coosata King" informed the board that he could "hear Nothing of them." Hastings admitted that the slaves had been sold, and the board ordered him to compensate the Coosata king 200 deerskins for each adult slave and 60 skins for each of the two children.[165] For the Coosata king, though, such a decision eliminated the prerogative of his own community, especially his female kinsmen, to determine the fate of his captives. Another trader, John Jones, also interfered with Creek men as they brought prisoners back from the Tuscarora War. Jones defied the commissioners' instructions by stopping two Lower Creeks at an Apalachee town and buying Tuscarora slaves from them before they returned home.[166] One wonders whether rum was involved; the commissioners forbade the sale of rum and the confiscation of captives to pay off rum debts, but the practice continued.[167] Whether the men, who were likely hungover and certainly without captives, received a scolding from their community members is unknown, but John Jones was specifically mentioned by name in April 1715 when the commissioners learned of Creek discontent with traders and a plot among them to kill Jones and his ilk.[168]

The most egregious misconduct of traders continued to be the kidnapping of captives who had undergone the transformation into kinsmen. From August 1711 until April 1715, traders either took or threatened to take fourteen Natives who belonged to indigenous communities.[169] Some of these cases were fairly straightforward. Carolinian traders simply took people away from their clients as payment for debts.[170] One of the most complicated of these cases involved a Chiaha woman named Toolodeha and her mother. The Chiahas then had a town among the Lower Creeks but had at one time lived among the Yamasees. The Cussitas took Toolodeha and her mother and gave them to traders working for John Pight, a leading Carolinian who claimed the Cussitas owed him five slaves. Toolodeha's husband, Tuskena, protested to the board for the theft of his wife and mother-in-law. The board was somewhat sympathetic to Tuskena's anguish. As part of their 1711 regulations, they declared that a town cannot be held responsible for an individual's debt, but Tuskena's case did not necessarily violate that rule. In this case a Native town held a Native individual responsible for their debt. Still, the board ordered that Pight surrender Toolodeha, whose abduction and enslavement did violate trade regulations. Toolodeha's mother, though, remained enslaved.[171] The terrible ordeal must have made the Chiahas suspicious not only of English traders but also of the more powerful Creek community of Cussita. In March 1713 the Chiahas asked Governor Craven for permission to reestablish their residency among the Yamasees.[172] No such permission was forthcoming, and the Chiahas apparently stayed among the Lower Creeks.

Creek discontent came to involve more than just the town of Chiaha. John Wright's actions in particular alienated Cussita and other Creek towns. One of Wright's misdeeds involved a "free" woman named Ahele, identified as a "Creek Indian" and "kinswom[an] of the Soogela King." Wright allegedly took this woman away and either detained or sold her. When he sent goods to the Cussita captain "for satisfaction," the Native leader refused them.[173] There is no way to determine whether the "Cussita Captain" and the "Soogela King" were members of the same clan, but the former man's refusal of gifts from Wright had much significance. Southeastern Natives considered their relatives who had been captured to be dead, and such deaths demanded retaliation.[174] The offending party could give gifts to assuage the family's grief, but when the Cussita captain refused Wright's gesture, it was a message that Ahele's abduction would be considered an act of war. Wright's ethnocentrism apparently blinded him to the consequences of his actions. He in fact continued to take part in the abduction of kinsmen from their communities. In November 1714 the commissioners heard a case in which Wright claimed a woman named Saluma, who had lived with another woman named Dorcas for ten years. Dorcas, whose community was not identified, continually hid Saluma, leading Wright to take a "slave man" from Dorcas and keep him until Saluma was produced. Dorcas originally agreed to surrender Saluma, but on their way to the Savannah, the alleged slave ran off, and Dorcas never showed up. Dorcas still wanted Wright to return the man, but the Englishman refused.[175] Through an arrogance stemming from the growing power of South Carolina and the growing weakness of their Native allies, Wright probably did not even consider that his actions would ultimately end in his violent death at the hands of Natives. But ultimately those aggrieved Natives had enough; they came to see their survival as free peoples jeopardized by widespread English practices of taking captives who could become kinsmen or had already become kinsmen.

Carolinian traders gave their indigenous clients ample reasons to fear for their future survival. Another, more surprising source of Native grievances involved the growing influence of Anglican missionaries. Several ministers working for the Church of England's missionary wing, the Society for the Propagation of the Gospel (SPG), arrived in South Carolina in the early eighteenth century. They came ostensibly to evangelize indigenous peoples within the English empire, and on the surface, some of South Carolina's allies seemed willing to host them. In 1708 the Apalachees, who had converted to Catholicism in Florida, asked for a priest as did the Yamasees, whose population consisted of large numbers of adopted captives from Spanish missions.[176] SPG ministers, however, showed little desire to work among Natives and instead had their hands full trying to reign in the large numbers of dissenters and unchurched Carolinians. Still, the influence of SPG ministers in Native affairs slowly increased over the years leading up to the Yamasee War. Instead of going to indigenous communities, Anglican ministers insisted that Native children be brought to them for instruction. Benjamin Dennis, for example, complained in 1714, "I cannot yet prevail on our Neighboring Indians to send their children, not withstanding all the Encouragement." He did manage to have a boy who was half Cherokee and half English committed to his care. Another SPG missionary was more optimistic. Thomas Haig wrote back to London that he sensed a willingness among Natives to convert, but he had resorted to actually buying children to accomplish his purposes. "I have bought several little Indians," he stated. "Their aptness to learn and tractable Temper makes me think with concern on ye multitudes that perish for want of good Instructions." One can only imagine the shock that a visiting Upper Creek chief had when Haig approached him and asked him to bring his son and daughter with him on his next trip so that they could remain in South Carolina and be educated.[177] Given the Native experience with Englishmen kidnapping their own kinsmen, it must have appeared to the visiting Creek leader that Haig had devious motives. Another SPG minister, Treadwell Bull, also added to Native suspicions of South Carolina. Bull bought a Native woman, a fifteen-year-old boy, and two small children, ostensibly to educate and convert them, but certainly to utilize their labor as well. He also baptized five "molatto children being those of [South Carolina's] Indian Traders by Indian women during their stay amongst them." After the father of one of those children died, she was then sent to live with an English family, who took "all imaginable care to give her a virtuous and Christian Education."[178] While Bull may have been well intentioned, his actions were probably interpreted by indigenous peoples as no less offensive than traders who had been involved in kidnapping directly from their communities. With matrilineal kinship systems, Native southeasterners undoubtedly believed that the offspring of Native women and Englishmen belonged to the mother's family. One wonders how many other cases there were in which children of indigenous women and English fathers were taken from their mother's custody. Such practices probably were more widespread than the documentary record reveals—Native complaints and fears of their children being enslaved reached the ears of the governors of New York and Florida.[179]

While a large majority of recorded instances of kidnappings and other abusive episodes involved Upper Path communities, Siouan peoples had similar reasons to distrust South Carolina. Siouans may not have accumulated astronomically high levels of debt, but they had experienced disastrous depopulation over the previous nineteen years and suffered from Carolinian actions that heightened their fears of enslavement. To be sure, episodes involving Carolina's northern allies show up in the documentary records with much less frequency than those involving Upper Path peoples. But there are reasons for the scarcity of evidence. Traders doing business in the Piedmont were not as heavily involved in the bitter factionalism among Carolinian traders that led to their abuses being entered into the written record. However faint they may be in the documentary record, the grievances of Carolina's northern allies do appear. In 1711, for example, South Carolinians heard Catawba complaints about a Savannah Shawnee attack that had left some of their people dead. Apparently, the Catawbas blamed traders for taking part in the raid. The Carolinians learned that the Catawbas had threatened retaliation against both the Shawnees and the "white men" of their colony and then vowed they would afterward "fly to the Virginians."[180] After hearing such complaints, the Commissioners of the Indian Trade promised to investigate, but the Tuscarora War intervened.[181] The Siouans must have temporarily put their differences with South Carolina aside, for hundreds of their warriors assisted Barnwell and Moore in their assaults on the Tuscaroras and the Algonquians.

During and after the Tuscarora War, Carolinians gave Siouans more reasons to distrust them. Not only did the Tuscarora War provide a visible lesson on how South Carolinians would use their stronger allies to enslave the weaker, but it led Siouans and Englishmen into conflict over captives. After his initial assault on the Tuscaroras, Barnwell complained of his Native allies, "[They] got all the slaves & plunder, only one girl we gott." He further lamented that after the Siouans departed there was "nothing left for the white men but their horses tired & their wounds to comfort them."[182] What happened to the captives that the Siouans took, of course, remains poorly known, but one fragment suggests that the Siouans intended most of them to be transformed into kinsmen. In July 1712 the Commissioners of the Indian Trade heard a complaint from the Waxhaws that an Englishman, John Ball, had shown up among them demanding that they give him one of their recent captives. Ball had alleged that his slave ran away to the Waxhaws, where a warrior allegedly harbored him. Both the slave and the warrior died—the former for unknown reasons and the latter from warfare. Ball nonetheless had insisted that the Waxhaws give him one of the "several slaves" that the deceased warrior left "behind with his Relations." Ball, as did many other Englishmen, probably did not realize that he was asking these Natives to give him one of their relatives. No further reference was made of the case, but one wonders whether the South Carolinians actually forced their allies to give up one of their kinsmen.[183] Carolinians did come into possession of at least one Waxhaw woman. Soon after the Yamasees began their hostilities, she escaped her master and made her way to the Saras. She told her fellow Siouans that the Carolinians had already begun to kill Natives among them, a charge that the Saras apparently believed since they joined the revolt. A prior visit by the Yamasees also helped prepare the Siouans for battle. In early 1715 Yamasee messengers arrived with stories of kidnappings and other abuses taking place on the Upper Path, stories that paled in comparison to the Siouans' own experience but that nonetheless gave the Siouans a warning that thefts of their kinsmen would continue and enslavement of all their people might follow if something was not done to destroy South Carolina's colonial regime.[184]

The voluminous examples of Englishmen taking kinsmen away from Native communities gave indigenous peoples ample reasons to go to war against South Carolina. Kidnapping was an action not of a kinsman but of an enemy. It was an action that demanded retaliation. That Carolinians had committed such crimes against communities that had lost 50 percent or more of their population over the previous nineteen years was all the more threatening. Even if disease had not depleted South Carolina's allies so substantially, indigenous peoples would have seen kidnapping as an act of war. Epidemics, however, had made kidnapping the only alternative for market-oriented traders, who absconded with kinsmen as payment for the debts that their Native clients owed. South Carolina's allies could not find enough captives to supply the traders, and the few that they did find were more valuable to them as adopted kinsmen than as exchange items. With Englishmen displaying such callousness in taking these valuable members away from their own disease-depleted allies, it is no wonder that the Yamasees and perhaps other Native groups saw something as innocuous as a census as a preliminary step to their ultimate enslavement. Native fears, though, were compounded by Natives' suspicions of one another. Those who took up arms against South Carolina may have believed that they were going to be enslaved, but they knew that the English would rely on Natives to do the work. For that reason, the way in which colonialism and its germs changed the social landscape also shaped Native decisions to go to war.

As the largest Native group that epidemics had left standing, the Choctaws commanded the attention of both South Carolina and their Native allies. Increasing English influence within this powerful confederacy over the few years before the Yamasee War could not have been lost on South Carolina's Upper Path allies. The relationship between the Choctaws and the Carolinians, of course, was just in gestation and not all the Choctaws welcomed an alliance with a colonial regime that had preyed on their people for slaves. Before South Carolina's Native allies revolted against them, some pro-French Choctaws in fact delivered Governor Bienville the heads of two Choctaw chiefs who had welcomed the English.[185] Nevertheless, English intrigue among the Choctaws had to be an ominous sign for the Creeks and the Chickasaws. All of Carolina's traders on the western end of the Upper Path were, in fact, hunted down and killed, suggesting that factions among the Creeks and the Chickasaws wanted to destroy any alliance between the Choctaws and the English before it got off the ground. The French were certainly not responsible for engineering Carolina's Upper Path allies to turn against them. As late as June 15, Bienville was unaware that the general revolt had begun and learned of it only when Creek emissaries later visited him in Mobile and asked him to send traders among them. The French governor, of course, had been working on bringing the Upper Creeks into a French alliance since 1712, and he welcomed the opportunity that the Yamasee War presented to bring in more defectors from South Carolina. It was the Creek's decision to approach Bienville, and they did so because of the "bad treatment" that they had received from the English.[186] John Wright was certainly among those badly behaved men. His kidnapping of a kinswoman of a prominent Creek chief and his other misdeeds led South Carolina's Commissioners of Indian Affairs to blame him for the defection of some Upper Creeks to the French in 1712.[187] Through the French the Creeks became acquainted with a quite different, nonmarket oriented model of colonialism. The French gave gifts as proper kinsmen did without making incessant and impossible demands for captives in return.[188] With English traders ingratiating themselves among the Choctaws, the Creeks found themselves in even greater need of a trustworthy trading partner.

The Creeks had only to consider their past experience with the Cherokees to see how willing South Carolinians were to use their allies to enslave one another. The relationship between the Cherokees and other Natives within South Carolina's trade network, of course, was complicated. The Cherokees maintained a friendly relationship with the Catawbas and other Siouan groups of the Piedmont. They may have fought one another in the seventeenth century, but they cooperated together in fighting a common enemy during the Tuscarora War. The Virginians helped in this process of bringing the Cherokees and the Siouans together, since they traded with both peoples and depended on Piedmont dwellers to guide them to remote Appalachian villages. The Cherokees also maintained an affiliation with the Yamasees, a group whose constituents included some Lower Cherokees who had left the upper Savannah in the 1670s and a group that the Cherokees considered in 1715 to be "their ancient people."[189] Nevertheless, violence plagued the Cherokees' relationship with other Upper Path peoples. Several communities whose members became Upper and Lower Creeks fled their eastern Tennessee homeland in the 1680s and 1690s due to Cherokee attacks. Conversely, the Cherokees experienced raids coming from the Upper Path, especially from Shawnees and Yuchis who had settled on the Savannah River. In the early 1700s major conflict between the Cherokees and their Upper Path enemies subsided as the English redirected the warring activities of their common friends toward French- and Spanish-allied Natives or toward the rebellious Tuscaroras and Algonquians, but the longstanding hostility between the two did not go away and flared up from time to time.

Unscrupulous traders tried to profit from some of those flareups and were often blamed for instigating Cherokee attacks. In 1703, for example, the Commons House of Assembly learned that the Cherokees had captured several individuals from Carolina's southern allies and sold them to traders. The assembly did not know how many had been shipped into the colony to be sold, but they succeeded in getting at least one Upper Creek man sent back to his home on the Coosa River.[190] According to Thomas Nairne such practices were more widespread than just the 1703 incident. "Those English traders, who live among [Natives] had gott a trick of setting them to surprize one another's towns," Nairne complained in 1708, "by that means to have the quicker sale of their goods for the prisoners taken, and to the end they might never be punished for actions of that kind." Nairne specifically mentioned James Child, who two years earlier "raised the people of some of the Chereckie towns, and led them to cutt off two or three small towns of [Carolina's] friends, pretending 'twas the Governor's order." The Cherokees allegedly destroyed the towns, took about 160 slaves, and gave Child 30 of the captives. Child then sold the captives in Charles Town. Since Child worked for Governor Johnson's son-in-law, Thomas Broughton, Nairne accused the governor of receiving a portion of the proceeds as a bribe. The assembly tried to prosecute Child but could not get him to come in for trial. He was later killed somewhere on the trading path.[191]

The Cherokees' conquest of the Yuchis sent an even more ominous message to South Carolina's other allies. In the early eighteenth century, the Yuchis maintained two large towns on the Savannah River. They also had at least one settlement on the Hiwassee, known as Chestowee, and possibly others downstream in the Tennessee Valley. In 1712 the South Carolinians learned that the "Uche or Round Town People" were abandoning their settlement, and it was feared that they were going to settle near the French.[192] Whether the Round Town settlement was at that time in the Savannah or the Tennessee river valley is not known, but what is clear is that South Carolinian intrigue with the Cherokees gave the Yuchis little incentive to stay. A trader named Alexander Longe especially disliked the Yuchis. Around the time the Yuchis were rumored to be leaving their settlements, they allegedly tried to scalp Longe following a dispute over a debt that they supposedly owed him. Longe, according to some rival traders, got his revenge in 1714 by inciting the Cherokees to attack Chestowee. Along with his accomplice, Eleazar Wiggen, Longe told the Cherokees that the governor had authorized such an attack and that they would be rewarded with a "brave parcel of slaves." Cherokee warriors indeed assaulted the town, taking numerous captives and forcing others to retreat into their council house, where the Yuchis killed several of their own people to prevent them from becoming enslaved. Longe and Wiggen received one woman and five children as payment for the debts that the Yuchis owed. When later examined about the affair, the two traders of course claimed that the Cherokees conducted the attack of their own volition. Wiggen, perhaps alluding to losses from the 1711–12 smallpox epidemic, claimed that the "Cherikees were dissatisfied for the loss of some of their people and for that reason cut off Chestowee." Longe flatly denied his culpability, claiming that "the Cherikees of their own Accord provided to goe against the Euches." The Commissioners of the Indian Trade did not buy their stories. They ordered the two men to surrender their licenses and bonds and stand trial.[193] Both escaped into the Appalachian Mountains, though, where they would later prove useful to the colony as diplomats during the Yamasee War. Before that war erupted, however, the Chestowee Yuchis who survived the Cherokee attack took up residence on the Upper Path, where their resentments only enflamed an already explosive situation.

The Cherokees' destruction of the Chestowee Yuchis should not be seen as a side note in the origins of the Yamasee War. It was not the first time South Carolinian traders instigated slave raids on their own allies, and it was not the first time that the Cherokees conducted raids on their weaker neighbors. It fit a common pattern of English behavior that understandably made South Carolina's allies fear their own enslavement. Nevertheless, fear that the Cherokees would be the agents of such a task worked in two ways in the growing conflict between South Carolina and its allies. On one hand, Carolinian activity among the Cherokees gave other Natives ample reason to believe that the powerful and numerous mountaineers would conduct more slave raids against them and that enslavement lay in the future for the most epidemiologically ravaged peoples if

South Carolina's trade network was not destroyed. On the other hand, war with South Carolina heightened the risk that the English would encourage the Cherokees to commit raids against Upper Path communities. For the latter reason, the Yamasees' decision to revolt was predicated on their belief that the Cherokees would join with them against South Carolina. The Cherokees, in fact, did meet with the Yamasees before the war and were among the 161 different communities that the Yamasees and the Lower Creeks told the Spanish stood behind them in their revolt.[194]

The Cherokees certainly had grievances against South Carolina. Carolinian slave dealers had been purchasing Cherokee captives since the 1680s. Even after they had become more fully integrated into South Carolina's trade network, some of their people wound up as prisoners on Carolinian plantations. In 1706, for example, Thomas Broughton's traders—the very individuals who used Cherokees to enslave others—held several Cherokees.[195] Perhaps the most interesting Cherokee who had fallen into possession of a Carolinian was a man referred to as Caesar, who had been owned by John Stephens but managed to escape back to his people. Stephens demanded that the Cherokees be made to compensate him for his loss, something with which the Commissioners of the Indian Trade agreed despite its own rules forbidding the sale of free Natives.[196] Also in 1713 the commissioners received complaints from the Cherokees that two of their kinswomen were being held at a Mr. St. Julien's plantation. The board ordered the two slaves to be freed.[197] The Cherokees' suspicions of South Carolina were further heightened by the actions of Alexander Longe. After fleeing from Charles Town, the renegade trader allegedly told the Cherokees that the "Einglish was goeing to macke warrs with them and that they did design to kill all their head warriers." Such rumors were confirmed by what the Cherokees had been hearing from other Natives and by the actions of traders who "had ben verry abusefull to them of latte and not as whitte men used to be to them."[198] The Cherokees' fears of their own enslavement, thus, propelled them into action in the early stages of the war.

Still, the Cherokees' commitment to the revolt was weak at best. One Englishman learned that sometime between April 15 and May 8, the Cherokees murdered several traders among them. The Cherokees, he observed, "appeared to be our friends, and made a feast, to which they invited the Whites in order to deceive them, after which they shot them."[199] Such actions were the green light that Siouans had been looking for to begin their assault on South Carolina. After the Yamasees initiated the war, the Catawbas and their affiliates took their cues from the Cherokees. If their more powerful neighbors had refused to join the revolt, Siouans would not likely have committed themselves either. The arrival of some seventy Cherokee warriors in their villages in early May and their participation in raids down the Santee Valley gave Siouans further reassurance that the revolt would end in the destruction of South Carolina and not their own enslavement through the agency of the Cherokees.²⁰⁰ When South Carolina sent peace overtures to the Cherokees shortly into the conflict, however, their fears of enslavement were assuaged, and they proved receptive to reconciliation. Some of the Cherokees, in fact, heard of Carolina's peace offerings on the night of June 12 and abandoned their Siouan friends as they were making their way into the Low Country. The following day, Carolinians under Colonel George Chicken inflicted a devastating defeat on the Siouans and sent them into retreat.²⁰¹

Indeed, as one of the nations that colonialism and its germs had damaged the least, the Cherokees saw much to gain by welcoming an alliance with South Carolina. South Carolina certainly pinned its hopes on the Cherokees. In July colonial officials compiled a gift of over five hundred guns along with powder and shot and enlisted the renegade trader Eleazar Wiggen to carry the cargo into the Appalachians.²⁰² The Cherokees warmly received the presents and sent a delegation to Charles Town in October to renew their kinship ties with the colony. "The Potent Nation of the Cherikee Indians came down . . . in a submissive manner," observed the Anglican missionary Francis Le Jau, "and made Peace with us with their wild Ceremonyes of a Grave dancing, wherein they Stripd themselves, and layd their cloaths by parcels att the feet of some of our most considerable men, who in return must do the like to them, this Exchanging of Cloaths and smoaking out of the same Pipe is a solemn token of reconciliation of friendship."²⁰³ With the breach in their relationship patched up, South Carolina turned its attention to getting the Cherokees to wage war in a way that fit a strategy of restoring its trade network. The Carolinians hoped the Cherokees would fall upon the Siouans of the Coastal Plain and the Piedmont and upon the Yamasees, the Apalachees, the Yuchis, and the Shawnees, who formerly inhabited the Savannah Basin but had dispersed into southern Georgia and even into Florida, where they received aid and encouragement from the Spanish. These smaller groups indeed seemed to be giving Carolina the most trouble, as their assault on English settlers continued into the winter of 1715–16. The English seemed hopeful that their relations with the Creeks and the Chickasaws could be restored.

The Cherokees, however, were deeply divided and had agendas that diverged from South Carolina's. In December 1715 Maurice Moore and George Chicken led a force of three hundred armed "settlement Indians," Africans, and Englishmen into the Appalachian Mountains. They first met with the Lower Cherokees, where the head priest of Tugalo Town informed the visiting Carolinians that his people would not go to war against the Yamasees but would fight against the Shawnees, the Yuchis, and the Apalachees. He also cleared the Catawbas of responsibility for continued attacks on the English and claimed that only one group of Siouans, the Keyauwees, remained hostile.[204] At the time the Lower Cherokees were awaiting a peace delegation from the Creeks. Warriors from the Middle and Upper Cherokees had different ideas. Caesar, the former slave and now spokesman for the warriors, informed the English that the Creeks had been his people's longstanding enemies and they were eager to go to war against them. They were surprised that the English did not want them to go after the Creeks, and they complained that if they remained at peace with their southern enemies, "they should have no way in getting of Slaves to buy ammunition & Clothing."[205] The advantages to be gained by exchanging captives for the Atlantic world's exotic and useful goods had taken a powerful hold on the Cherokees, even on a man who knew firsthand what it meant to be enslaved to the English.

As Chicken's forces negotiated the terms of their alliance with the Cherokees, an event happened that forced the issue. The delegation of Creeks finally reached Tugalo to discuss peace terms, but as they slept in the council house, eleven of them were murdered. The Cherokees gave a twelfth Creek man to a Carolinian, who promptly shot the captive in the night, suggesting that the English played some role in instigating what would become a nearly forty-year conflict between the Cherokees and the Creeks.[206] After the momentous event at Tugaloo, the Carolinians knew that their hands had been forced, and in a council of war they decided to support the Cherokees against the Creeks.[207] Given the way epidemics had severely depleted their neighbors and elevated them by default to a position of superior strength, the Cherokees now had a golden opportunity to become South Carolina's premier partner in the Native slave trade. To be sure, Cherokee demographic needs also motivated them; they too needed to adopt people to recover from previous epidemics and knew that they now had an advantage over the Creeks, whose women and children could augment their own numbers. But as Caesar's comments confirmed, the Cherokees were also thinking about how they could exchange Creek captives for more of the cargo that English colonialism had made such an important part of their everyday lives. Their reentry into South Carolina's trade network tragically confirmed those fears of enslavement that colonialism and its germs had made acute among peoples of the Upper Path.

The violence of the Yamasee War accelerated the changes in the social landscape that the cycle of enslavement and epidemics had begun many decades before. The Cherokees, according to South Carolina officials, "have done us a signal piece of service, in Compelling ye Cattawbaws, and those other Small Nations about them to make Peace with us, whom otherwise they threatened to Destroy."[208] The Catawbas exercised their own force and persuasion in getting the Waxhaws, the Waccamaws, the Saras, and other Siouans to give up the fight. Many joined the Catawbas in their homeland and over the years became more fully merged into one collective body.[209] To the south the Cherokees finished what the Carolinians had started in the summer of 1715. After their initial assaults on English settlements, the Yamasees, the Apalachees, the Yuchis, and the Shawnees saw vengeful Carolinians invade their villages and put them to the torch. The Yamasees lost three hundred of their people to death or enslavement during the English counterattack.[210] Survivors from the Savannah Basin became dispersed. Some evacuated to the Lower Creeks; some hid in the swamps of southern Georgia; and others moved to St. Augustine, where they received the support and protection of the Spanish. When the Cherokees entered the conflict on the side of South Carolina, they chased some of those refugee groups but directed most of their attacks toward the Creeks. By the end of April, Lower Creeks had evacuated the Ocmulgee area and moved to their old homeland, the Chattahoochee region.[211] The Cherokees also inflicted a serious defeat on the Upper Creeks.[212]

Such actions did little to protect the colony of South Carolina. Natives continued to harass English settlers and then disappear to their hiding places. "As for the Cherokees they have so often promised that they would fall upon our enemies to ye Southward (vizt) the Creeks, Euchees, & etc and so often Disappointed us," Carolinians complained in August 1716, "that we can but little to Depend on them in that affair."[213] Carolinians, moreover, grew tired of giving the copious amount of gifts to the Cherokees. "We are become their Tributaries," the governor and council of South Carolina complained. "We buy their Friendship at too dear a rate."[214] The Cherokees, they believed, had "insulted [them] to the last degree," and they were delighted that in June 1717 the Creeks had sent them a peace overture. In the summer of 1717 Carolinians carried presents to the Lower Creeks, and the following fall Creek leaders traveled to Charles Town to conclude a peace. Early in 1718 Carolinian traders were once again traveling the Upper Path through the various Creek towns and then to the Chickasaws. Meanwhile, the Cherokees and the Creeks remained at war. One Carolinian was quite candid about how such conflict benefited his colony. "To hold both as our friends, for some time, and assist them in cutting one anothers

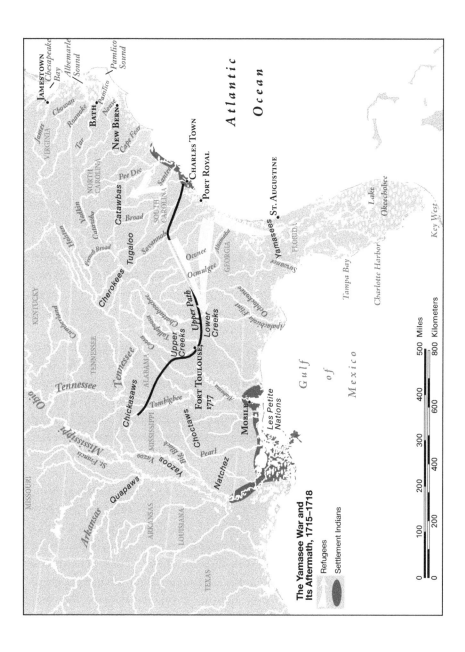

The Yamasee War and
Its Aftermath, 1715–1718

Refugees
Settlement Indians

throat w[ith]out offending either," Joseph Boone revealed. "This is the Game we intend to play . . . for if [we] cannot Destroy one nation of Indians by another— Our country must be lost."[215] The lesson of divide and conquer, which had played such a central role in facilitating the Native slave trade, had not been lost on Carolinians, and they used it successfully for the next several decades to keep their two most powerful allies from uniting.

Conclusion

With South Carolina reestablishing its relations with the Creeks, the Yamasee War essentially came to an end. South Carolinians still experienced the occasional raid from Yamasees who lived in Florida, but their colony had survived a great test. The Native slave trade did not. Carolinians bought some of the prisoners that their allies possessed, especially Yamasee captives from Florida, but the days of an essentially unregulated trade in which a high volume of prisoners flowed into Charles Town were over. Carolinians would also no longer organize and take part in the large-scale slaving expeditions as they had before 1715; instead their role in human trafficking switched to importing Africans rather than exporting indigenous peoples. Catastrophic depopulation of Natives from germs and violence undoubtedly lay behind that transformation. The Yamasee War may have brought the Native slave trade to a climactic finish, but disease and depopulation undermined the economic basis of South Carolina's relations with its indigenous partners and laid the basis for the conflict. After the Yamasee War the only sizable Native polities left were the Cherokees, the Creeks, the Chickasaws, and the Choctaws, and imperial considerations tempered the desires of Carolinians to profit from a continued slave trade. They could supply the Cherokees and the Creeks with the guns, powder, and shot that the respective groups used against each other and still enjoy a profit from the deerskins that were given in return, but playing an active role in organizing raids or purchasing captives put them at risk of driving their allies into the hands of the French. The French could never supply Natives as the English could, but through gift giving and diplomacy, they expanded their influence during the Yamasee War. They regained their ties with the Choctaws and gained more support among the Creeks. A sign of this growing influence was the construction of Fort Toulouse in 1717 at the junction of the Coosa, Tallapoosa, and Alabama rivers. Even South Carolinians, whose colony began with an aggressive profit-seeking group of people who eagerly sought to transform human captives into commodities, came to recognize that at times they too had to act as proper kinsmen.[216]

Chapter Five

Conclusion

It is often said that historians do not like to talk about epidemics because of their supposed accidental nature.[1] Epidemics after all seem out of human control, whereas other historical events such as wars and revolutions can be seen as the consequences of the decisions and actions, either collectively or individually, of politicians, generals, merchants, workers, intellectuals, or other human actors. Epidemics in the Southeast may not have resulted directly from the conscious decisions of historical actors, and there is no evidence that Europeans, who did not yet have the germ theory, deliberately attempted to spread diseases to the region's indigenous peoples between 1492 and 1715.[2] The impact of diseases on Natives, however, should not be seen as merely an accident of Europeans and Africans arriving among a people who had no prior experience with the Atlantic world's deadliest microbes. Instead, the larger aspects of colonialism shaped the impact that epidemics had on indigenous peoples. In the Southeast, English commerce in Native slaves was the aspect of colonialism most responsible for transforming the disease ecology of the region and facilitating widespread depopulation.

Although the Spanish explored the Southeast and established a series of missions on the perimeter of the region long before the English arrived, there is very little reason to believe that they sparked epidemics that spread as extensively and did as much regionwide damage as did the Great Southeastern Smallpox Epidemic. To be sure, such a conclusion might appear biased by a historian's preference for documentary evidence over evidence derived from the archaeological record. This study, however, has aimed not to dismiss the archaeological record but instead to look at it more critically. Demographic changes did occur among Native societies during the protohistoric period, but dramatic alterations did not characterize the entire social landscape, and alterations that occurred can be explained by nonepidemiological causes. In fact, when the evidence is scrutinized through an epidemiological lens, it becomes even more problematic to explain protohistoric demographic changes as a result of newly introduced diseases. The documents associated with the various Spanish expeditions indicate that early exploration could not have resulted in the introduction of the Atlantic world's deadliest diseases. At most, early European intruders seeded the region with malaria, a disease that could have caused some casualties and some alterations in the social landscape but that by itself would not have resulted in massive regionwide depopulation. Still, Spanish explorers, especially Hernando de Soto, did great damage, but instead of introducing history's most notorious germ killers, Spanish invaders stole food, killed Natives, enflamed violence between rival polities, and contaminated indigenous communities with ordinary pathogens that were not necessarily new to the southeastern environment. Rather than some undocumented introduction of smallpox, measles, typhus, or influenza, then, a combination of malaria, psychological trauma, and physical brutality can explain the collapse of sixteenth-century polities. Epidemiological reasoning also suggests that the establishment of Florida did very little to facilitate the spread of colonialism's worst biological scourges throughout the greater Southeast. Catholic missions certainly brought Native converts into the flow of the Atlantic world's deadliest microbes, but Spanish colonialism did not provide the means for those diseases to travel very far beyond direct European contact. Spanish trade remained minimal and did not escalate to the volume at which it could be suspected of spreading acute infectious diseases into the interior. While scholars—both historians and archaeologists—have made great strides in understanding the mysterious protohistoric period, there is still much to be done. It is hoped that future scholarship will begin with a better understanding of those viruses and bacteria that have been so casually cited as the causes of demographic changes in the sixteenth and seventeenth centuries.

Certainly scholars feel more comfortable making conclusions about the late seventeenth and early eighteenth century, when the documentary evidence becomes richer. Such evidence demonstrates that English-inspired slave raids mediated the spread and impact of newly introduced germs in very powerful ways. The high volume of human traffic involved in the slave trade caused newly introduced diseases to be more widely circulated than they otherwise would have. The biological consequences of the noxious commerce included the Great Southeastern Smallpox Epidemic and a series of aftershocks that gave a large number of Native communities an experience with virgin-soil epidemics as devastating as historian Alfred Crosby's model suggests. The violence associated with the slave trade created ecological conditions in which mortality rates skyrocketed. By 1715 the synergy of germs and slave raids had widowed much of the region of its indigenous population. Carolina's Coastal Plain and Piedmont lost vast numbers of its original Tuscarora, Algonquian, and Siouan population, and those who remained existed either as "settlement Indians" or as heterogeneous peoples such as the Catawbas or the Yamasees, who were overshadowed by more powerful confederacies in the interior. Florida was essentially vacant with the exception of a few hundred Natives huddled around St. Augustine and some scattered bands of Calusas who hid from English-allied slave raiders in the Everglades; the majority of Apalachees, Timucuas, and Guales only survived by becoming adopted members of South Carolina's allies or by fleeing to French Louisiana and amalgamating with other refugee groups. The formerly large towns that had been located uncomfortably close to one another along the Gulf Coast and the lower Mississippi Valley had also tragically shrunk into *les petite nations,* which depended heavily on the French for protection. This dramatic alteration in the social landscape was not the inevitable result of the introduction of new germs but instead occurred as a consequence of English colonialism creating conditions for those germs to reach their deadliest potential.

In 1715 the combination of enslavement and epidemics had brought the Native Southeast to a turning point. English commerce in indigenous captives had become unsustainable, the economic basis of South Carolina's relationship with its Native allies collapsed, and the consequent tensions between Natives and their trading partners erupted into the Yamasee War. South Carolina's traders and officials seemed unwilling or unable to change their orientation from market imperatives to more reciprocal forms of exchange that did not violate Native understandings of how kinsmen treated one another. But the tensions were so explosive because they occurred within a context that the Great Southeastern Smallpox Epidemic and its aftershocks had created. Carolinians and their indigenous allies increasingly saw captives fulfilling different purposes. The English saw them as property that could be confiscated from debtors; indigenous peoples saw them as potential kinsmen who could add valuable numbers to their disease-depleted communities. Widespread Carolinian practices of kidnapping kinsmen threatened the survival of their Native clients and helped Yamasees and others decide that war against South Carolina was necessary for their survival. War was certainly not an unthinking decision. The way epidemics had changed the social landscape affected the decision of South Carolina's allies to revolt. Increased English intercourse with the Choctaws and the Cherokees posed the frightening specter of enslavement for those groups whose numbers had plummeted much more dramatically; the Carolinians had given their allies several examples in which they used stronger groups to raid weaker ones for captives. The Tuscarora

War and the Cherokees' destruction of the Chestowee Yuchis in particular taught South Carolina's allies a valuable lesson—South Carolina's slave trade would only continue with English-allied tribes attacking one another. That lesson led the Yamasees and other peoples of the Upper Path to engage in a complex set of talks with one another and with Cherokees and Siouans to the north. The more demographically stressed Yamasees misperceived the level of discontent among the more numerous Cherokees, and the decision of the latter to drop out of the revolt and fight against Carolina's enemies only confirmed what slave traders had managed to do so successfully since their arrival in the Southeast.

While hundreds of Yamasees wound up enslaved and the survivors became scattered either in Florida or among the Creeks, the conflict that they had begun did destroy what they had sought to free themselves from. The deadly cycle of germs and violence had made the Native slave trade untenable, and the Yamasee War brought the noxious commerce to its ultimate end.[3] A generation of traders who had staked their prospects on slavery were wiped out in a quick moment, and the flow of indigenous captives into South Carolina after the conflict consisted of a mere trickle in comparison to the voluminous torrent of days past. A new generation of Carolinian traders made their way to Native villages with little desire to purchase human captives or become directly involved in captive raids. The colony's role in the international slave trade completed its transition from a supplier of indigenous labor to an importer of Africans. For those Native polities that survived the deadly cycle of epidemics and enslavement that the English had unleashed, a new order emerged after the Yamasee War, one in which their European partners valued their friendship more than the commodities that they could produce for the Atlantic market. Both the English and the French sought profits from deerskins acquired from the Cherokees, the Creeks, the Choctaws, and the Chickasaws, but the European rivals also depended on their respective Native allies for support in the imperial competition against each other. Both found it necessary to operate under nonmarket imperatives by giving gifts, adjusting prices of trade goods to below market values, and participating in Native rituals and ceremonies. This continued interaction kept the Native Southeast connected to the larger Atlantic world, and epidemics continued to be a problem among the region's surviving indigenous communities. Nevertheless, no epidemiological event that indigenous peoples suffered after 1715 was to equal the magnitude of what they endured when the Native slave trade was at its height, a time in which English colonialism unleashed potent biological forces that forever changed the Native Southeast's destiny.[4]

NOTES

Source Abbreviations

BPROSC   *Records in the British Public Records Office relating to South Carolina.* Transcribed by W. Noel Sainsbury. 36 vols. Columbia: South Carolina Department of History and Archives, 1955. Microfilm.

CCLJ   *The Carolina Chronicle of Dr. Francis Le Jau.* Edited by Frank Klingberg. Berkeley: University of California Press, 1956.

CRNC   *The Colonial Records of North Carolina.* Edited by William L. Saunders. 10 vols. Raleigh NC: P. M. Hale, 1886–90.

C.O.   Colonial Office. British Public Record Office.

DSC   *The De Soto Chronicles: The Expedition of Hernando de Soto to the United States, 1539–1543.* Edited by Langdon Clayton, Vernon James Knight Jr., and Edward C. Moore. 2 vols. Tuscaloosa: University of Alabama, 1993.

EJCCV   *Executive Journals of the Council of Colonial Virginia.* Edited by H. R. McIlwaine. 6 vols. Richmond: D. Bottom, 1925–45.

JCHASC   *The Journal of the Commons House of Assembly of South Carolina.* Edited by Alexander S. Salley. 21 vols. Columbia: South Carolina Department of Archives and History, 1907–49.

JCHASC transcripts   The Journal of the Commons House of Assembly of South Carolina. South Carolina Department of Archives and History, Columbia. Microfilm.

JCIT   *Journals of the Commissioners of the Indian Trade, September 20, 1710–August 29, 1718.* Edited by William L. McDowell. Columbia: South Carolina Department of History and Archives, 1955.

JPE   *The Juan Pardo Expeditions: Exploration of the Carolinas and Tennessee, 1566–1568.* Edited by Charles Hudson, with documents relating to the Pardo Expedition transcribed, translated, and annotated by Paul E. Hoffman. Washington: Smithsonian Institution Press, 1990.

LP   *The Luna Papers.* Translated and edited by Herbert Priestly. 2 vols. Deland: Florida State Historical Society, 1928.

MPAFD   *Mississippi Provincial Archives, French Dominion.* Edited by Dunbar Rowland, A. G. Sanders, and Patricia Galloway. 5 vols. Jackson: Mississippi Department of Archives and History, 1927–32 and 1984.

NA/PRO   National Archives of the United Kingdom, formerly known as the British Public
          Record Office. Kew, England.

NAW   *New American World: A Documentary History of North America to 1612.* Edited
          by David B. Quinn. 5 vols. New York: Arno Press, 1979.

PGJ   *Carolina Chronicle: The Papers of Gideon Johnston.* Edited by Frank Klingberg.
          University of California Publications in History 35. Berkeley: University of
          California Press, 1946.

SCHGM   *South Carolina Historical and Genealogical Magazine.*

SPG   Records of the Society for the Propagation of the Gospel in Foreign Parts. Society
          for the Propagation of the Gospel. London. Microfilm.

Introduction

1. Alfred Crosby has offered the most extensive work on the role of epidemic disease in facilitating European conquest. See Crosby, *Columbian Exchange;* Crosby, "Virgin Soil Epidemics"; Crosby, *Ecological Imperialism;* Crosby, *Germs, Seeds, and Animals.* Other works
have borrowed heavily from Crosby; see McNeill, *Plagues and Peoples;* Watts, *Epidemics and
History;* Diamond, *Guns, Germs, and Steel;* Cook, *Born to Die.*

2. Work on the Columbian Exchange subsequent to Crosby's explains well why indigenous
peoples did not have the same experience with disease as did people in the Eastern Hemisphere before 1492. Subsequent work also describes the devastating impact those diseases had
on Native peoples. But in general Columbian Exchange scholarship fails to address the connection between epidemics and the larger aspects of colonialism. Jared Diamond, for example, lists infectious diseases as one of the proximate causes for Europe's success in conquering
the Americas, but he leaves his readers to believe that novel germs damaged Native populations simply due to their arrival, thus obscuring how European invaders brought indigenous
peoples into larger colonial systems in which diseases could spread to them and exact severe
mortality rates. He specifically mentions the American Southeast as a region in which newly
introduced germs spread in advance of European colonialism, a point that this book will argue against. See Diamond, *Guns, Germs, and Steel,* esp. 77–78 and 210–11. William Cronon,
Richard White, and Timothy Silver have offered exceptional studies of the ecological aspects
of European colonization that do place disease in a larger context of a larger Atlantic market
economy. Cronon, White, and Silver, however, do not make the connection between epidemics and the Atlantic market economy as explicit as this study does. See Cronon, *Changes
in the Land;* White, *Roots of Dependency;* Silver, *New Face on the Countryside.*

3. Alan Gallay and Steven Oatis have expanded our insights into the Native slave trade, and
this work builds on theirs by emphasizing something they overlook: the trade's epidemiological importance. See Gallay, *Indian Slave Trade;* Oatis, *Colonial Complex.*

4. Anthropologist Henry Dobyns has made the boldest estimates of population decline
during the protohistoric. See *Their Number Become Thinned.* Ann Ramenofsky offers support
to Dobyns's views in *Vectors of Death.* Others have greeted Dobyns's and Ramenofsky's conclusions with a great deal of skepticism. See Henige, *Numbers from Nowhere.*

5. Marvin Smith has done a remarkable job tracing population movements of indigenous

communities out of the Tennessee and Coosa valleys and attributes such movements to various possibilities, including disease-induced depopulation deriving from Spanish colonialism and English-inspired slave raids. My analysis offers a complement to Smith's work by examining in more detail what led to those movements. See Smith, *Archaeology of Aboriginal Culture Change;* Smith, *Coosa.*

6. Charles Hudson, while maintaining that Spanish colonialism had a greater epidemiological significance than my analysis does, nonetheless attributes the emergence of coalescent societies to their incorporation into the modern world system as theorized by Immanuel Wallerstein. See Hudson, introduction to *Transformation of the Southeastern Indians,* ed. Robbie Ethridge and Charles Hudson, xi–xxxix. That the Columbian Exchange was a contingent process that depended on Native incorporation into the larger Atlantic market economy indeed suggests that scholars should pay more attention to the political economist Wallerstein than the biologist Diamond in explaining European global expansion. See Wallerstein, *Capitalist Agriculture;* Wallerstein, *Mercantilism.* For a global history based on a modified version of Wallerstein's world system theory, see Wolf, *Europe and the People without History.*

7. While Ramenofsky places the timing of the Southeast's worst experience with the Columbian Exchange in the protohistoric period, her ideas of differential persistence still have applicability to this study. See Ramenofsky, "Loss of Innocence." Other works that discuss the differential impact of epidemics include White, "Winning the West"; Newson, "Highland-Lowland Contrasts," 1190; Milner, "Epidemic Disease"; Thornton, "American Indian Population Recovery"; Baker and Kealhofer, *Bioarchaeology of Native American Adaptation.*

8. For a discussion of ethnohistorical methodology, see Axtell, "Ethnohistory of Early America"; Axtell, "Ethnohistory"; Jennings, "Discovery of Americans"; and Trigger, "Ethnohistory."

9. For different perspectives on environmental history, see Worster, "Transformations of the Earth," 1087–106; Alfred W. Crosby, "An Enthusiastic Second," 1107–10; Richard White, "Environmental History, Ecology and Meaning," 1111–16; Carolyn Merchant, "Gender and Environmental History," 1117–21; William Cronon, "Modes of Prophecy and Production: Placing Nature in History," 1122–31; Stephen J. Pyne, "Firestick History," 1132–41; Donald Worster, "Seeing beyond Culture," 1142–47, all published in *Journal of American History* 76 (March 1990).

1. Disease Ecology of the Native Southeast

1. Alfred Crosby disputes assertions that indigenous peoples had weak genes, but subsequent works that utilize the virgin soil thesis make specific reference to indigenous peoples lacking genetic immunity. For discussion of this controversy, see David S. Jones, "Virgin Soils Revisited."

2. On the environmental history of the Southeast, see Cowdrey, *This Land, This South;* Silver, *New Face on the Countryside,* 7–14; Hudson, *Southeastern Indians,* 14–22.

3. Hudson, *Southeastern Indians,* 272–89; Silver, *New Face on the Countryside,* 36–37.

4. Bruce D. Smith, "Origins of Agriculture in Eastern North America"; Bruce D. Smith, "Origins of Agriculture in the Americas"; Kelly, "Emergence of Mississippian Culture."

5. Kelly, "Emergence of Mississippian Culture," 113–52; Claire Monod Cassidy, "Prehistoric Subsistence in the Central Ohio River Valley," in Cohen and Armelagos, *Paleopathology at the Origins of Agriculture,* 307–45; Hudson, *Southeastern Indians,* 80–81; William Baden, "Dynamic Model," 48.

6. Cohen, *Health and the Rise of Civilization,* 71 and 103.

7. Kelly, "Emergence of Mississippian Culture," 113–52; Larsen, "Biological Changes in Human Populations"; Bentley, Jasieńska, and Goldberg, "Is the Fertility of Agriculturalists Higher?"

8. Jane E. Buikstra, "The Lower Illinois River Region: A Prehistoric Context for the Study of Ancient Diet and Health," in *Paleopathology at the Origins of Agriculture,* 226–27.

9. Thomas McKeown, *Origins of Human Disease* (New York: Blackwell, 1988), 61; Cassidy, "Prehistoric Subsistence in the Central Ohio River Valley," 337; Jane E. Buikstra, "Diseases of the Pre-Columbian Americas," in Kiple, *Cambridge World History of Human Disease,* 311–13.

10. Neel, "Health and Disease in Unacculturated Amerindian Populations."

11. Cohen, *Health and the Rise of Civilization,* 129.

12. Bentley, Jasieńska, and Goldberg, "Fertility of Agricultural and Nonagricultural Traditional Societies."

13. For an overview of this process, see the series of articles in *Mississippian Settlement Patterns,* ed. Bruce D. Smith.

14. Muller, *Mississippian Political Economy,* 217.

15. Bruce D. Smith, "Variation in Mississippian Settlement Patterns," in *Mississippian Settlement Patterns,* 490; Bruce D. Smith, "Mississippian Patterns of Subsistence and Settlement," in Badger and Clayton, *Alabama and the Borderlands from Prehistory to Statehood,* 75–77.

16. David Anderson, *Savannah River Chiefdoms,* 283.

17. Baden, "Dynamic Model," 30, 56–59.

18. Blitz, *Ancient Chiefdoms of the Tombigbee,* 113–14; Muller, *Mississippian Political Economy,* 222–23.

19. Larson, "Functional Considerations of Warfare."

20. Blitz, *Ancient Chiefdoms of the Tombigbee,* 98–101; Phyllis Morse and Dan F. Morse, "The Zebree Site: An Emerged Early Mississippian Expression in Northeast Arkansas," in Bruce D. Smith, *Mississippian Emergence,* 57.

21. Scholars disagree on the reasons why indigenous peoples of the Native Southeast warred with one another, but they agree that they preferred the same general tactics of ambushes and raids. See Larson, "Functional Considerations of Warfare," 383–92; Gibson, "Aboriginal Warfare in the Protohistoric Southeast"; Dickson, "Yanomamö of the Mississippi Valley?"; Steinen, "Ambushes, Raids, and Palisades."

22. Bruce D. Smith, "Mississippian Patterns of Subsistence and Settlement," 75–77.

23. Muller, *Mississippian Political Economy,* 222–23.

24. Blitz, *Ancient Chiefdoms of the Tombigbee,* 98–104; Bruce D. Smith, "Mississippian Patterns of Subsistence and Settlement," 77; Bruce D. Smith, "Variation in Mississippian Settlement Patterns," 490–95.

25. Winterville, one of the largest mound centers in the eastern woodlands, stood in the

Mississippi Valley, but its residential population was dispersed throughout the countryside. See Brain, *Winterville,* 110. For much of its history, the Cahokia chiefdom included both nucleated and dispersed patterns as well. Most people belonging to the chiefdom in this highly fertile area lived dispersed over the countryside. See Milner, "Late Prehistoric Cahokia Cultural System." On the other hand, several communities in the narrow valleys of the Appalachian highlands were compact and fortified in the years before the European invasion. See Ward and Davis, *Time before History,* 160–61; Roy S. Dickens, "Mississippian Settlement Patterns in the Appalachian Summit Area: The Pisgah and Qualla Phases," in Bruce D. Smith, *Mississippian Settlement Patterns,* 115–39; Dickens, *Cherokee Prehistory,* 46–51.

26. This paradox can be seen across the globe as hunter-gatherers became farmers. See Karlen, *Man and Microbes,* 34–42.

27. Goodman and Armelagos, "Disease and Death at Dr. Dickson's Mounds."

28. Kenneth Parham, "Toqua Skeletal Biology: A Biocultural Approach," in Polhemus, *Toqua Site,* 544.

29. Leslie Eisenberg, "Mississippian Cultural Terminations in the Middle Tennessee: What the Bioarchaeological Evidence Can Tell Us," in Powell, Bridges, and Mires, *What Mean These Bones?* 86.

30. Crawford, *Origins of Native Americans,* 68.

31. El-Najjar, "Maize, Malaria, and the Anemias"; Parham, "Toqua Skeletal Biology," 488, 491.

32. Goodman and Armelagos, "Disease and Death at Dr. Dickson's Mounds," 15–16.

33. George Milner, "Health and Cultural Change in the Late Prehistoric American Bottom, Illinois," in Powell, Bridges, and Mires, *What Mean These Bones?* 65.

34. Eisenberg, "Mississippian Cultural Terminations in the Middle Tennessee," 86; Parham, "Toqua Skeletal Biology," 493.

35. Clark Spencer Larsen, "Health and Disease in Prehistoric Georgia," in Cohen and Armelagos, *Paleopathology at the Origins of Agriculture,* 367–92; Parham, "Toqua Skeletal Biology," 492. It remains theoretically possible for women to have shorter life expectancies and still outnumber men. In communities with high levels of iron-deficiency anemia, more women died in their early teens than did boys, but those women who survived past their teen years lived longer than did their male cohorts who had higher death rates in their late teens and early twenties due to warfare and hunting accidents. Moreover, among communities not as highly compromised as those on the Cumberland, life expectancies for women were as long if not longer than those for men.

36. Parham, "Toqua Skeletal Biology," 492.

37. Buikstra, "Diseases of the Pre-Columbian Americas," 314.

38. Cohen, *Health and the Rise of Civilization,* 14.

39. Merbs, "New World of Infectious Disease," 14. Merbs identifies tularemia as a likely aboriginal disease. Calvin Martin does not label this disease as either pre- or post-Columbian but does attribute human epidemics of this disease to higher demands for beaver pelts that came with the fur trade. See Martin, "Wildlife Diseases."

40. Chin, *Control of Communicable Diseases Manual,* 20–25.

41. Reinhard, "Archaeoparasitology in North America."

42. Chin, *Control of Communicable Diseases Manual,* 508–11.

43. Chin, *Control of Communicable Diseases Manual,* 75–78.

44. Scholars have perpetuated the idea that European livestock infected both humans and the wildlife populations in the Americas with trichinosis, brucellosis, and other diseases. (For the popularization of this notion, see Mann, "1491," 45.) Such assertions are flawed because they assume that wildlife populations in America were virgin populations, which is not necessarily the case. Moreover, assuming that wildlife diseases were introduced to indigenous animals, none of these zoonotic infections would have sparked major epidemics among Native peoples, who would have served as a dead end in the chain of infection.

45. Buikstra, "Diseases of the Pre-Columbian Americas," 305–17.

46. Marvin J. Allison, "Chagas' Disease," 636–38; Marvin J. Allison, "Leishmaniasis," 832–33, both in Kiple, *Cambridge World History of Human Disease.*

47. Chin, *Control of Communicable Diseases Manual,* 430–32.

48. Merbs, "New World of Infectious Disease," 14 and 26–27.

49. Chin, *Control of Communicable Diseases Manual,* 302–06; Merbs, "New World of Infectious Disease," 14–15.

50. Cohen, *Health and the Rise of Civilization,* 17.

51. Cohen, *Health and the Rise of Civilization,* 36–37.

52. Karlen, *Man and Microbes,* 19; Cohen, *Health and the Rise of Civilization,* 35.

53. Goodman and Armelagos, "Disease and Death at Dr. Dickson's Mounds," 15. See also Clark Spencer Larsen, "Health and Disease in Prehistoric Georgia," in Cohen and Armelagos, *Paleopathology at the Origins of Agriculture,* 367–92.

54. Parham, "Toqua Skeletal Pathology," 508.

55. David J. Hally, "The Chiefdom of Coosa," in Hudson and Tesser, *Forgotten Centuries,* 232.

56. K. David Patterson, "Amebic Dysentery," in Kiple, *Cambridge World History of Human Disease,* 568–71; Merbs, "New World of Infectious Disease," 10.

57. Ann Ramenofsky, "Diseases of the Americas, 1492–1700," in Kiple, *Cambridge World History of Human Disease,* 323.

58. Chin, *Control of Communicable Diseases Manual,* 535–41.

59. Charles W. LeBaron and David W. Taylor, "Typhoid Fever," in Kiple, *Cambridge World History of Human Disease,* 1071–77; Cockburn, "Where Did Our Infectious Diseases Come From?" 108.

60. Chin, *Control of Communicable Diseases Manual,* 535–41.

61. Taylor, *American Colonies,* 130–31.

62. Francis L. Black, "Infectious Hepatitis," in Kiple, *Cambridge World History of Human Disease,* 794–800.

63. Chin, *Control of Communicable Diseases Manual,* 68–70.

64. Eisenberg, "Mississippian Cultural Terminations in the Middle Tennessee," 78 and 84.

65. Falkner, Patton, and Johnson, "Prehistoric Parasitism in Tennessee"; Reinhard, "Archaeoparasitology in North America."

66. The current weight of scholarly opinion suggests a pre-Columbian presence of hookworm. See John Ettling, "Hookworm Disease," in Kiple, *Cambridge World History of Human Disease,* 784–88. For a dissenting view, see Kathleen Fuller, "Hookworm." Fuller's views, though, have been challenged. See "Commentaries," 91.

67. For the characteristics of helminths, see Chin, *Control of Communicable Diseases Manual,* 186–88 (pinworm), 265–68 (hookworm), and 513–14 (whipworm).

68. Chin, *Control of Communicable Diseases Manual,* 521–30. Ingestion is another mode of transmission, usually through unpasteurized cows' milk. Bovine tuberculosis, though, would not have been common among precontact American populations for obvious reasons.

69. Jane E. Buikstra, introduction to *Prehistoric Tuberculosis in the Americas,* 7; Robert L. Blakely and David S. Mathews, "What Price Civilization? Tuberculosis for One," in Richardson and Webb, *Burden of Being Civilized,* 11–23. For two good summaries of this topic, see Paulsen, "Tuberculosis in the Native American"; Reider, "Notes on the History of an Epidemic Tuberculosis"; Mahmoud Y. El-Najjar, "Skeletal Changes in Tuberculosis: The Hamman-Todd Collection," in Buiksta, *Prehistoric Tuberculosis in the Americas,* 85–86 and 91; El-Najjar, "Human Treponematosis and Tuberculosis," 608.

70. Salo et al., "Identification of *Mycobacterium tuberculosis* DNA."

71. William Stead et al., "When Did *Mycobacterium tuberculosis* Infection First Occur in the New World?"

72. Sousa et al., "Epidemic of Tuberculosis"; Fackelmann, "Tuberculosis Outbreak."

73. McNeill, *Plagues and Peoples,* 226–28.

74. Mary Lucas Powell, "Ancient Disease, Modern Perspectives: Treponematosis and Tuberculosis in the Age of Agriculture," in Lambert, *Bioarchaeological Studies,* 6–34.

75. Chin, *Control of Communicable Diseases Manual,* 481–86.

76. Black, "Infectious Diseases in Primitive Societies," 517.

77. Chin, *Control of Communicable Diseases Manual,* 243–51; Francis L. Black, "Infectious Hepatitis," in Kiple, *Cambridge World History of Infectious Disease,* 794–800.

78. Black, "Infectious Diseases in Primitive Societies," 517.

79. Haddler et al., "Delta Virus and Severe Hepatitis."

80. Jacobson and Dienstag, "Viral Hepatitis, Type D."

81. Spiess and Spiess, "New England Pandemic of 1616–22."

82. Starr, "Novel Mechanism of Immunosuppression after Measles."

83. Chin, *Control of Communicable Diseases Manual,* 310–23.

84. Harder, "Seeds of Malaria."

85. Chin, *Control of Communicable Diseases Manual,* 381–87.

86. McNeil, *Plagues and Peoples,* 161–207. For a more detailed history of plague in a single nation, see Alexander, *Bubonic Plague in Early Modern Russia.*

87. Dobyns, *Their Number Become Thinned,* 18–20 and 264–65.

88. McNeil, *Plagues and Peoples;* 168; Merbs, "New World of Infectious Diseases," 20–21.

89. Chin, *Control of Communicable Diseases Manual,* 553–58.

90. Ackerknecht, *History and Geography of the Most Important Diseases,* 51–55.

91. Humphreys, *Yellow Fever in the South.* Although popularly accepted, the notion that Africans withstood yellow fever better is debatable. See Donald B. Cooper and Kenneth F. Kiple, "Yellow Fever," in Kiple, *Cambridge World History of Human Disease,* 1100–1107.

92. Chin, *Control of Communicable Diseases Manual,* 541–44.

93. Ackerknecht, *History and Geography of the Most Important Diseases,* 34–35. The history of typhus is told in Hans Zinsser's classic work *Rats, Lice, and History.*

94. Cook, "Sickness, Starvation, and Death in Early Hispaniola."

95. Kenneth Kiple, "Typhus," in Kiple, *Cambridge World History of Disease,* 1080.

96. Some may consider influenza an exception to this since hogs are known to become infected with the same viruses that cause this disease and then can transmit the virus back to humans. For reasons to be discussed in chapter 2, there are barriers to such transmission. The vast majority of human influenza cases come from human-to-human transmission, making it most likely that when indigenous peoples experienced this dreaded disease during colonization, they did so after being infected by Europeans and Africans rather than by their livestock. Influenza also is endemic among a variety of wild waterfowl and occasionally makes the jump to humans, usually through domestic poultry. Avian flu, however, is not readily transmitted from person to person and only becomes so after undergoing genetic transformation usually as a result of reassortment with a human strain. Since pigs can contract both human and avian influenza, they may serve as a "mixing vessel" for this transformation to occur. See Perdue and Swayne, "Public Health Risk from Avian Influenza Viruses."

97. Chin, *Control of Communicable Diseases Manual,* 455–57; Shurkin, *Invisible Fire,* 26–27.

98. Native virginity to influenza is misleading because the virus mutates so frequently and rapidly that antibodies produced during earlier bouts can be ineffective against significantly different strains of the germ. These strains have been continually emerging, keeping peoples from all racial, ethnic, and geographic backgrounds vulnerable. Indigenous peoples of the Americas may have missed out on influenza before 1492, resulting in their lack of acquired immunity to strains commonly circulated throughout Europe. But Europeans, Africans, and Asians were not impervious either, as influenza continually came back to them in forms that previously produced antibodies failed to recognize. One of the world's deadliest epidemics was the influenza pandemic of 1918–19, which spread across the globe by a network of steamships, railroads, and soldiers going to and returning from war. See Crosby, *America's Forgotten Pandemic.*

99. To compare the characteristics of smallpox and influenza, see Chin, *Control of Communicable Diseases Manual,* 455–57 and 270–76.

100. Chin, *Control of Communicable Diseases Manual,* 330–35.

101. Chin, *Control of Communicable Diseases Manual,* 375–79. Whooping cough is not as deadly as smallpox; death disproportionately strikes children.

102. Chin, *Control of Communicable Diseases Manual,* 455–57; Shurkin, *Invisible Fire,* 26–27; Snow and Lanphear, "European Contact and Indian Depopulation in the Northeast."

103. For this theoretical model of chiefdoms, see Service, *Primitive Social Organization;* and Sahlins, *Tribesmen.* For critical views, see Earle, *Chiefdoms.*

104. Blitz, *Ancient Chiefdoms of the Tombigbee,* 182.

105. Muller, *Mississippian Political Economy,* 252.

106. Welch, *Moundville's Economy,* 132–33; Blitz, *Ancient Chiefdoms of the Tombigbee,* 22.

107. Blitz, *Ancient Chiefdoms of the Tombigbee,* 22.

108. On the cycling of southeastern chiefdoms, see David Anderson, *Savannah River Chiefdoms.*

109. Jarcho, "Some Observations on Disease in Prehistoric North America," 14.

110. For incoming items, see Wayne D. Roberts, "Lithic Artifacts," in Polhemus, *Toqua Site,* 822–24; Peebles and Kus, "Some Archaeological Correlates of Ranked Societies," 443;

Vincas P. Steponaitis, "Contrasting Patterns of Mississippian Development," in Earle, *Chiefdoms,* 208–16. For outgoing items, see Dickens, *Cherokee Prehistory,* 156–58; Ralf Lane's "Narrative," in NAW, 3:298–99; David Hurst Thomas, "The Spanish Missions of La Florida: An Overview," in Thomas, *Columbian Consequences,* 363.

111. Hally, "Chiefdom of Coosa," 243.

112. Welch, *Moundville's Economy,* 194–97.

113. George R. Milner, David G. Anderson, and Marvin T. Smith, "Distribution of Eastern Woodlands Peoples at the Prehistoric and Historic Interface," in Brose, Cowan, and Mainfort, *Societies in Eclipse,* 16; James B. Griffin, "Comments on the Late Prehistoric Societies in the Southeast," in Dye and Cox, *Towns and Temples along the Mississippi,* 10–11.

114. Hickerson, *Southwestern Chippewa,* 12–29.

115. Calderón, "Seventeenth-Century Letter," 11–12.

116. [Anonymous], "The First Published Report of the Laudonnière Colony," in NAW, 2:362.

117. René de Laudonnière, "The Second Voyage unto Florida [1564–1565]," in NAW, 2:329–330 and 342. John Hann also notes the presence of buffer zones as deterrents of the spread of disease up the Florida peninsula; see Hann, *Apalachee,* 179.

118. Alvar Núñez Cabeza de Vaca, "The Relation of Alvar Núñez Cabeza de Vaca," in NAW, 2:21.

119. Hudson, *Knights of Spain, Warriors of the Sun,* 124–25. For an ethnohistorical overview of the various Native groups of Florida, see Milanich, *Florida Indians.*

120. "The Account by a Gentleman from Elvas," in DSC, 1:168; Luys Hernández de Biedma, "Relation of the Island of Florida," in DSC, 1:229. Two types of leagues were used by the Spaniards. One was a statute league, equaling 4.19 kilometers; the other was a common league, equaling about 5.5 kilometers. It is unclear which of the two measurements the Soto expedition used. On the problem of the Spanish league, see Ross Hassig, "Leagues in Mexico versus Leagues in Florida: How Good Were Estimates?" in Galloway, *Hernando de Soto Expedition,* 234–45.

121. David Anderson, "Stability and Change," 208.

122. Hudson, *Knights of Spain, Warriors of the Sun,* 278.

123. [Jean-Baptiste] Minet, "Voyage Made from Canada Inland Going Southward during the Year 1682," in Weddle, *La Salle, the Mississippi, and the Gulf,* 50–51.

124. Pénicaut, *Fleur de Lys and Calumet,* 25–26.

125. Fackelmann, "Tuberculosis Outbreak," 73–75; Sousa et al., "Epidemic of Tuberculosis."

126. J. M. McNicholl et al., "Host-Pathogen Interactions."

127. Neel, Centerwall, Chagnon, and Casey, "Notes on the Effects of Measles"; Neel, "Health and Disease in Unacculturated Amerindian Populations," 155–77.

128. Black, "Infectious Diseases in Primitive Societies," 515–18.

129. Barquet and Domingo, "Smallpox."

130. Jared Diamond leans toward the view that people of European descent had developed genetic advantages in fighting infectious diseases, while indigenous peoples of the Americas lacked those advantages. See Diamond, "Nature's Infinite Book." Diamond's view is discredited by David Jones. See Jones, "Virgin Soils Revisited."

131. Black, "Why Did They Die?"; Black, "Explanation of High Death Rates."
132. Crawford, *Origins of Native Americans*, 147.
133. McKeown, *Origins of Human Disease*, 22–23.

2. The Protohistoric Puzzle

1. John Archdale, "A New Description of That Fertile and Pleasant Province of South Carolina," in Carroll, *Historical Collections of South Carolina*, 2:12. Archdale emphasized "Spaniard" and "Indian."
2. Archdale, "New Description," 2:12.
3. Paul Kelton, "The Great Southeastern Smallpox Epidemic: The Region's First Major Epidemic?" in Ethridge and Hudson, *Transformation of the Southeastern Indians*, 21–37.
4. Dobyns, *Their Number Become Thinned*, 267 and 287; Ramenofsky, *Vectors of Death*, 171.
5. Cook, "Sickness, Starvation, and Death in Early Hispaniola," 375.
6. For epidemics in Latin America, see Cook and Lovell, *"Secret Judgements of God"*; Cook, *Born to Die*.
7. Crosby, *Columbian Exchange*, 47–48; Crosby, *Ecological Imperialism*, 200–201.
8. Muller, *Mississippian Political Economy*, 363. Saul Jarcho is also critical of the idea of a hypothetical spread of acute infectious disease by way of aboriginal exchange. See Jarcho, "Some Observations on Disease in Prehistoric North America," 14.
9. Dobyns and Crosby both assert that this is what happened. See Crosby, *Ecological Imperialism*, 201; Dobyns, *Their Number Become Thinned*, 259.
10. Hann, *Apalachee*, 178–79.
11. David Henige has been especially critical of the idea that pandemics spread into North America by way of aboriginal exchange networks, particularly involving the Calusas. See Henige, "Primary Source by Primary Source?"
12. Dean Snow and Kim Lanphear also doubt that undocumented visits spread diseases to the Northeast. See Snow and Lanphear, "European Contact and Indian Depopulation in the Northeast," 15–33.
13. Documentary accounts of Ponce de León's two expeditions can be found in *NAW*, 1:231–47. See also Milanich, *Florida Indians*, 106–13.
14. "Gomera on the First Voyage Sponsored by Lucas Vázquez de Ayllón," in *NAW*, 1:248–57.
15. Gonzalo Fernández de Oviedo, "Historia general y natural de las Indias," in *NAW*, 1:260–63. For a secondary account of the expedition, see Hoffman, *New Andalucia*, 66–79.
16. "Account by a Gentleman from Elvas," 84; Hernández de Biedma, "Relation of the Island of Florida," 231.
17. "Account by a Gentleman from Elvas," 83.
18. Garcilaso de la Vega, "La Florida by the Inca," in *DSC*, 2:286. Postmodern analysis suggests that scholars should exercise a great deal of caution in using the Soto chronicles, especially Garcilaso's account. See Patricia Galloway, "The Incestuous Soto Narratives," in Galloway, *Hernando de Soto Expedition*, 11–44.
19. Although many scholars believe that the plague of Cofitachequi was indeed due to Eu-

ropean introduced diseases, some argue that famine rather than disease afflicted the chiefdom. See Randolph J. Widmer, "The Structure of Southeastern Chiefdoms," in Hudson and Tesser, *Forgotten Centuries*, 137–38; Chester DePratter, "The Chiefdom of Cofitachequi," in Hudson and Tesser, *Forgotten Centuries*, 215–16.

20. These dates are corrected to accord with modern calendars. The chroniclers of the Vázquez de Ayllón expedition were given according to the Julian system, which was ten days behind modern calendars. See Hoffman, *New Andalucia*, 66–76.

21. "Account by a Gentleman from Elvas," 83–84; Garcilaso de la Vega, "La Florida by the Inca," 286. On the impact of malaria on agricultural production, see Rutman and Rutman, "Of Agues and Fevers," 55–57.

22. Antonio de Herrera, "Herrera's Account of the Breakup of the Narváez Expedition," in *NAW*, 2:10.

23. Cabeza de Vaca, "Relation," 24.

24. Cabeza de Vaca, "Relation," 25; Herrera, "Herrera's Account," 11.

25. Cabeza de Vaca, "Relation," 25; Herrera, "Herrera's Account," 11–13.

26. Cabeza de Vaca, "Relation," 30–31.

27. "Account by a Gentleman from Elvas," 55.

28. Charles Hudson has convincingly retraced Soto's route through the Southeast, and his research has culminated in the best secondary account of this Spanish expedition. See Hudson, *Knights of Spain, Warriors of the Sun*.

29. "Account by a Gentleman from Elvas," 69–74.

30. Rodrigo Rangel, "Account of the Northern Conquest and Discovery of Hernando de Soto," in *DSC*, 1:281.

31. "Account by a Gentleman from Elvas," 91.

32. "Account by a Gentleman from Elvas," 104.

33. Garcilaso de la Vega, "La Florida by the Inca," 446–47.

34. Gabriele A. Landolt et al., "Restricted Infectivity of a Human-Lineage H3N2 Influenza A Virus"; Gabriele A. Landolt et al., "Comparison of the Pathogenesis of Two Genetically Different H3N2 Influenza A Viruses in Pigs." The author wishes to thank Christopher Olsen for these references.

35. Robert G. Webster and William J. Bean Jr., "Evolution and Ecology of Influenza Viruses: Interspecies Transmission," in Nicholson, Webster, and Hay, *Textbook of Influenza*, 112.

36. Scholtissek, "Source for Influenza Pandemics," 455–58; Christopher Scholtissek, Virginia S. Hinshaw, and Christopher W. Olsen, "Influenza in Pigs and Their Role as the Intermediate Host," in Nicholson, Webster, and Hay, *Textbook of Influenza*, 137–45.

37. Christopher W. Potter, "Chronicle of Influenza Pandemics," in Nicholson, Webster, and Hay, *Textbook of Influenza*, 3–18; Potter, "History of Influenza." The 1918 influenza pandemic may be an exception in that it may have originated in the United States, but scientists have yet to pinpoint the origin of this deadly event. See Reid and Taubenberger, "Origin of the 1918 Pandemic Influenza Virus." For an overview of the 1918 epidemic, see Crosby, *America's Forgotten Pandemic*.

38. Rangel, "Account of the Northern Conquest and Discovery of Hernando de Soto," 289.

39. Rangel, "Account of the Northern Conquest and Discovery of Hernando de Soto," 257.

40. "Letter of Hernando de Soto at Tampa Bay to the Justice and Board of Magistrates in Santiago de Cuba, July 9, 1539," in DSC, 1:375–76.

41. The chronicles of the Soto expedition are filled with accounts of Spanish brutality. I will discuss a few examples in the text that follows. For more details, see Rangel, "Account of the Northern Conquest and Discovery of Hernando de Soto," 270, 275–76, 283–85, 292, 296, and 301; "Account by a Gentleman from Elvas," 65, 70, 72, 74, 93, 105–6, 109, 112, 154, and 156; and Hernández de Biedma, "Relation of the Island of Florida," 231.

42. Hernández de Biedma, "Relation of the Island of Florida," 231.

43. Rangel, "Account of the Northern Conquest and Discovery of Hernando de Soto," 284.

44. "Account by a Gentleman from Elvas," 89.

45. "Account by a Gentleman from Elvas," 89.

46. "Account by a Gentleman from Elvas," 89, 104–5; Rangel, "Account of the Northern Conquest and Discovery of Hernando de Soto," 294. Rangel places the Indian casualties at three thousand while listing only twenty-two fatalities among the Spaniards.

47. Hernández de Biedma, "Relation of the Island of Florida," 238.

48. "Account by a Gentleman from Elvas," 135–36.

49. The Provincials to His Majesty [Phillip II], May 1, 1559, in LP, 2:210–11; Hoffman, New Andalucia, 157–59.

50. Tristán de Luna to His Majesty [Phillip II], September 24, 1559, in LP, 2:245–48.

51. Hoffman, New Andalucia, 159.

52. Hoffman, New Andalucia, 169–70.

53. The Captains to Tristán de Luna, in LP, 1:163. This provides further evidence that scholars should not always attribute archaeologically observed population movements to epidemic disease.

54. Married Soldiers to Tristán de Luna, May 11, 1560, in LP, 1:132–35. Other letters confirmed famine; see LP, 1:132–97. No specific mention of disease is found. One letter refers to la enfermedad, translated by Priestly as "illness," but given the circumstances, famine was most likely what plagued the expedition (Luis de Velasco to Tristán de Luna, LP, 1:180–81).

55. Hoffman, New Andalucia, 173.

56. Hoffman, New Andalucia, 173–74.

57. Dobyns, Their Number Become Thinned, 18–19.

58. Mateo del Sauz to Tristán de Luna, July 6, 1560, in LP, 1:219.

59. Fray Domingo de la Anunciación et al. to Tristán de Luna, July 6, 1560, in LP, 1:223 and 225.

60. Fray Augustín Davíla Padilla, "Padilla's Account of Coosa," in NAW, 2:241.

61. Padilla, "Padilla's Account of Coosa," 240.

62. This is the conclusion of Charles Hudson, the editor of the published Juan Pardo accounts. See JPE, 176.

63. "The Pardo Relation," in JPE, 311.

64. "The 'Short' Bandera Relation," in JPE, 302.

65. "The 'Long' Bandera Relation," in JPE, 264.

66. "'Long' Bandera Relation," 267; "Pardo Relation," 314.

67. "The Martinez Relation," in *JPE*, 320.

68. "'Short' Bandera Relation," 303.

69. The ratio of one adult male to every 3.5 women and children is Peter Wood's calculation, which derives from painstaking research of demographic data on the historic Southeast. See Wood, "The Changing Population of the Colonial South," in Wood, Waselkov, and Hatley, *Powhatan's Mantle,* 35–103. Archaeologists, furthermore, estimate town size in the Coosa and Tennessee valleys between 350 and 652 inhabitants. See David J. Hally, Marvin T. Smith, and James B. Langford Jr., "The Archaeological Reality of de Soto's Coosa," in Thomas, *Columbian Consequences,* 2:121–38.

70. "'Long' Bandera Relation," 270–71; and "Pardo Relation," 315.

71. "'Short' Bandera Relation," 303.

72. "'Long' Bandera Relation," 267; and "Martinez Relation," 320.

73. Jean Ribault, "The True Discoveries of Terra Florida," in *NAW*, 2:291–92.

74. "Expedition of Hernando Manrique de Rojas," in *NAW*, 2:311–12 and 315.

75. "Expedition of Hernando Manrique de Rojas," 332.

76. "Expedition of Hernando Manrique de Rojas," 356.

77. Hoffman, *New Andalucia,* 229–30; Paar, "'To Settle Is to Conquer.'"

78. Father Francis Villarreal to Father Francisco Borgiae, March 5, 1570, and Antonio Sedeño to Borgiae, March 6, 1570, in Zubillaga, *La Florida,* 412–28. The author wishes to thank Ernest Jenkins for translating these two documents.

79. Barcia Carballido y Zúñiga, *Barcia's Chronological History,* 153; Grant Jones, "Ethnohistory of the Guale Coast," 182.

80. Luis de Quirós and Juan Baptista de Segura to Juan de Hinistrosa, September 12, 1570, in *NAW*, 2:557.

81. Juan Rogel to Father Francisco Borgiae, August 28, 1572, in *NAW*, 2:560.

82. Cook, "Sickness, Starvation, and Death in Early Hispaniola," 369.

83. Early European visitors noticed this period of want among coastal Natives. See Cabeza de Vaca, "Relation," 31; René de Laudonnière, "Description of Florida and Its Indians," in *NAW*, 2:283; Ralph Lane, "Ralph Lane's Narrative of the Roanoke Island Colony, 1585–86," in *NAW*, 3:302. The classic secondary work on subsistence patterns for southeastern coastal natives is Larson, *Aboriginal Subsistence Technology.* For comparison with Natives of New England, see Cronon, *Changes in the Land,* 34–53.

84. Rebecca Saunders, "The Guale Indians of the Lower Atlantic Coast: Change and Continuity," in McEwan, *Indians of the Greater Southeast,* 26–56; Rebecca Saunders, "Seasonality, Sedentism, Subsistence, and Disease in the Protohistoric: Archaeological versus Ethnohistoric Data along the Lower Atlantic Coast," in Wesson and Rees, *Between Contacts and Colonies,* 32–48.

85. Kupperman, *Roanoke, the Abandoned Colony;* Quinn, *Set Fair for Roanoke.*

86. Thomas Harriot, "A Briefe and True Report of the New Found Land of Virginia," in *NAW*, 3:152.

87. Lane, "Ralph Lane's Narrative," 3:301.

88. Mackenthun, *Metaphors of Dispossession,* 142–53.

89. Harriot, "Briefe and True Report," 154.

90. [Bigges], *Summary and True Discourse*, 14.

91. [Bigges], *Summary and True Discourse*, 25.

92. "The *Primrose* Journal of Drake's Voyage to Florida and Virginia," in *NAW*, 3:307.

93. Duffy, *Epidemics in Colonial America*, 139. Erwin Ackerknecht is not convinced yellow fever came with Drake but does suggest the possibility. He also discusses the possibility that the virus was in the Caribbean as early as the 1620s and identifies it as responsible for an outbreak of *mal de siam* that spread through the Caribbean from 1668 to 1690. See Ackerknecht, *History and Geography of the Most Important Diseases*, 51–55.

94. Kenneth F. Kiple and Brian T. Higgins, "Yellow Fever and the Africanization of the Caribbean," in Verano and Ubelaker, *Disease and Demography in the Americas*, 237–48.

95. Lane, "Ralph Lane's Narrative," 3:304–5.

96. For an overview, see Jerald T. Milanich, "Franciscan Missions and Native Peoples in Spanish Florida," in Hudson and Tesser, *Forgotten Centuries*, 276–303; Thomas, "Spanish Missions of La Florida," 357–98.

97. There is a growing list of ethnohistorical studies of Spanish colonialism and indigenous peoples in Florida. See Worth, *Timucuan Chiefdoms of Spanish Florida*; Hann, *Apalachee*; Hann and McEwan, *Apalachee Indians and Mission San Luis*; Milanich, *Florida Indians*.

98. Quoted in Worth, *Timucuan Chiefdoms*, 2:10–11.

99. Hann, *Apalachee*, 176–77.

100. Hann, "Translation of Governor Robolledo's 1657 Visitation," 109.

101. Epidemiological events in other parts of North America suggest that the diseases striking Florida Natives in the second decade of the seventeenth century were part of larger pandemics occurring among Native peoples who had become integrated into ever-expansive Atlantic shipping networks. By 1616 Native communities of coastal New England had become active commercial partners with the French, the English, and the Dutch, whose ships frequently arrived with trade goods to exchange for beaver pelts and other furs. Tragically, indigenous peoples paid an epidemiological price for such commerce. Beginning in 1616 multiple outbreaks erupted among coastal communities from Maine to Rhode Island, widowing a landscape for the Pilgrims to discover when they landed on Plymouth Rock in 1620. (See Spiess and Spiess, "New England Pandemic of 1616–22," 71–83.) Conceivably, the various European sailors passed the deadliest diseases of the Columbian Exchange to one another as they sailed along the Atlantic coast, pirating their enemies and trading with their friends, and infecting indigenous peoples, who had just recently become acquainted with the newcomers' god, goods, and germs. See Ceci, "Native Wampum as a Peripheral Resource."

102. See, for example, Hann, "Translation of Governor Robolledo's 1657 Visitation," 127. On one trip to St. Augustine, only ten of two hundred Apalachee laborers survived the journey. Robolledo reported they were denied food and died of hunger, but such high mortality suggests disease as well.

103. Worth, *Timucuan Chiefdoms of Spanish Florida*, 2:10.

104. See chapter 1.

105. Marianne Reeves, "Dental Health at Early Historic Fusihatchee Town: Biocultural Implications of Contact in Alabama," in Lambert, *Bioarchaeological Studies*, 78–95; Larson, "Inferring Iron-Deficiency Anemia" in Lambert, *Bioarchaeological Studies*, 116–33.

106. Hann, "Translation of Governor Robolledo's 1657 Visitation," 96–97 and 127.

107. Hann, "Translation of Governor Robolledo's 1657 Visitation," 92.

108. Gregory A. Waselkov characterizes the flow of Spanish items into the interior as an "extended period of low volume, indirect trade." The items that do appear in the archeological record could have just as easily come from raiding. See Waselkov, "Macon Trading House," 194; Waselkov, "Seventeenth-Century Trade in the Colonial Southeast."

109. Alfred Crosby suggests this (see *Ecological Imperialism,* 210–13), but recent archaeological studies were not taken into account. For an overview, see Milner, "Late Prehistoric Cahokia Cultural System," 1–43.

110. "The Account by a Gentleman from Elvas," 116.

111. Hudson, *Knights of Spain, Warriors of the Sun,* 309.

112. Some of the more recent and sophisticated works on Cahokia include Pauketat, *Ascent of Chiefs;* Pauketat and Emerson, *Cahokia;* Emerson, *Cahokia and the Archaeology of Power.*

113. David Anderson, *Savannah River Chiefdoms,* 283–88 and 326–29. Anderson derives the years that bracketed the drought period through dendrochronology.

114. Hudson, *Knights of Spain, Warriors of the Sun,* 274–314.

115. Father Claudius Dablon, "Relation of the Voyages, Discoveries, and Death of Father James Marquette," in Shea, *Discovery and Exploration of the Mississippi Valley,* 47–48.

116. Father Zenobius Membré, Recollect, "Narrative of La Salle's Voyage down the Mississippi," in Shea, *Discovery and Exploration of the Mississippi Valley,* 171–74; Minet, "Voyage Made from Canada Inland," 44–47.

117. Phyllis A. Morse, "The Parkin Site and the Parkin Phase," in Dye and Cox, *Towns and Temples,* 118–34; Gerald P. Smith, "The Walls Phase," in Dye and Cox, *Towns and Temples,* 135–69; and Dan Morse, "The Nodena Phase," in Dye and Cox, *Towns and Temples,* 69–97.

118. For other studies critical of a massive depopulation due to Soto's germs, see Burnett and Murray, "Death, Drought, and De Soto"; Robert C. Mainfort, Jr., "The Late Prehistoric and Protohistoric Periods in the Central Mississippi Valley," in Brose, Cowan, and Mainfort, *Societies in Eclipse,* 182–89.

119. Hernández de Biedma, "Relation of the Island of Florida," 239; Hudson, *Knights of Spain, Warriors of the Sun,* 291.

120. Marvin Jeter does not agree with this particular interpretation, but he does discuss various theories of the Quapaws' origins. See Jeter, "From Prehistory through Protohistory to Ethnohistory in and near the Northern Lower Mississippi Valley," in Ethridge and Hudson, *Transformation of the Southeastern Indians,* 177–223.

121. Richter, *Ordeal of the Longhouse,* 60 and 145; White, *Middle Ground,* 1.

122. Dablon, "Relation of the Voyages," 45.

123. Dablon, "Relation of the Voyages," 35.

124. Minet, "Voyage Made from Canada Inland," 35–38.

125. Minet, "Voyage Made from Canada Inland," 40.

126. Jeter, "From Prehistory through Protohistory to Ethnohistory," 177–223.

127. Minet, "Voyage Made from Canada Inland," 49.

128. Membré, "Narrative of La Salle's Voyage," 176.

129. Gallay, *Indian Slave Trade,* 28.

130. Marvin Smith, *Coosa,* 96–117.

131. It is interesting to note that also during the late sixteenth century the upper Oconee watershed experienced an influx of settlement, further weakening the case for regionwide epidemics and massive depopulation at that time. See Kowalewski and Hatch, "Sixteenth-Century Expansion of Settlement"; Mark Williams, "Growth and Decline of the Oconee Province," in Hudson and Tesser, *Forgotten Centuries*, 179–96. It cannot be demonstrated, however, that the people who moved into the Oconee came from the Coosa. Coosa's inhabitants who were not captured or killed by enemies certainly moved downriver. It is also possible that some of Coosa's inhabitants fled to places that archaeologists have not discovered, although exhaustive surveys of the archaeological record have not uncovered any of those places.

132. DePratter, "Chiefdom of Cofitachequi," 197–226.

133. Ward and Stephen Davis, "Impact of Old World Diseases"; Ward and Davis, *Time before History*, 257–60 and 265–66.

134. Population movements did occur within the Appalachian highlands but signs of massive depopulation—evacuation of river valleys and abandoned towns—are not visible. Christopher B. Rodning, "Reconstructing the Coalescence of Cherokee Communities in Southern Appalachia," in Ethridge and Hudson, *Transformation of the Southeastern Indians*, 155–75; Ward and Davis, *Time before History*, 160–81; Dickens, "Mississippian Settlement Patterns," 115–39; Dickens, *Cherokee Prehistory;* Keel, *Cherokee Archaeology.*

135. Keith J. Little and Caleb Curren, "Conquest Archaeology of Alabama," in Thomas, *Columbian Consequences*, 2:174, 177, 184.

136. Hudson, *Knights of Spain, Warriors of the Sun*, 250–61.

137. Moundville and its affiliated towns in the Black Warrior River valley have been the subject of numerous scholarly studies. Some argue that the valley must have been depopulated by European diseases in the sixteenth century, while others conclude that indigenous peoples remained there until the late seventeenth century. None of these takes a critical view of the Columbian Exchange. For studies that place the Columbian Exchange in the protohistoric, see Curren, *Protohistoric Period in Central Alabama*, 242; and Charles Hudson, Marvin Smith, and Chester DePratter, "The Hernando de Soto Expedition: From Mabila to the Mississippi River," in Dye and Cox, *Towns and Temples*, 190–91. For studies that depict residential continuity in the Black Warrior River valley, see Peebles, "Rise and Fall of the Mississippian in Western Alabama"; Peebles, "Paradise, Lost, Strayed, and Stolen: Prehistoric Social Devolution in the Southeast," in Richardson and Webb, *Burden of Being Civilized*, 24–40. Peebles's view receives further support by Margaret J. Schoeninger and Mark R. Schurr, "Human Subsistence at Moundville: The Stable-Isotope Data," in Knight and Steponaitis, *Archaeology of the Moundville Chiefdom*, 120–32.

138. Reverend Father Beaudouin to Mr. Salmon, November 23, 1732, in *MPAFD*, 1:156–57.

139. "Account by a Gentleman from Elvas," 105–6.

140. Johnson and Sparks, "Protohistoric Settlement Patterns in Northeastern Mississippi"; Jay K. Johnson, "The Chickasaws" in McEwan, *Indians of the Greater Southeast*, 85–121; Jay K. Johnson and Geoffrey R. Lehmann, "Sociopolitical Devolution in Northeast Mississippi and the Timing of the De Soto Entrada," in Baker and Kealhofer, *Bioarchaeology of Native American Adaptation*, 38–55.

3. Slave Raids and Smallpox

1. Nicholas Carteret, "Nicholas Carteret's Relation of Their Planting at Ashley River [1670]," in Salley, *Narratives of Early Carolina*, 117.

2. On the contrast between indigenous and English views of the land, see Cronon, *Changes in the Land*. Cronon, however, does not imply that New England colonists sought Natives as a source of slaves.

3. Thomas Nairne to Ralph Izard, April 12, 1708, in Moore, *Nairne's Muskhogean Journals*, 47.

4. Dunn, *Sugar and Slaves*.

5. Thomas Nairne to Landgrave Smith, January 20, 1708, in Moore, *Nairne's Muskhogean Journals*, 34.

6. Reid, *Law of Blood*.

7. Perdue, *Cherokee Women*, 53–55.

8. Several primary sources depict the practices of capture and torture or adoption in the Native Southeast. See Lawson, *New Voyage to Carolina*, 53–55, 177, 207–8, 210; Bossu, *Travels in the Interior of North America*, 64–65; Adair, *History of the American Indians*, 380–90.

9. Norton, *Journal of Major John Norton*, 46. In this regard captive taking played similar roles among Southwestern and Southeastern Natives. See Brooks, *Captives and Cousins*.

10. Lawson, *New Voyage to Carolina*, 207–10.

11. "Letter of J. F. Buisson St. Cosme, Missionary Priest, to the Bishop [of Quebec]," in Shea, *Early Voyages up and down the Mississippi*, 72–73.

12. Bossu, *Travels in the Interior of North America*, 169.

13. Perdue, *Slavery and the Evolution of Cherokee Society*, 3–18.

14. John Stewart to Queen Anne, October 1711, Archives des Colonies, Archives Nationales, Paris, microfilm copies in Manuscript Reading Room, Library of Congress, C13C, 2:72, photocopy provided by Alan Gallay.

15. Crane, *Southern Frontier*, 112–14; Wood, *Black Majority*, 55n.

16. Wright, *Only Land They Knew*, 148–50.

17. The most thorough study of alcohol and indigenous peoples is Mancall, *Deadly Medicine*. Mancall emphasizes Native agency in their struggle with liquor. Richard White emphasizes alcohol as a commodity that fostered dependency. White, *Roots of Dependency*, 58–59.

18. John Lederer, "The Discoveries of John Lederer," in Alvord and Bidgood, *First Explorations of the Trans-Allegheny Region*, 170.

19. John Stewart to Queen Anne, October 1711, Archives des Colonies, Archives Nationales, Paris, microfilm copies in Manuscript Reading Room, Library of Congress, C13C, 2:72.

20. Several scholars advance the argument that Natives turned to firearms because of their supposed technological advantages. See Jennings, *Ambiguous Iroquois Empire*, 80–81; White, *Roots of Dependency*, 44; Bowne, *Westo Indians*, 65–71. To this author's knowledge, scholars have yet to offer an interpretation of Native adoption of firearms as labor-saving devices, but such a view is supported by ethnographic information regarding Native arms production. See Swanton, *Indians of the Southeastern United States*, 571–82.

21. Membré, "Narrative of La Salle's Voyage," 180.

22. John Stewart to Queen Anne, October 1711, Archives des Colonies, Archives Nationales, Paris, microfilm copies in Manuscript Reading Room, Library of Congress, C13C, 2:72.

23. Numerous ethnohistories utilize the concept of kinship in depicting Native conceptions of their interactions with Europeans and European Americans. Two important works that make kinship central to their analyses are Gary Clayton Anderson, *Kinsmen of Another Kind;* White, *Middle Ground.* Such work has drawn heavily from the anthropological studies of Marcel Mauss. See Mauss, *Gift.*

24. John Stewart to William Dunlop, April 27, 1690, in *SCHGM* 32 (January 1931): 29.

25. Older studies, which incorporate dependency theory, depict indigenous peoples as having their modes of production and concepts of exchange obliterated by capitalist hegemony and thus becoming proletarians within a larger world system. Recent theoretical works depict Natives as maintaining kinship modes of production in which their conceptions of exchange did not necessarily change, even though their participation in the North Atlantic market economy subsidized an emerging capitalist world system. For the concept of articulation, see Wolf, *Europe and the People without History;* Mallon, *Defense of Community in Peru's Central Highlands.*

26. For an excellent summary of anthropological theory pertaining to indigenous perceptions of power, see O'Brien, *Choctaws in a Revolutionary Age,* 1-10.

27. Welch, *Moundville's Economy.*

28. Nairne to Izard, April 12, 1708, 38-39.

29. On how the slave trade altered the balance of power between men and women in Native societies, see Perdue, *Cherokee Women,* 66-70.

30. Alvord and Bidgood, *First Explorations of the Trans-Allegheny Region,* 15-97; Franklin, "Virginia and the Cherokee Indian Trade"; Briceland, *Westward from Virginia.*

31. William Byrd II, "A History of the Dividing Line Run in the Year 1728," in *Writings of Colonel William Byrd of Westover in Virginia,* 235.

32. Abraham Wood to John Richards, August 22, 1674, in Alvord and Bidgood, *First Explorations of the Trans-Allegheny Region,* 211.

33. Hening, *Statutes at Large,* 1:415 and 441.

34. Hening, *Statutes at Large,* 1:525.

35. Hening, *Statutes at Large,* 2:337 and 350.

36. The standard accounts of Bacon's Rebellion are Morgan, *American Slavery/American Freedom,* 250-70; Webb, *1676.* On Virginia's tributary communities, see Rountree, *Pocahontas's People.*

37. Hening, *Statutes at Large,* 2:350.

38. Hening, *Statutes at Large,* 2:410-12.

39. Hening, *Statutes at Large,* 2:480.

40. Hening, *Statutes at Large,* 3:69.

41. Hening, *Statutes at Large,* 2:143-44.

42. Hening, *Statutes at Large,* 2:283.

43. Hening, *Statutes at Large,* 2:346.

44. Hening, *Statutes at Large,* 2:404.

45. Hening, *Statutes at Large,* 2:440.

46. Hening, *Statutes at Large*, 2:490–91.

47. The most comprehensive study of the Westos is Bowne, *Westo Indians*. My analysis follows Bowne's interpretation. For alternative views of the Westos' origins, see Juricek, "Westo Indians"; Swanton, "Westo."

48. John Worth, overview of *Struggle for the Georgia Coast*, 17.

49. Governor Aranguiz y Cotes to the King of Spain, November 15, 1661, quoted in Worth, overview, 15.

50. Statements of Fray Carlos de Anguiano, Fray Gabriel Fernández, and Jacinto de Barreda, April 1663, in Worth, *Struggle for the Georgia Coast*, 92–94.

51. On the scattering of Hitchiti speakers, see Worth, overview, 18 and 27; Oatis, *Colonial Complex*, 25; Hahn, *Invention of the Creek Nation*, 28–30.

52. Marvin Smith claims that the evacuation of the upper Coosa was complete by 1630, but it cannot be ruled out that English-inspired slave raids in the 1660s led to further turmoil for the descendants of the collapsed Coosa chiefdom in their downriver location. Smith, *Coosa*, 96–117.

53. Carteret, "Nicholas Carteret's Relation of Their Planting at Ashley River [1670]," 118.

54. William Owen to Lord Ashley, September 15, 1670, in South Carolina Historical Society, *Collections*, 5:200–201.

55. Stephen Bull to Lord Ashley, September 12, 1670, in South Carolina Historical Society, *Collections*, 5:194.

56. Henry Woodward, "A Faithfull Relation of my Westoe Voiage," in Salley, *Narratives of Early Carolina*, 133.

57. Edward Bland, "The Discovery of New Brittaine," in Alvord and Bidgood, *First Explorations of the Trans-Allegheny Region*, 116–17; Parramore, "Tuscarora Ascendancy."

58. Lederer, "Discoveries of John Lederer," 162.

59. Palmer, *Calendar of Virginia State Papers*, 1:65; William Byrd I to Stephanus Van Cortland, August 3, 1691, in Tinling, *Correspondence of the Three William Byrds*, 1:163; Lawson, *New Voyage to Carolina*, 232.

60. Lawson, *New Voyage to Carolina*, 233.

61. Lawson, *New Voyage to Carolina*, 225.

62. Lederer, "Discoveries of John Lederer," 155–56. Lederer referred to the Westos as "Rickohockan," as did others in Virginia. That these were the same people as the Westos, see Bowne, *Westo Indians*, 21–27 and 80.

63. Wood to Richards, August 22, 1674, 225.

64. On the Tomahitans' location in Tennessee, see Alvord and Bidgood, *Early Explorations in the Trans-Allegheny Region*, 82; and "Letter of Abraham Wood Describing Needham's Journey (1673)," in Williams, *Early Travels in the Tennessee Country*, 17–38. A more recent and thorough recreation of the route is offered by Briceland, *Westward from Virginia*, 147–70.

65. Wood to Richards, August 22, 1674, 214.

66. Several scholars have claimed the guns to be from the Spanish. See Alvord and Bidgood, *First Explorations of the Trans-Allegheny Region*, 83; Waselkov, "Seventeenth-Century Trade in the Colonial Southeast," 120–21; Bowne, *Westo Indians*, 13. But the origins of the guns cannot be determined with any degree of certainty.

67. "Discourse between Long Warrior of Tunnisee, Head Warrior, and President of South Carolina Council, January 24, 1727," C.O. 5:387, fols. 237–38, NA/PRO.

68. Wood to Richards, August 22, 1674, 213.

69. Wood to Richards, August 22, 1674, 213–14.

70. Wood to Richards, August 22, 1674, 220–21.

71. Wood to Richards, August 22, 1674, 218. Wood identified these children as "weesocks"—a clear reference to the Waxhaws, a Siouan tribe of the Carolina Piedmont. Wood wrote: "[Y]e wesocks children they take are brought up with them as ye Ianesaryes are a mongst ye Turkes." The Virginian's analogy was to the Janissaries, young boys captured by the Ottomans, raised to be fierce fighters, and impressed into service as an elite force loyal only to the sultan. The author wishes to thank his supremely intelligent colleague Jeff Moran for pointing out the meaning of Wood's obscure reference.

72. John Lawson reported that he had met a Native woman who "had been brought from beyond the Mountains, and was sold a slave into Virginia." Interestingly, the woman's language was mutually intelligible to a coastal tribe. They were probably both Algonquian speakers. See Lawson, *New Voyage to Carolina*, 174.

73. Adair, *History of the American Indians*, 273. For a view that proposes a non-Cherokee affiliation for the Tomahitans, see Davis, "Travels of James Needham and Gabriel Arthur."

74. Wood to Richards, August 22, 1674, 221.

75. Keel, *Cherokee Archaeology*; Dickens, *Cherokee Prehistory*; Dickens, "Mississippian Settlement Patterns," 132–35; Ward and Davis, *Time before History*, 180.

76. Norton, *Journal*, 46; Charles Hicks to John Ross, February 1, 1826, in Moulton, *Papers of Chief John Ross*, 1:112.

77. Norton, *Journal*, 263.

78. James Mooney, *History, Myths, and Sacred Formulas*, 380–81.

79. Byrd, *Writings*, 185.

80. Alvord and Bidgood, *First Explorations of the Trans-Allegheny Region*, 31.

81. This map is reprinted in Harrison, "Western Exploration in Virginia."

82. Chapman, *Tellico Archaeology*, 99–100. Marvin Smith is essentially correct that Cherokees replaced Muskogeans in the Little Tennessee Valley, but he places too much emphasis on epidemic disease in facilitating this transition. The area was well on its way to being vacated because of slave raids that preceded smallpox by about ten years. See Smith, *Archaeology of Aboriginal Culture Change*, 71–72.

83. "1681 Census of Guale and Mocama," in Worth, *Struggle for the Georgia Coast*, 101.

84. Boyd, "Expedition of Marcus Delgado," 26.

85. *JCHASC*, 1693, 12.

86. James Mooney, *History, Myths, and Sacred Formulas*, 389.

87. Norton, *Journal*, 112; Charles Hicks also records Cherokee memories of Creeks living in eastern Tennessee. See Hicks to John Ross, March 1, 1826, in *Papers of Chief John Ross*, 1:114–15.

88. Charles Hicks to John Ross, May 4, 1826, in Moulton, *Papers of Chief John Ross*, I, 117.

89. Dablon, "Relation of the Voyages," 47.

90. Gallay, *Indian Slave Trade*, 103–4.

91. "Memoir by the Sieur de La Tonty [1693]," in French, *Historical Collections of Louisiana,* 1:60.

92. That they were Tuscaroras, see Parramore, "Tuscarora Ascendancy," 310–11. That they were Chickasaws, see Gallay, *Indian Slave Trade,* 103.

93. Dablon, "Relation of the Voyages," 50.

94. Dablon, "Relation of the Voyages," 47.

95. Nairne to Izard, April 12, 1708, 37.

96. Minet, "Voyage Made from Canada Inland," 54. Other accounts of La Salle's expedition confirm this episode. See Membré, "Narrative of La Salle's Voyage down the Mississippi," 178; "Memoir by the Sieur de La Tonty [1693]," 63.

97. Minet, "Voyage Made from Canada Inland," 54.

98. Minet, "Voyage Made from Canada Inland," 49; "Memoir by the Sieur de La Tonty [1693]," 62.

99. Membré, "Narrative of La Salle's Voyage down the Mississippi," 180; "Memoir by the Sieur de La Tonty [1693]," 65.

100. Francis Nicholson to Board of Trade, April 24, 1700, C.O. 5:1311, pp. 149–50, NA/PRO

101. Merrell, "Some Thoughts on Colonial Historians," 100–107; Wright, *Only Land They Knew,* 135–36.

102. Morgan, *American Slavery, American Freedom,* 330.

103. Lawson, *New Voyage to Carolina,* 35–36 and 191–92.

104. Byrd, *Writings,* 235.

105. "The Fundamental Constitutions of Carolina, March 1, 1669," in CRNC, 1:204.

106. "Temporary Laws" [Lords Proprietors to Governor and Council of Carolina, 1671], in Rivers, *Sketch of the History of South Carolina,* 353. The law was reiterated verbatim one year later. See Lords Proprietors to Governor and Council of Carolina, June 21, 1672, "Agrarian Laws or Instructions from the Lords Proprietors to the Governor and Council of Carolina," in Rivers, *Sketch of the History of South Carolina,* 358.

107. Alan Gallay has offered an excellent and thorough study of Carolina's commerce in Native captives, and my analysis follows the sequence of events that he lays out. I wish to emphasize, however, that the Native slave trade had a dramatic demographic impact before epidemics struck, leading to population movements and the coalescence process that produced the historic confederacies known as the Catawbas, the Cherokees, the Creeks, the Chickasaws, and the Choctaws. And, of course, my analysis adds an epidemiological component missing from Gallay's work. See Gallay, *Indian Slave Trade.*

108. Woodward, "Faithfull Relation of my Westoe Voiage," 134.

109. Reding, "Plans for the Colonization and Defense of Apalachee," 173.

110. Hahn, *Invention of the Creek Nation,* 30, 71, and 76; Oatis, *Colonial Complex,* 25.

111. Worth, overview, 27.

112. Proprietors to Governor and Grand Council, October 22, 1677, in BPROSC, 1:60–61.

113. Information concerning the conflict involving the proprietors, colonists, and Westos are discussed in the following: Proprietors to Governor and Council, February 21, 1681, in BPROSC, 1:104–5; "Instructions for Mr. Andrew Percivall, February 21, 1681," in BPROSC,

1:106–8; Proprietors to Governor and Council, March 7, 1681, in *BPROSC*, 1:115–20; Proprietors to Governor and Grand Council, September 30, 1683, in *BPROSC*, 1:255–63.

114. Francis Le Jau to Secretary of the Society for the Propagation of the Gospel, February 1, 1710, in *CCLJ*, 68; Francis Le Jau to Secretary of the Society for the Propagation of the Gospel, June 13, 1710, in *CCLJ*, 79.

115. Woodward, "Faithfull Relation of my Westoe Voiage," 133–34.

116. "Instructions for the Commissioners appoynted to heare and determine differences between the Christians and the Indians [1680]," in *BPROSC*, 1:99.

117. Proprietors to Governor and Grand Council, September 30, 1683, in *BPROSC*, 1:258.

118. "Pablo de Hita Salazar, Governor of Florida, to the Crown, March 6, 1680," trans. by José Miguel Gallardo, in *SCHGM* 37 (October 1936): 137–38.

119. Worth, overview, 25–26.

120. Worth, overview, 33.

121. "The Examination of Several Yamasse Indians," May 6, 1685, in *BPROSC*, 2:66.

122. Caleb Westbrooke to [Deputy-Governor Godfrey?], February 21, 1685, Sainsbury et al., *Calendar of State Papers,* 12:5–6.

123. Oatis, *Colonial Complex,* 26–29.

124. Crane, *Southern Frontier,* 40.

125. John Stewart to William Dunlop, April 27, 1690, in *SCHGM* 32 (January 1931): 29–30.

126. Quoted in Crane, *Southern Frontier,* 41; John Stewart to William Dunlop, June 23, 1690, in *SCHGM* 32 (April 1931): 107.

127. Lords Proprietors to Seth Sothell et al., May 13, 1691, in *BPROSC*, 2:14–15.

128. Crane, *Southern Frontier,* 41.

129. *JCHASC* (1693), 12.

130. Hewatt, *Historical Account,* 1:116.

131. *JCHASC* (1698), 30.

132. Harrison, "Western Exploration in Virginia," 323–40.

133. Hahn, *Invention of the Creek Nation,* 26–29.

134. The migration story of the Cussitas and the Cowetas is often referred to as "Chekilli's Legend." Georgia's English settlers recorded the story in 1735, and it has been reprinted in a variety of different sources. For a verbatim reprint, see "Some Ancient Georgia Indian Lore," *Georgia Historical Quarterly* 15 (June 1931): 192–98.

135. Reding, "Plans for the Colonization and Defense of Apalachee," 175.

136. Such distant trade alarmed the proprietors, who ordered it stopped. See *BPROSC*, 1:60–61.

137. Hahn, *Invention of the Creek Nation,* 34.

138. Hahn, *Invention of the Creek Nation,* 36–37.

139. Hahn, *Invention of the Creek Nation,* 37–39.

140. Hahn, *Invention of the Creek Nation,* 42.

141. Hahn, *Invention of the Creek Nation,* 42–47.

142. Hahn, *Invention of the Creek Nation,* 48–52.

143. John Stewart to William Dunlop, April 27, 1690, in *SCHGM* 32 (January 1931): 30.

144. Hann, "Translation of Alonso De Leturiondo's Memorial," 175.

145. Nairne to Izard, April 12, 1708, 50.

146. Knight and Adams, "Voyage to the Mobile and Tomeh in 1700," 35–36.

147. Hudson, *Knights of Spain, Warriors of the Sun,* 250–61 and 305–7.

148. Hann, *Apalachee,* 77.

149. Patricia Galloway, while assuming that sixteenth-century exploration initiated major disease depopulation, nonetheless, acknowledges slave raids as a major cause for the coalescence of the Choctaws. On the origins of the Choctaw confederacy, see Galloway, *Choctaw Genesis,* 172–73, 193, 197–98, 203, 345, and 356.

150. Beaudouin to Salmon, November 23, 1732, in *MPAFD,* 1:156–57. See also Timothy Paul Mooney, "Migration of the Chickasawhay."

151. Nairne to Izard, April 12, 1708, 50.

152. "At a Meeting of His Majesties Commissioners for Trade and Plantations," December 12, 1699, in *BPROSC,* 4:127.

153. Crane, *Southern Frontier,* 46–47.

154. John Stewart to William Dunlop, October 20, 1693, in *SCHGM* 32 (July 1931): 172.

155. Stewart to Dunlop, October 20, 1693, 172.

156. Edward Loughton and Richard Tranter to Lords Commissioners for Trade and Plantations, n.d., in *BPROSC,* 4:194–96. See also Crane, "Tennessee River as the Road to Carolina."

157. Le Moyne d'Iberville, *Gulf Journals,* 144–45.

158. Du Ru, *Journal,* 56.

159. Le Moyne de Sauvole de La Villantray, *Journal,* 52–53. The ethnic affiliation of the "Calés" is uncertain. They were probably Yuchis, who were later expelled from the Tennessee Valley by the Cherokees.

160. "Letter of J. F. Buisson St. Cosme," 60–61.

161. Le Moyne d'Iberville, *Gulf Journals,* 119 and 132.

162. Le Moyne d'Iberville, *Gulf Journals,* quote on 110, see also 119 and 132.

163. Le Moyne de Sauvole de La Villantray, *Journal,* 36.

164. Le Moyne de Sauvole de La Villantray, *Journal,* 36.

165. Le Moyne d'Iberville, *Gulf Journals,* 172.

166. Patricia Galloway, "Confederacy as a Solution to Chiefdom Dissolution: Historical Evidence in the Choctaw Case," in Hudson and Tesser, *Forgotten Centuries,* 393–420.

167. Gallay, *Indian Slave Trade,* 294–99.

168. Edmond Andros to Duke of Shrewsbury, June 27, 1696, C.O. 5:1307, p. 83, NA/PRO; Blanton, *Medicine in Virginia in the Seventeenth Century,* 61.

169. Curtain, "Epidemiology and the Slave Trade." For an interesting model of how the African slave trade spread disease to Brazil, see Alden and Miller, "Unwanted Cargoes."

170. Berlin, *Many Thousands Gone,* 110.

171. Rutman and Rutman, "Of Agues and Fevers," 32–60; Carr and Walsh, "Planter's Wife"; Walsh and Menard, "Death in the Chesapeake."

172. Edmond Andros to Lords of the Council for Trade and Plantations, July 1, 1697, C.O. 5:1309, p. 108, NA/PRO. On the persistence of Native communities within Virginia, see Rountree, *Pocahontas's People.*

173. Archdale, "New Description," 89.

174. Lawson, *New Voyage to Carolina,* 17 and 34.

175. Lawson, *New Voyage to Carolina*, 232.

176. Francis Nicholson, "Proclamation Prohibiting the Entertainment of Indians," C.O. 5:1311, pp. 361–62, NA/PRO. In 1699 Englishmen who had settled near Albemarle Sound complained that their bound laborers kept running away to South Carolina and Virginia. In one instance four servants sought their freedom by fleeing southward; all four ended up sick, with three of them dying from an undisclosed ailment that, given the timing, could have been smallpox. Although the backgrounds of these particular runaways were not identified, if they were Natives, it would not have been the first time that English masters complained about their indigenous laborers running away. See Henderson Walker to Francis Nicholson, October 10, 1699, C.O. 5:1311, p. 388, NA/PRO; Henderson Walker to Francis Nicholson, November 18, 1699, C.O. 5:1311, pp. 393–94, NA/PRO.

177. William Byrd I to Francis Howard, June 10, 1689, in Tinling, *Correspondence of the Three William Byrds*, 1:108.

178. Merrell, *Indians' New World*, 22–23.

179. Lawson, *New Voyage to Carolina*, 45.

180. Lawson, *New Voyage to Carolina*, 53.

181. Lawson, *New Voyage to Carolina*, 61–62. Lawson records these groups with the following names respectively: "Enoes," "Shoccories," and "Adshusheers."

182. Lawson, *New Voyage to Carolina*, 193.

183. Lawson, *New Voyage to Carolina*, 177.

184. *JCHASC* (1697), 9–12.

185. Joseph Blake and Council to Lords Proprietors of Carolina, March 12, 1698, in Salley, *Commissions and Instructions*, 103.

186. Quoted in McCrady, *History of South Carolina*, 1:308.

187. Joseph Blake and Council to Lords Proprietors, April 23, 1698, in Salley, *Commissions and Instructions*, 105.

188. Blake and Council to Lords Proprietors, April 23, 1698, 105.

189. Thomas Nairne to Ralph Izard, April 15, 1708, in Moore, *Nairne's Muskhogean Journal*, 63.

190. Pénicaut, *Fleur de Lys and Calumet*, 11.

191. Le Moyne d'Iberville, *Gulf Journals*, 38.

192. Pénicaut, *Fleur de Lys and Calumet*, 11.

193. Le Moyne d'Iberville, *Gulf Journals*, 63.

194. Le Moyne d'Iberville, *Gulf Journals*, 61.

195. Le Moyne de Sauvole de La Villantray, *Journal*, 31.

196. Le Moyne d'Iberville, *Gulf Journals*, 139–40.

197. Le Moyne de Sauvole de La Villantray, *Journal*, 28–29.

198. "Letter of Thaumur de La Source, [1699]," in Shea, *Early Voyages up and down the Mississippi*, 79.

199. "Letter of J. F. Buisson St. Cosme," 72.

200. "Letter of J. F. Buisson St. Cosme," 72.

201. "Letter of J. F. Buisson St. Cosme," 73.

202. Le Moyne d'Iberville, *Gulf Journals*, 128.

203. "Letter of Thaumur de La Source, [1699]," 79.

204. "Letter of Mr. de Montigny, [1699]," in Shea, *Early Voyages up and down the Mississippi,* 78.

205. "Letter of Thaumur de La Source, [1699]," 81.

206. Usner, *Indians, Settlers, and Slaves in a Frontier Exchange Economy.*

207. Blasingham, "Depopulation of the Illinois Indians," 383.

208. Longe, "Small Postscript," 40–42.

209. [Barnwell Map, 1722], C.O. 700, North American Colonies 7, NA/PRO.

210. James Mooney, *History, Myths, and Sacred Formulas,* 341–42. A Cherokee story about the downfall of an ancient priesthood known as the Aní-Kutánî might be read as evidence of an early and unrecorded smallpox epidemic, but none of the accounts of this story specifically mentions disease. The Cherokees executed these priests for allegedly violating the wives of hunters when they were away hunting. In "Who Were the Aní-Kutánî?" Raymond Fogelson analyzes the various accounts of this priesthood and argues persuasively that the story symbolizes the tensions between egalitarianism and hierarchy.

211. In their correspondence with the Crown in the 1690s, Spanish officials in Florida make no reference to smallpox striking their missions. Such correspondence is included in Boyd, *Here They Once Stood.* Also, Alonso Leturiondo resided in Florida at the time of the Great Southeastern Smallpox Epidemic and wrote a memorial to the Crown decrying the lack of protection that Catholic Natives had against English-inspired slave raids. Leturiondo made no mention of smallpox in Florida. See Hann, "Translation of Alonso Leturiondo's Memorial." None of the secondary works on Spanish colonialism in Florida makes reference to smallpox in the 1690s. See Hann, *Apalachee;* Worth, *Timucuan Chiefdoms of Spanish Florida;* Amy Turner Bushnell, "Ruling the 'Republic of Indians' in Seventeenth-Century Florida," in Wood, Waselkov, and Hatley, *Powhatan's Mantle,* 134–50.

212. "Discussion of Choctaw History by Nathaniel Folsom [1826]," MSS, Thomas Gilcrease Museum of American Art and History, Archives, Tulsa, Oklahoma.

213. Cronon, *Changes in the Land,* 125.

214. Merrens and Terry, "Dying in Paradise"; Wood, *Black Majority,* 63–91.

215. Lawson, *New Voyage to Carolina,* 17.

216. Le Moyne d'Iberville, *Gulf Journals,* 122.

217. Le Moyne d'Iberville, *Gulf Journals,* 125 and 132; Du Ru, *Journal,* 34.

218. Du Ru, *Journal,* 24.

219. Le Moyne de Sauvole de La Villantray, *Journal,* 27 and 33.

220. Le Moyne d'Iberville, *Gulf Journals,* 120–21.

221. On the location of the Choctaws around 1700, see Galloway, *Choctaw Genesis,* 183–99. John Stewart reported that the Choctaws lived in scattered homesteads along various cane swamps. See John Stewart to Queen Anne, March 10, 1711, Archives des Colonies, Archives Nationales, Paris, microfilm copies in Manuscript Reading Room, Library of Congress, C13C, 2:80.

222. On Chickasaw settlement patterns, see Nairne to Landgrave Smith, January 20, 1708, 36.

4. Epidemiological Origins of the Yamasee War

Note to Table 1. 1698 Virginia: "Proclamation for a Publick Fast" by Edmond Andros, July 8, 1698, C.O. 5:1309, fol. 193, NA/PRO. Blanton misses this epidemic but notes that New England suffered especially severely from influenza from 1697 to 1699. See Blanton, *Medicine in Virginia in the Seventeenth Century*, 56.

1699 Gulf Coast: Le Moyne d'Iberville, *Gulf Journals*, 20–21. Because the outbreak occurred in winter, the disease was more likely to be one that flourished in cold weather, such as typhus or influenza, rather than yellow fever. The disease was possibly responsible for the grave illness that Spanish soldiers at Pensacola suffered after receiving a visit from the French. See *Gulf Journals*, 94.

1699 Charles Town: Governor Joseph Blake et al. to Lords Proprietors, January 17, 1700, in Salley, *Commissions and Instructions*, 129. The disease involved was certainly yellow fever because it had case fatality rates more severe than one would expect from malaria and because it occurred in the summer and did not spread outside Charles Town. Duffy agrees. See his *Epidemics in Colonial America*, 143.

1703 Florida: Hann, *Apalachee*, 167. The epidemic likely spread to other Apalachee missions as well.

1704 Mobile: Bienville to Pontchartrain, September 6, 1704, in MPAFD, 3:24; Bienville, "Memoir [1726]," in MPAFD, 3:536; Bénard de La Harpe, *Historical Journal*, 47. For reasons that will be discussed later in this chapter, the responsible disease appears to be not yellow fever but instead a disease more capable of spreading inland and of producing severe mortality rates. Measles seems the most likely culprit, but typhus or influenza cannot be ruled out.

1706 Charles Town and James River: This is one of the best documented single epidemics in the early eighteenth century, and all sources indicate that yellow fever was involved. The simultaneous occurrence of another disease cannot be ruled out. For its occurrence in South Carolina, see "Account of the Invasion made by the French and Spaniards upon Carolina," in BPROSC, 5:172; Mr. Auchinleck to Secretary, October 29, 1706, SPG, ser. A, vol. 3; November 20, 1706, JCHASC, 5; Le Jau to Secretary, December 2, 1706, in CCLJ, 17–18; Lords Proprietors to Governor Nathaniel Johnston, March 8, 1707, in Salley, *Commissions and Instructions*, 189; Thomas Hasell to Secretary, September 6, 1707, SPG, ser. A, vol. 3; Thomas Hasell to Secretary, November 30, 1707, SPG, ser. A, vol. 3. For its occurrence in Virginia, see President and Council of Virginia to Lords Commissioners of Trade and Plantations, August 29, 1706, C.O. 5:1315, pt. 1, fol. 82, NA/PRO; Le Jau to Secretary, September 9, 1706, in CCLJ, 15; Le Jau to Secretary, December 2, 1706, in CCLJ, 18.

1706 Louisiana: French sailors, as well as Louisiana's founder, Le Moyne d'Iberville, contracted yellow fever and died in the Caribbean during the summer of 1706. Later it was reported that the French in Louisiana suffered from a "general sickness" during 1706. See Bénard de La Harpe, *Historical Journal*, 54; King Louis XIV to de Muy, June 30, 1707, in MPAFD, 3:56.

1708 Virginia: Col. Edmund Jennings to Lords Commissioners for Trade and Plantations, September 20, 1708, C.O. 5:1316, fol. 33, NA/PRO. Yellow fever may have been present among coastal populations, but at least one disease capable of spreading inland was also involved since the Tuscaroras were said to have had a "violent distemper" in September 1708.

The epidemic may have been sparked by the arrival of the *Oxford* with one hundred "dangerous sick" crewmen; thirty had died at sea. See Mr. Black to the Secretary, June 19, 1708, SPG, ser. A., vol. 4; *EJCCV*, 3:189.

1708 Pensacola: Bienville to Pontchartrain, October 12, 1708, in *MPAFD*, 2:41. Fifty-five Spanish soldiers died of this "plague."

1709 South Carolina: Le Jau to Secretary, February 18, 1709, in *CCLJ*, 49, 53.

1709 Virginia: "A Proclamation for a publick fast by Edmund Jennings," April 15, 1709, in *EJCCV*, 3:568–69.

1709–10 Virginia: "A Proclamation for a publick fast by Edmund Jennings," December 8, 1709, in *EJCCV*, 3:572. Jennings later reported that the epidemic was widespread and "rage[d] most in the coldest weather." Jennings to Lords Commissioners of Trade and Plantations, January 11, 1710, C.O. 5:1316, fol. 134, NA/PRO. The epidemic continued into 1710. Jennings to Lords Commissioners of Trade and Plantations, April 24, 1710, C.O. 5:1316, fol. 141, NA/PRO.

1711 Virginia: "A Proclamation of Alexander Spotswood," January 15, 1711, in *EJCCV*, 3:582–83.

1711 South Carolina: Gideon Johnston to Secretary, January 27, 1711, in *PGJ*, 67, 91; Francis Le Jau to Secretary, February 9, 1711, in *CCLJ*, 85.

1711–12 South Carolina: May 15, 1711, JCHASC transcripts, 303, 333; October 26, 1711, JCHASC transcripts, 341; Gideon Johnston to Secretary, November 16, 1711, in *PGJ*, 99; Thomas Hasell to Secretary, March 12, 1712, SPG, ser. A, vol. 7; Commissary Johnston's Notitia Parochialis, 1711–12, SPG, Ser. A, vol. 7; "An Act for the More Effectual Preventing the Spreading of Contagious Distempers," in Cooper, *Statutes at Large of South Carolina*, 2:382.

1711 North Carolina: "De Graffenried's Manuscript," in *CRNC*, 1:909; John Urmstone to the Secretary, July 17, 1711, in *CRNC*, 1:773–75. Yellow fever was a possible contagion afflicting the Palatines during the summer of 1711. See Dill, "Eighteenth-Century New Bern." Typhus could also have been the culprit, especially if the same disease lingered into the winter and was the cause of the "pestilential distemper" that struck that December. See below.

1711 North Carolina: Spotswood to Lord Dartmouth, December 28, 1711, in Brock, *Official Letters of Alexander Spotswood*, 1:137. Typhus is suspected because Palatine settlers who had recently arrived in Virginia and then settled in North Carolina had contracted "ship's fever." The timing in the winter is also indicative of typhus.

1711–12 South Carolina: Mr. Dennis to the Secretary, October 7, 1711, SPG, ser. A, vol. 6; Gideon Johnston to Secretary, November 16, 1711, in *PGJ*, 99. One of the many illnesses to ravage South Carolina during this period was a disease that struck in August and let up when the cold weather set in, making a diagnosis of yellow fever likely. Early modern Europeans often identified influenza as "pleurisy" because it often led to pneumonia. For reference to pleurisy, see Gideon Johnston to Secretary, November 16, 1711 in *PGJ*, 99; Le Jau to Secretary, January 4, 1712, in *CCLJ*, 104; Le Jau to Secretary, February 20, 1712, in *CCLJ*, 108; Mr. Dennis to Secretary, February 26, 1712, SPG, ser. A, vol. 7; Thomas Hasell to Secretary, March 12, 1712, SPG, ser. A, vol. 7. Malignant fever may also be a reference to influenza or possibly typhus. For reference to malignant fever, see Thomas Hasell to Secretary, March 12, 1712, SPG, ser. A, vol. 7; "An Act for the More Effectual Preventing the Spreading of Contagious Distempers," in Cooper, *Statutes at Large of South Carolina*, 2:382. Both typhus and measles involve small macular eruptions. For reference to spotted fever, see "An Act for the More Effectual Preventing the Spreading of Contagious Distempers," in Cooper, *Statutes at Large of South Carolina,* 2:382.

Note to Table 2 (p. 171). "An exact account of the number and strength of all the Indian nations that were subject to the government of South Carolina . . . in the beginning of the year 1715." Included in Governor Robert Johnson to Lords Commissioners of Trade and Plantations, January 12, 1720, *BPROSC,* 7:233–50. The letter and census is also reprinted in H. Roy Merrens, ed., *The Colonial South Carolina Scene: Contemporary Views, 1697–1774* (Columbia: University of South Carolina Press, 1977), 56–66. Some of the calculations in the census were incorrect. The totals for the Yamasees, the Apalachees, the Shawnees, the Cherokees, and the Saras have been corrected. The uncorrected numbers for these groups are as follows: Yamasees, 1,215; Apalachees, 638; Shawnees, 283; Cherokees, 11,530; and Saras, 570. The uncorrected total population of Natives is 28,041. I have also corrected the spellings of tribal names to correspond with the most common usages.

1. Mr. Dennis to the Secretary, January 3, 1715, SPG, ser. A, vol. 10.
2. Robert Maule to Secretary, February 18, 1716, SPG, ser. A, vol. 10.
3. Crosby, "Virgin Soil Epidemics," 289–99.
4. Lawson, *New Voyage to Carolina,* 66.
5. "Mr. Randolph's Memorial about Illegal Trade," November 10, 1696, *CRNC,* 1:46.
6. Parramore, "Tuscarora Ascendancy," 307–26.
7. Parramore, "Tuscarora Ascendancy," 318–21.
8. Edmund Jennings to Lords Commissioners of Trade and Plantations, September 20, 1708, C.O. 5:1316, fol. 33, NA/PRO. Douglas Boyce also cites this letter and mistakenly dates the epidemic to 1707. See Boyce, "Notes on Tuscarora Political Organization," 54. Parramore citing Boyce perpetuates the mistake and adds that the epidemic was smallpox when no specific disease was mentioned or discernable. See Parramore, "Tuscarora Ascendancy," 324.
9. Lawson, *New Voyage to Carolina,* 232.
10. Edmund Jennings to Lords Commissioners of Trade and Plantations, November 27, 1708, C.O. 5:1316, fol. 53–54, NA/PRO; *EJCCV,* 3:193; Jennings to Lords Commissioners of Trade and Plantations, October 8, 1709, C.O. 5:1316, NA/PRO.
11. John Urmston to Secretary, July 17, 1711, in *CRNC,* 1:775.
12. "De Graffenried's Manuscript," in *CRNC,* 1:909; "A Letter from Major Christopher Gale, November 2, 1711," in *CRNC,* 1:826.
13. Gallay, *Indian Slave Trade,* 265.
14. *Minutes of the Provincial Council of Pennsylvania,* 2:533.
15. Oatis, *Colonial Complex,* 84.
16. The most thorough secondary account of the Tuscarora War is Gallay, *Indian Slave Trade,* 259–87. See also Oatis, *Colonial Complex,* 84–91.
17. *EJCCV,* 3:295.
18. John Barnwell to the Governor, February 4, 1711, in Barnwell, "Tuscarora Expedition," 30–31.
19. John Barnwell to the Governor, April 20, 1712, in Barnwell, "Tuscarora Expedition," 53.

20. Alexander Spotswood to Lord Dartmouth, December 28, 1711, in Brock, *Official Letters of Alexander Spotswood,* 1:137.

21. Barnwell to the Governor, April 20, 1712, 53.

22. Barnwell to the Governor, April 20, 1712, 47.

23. Brickell, *Natural History of North Carolina,* 397. On smallpox in South Carolina at the time, see table 1 in this chapter.

24. Pollock to Lords Proprietors, September 20, 1712, in *CRNC,* 1:875.

25. "De Graffenried's Manuscript," 1:956.

26. Gallay, *Indian Slave Trade,* 274–75.

27. Mr. Hyde to Mr. Rainsford, May 30, 1712, SPG, ser. A, vol. 8.

28. Pollock to Spotswood, October 5, 1712, in *CRNC,* 1:881; "De Graffenried's Manuscript," 1:966.

29. Gallay, *Indian Slave Trade,* 278.

30. August 6, 1712, JCHASC transcripts

31. These numbers are derived from the map that Moore produced depicting his assault on the Tuscaroras. The Cherokees were the only Natives in his army specifically identified. The map and primary documents related to Moore's campaign are reprinted in Joseph W. Barnwell, "The Second Tuscarora Expedition," *SCHGM* 10 (January 1909): 33–48.

32. Barnwell, "Second Tuscarora Expedition," 39–40.

33. Adair, *History of the American Indian,* 246.

34. Lawson, *New Voyage to Carolina,* 38–52.

35. In 1708 the Saponies moved to Virginia, while in 1712 the Saxapahaws moved south and joined the Catawbas.

36. Gideon Johnston to Secretary, November 16, 1711, in *PGJ,* 99.

37. Aquila, *Iroquois Restoration,* 205–10.

38. This episode involving the Catawbas and the Shawnees is chronicled in *JCHASC.* See entry of June 12, 1707, in *JCHASC,* 26–27 and 50; November 6, 1707, in *JCHASC,* 28; November 12, 1707, in *JCHASC,* 38–39; November 20, 1707, in *JCHASC,* 45.

39. Lawson, *New Voyage to Carolina,* 242; *EJCCV,* 3:188; Col. Edmund Jennings to Lords Commissioners for Trade and Plantations, September 20, 1708, C.O. 5:1316, fol. 33, NA/PRO.

40. Barnwell to [Governor Craven], February 4, 1712, in Barnwell, "Tuscarora Expedition," 31–32.

41. The Ocaneechis, the Saponis, and the Tutelos wound up as tributaries to Virginia, while the Saras (also spelled Cheraws) and the Keyauwees took up residence on the Pee Dee River. Alexander Spotswood to Council of Trade, July 26, 1712, in Brock, *Official Letters of Alexander Spotswood,* 1:167. See also Merrell, *Indians' New World,* 96.

42. April 9, 1712, JCHASC transcripts.

43. Merrell, *Indians' New World,* 94.

44. Merrell, *Indians' New World,* 51.

45. Nathaniel Johnson et al. to Lords Commissioners, September 17, 1708, in *BPROSC,* 5:209.

46. Thomas Nairne to His Lordship, July 10, 1708, in *BPROSC,* 5:199.

47. On the Cherokees' emergence as a primary trading partner with South Carolina, see Reid, *Better Kind of Hatchet*.

48. Charles Hicks to John Ross, May 4, 1826, in Moulton, *Papers of Chief John Ross*, 1:117.

49. Le Jau to Secretary, June 13, 1710, in *CCLJ*, 78.

50. Le Jau to Secretary, February 9, 1711, in *CCLJ*, 87.

51. Le Jau to Secretary, February 20, 1712, in *CCLJ*, 109.

52. On Native population, see table 1 in this chapter. On whites and blacks, see Wood, "Changing Population of the Colonial South," 38. Wood counts 5,100 natives in South Carolina "east of the mountains." His figures must include non-Siouan Yamasees, Apalachees, Shawnees, Yuchis, and Apalachicolas. I discuss those groups in the next section.

53. Marston to Secretary, February 2, 1703, SPG, ser. A, vol. 1.

54. April 28, 1703, *JCHASC*, 75.

55. Oatis, *Colonial Complex*, 47; Crane, *Southern Frontier*, 76.

56. John Stewart to Queen Anne, October 1711, Archives des Colonies, Archives Nationales, Paris, microfilm copies in Manuscript Reading Room, Library of Congress, C13C, 2:72.

57. "Account of the Invasion made by the French and Spaniards upon Carolina, [1706]" in *BPROSC*, 5:171–87.

58. November 20, 1706, *JCHASC*, 5.

59. "Account of the Invasion made by the French and Spaniards upon Carolina [1706]," in *BPROSC*, 5:172.

60. Barnwell to the Governor, April 20, 1712, 47.

61. Barnwell to the Governor, April 20, 1712, 54.

62. May 21, 1712, JCHASC transcripts; see also "An Act for the More Effectual Preventing the Spreading of Contagious Distempers," in Cooper, *Statutes at Large of South Carolina*, 2:382.

63. Le Jau to Secretary, August 10, 1713, in *CCLJ*, 184.

64. See table 1.

65. Gallay, *Indian Slave Trade*, 330–31; Wood, *Black Majority*, 58–62.

66. *JCIT*, 11, 27–28.

67. Hann, *Apalachee*, 167.

68. [Barnwell Map, 1722], C.O. 700, North American Colonies 7, NA/PRO.

69. Alan Gallay suggests that Carolinians ended up with between two thousand and four thousand Apalachee slaves, but he does not take into consideration the number that must have been adopted into the communities of Carolina's Native allies. He also bases his figure on the dwindling number of free Apalachees along the Savannah but does not consider the possibility that they suffered from disease or relocated to live in the interior. John Hann puts the number enslaved at little more than one thousand. See Gallay, *Indian Slave Trade*, 146–49; Hann, *Apalachee*, 168–69.

70. Hann, *Apalachee*, 167.

71. Moore counted 1,300, but Nairne counted 1,600. See "An Account of What the Army Did, under the Command of Col. Moore, in His Expedition Last Winter against the Spaniards and Spanish Indians," in South Carolina Historical Society, *Collections*, 2:573–76; Thomas Nairne to Doctor Marsden, August 20, 1704, SPG, series A., vol.2.

72. Nathaniel Johnson et al. to Lords Proprietors, September 17, 1708, in *BPROSC*, 5:208.

73. The destruction of the Apalachees is covered in secondary works. My summary is based on Hahn, *Invention of the Creek Nation,* 58–65; Gallay, *Indian Slave Trade,* 144–49; Oatis, *Colonial Complex,* 49–51.

74. Hann, *Apalachee,* 167.

75. See table 1.

76. Nairne to Izard, April 15, 1708, 63.

77. Bienville to Pontchartrain, September 6, 1704, 3:20–22.

78. John Stewart to William Dunlop, April 27, 1690, in Stewart, "Letters," 30.

79. "Memoir by the Sieur de La Tonty [1693]," 60.

80. Nine villages in 1701: Bénard de La Harpe, *Historical Journal,* 26–27; six villages in 1715: see table 1 in this chapter.

81. Governor Francisco Corcoles y Martínez to the King, January 14, 1708, in Boyd, *Here They Once Stood,* 90–91.

82. Thomas Nairne to Lords Proprietors, July 10, 1708, in *BPROSC*, 5:196–97.

83. Hahn, *Invention of the Creek Nation,* 76.

84. "An Account Shewing the quantity of Skins and Furrs Imported annually into this Kingdom from Carolina from Christmas 1698 to Christmas 1715," C.O. 5:1265, p. 53, NA/PRO.

85. William L. Ramsey, "'Something Cloudy in Their Looks,'" 56.

86. Le Jau to Secretary, August 10, 1713, in *CCLJ*, 134.

87. Boyd, "Diego Peña's Expedition," 26.

88. Bénard de La Harpe, *Historical Journal,* 15; Le Moyne d'Iberville, *Gulf Journals,* 170.

89. Bienville, "Memoir [1726]," 3:537.

90. Le Moyne de Sauvole de La Villantray, *Journal,* 40.

91. Le Moyne de Sauvole de La Villantray, *Journal,* 45. These tribes are listed as "Conchas" and "Piniscas" in Higgenbotham's translation of Le Moyen de Sauvole de La Villantray's journal. Higginbotham mistakenly identifies the former as Choctaws and the later as Colapissas. Conchacs, however, was a widely used name for the Koasatis, while Piniscas has a closer resemblance to one of the Koasatis' allies in the emerging Upper Creek Confederacy, the Pacanas.

92. Pénicaut, *Fleur de Lys and Calumet,* 72.

93. Bienville to Pontchartrain, September 6, 1704, 3:20–22.

94. Bienville to Pontchartrain, September 6, 1704, 3:24.

95. Bienville, "Memoir [1726]," 536.

96. Bénard de La Harpe, *Historical Journal,* 47. The dramatic decline in deerskins that South Carolina collected from its Native partners offers more evidence that the epidemic was quite widespread and thus involved something other than yellow fever. See note to table 1.

97. Bienville, "Memoir [1726]," 537.

98. Hann and McEwan, *Apalachee Indians and Mission San Luis,* 171. Hann and McEwan claim the epidemic was yellow fever, which I have argued was probably something else.

99. Bienville, "Memoir [1726]," 536. Bienville mistakenly records the arrival of the Apalachees near Mobile Bay in 1702. He also does not give total population figures but records the number of Apalachees at one hundred men. I used a multiplier of 3.5 to arrive at the total Apalachee population. These Apalachees continued to be tied to the French and ultimately

moved west of the Mississippi after 1763. Today descendants of these Apalachees are attempting to gain federal recognition. See "Apalachee Tribe, Missing for Centuries, Comes Out of Hiding," *Wall Street Journal*, March 9, 2005.

100. Bénard de La Harpe stated that the three groups combined had 130 warriors in 1699. Bienville lists the Pascagoulas having 200 men when the French first arrived, a figure that probably included the Biloxis and the Moctobis as well. Bénard de La Harpe, *Historical Journal*, 14; Bienville, "Memoir [1726]," 535.

101. Pénicaut, *Fleur de Lys and Calumet*, 81.

102. Bienville, "Memoir [1726]," 535.

103. Bénard de La Harpe, *Historical Journal*, 14; Du Ru, *Journal*, 65–66.

104. Le Moyne d'Iberville, *Gulf Journals*, 133.

105. Pénicaut, *Fleur de Lys and Calumet*, 146.

106. Pénicaut, *Fleur de Lys and Calumet*, 219; Bienville, "Memoir [1726]," 535.

107. Du Ru, *Journal*, 19.

108. Le Moyne d'Iberville, *Gulf Journals*, 143; Bénard de La Harpe, *Historical Journal*, 25.

109. Bénard de La Harpe, *Historical Journal*, 48.

110. Pénicaut, *Fleur de Lys and Calumet*, 71.

111. Bénard de La Harpe, *Historical Journal*, 53.

112. Bienville to Pontchartrain, June 15, 1715, in *MPAFD*, 3:183; Bénard de La Harpe, *Historical Journal*, 53; Bienville, "Memoir [1726]," 536.

113. Bienville, "Memoir [1726]," 536.

114. Pierre de Charlevoix, "Historical Journal," in French, *Historical Collections of Louisiana*, 3:176.

115. Bienville, "Memoir [1726]," 536.

116. Pénicaut, *Fleur de Lys and Calumet*, 33.

117. Le Moyne d'Iberville, *Gulf Journals*, 144.

118. "Letter of Mr. de Montigny [1699]," 75–76, "Letter Thaumur de La Source [1699]," 80–81.

119. Bienville to Pontchartrain, September 6, 1704, 3:22–23.

120. Bénard de La Harpe, *Historical Journal*, 48–49.

121. Bénard de La Harpe, *Historical Journal*, 54; Pénicaut, *Fleur de Lys and Calumet*, 129–30; Bienville, "Memoir [1726]," 528. Pénicaut placed the Houma-Tunica conflict in 1709, while Bénard de La Harpe, whose dates were consistently more accurate, placed it in 1706.

122. Bienville, "Memoirs [1726]," 530.

123. Le Moyne d'Iberville, *Gulf Journals*, 72–73, 125, and 132; Pénicaut, *Fleur de Lys and Calumet*, 84; Bénard de La Harpe, *Historical Journal*, 22. Bénard de La Harpe estimated that the Natchez had twelve hundred warriors, which was the same number that Bienville claimed they had in 1699. Bienville, "Memoir [1726]," 530–31.

124. Bienville to Pontchartrain, February 20, 1707, in *MPAFD*, 3:37.

125. Bienville to Pontchartrain, February 25, 1708, in *MPAFD*, 3:113. Bienville called the Englishmen's Native escorts "Tchitchiatchys," which resembles "Hitchitis" more closely than "Chickasaws," as the editor of Bienville's letters claims. Moreover, "Chickasaw" had become standard usage by 1708, meaning that the French would not have referred to them by anything other than that name.

126. Bienville to Pontchartrain, October 12, 1708, in *MPAFD*, 2:39.

127. Pénicaut, *Fleur de Lys and Calumet,* 159.

128. Bienville, "Memoir [1726]," 530–31.

129. Nairne to Landgrave Smith, January 20, 1708, 48.

130. Thomas Nairne to Charles Spencer, July 10, 1708, in Moore, *Nairne's Muskhogean Journal,* 75–76.

131. Bienville, "Memoir [1726]," 537–38.

132. Bénard de La Harpe, *Historical Journal,* 51.

133. Bienville to Pontchartrain, April 1705, in *MPAFD*, 3:34.

134. Bénard de La Harpe, *Historical Journal,* 52.

135. November 6, 1707, in *JCHASC*, 27–28; Gallay, *Indian Slave Trade,* 153.

136. Nairne to Landgrave Smith, January 20, 1708, 53.

137. Pénicaut, *Fleur de Lys and Calumet,* 130.

138. Pénicaut, *Fleur de Lys and Calumet;* Bénard de La Harpe, *Historical Journal,* 48, 52, and 56. Bienville to Pontchartrain, August 20, 1709, in *MPAFD*, 3:136.

139. Crane, *Southern Frontier,* 96. Bienville learned of this expedition and estimated that sixty Englishmen and three thousand Native warriors were involved. His letters do not indicate what actually took place and how many slaves the English obtained. See Bienville to Pontchartrain, October 27, 1711, in *MPAFD*, 3:159–60.

140. Bienville to Pontchartrain, August 20, 1709, in *MPAFD*, 3:136.

141. Bienville to Pontchartrain, August 20, 1709, 3:136.

142. John Stewart to Queen Anne, March 10, 1711, Archives des Colonies, Archives Nationales, Paris, microfilm copies in Manuscript Reading Room, Library of Congress, C13C, 2:80, photocopy provided by Alan Gallay.

143. John Stewart to My Lord [Lord Dunmore?], June 8, 1712, C.O. 5:9, fols. 76–77, NA/PRO.

144. Bienville to Pontchartrain, June 15, 1715, in *MPAFD*, 3:183. Bienville had not yet heard about the Yamasee War, thus showing he had no role in any French conspiracy to engineer South Carolina's Native allies to revolt against them.

145. Pénicaut, *Fleur de Lys and Calumet,* 159–62; Bénard de La Harpe, *Historical Journal,* 66.

146. Chicken, "Journal from Carolina in 1715 [1716]," 336.

147. On the rapprochement between the Upper Creeks and the French, see Bénard de La Harpe, *Historical Journal,* 60; Cadillac to Pontchartrain, October 26, 1713, *MPAFD*, 2:172.

148. The events of the Yamasee War are covered in Oatis, *Colonial Complex,* 112–39; Gallay, *Indian Slave Trade,* 327–38.

149. Letter of Captain Jonathan St. Lo and Enclosure, July 12, 1715, Admiralty Office, 1:2451, NA/PRO.

150. Córcoles y Martínez to King Philip V, July 5, 1715, Archivo General de las Indias, Audiencia of Santo Domingo, 834, fol. 4, microfilm in Stetson Manuscript Collection, P. K. Yonge Library of Florida History, University of Florida, Gainesville, photocopy provided by Steven C. Hahn. The author wishes to thank Ryan Gaston for help translating this document.

151. Swanton, *Early History of the Creeks and Their Neighbors,* 100.

152. Colonel Caleb Heathcote to Lord Townsend, July 16, 1715, in *Documents Relative to*

the Colonial History of the State of New York (Albany: Weed, Parsons and Company, 1855), 5:433.

153. The origins of the Yamasee War have received a refreshing wave of scholarly interpretations. Scholars have long identified debt, trader's abuses, and Native fears of enslavement as causes for the revolt, but more recently scholars have debated the underlying origins of the conflict. In particular, Richard L. Haan places the conflict in the larger context of the Columbian Exchange. He emphasizes that a declining population of potential slaves helped bury the Yamasees under a mountain of debt, but he does not include the impact of epidemics on South Carolina's own allies and their differential impact in his analysis. He also argues less convincingly that Yamasee debt stemmed from declining deer populations without much evidence for a deer shortage. (See Haan, " 'Trade Do's Not Flourish as Formerly.' ") William L. Ramsey is persuasive in characterizing the conflict as deriving from a fundamental misunderstanding between Carolinian traders and their Native clients about proper economic behavior. Driven by market imperatives to pay off their debts, traders violated the Native conception of reciprocal exchange. Ramsey, moreover, sees South Carolina officials failing miserably to ameliorate the market-generated tensions that their colonial regime produced. Ramsey's analysis, though, does not take into consideration the epidemiological context in which the growing indebtedness occurred. (See Ramsey, " 'Something Cloudy in Their Looks,' " 44–75.) Steven J. Oatis appropriately cautions scholars about reducing the war's origins to a singular cause and effect. Multiple tribes took part, had multiple considerations for doing so, and fought to varying degrees of intensity and commitment. (See Oatis, *Colonial Complex,* 113–39.) All tribes, however, had disastrous experience with diseases, and the differential impact of epidemics shaped the multiple decisions that were made. The rest of this chapter will show how changes in the social landscape factored into Native decisions to go to war, the planning of the war, and the different paths that Native participants would take during the war. Although Steven Hahn does not place English kidnapping in the context of disease and depopulation, I agree with his assessment that the taking of adopted captives by traders was instrumental in driving South Carolina's allies to revolt. (See Hahn, *Invention of the Creek Nation,* 74–80.)

154. Perdue, *Cherokee Women,* 63, 68–70.

155. April 28, 1703, in *JCHASC,* 75.

156. December 11, 1706, in *JCHASC,* 21–22.

157. Gallay, *Indian Slave Trade,* 213–14.

158. *JCIT,* 3, 4, 5, 11, and 12.

159. *JCIT,* 11.

160. *JCIT,* 11 and 12.

161. *JCIT,* 4–5.

162. *JCIT,* 15–16 (emphasis added).

163. *JCIT,* 23–24.

164. *JCIT,* 25.

165. *JCIT,* 53.

166. *JCIT,* 57.

167. *JCIT,* 49–50.

168. *JCIT*, 65.

169. *JCIT*, 26–27 (two individuals), 28, 33, 38 (two individuals), 42, 47, 49, 50 (three), 58, and 60.

170. *JCIT*, 28, 42, and 58.

171. *JCIT*, 26–27.

172. *JCIT*, 42.

173. *JCIT*, 47–48. The Soogela king may have been the headman of the Lower Creek town of Savacola, which sometimes appears in English documents as "Sowagles" or variants thereof, or it may have been the Upper Creek town of Sogey hatchy. See [Map of Southeast], C.O. 700, Carolina 3, NA/PRO; and "Captain Glover's Account of Indian Tribes," in *SCHGM* 32 (July 1931): 241–42.

174. Nairne to Izard, April 15, 1708, 62

175. *JCIT*, 60.

176. Le Jau to Secretary, April 22, 1708, in *CCLJ*, 39; and Le Jau to Secretary, March 13, 1708, in *CCLJ*, 37.

177. Extract of a letter from Mr. Haig, n.d., SPG, ser A., vol. 10.

178. Treadwell Bull to Secretary, January 20, 1715, SPG, ser. A, vol. 10.

179. Heathcote to Townsend, July 16, 1715, 5:433; Córcoles y Martínez to King Philip V, July 5, 1715.

180. June 14, 1711, JCHASC transcripts, 309.

181. JCHASC, 14.

182. Barnwell to Governor Craven, February 4, 1711, in Barnwell, "Tuscarora Expedition," 33.

183. JCHASC, 33–34.

184. *EJCCV*, 3:412; Merrell, *Indians' New World*, 75–80.

185. Bienville, "Memoir [1726]," 491.

186. Bienville to Pontchartrain, June 15, 1715, 3:181–83; Bienville to Pontchartrain, September 1, 1715, in *MPAFD*, 3:188.

187. *JCIT*, 49.

188. Ramsey, "'Something Cloudy in Their Looks,'" 68.

189. Chicken, "Journal from Carolina in 1715 [1716]," 330–31. On Cherokees' and the Yamasees' relationship, see "Discourse between the Long Warrior of Tunnisee . . . and President of South Carolina Council, January 24, 1727," C.O. 5:387, fols. 237–38, NA/PRO.

190. April 29, 1703, in *JCHASC*, 75 and 78.

191. Thomas Nairne to [the Earl of Sunderland?], July 28, 1708, in Sainsbury et al., *Calendar of State Papers*, 24:133.

192. May 19, 1712, JCHASC transcripts; *JCIT*, 24.

193. For the Cherokees' destruction of Chestowee, see *JCIT*, 53–56.

194. Treadwell Bull to Secretary, October 31, 1715, SPG, ser. A, vol. 11; Córcoles y Martínez to King Philip V, July 5, 1715; Oatis, *Colonial Complex*, 113.

195. Gallay, *Indian Slave Trade*, 220.

196. *JCIT*, 45.

197. *JCIT*, 49.

198. Chicken, "Journal from Carolina in 1715 [1716]," 334–35.

199. Charles Rodd to His Employer in London, May 8, 1715, in Sainsbury et al., *Calendar of State Papers*, 28:169.

200. Merrell, *Indians' New World*, 74.

201. Merrell, *Indians' New World*, 76–77.

202. Charles Craven et al. to Lords Commissioners of Trade and Plantations, July 19, 1715, C.O. 5:1265, NA/PRO.

203. Le Jau to Secretary, November 28, 1715, in *CCLJ*, 169.

204. Chicken recorded this group as the "Wawwees," a name that most closely resembles "Keyauwees." Chicken, "Journal from Carolina in 1715 [1716]," 331.

205. Chicken, "Journal from Carolina in 1715 [1716]," 344.

206. Chicken records a total of twelve Creeks being killed, but other Carolinian sources pushed the number to nineteen. See Le Jau to Secretary, March 19, 1716, in *CCLJ*, 175; Commons House of Assembly to Their Agents in Great Britain, March 15, 1716, C.O. 5:1265, fols. 48–49, NA/PRO.

207. Chicken, "Journal from Carolina in 1715 [1716]," 347.

208. Ralph Izard, B. Gochin, and Edward Hyrne to Joseph Boone and Richard Berresford, August 6, 1716, C.O. 5:1265, fols. 86–87, NA/PRO.

209. Izard, Gochin, and Hyrne to Boone and Berresford, August 6, 1716.

210. Oatis, *Colonial Complex*, 178–80.

211. Commons House of Assembly to Agents in Great Britain, April 28, 1716, C.O. 5:1265, fol. 64, NA/PRO.

212. *JCIT*, 141.

213. Izard, Gochin, and Hyrne to Boone and Berresford, August 6, 1716.

214. Thomas Smith, Nicholas Trott, Francis Younge, Robert Daniel, Samuel Everleigh, Charles Hart, and Charles Craven to Lords Commissioners of Trades and Plantations, C.O. 5:1265, fol. 129, NA/PRO.

215. Joseph Boone to Lords Commissioners of Trades and Plantations, April 2, 1717, C.O. 5:1265, fol. 140, NA/PRO.

216. After the Yamasee War, the English moved closer to a type of relationship with their Native allies that historian Richard White has described with the metaphor of the "middle ground." See White, *Middle Ground*.

Conclusion

1. McNeill, *Plagues and Peoples*, 22.

2. Although I did not find evidence that pertains to the Southeast before 1715, Elizabeth Fenn makes a compelling argument that later in the eighteenth century Europeans had the knowledge, the technology, and the will to spread smallpox and that "actual incidents [of biological warfare] may have occurred more frequently than scholars have previously acknowledged." See Fenn, "Biological Warfare in Eighteenth-Century North America," 1553.

3. Most historians agree that the Yamasee War marked the end of South Carolina's Native slave trade. See Gallay, *Indian Slave Trade*, 338 and 346; William L. Ramsey, "'All Singular the Slaves.'"

NOTES TO PAGE 224 | 261

4. Eighteenth-century epidemics in the Southeast have been the subject of several works. See Peter Wood, "The Impact of Smallpox on the Native Population of the 18th-Century South," *New York State Journal of Medicine* 87 (1987): 30–36; Russell Thornton, *The Cherokees: A Population History* (Lincoln: University of Nebraska Press, 1987). The Southeast was also affected by what Elizabeth Fenn has called "the Great Smallpox Epidemic of 1775–1782," a pandemic that swept North America during the heightened human traffic related to the Revolutionary War. See her *Pox Americana*. Fenn indeed skillfully reconstructs the wide-ranging and devastating impact of smallpox during the American Revolution, but the pandemic was not as significant for the Native Southeast as were previous epidemics. By 1775 indigenous leaders in the Southeast had learned effective ways to avoid exposure and to retard mortality rates. See Kelton, "Avoiding the Smallpox Spirits."

BIBLIOGRAPHY

Archival Sources

Colonial Office Records. National Archives (formerly British Public Record Office). Kew, United Kingdom.

Folsom, Nathaniel. Discussion of Choctaw History. MSS. Thomas Gilcrease Museum of American Art and History, Tulsa OK.

Journal of the Commons House of Assembly of South Carolina. Transcripts of the original. South Carolina Department of Archives and History. Columbia SC. Microfilm.

Records in the British Public Record Office relating to South Carolina, 1663–1782. 36 vols. Transcribed by W. Noel Sainsbury. South Carolina Department of History and Archives, Columbia SC. Microfilm.

Records of the Society for the Propagation of the Gospel in Foreign Parts. Society for the Propagation of the Gospel. London. Microfilm.

Published Primary Sources

Adair, James. *The History of the American Indians.* Edited by Kathryn E. Holland Braund. Tuscaloosa: University of Alabama Press, 2005.

Alvord, Clarence Walworth, and Lee Bidgood, eds. *The First Explorations of the Trans-Allegheny Region by the Virginians, 1650–1674.* Cleveland: Arthur H. Clark, 1912.

Barcia Carballido y Zúñiga, Andrés González. *Barcia's Chronological History of the Continent of Florida.* Translated by Anthony Kerrigan. Westport CT: Greenwood Press, 1951.

Barnwell, John. "The Tuscarora Expedition: Letters of Colonel John Barnwell." *South Carolina Historical and Genealogical Magazine* 9 (January 1908): 28–54.

Bénard de La Harpe, Jean Baptiste. *Historical Journal of the Establishment of the French in Louisiana.* Edited by Glenn R. Conrad. Translated by Joan Cain and Virginia Koenig. Lafayette: University of Southwest Louisiana Press, 1971.

[Bigges, Walter]. *A Summary and True Discourse of Sir Francis Drake's West Indian Voyage.* London, 1589.

Bossu, [Jean-Bernard]. *Travels in the Interior of North America, 1751–1762.* Edited and translated by Seymour Feiler. Norman: University of Oklahoma Press, 1962.

Boyd, Mark F., trans. "Diego Peña's Expedition to Apalachee and Apalachicola in 1716." *Florida Historical Quarterly* 28 (July 1949): 1–27.

———, trans. "The Expedition of Marcus Delgado from Apalachee to the Upper Creek Country in 1686." *Florida Historical Quarterly* 16 (January 1937): 3–48.

263

————. *Here They Once Stood: The Tragic End of the Apalachee Missions*. Gainesville: University Press of Florida, 1951.

Brickell, John. *The Natural History of North Carolina*. London, 1737. Reprint, Raleigh: North Carolina Public Libraries, 1911.

Brock, R. A., ed. *The Official Letters of Alexander Spotswood*. 2 vols. Richmond: Virginia Historical Society, 1882–85.

Byrd, William, II. *The Writings of Colonel William Byrd of Westover in Virginia*. Edited by John Spencer Bassett. New York: Doubleday, Page, and Company, 1901.

Calderón, Gabriel Diaz Vara, Bishop of Cuba. *A Seventeenth-Century Letter of Gabriel Diaz Vara Calderón, Bishop of Cuba, describing the Indians and Indian Missions of Florida*. Translated by Lucy Wenhold. Smithsonian Miscellaneous Collections, vol. 95, no. 16. Washington DC: Smithsonian Institution Press, 1936.

Carroll, Bartholomew R., ed. *Historical Collections of South Carolina*. 2 vols. New York: Harper and Brothers, 1836.

Chicken, George. "A Journal from Carolina in 1715 [1716]." In *Yearbook of the City of Charleston*, 324–54. Charleston SC: Walker, Erono, and Cogswell, 1894.

Clayton, Langdon, Vernon James Knight Jr., and Edward C. Moore, eds. *The De Soto Chronicles: The Expedition of Hernando de Soto to the United States, 1539–1543*. 2 vols. Tuscaloosa: University of Alabama, 1993.

Cooper, Thomas, ed. *Statutes at Large of South Carolina*. 10 vols. Columbia SC: A. S. Johnston, 1836–41.

Du Ru, Paul. *Journal of Paul du Ru [February 1 to May 8, 1700] Missionary Priest of Louisiana*. Translated by Ruth Lapham Butler. Chicago: Caxton Club, 1934.

French, B. F., ed. *Historical Collections of Louisiana*. 5 vols. New York: Lamport, Blakeman, and Law, 1846–75.

Gallardo, José Miguel, trans. "Pablo de Hita Salazar, Governor of Florida, to the Crown, March 6, 1680." *South Carolina Historical and Genealogical Magazine* 37 (April 1936): 49–99; (October 1936): 131–41.

Hann, John, trans. "Translation of Alonso de Leturiondo's Memorial to the King of Spain [c.1700]." *Florida Archaeologist* 2 (1986): 165–225.

————. "Translation of Governor Robolledo's 1657 Visitation of Three Florida Provinces and Related Documents." *Florida Archaeology* 2 (1986): 81–145.

Hening, William Waller. *The Statutes at Large: Being a Collection of all the Laws of Virginia*. 13 vols. Richmond: Samuel Pleasants, 1810–23.

Hudson, Charles, ed. *The Juan Pardo Expeditions: Exploration of the Carolinas and Tennessee, 1566–1568*. Transcribed, translated, and annotated by Paul E. Hoffman. Washington DC: Smithsonian Institution Press, 1990.

Klingberg, Frank, ed. *The Carolina Chronicle of Dr. Francis Le Jau*. University of California Publications in History vol. 53. Berkeley: University of California Press, 1956.

————, ed. *Carolina Chronicle: The Papers of Gideon Johnston*. University of California Publications in History 35. Berkeley: University of California Press, 1946.

Knight, Vernon James, Jr., and Sherée L. Adams, trans. "A Voyage to the Mobile and Tomeh in 1700, with Notes on the Interior of Alabama [by Charles Levassuer]." *Journal of Alabama Archaeology* 27 (June 1981): 32–56.

Lawson, John. *A New Voyage to Carolina*. Edited by Hugh Talmage Lefler. Chapel Hill: University of North Carolina Press, 1967.

Le Moyne de Sauvole de La Villantray, Antoine. *Journal of Sauvole [1699–1701]*. Edited by Prieur Jay Higginbotham. Mobile AL: Colonial Books, 1969.

Le Moyne, sieur d'Iberville, Pierre. *Iberville's Gulf Journals*. Translated by Richebourg Gaillard McWilliams. Tuscaloosa: University of Alabama Press, 1981.

Longe, Alexander. "A Small Postscript on the Ways and Manners of the Indians called Cherokees [c. 1711]." *Southern Indian Studies* 21 (October 1969): 6–49.

McDowell, William L., ed. *Journals of the Commissioners of the Indian Trade, September 20, 1710–August 29, 1718*. Columbia: South Carolina Department of History and Archives, 1955.

McIlwaine, H. R., ed. *Executive Journals of the Council of Colonial Virginia*. 6 vols. Richmond: D. Bottom, 1925–45.

Minutes of the Provincial Council of Pennsylvania. 10 vols. Philadelphia: Joseph Severns, 1852.

Moore, Alexander, ed. *Nairne's Muskhogean Journals: The 1708 Expedition to the Mississippi River*. Jackson: University Press of Mississippi, 1988.

Moulton, Gary, ed. *The Papers of Chief John Ross*. 2 vols. Norman: University of Oklahoma Press, 1985.

Norton, John. *The Journal of Major John Norton, 1816*. Edited by Carl F. Klinck and James J. Talman. Toronto: Champlain Society, 1970.

Palmer, William P. *Calendar of Virginia State Papers*. 11 vols. Richmond, 1875. Reprint, New York: Kraus Reprint, 1968.

Pénicaut, André. *Fleur de Lys and Calumet: Being the Pénicaut Narrative of French Adventure in Louisiana*. Translated and edited by Richebourg Gaillard McWilliams. Tuscaloosa: University of Alabama Press, 1987.

Priestly, Herbert, trans. and ed. *The Luna Papers*. 2 vols. Deland: Florida State Historical Society, 1928.

Quinn, David B., ed. *New American World: A Documentary History of North America to 1612*. 5 vols. New York: Arno Press, 1979.

Reding, Katherine, trans. "Plans for the Colonization and Defense of Apalachee, 1675." *Georgia Historical Quarterly* 9 (June 1925): 169–75.

Rowland, Dunbar, A. G. Sanders, and Patricia Galloway, eds. *Mississippi Provincial Archives, French Dominion*. 5 vols. Jackson: Mississippi Department of Archives and History, 1927–32 and 1984.

Sainsbury, Noel, J. W. Fortesque, Cecil Hedlam, and A. P. Newton, eds. *Calendar of State Papers, Colonial Series, American and the West Indies*. 38 vols. London: His Majesty's Stationary Office, 1860–1930.

Salley, Alexander, Jr., ed. *Commissions and Instructions from the Lords Proprietors of Carolina to Public Officials of South Carolina, 1685–1715*. Columbia: South Carolina Department of History and Archives, 1916.

———, ed. *The Journal of the Commons House of Assembly of South Carolina*. 21 vols. Columbia: South Carolina Department of Archives and History, 1907–49.

———, ed. *Narratives of Early Carolina, 1650–1708*. New York: Scribner's Sons, 1911.

Saunders, William L., ed. *The Colonial Records of North Carolina.* 10 vols. Raleigh NC: P. M. Hale, 1886–90.

Shea, John D., ed. *Discovery and Exploration of the Mississippi Valley.* Albany: Joseph McDonough, 1906.

———, ed. *Early Voyages up and down the Mississippi by Cavelier, St. Cosme, Le Seur, Gravier, and Guignas.* Albany: Joel Munsell, 1861.

South Carolina Historical Society. *Collections of the South Carolina Historical Society.* 5 vols. Columbia: South Carolina Historical Society, 1857.

Stewart, John. "Letters from John Stewart to William Dunlop." *South Carolina Historical and Genealogical Magazine* 32 (1931): 1–33, 81–114, and 170–74.

Tinling, Marion, ed. *The Correspondence of the Three William Byrds of Westover, Virginia, 1684–1776.* 2 vols. Charlottesville: University Press of Virginia, 1977.

Weddle, Robert S., ed. *La Salle, the Mississippi, and the Gulf: Three Primary Documents.* Translated by Linda Bell. College Station: Texas A&M University Press, 1987.

Williams, Samuel Cole, ed. *Early Travels in the Tennessee Country.* Johnson City TN: Watauga Press, 1928.

Worth, John, ed. and trans. *The Struggle for the Georgia Coast: An 18th-Century Spanish Retrospective on Guale and Mocama.* Anthropological Papers of the American Museum of Natural History 75. Athens: University of Georgia Press, 1995.

Zubillaga, Félix, ed. *La Florida: La Mission Jesuitica (1566–1572).* Rome: Institutum Historicum S.I., 1941.

Secondary Sources

Ackerknecht, Erwin. *History and Geography of the Most Important Diseases.* New York: Hafner, 1965.

Alden, Dauril, and Joseph C. Miller. "Unwanted Cargoes: the Origins and Dissemination of Smallpox via the Slave Trade from Africa to Brazil, c. 1560–1830." In *The African Exchange: Toward a Biological History of Black People,* edited by Kenneth F. Kiple, 35–109. Durham NC: Duke University Press, 1987.

Alexander, John T. *Bubonic Plague in Early Modern Russia.* New York: Oxford University Press, 2003.

Anderson, David. "Stability and Change in Chiefdom-Level Societies: An Examination of Mississippian Political Evolution on the South Atlantic Slope." In *Lamar Archaeology,* edited by Gary Shapiro, 187–252. Tuscaloosa: University of Alabama, 1987.

———. *The Savannah River Chiefdoms: Political Change in the Late Prehistoric Southeast.* Tuscaloosa: University of Alabama Press, 1994.

Anderson, Gary. *Kinsmen of Another Kind: Dakota-White Relations in the Upper Mississippi Valley, 1650–1862.* Lincoln: University of Nebraska Press, 1984.

Aquila, Richard. *The Iroquois Restoration: Iroquois Diplomacy on the Colonial Frontier, 1701–1754.* Detroit: Wayne State University Press, 1983.

———. "Ethnohistory of Early America: A Review Essay." *William and Mary Quarterly,* 3d ser., 35 (January 1978): 110–44.

———. *The European and the Indian: Essays in the Ethnohistory of Colonial North America.* New York: Oxford University Press, 1981.

Baden, William. "A Dynamic Model of Stability and Change in the Mississippian Agricultural Systems." PhD diss., University of Tennessee, 1987.

Badger, R. Reid, and Lawrence A. Clayton, eds. *Alabama and the Borderlands from Prehistory to Statehood.* Tuscaloosa: University of Alabama Press, 1985.

Baker, Brenda J., and Lisa Kealhofer, eds. *Bioarchaeology of Native American Adaptation in the Spanish Borderlands.* Gainesville: University Press of Florida, 1996.

Barnwell, Joseph W. "The Second Tuscarora Expedition." *South Carolina Historical and Genealogical Magazine* 10 (January 1909): 33–48.

Barquet, Nicolau, and Pere Domingo. "Smallpox: The Triumph over the Most Terrible of the Ministers of Death." *Annals of Internal Medicine* 127 (1997): 635–42.

Bell, Stephanie, John F. Henry, and L. Randall Wray. "A Chartalist Critique of John Locke's Theory of Property, Accumulation and Money: Or, Is it Moral to Trade Your Nuts for Gold." *Review of Social Economy* 62 (March 2004): 51–65.

Bentley, Gillian R., Brazyna Jasieńska, and Tony Goldberg. "Is the Fertility of Agriculturalists Higher than that of Nonagriculturalists?" *Current Anthropology* 34 (December 1993): 778–85.

———. "The Fertility of Agricultural and Nonagricultural Traditional Societies." *Population Studies* 47 (July 1993): 269–81.

Berlin, Ira. *Many Thousands Gone: The First Two Centuries of Slavery in North America.* Cambridge MA: Belknap Press of Harvard University, 1998.

Black, Francis. "An Explanation of High Death Rates among New World Peoples When in Contact with Old World Diseases." *Perspectives in Biology and Medicine* 37 (Winter 1994): 292–307.

———. "Infectious Diseases in Primitive Societies." *Science* 187 (February 14, 1975): 515–18.

———. "Why Did They Die?" *Science* 258 (December 11, 1992): 1738–40.

Blanton, Wyndham. *Medicine in Virginia in the Seventeenth Century.* Richmond VA: William Byrd Press, 1930.

Blasingham, Emily J. "The Depopulation of the Illinois Indians, part 2." *Ethnohistory* 4 (Fall 1956): 361–412.

Blitz, John. *Ancient Chiefdoms of the Tombigbee.* Tuscaloosa: University of Alabama Press, 1993.

Bowne, Eric. *The Westo Indians: Slave Traders of the Early Colonial South.* Tuscaloosa: University of Alabama Press, 2005.

Boyce, Douglas. "Notes on Tuscarora Political Organization, 1650–1713." Masters thesis, University of North Carolina at Chapel Hill, 1971.

Brain, Jeffrey P. *Winterville: Late Prehistoric Culture Contact in the Lower Mississippi Valley.* Archaeological Report 23. Jackson: Mississippi Department of Archives and History, 1989.

Braund, Kathryn E. Holland. *Deerskins and Duffels: The Creek Indian Trade with Anglo-America, 1685–1815.* Lincoln: University of Nebraska Press, 1993.

Briceland, Vance. *Westward from Virginia: The Exploration of the Virginia-Carolina Frontier, 1650–1710.* Charlottesville: University Press of Virginia, 1987.

Brooks, James. *Captives and Cousins: Slavery, Kinship, and Community in the Southwest Borderlands.* Chapel Hill: University of North Carolina Press, 2002.

Brose, David S., C. Wesley Cowan, and Robert C. Mainfort Jr. *Societies in Eclipse: Archaeology of the Eastern Woodland Indians, AD 1400–1700.* Washington DC: Smithsonian Institution Press, 2001.

Buikstra, Jane, ed. *Prehistoric Tuberculosis in the Americas.* Northwestern University Archaeological Program, Scientific Papers 5. Evanston IL: Northwestern University Archaeological Program, 1976.

Burnett, Barbara A., and Katherine A. Murray. "Death, Drought, and De Soto: The Bioarchaeology of Depopulation." In *The Expedition of Hernando De Soto West of the Mississippi,* edited by Gloria A. Young and Michael P. Hoffman, 227–36. Fayetteville: University of Arkansas Press, 1993.

Carr, Lois Green, and Lorena S. Walsh. "The Planter's Wife: The Experience of White Women in Seventeenth-Century Maryland." *William and Mary Quarterly,* 3d ser., 34 (October 1977): 542–71.

Ceci, Lynn. "Native Wampum as a Peripheral Resource in the Seventeenth-Century World System." In *The Pequots in Southern New England: The Fall and Rise of an American Indian Nation,* edited by Laurence M. Hauptman and James D. Wherry, 48–63. Norman: University of Oklahoma Press, 1990.

Chapman, Jefferson. *Tellico Archaeology: 12,000 Years of Native American History.* Knoxville: University of Tennessee Press, 1985.

Chin, James, ed. *Control of Communicable Diseases Manual.* 17th ed. Washington DC: American Public Health Association, 2000.

Cockburn, A. "Where Did Our Infectious Diseases Come From?" In *Health and Disease in Tribal Societies,* Ciba Foundation Symposium 49, 103–112. New York: Elsevier/Excerpta Medica/North-Holland, 1977.

Cohen, Mark. *Health and the Rise of Civilization.* New Haven CT: Yale University Press, 1989.

Cohen, Mark, and George Armelagos, eds. *Paleopathology at the Origins of Agriculture.* Orlando FL: Academic Press, 1984.

"Commentaries: American Hookworm Antiquity." *Medical Anthropology* 20 (January 2001): 101–4.

Cook, Noble David. *Born to Die: Disease and New World Conquest, 1492–1650.* Cambridge: Cambridge University Press, 1998.

———. "Sickness, Starvation, and Death in Early Hispaniola." *Journal of Interdisciplinary History* 32 (Winter 2002): 349–63.

Cook, Noble David, and W. George Lovell, eds. *"Secret Judgements of God": Old World Disease in Colonial Spanish America.* Norman: University of Oklahoma Press, 1991.

Cowdrey, Albert. *This Land, This South: An Environmental History.* Lexington: University of Kentucky Press, 1983.

Crane, Verner. *The Southern Frontier, 1670–1732.* Ann Arbor: University of Michigan, 1929.

———. "The Tennessee River as the Road to Carolina: The Beginnings of Exploration and Trade." *Mississippi Valley Historical Review* 3 (June 1916): 3–18.

Crawford, Michael. *Origins of Native Americans: Evidence from Anthropological Genetics.* New York: Cambridge University Press, 1998.

Cronon, William. *Changes in the Land: Indians, Colonists, and the Ecology of New England.* New York: Hill and Wang, 1983.

Crosby, Alfred. *America's Forgotten Pandemic: The Influenza of 1918.* New York: Cambridge University Press, 1989.

———. *The Columbian Exchange: Biological and Cultural Consequences of 1492.* Westport CT: Greenwood, 1972.

———. *Ecological Imperialism: The Biological Expansion of Europe, 900–1900.* New York: Cambridge University Press, 1986.

———. *Germs, Seeds, and Animals: Studies in Ecological History.* Armonk, NY: M. E. Sharpe, 1994.

———. "Virgin Soil Epidemics as a Factor in the Aboriginal Depopulation in America." *William and Mary Quarterly,* 3d ser., 33 (April 1976): 289–99.

Curren, Caleb. *The Protohistoric Period in Central Alabama.* Camden AL: Alabama-Tombigbee-Regional Commission, 1984.

Curtain, Philip D. "Epidemiology and the Slave Trade." *Political Science Quarterly* 83 (June 1968): 191–216.

Davis, R. P. Stephens, Jr. "The Travels of James Needham and Gabriel Arthur through Virginia, North Carolina, and Beyond, 1673–1674." *Southern Indian Studies* 39 (January 1990): 31–55.

Diamond, Jared. *Guns, Germs, and Steel: The Fates of Human Societies.* New York: W. W. Norton, 1997.

———. "Nature's Infinite Book: A Pox upon Our Genes." *Natural History* 99 (February 1990): 26–30.

Dickens, Roy S. *Cherokee Prehistory: The Pisgah Phase in the Appalachian Summit Region.* Knoxville: University of Tennessee Press, 1976.

Dickson, D. Bruce. "The Yanomamö of the Mississippi Valley? Some Reflections on Larson (1972), Gibson (1974) and Mississippian Warfare in the Southeastern United States." *American Antiquity* 46 (October 1981): 909–16.

Dill, Alonzo Thomas, Jr. "Eighteenth-Century New Bern: A History of the Town and Craven County, 1700–1800." *North Carolina Historical Review* 22 (July 1945): 293–319.

Dobyns, Henry. *Their Number Become Thinned: Native American Population Dynamics in Eastern North America.* Knoxville: University of Tennessee Press, 1983.

Duffy, John. *Epidemics in Colonial America.* Baton Rouge: Louisiana State University Press, 1953.

Dunn, Richard S. *Sugar and Slaves: The Rise of the Planter Class in the English West Indies, 1624–1713.* New York: W. W. Norton, 1972.

DuVal, Kathleen. *The Native Ground: Indians and Colonists in the Heart of the Continent.* Philadelphia: University of Pennsylvania Press, 2006.

Dye, David H., and Cheryl Anne Cox, eds. *Towns and Temples along the Mississippi.* Tuscaloosa: University of Alabama Press,1990.

Earle, Timothy K., ed. *Chiefdoms: Power, Economy, and Ideology.* New York: Cambridge University Press, 1991.

El-Najjar, Mahmoud Y. "Human Treponematosis and Tuberculosis: Evidence from the New World." *American Journal of Physical Anthropology* 51 (1979): 600–608.

———. "Maize, Malaria, and the Anemias in the Pre-Columbian New World." *Yearbook of Physical Anthropology* 20 (1976): 329–37.

Emerson, Thomas E. *Cahokia and the Archaeology of Power.* Tuscaloosa: University of Alabama Press, 1997.

Ethridge, Robbie, and Charles Hudson, eds. *The Transformation of the Southeastern Indians: 1540–1760.* Jackson: University of Mississippi Press, 2002.

Fackelmann, Kathleen. "Tuberculosis Outbreak." *Science News* 153 (January 31, 1998): 73–75.

Falkner, Charles T., Sharon Patton, and Sandra S. Johnson. "Prehistoric Parasitism in Tennessee: Evidence from the Analysis of Desiccated Fecal Material Collected from Big Bone Cave, Van Buren County, Tennessee." *Journal of Parasitology* 75 (June 1989): 461–63.

Fenn, Elizabeth. "Biological Warfare in Eighteenth-Century North America: Beyond Jeffery Amherst." *Journal of American History* 86 (March 2000): 1552–80.

———. *Pox Americana: The Great Smallpox Epidemic of 1775–1782.* New York: Hill and Wang, 2001.

Fogelson, Raymond D. "Who Were the Aní-Kutání? An Excursion into Cherokee Historical Thought." *Ethnohistory* 31 (Winter 1984): 255–63.

Franklin, W. Neill. "Virginia and the Cherokee Indian Trade." *East Tennessee Historical Society's Publications* 4 (January 1932): 3–21.

Fuller, Kathleen. "Hookworm: Not a Pre-Columbian Pathogen." *Medical Anthropology* 17 (1996): 297–308.

Gallay, Alan. *The Indian Slave Trade: The Rise of the English Empire in the American South, 1670–1717.* New Haven CT: Yale University Press, 2002.

Galloway, Patricia. *Choctaw Genesis, 1500–1700.* Lincoln: University of Nebraska Press, 1995.

———, ed. *The Hernando de Soto Expedition: History, Historiography, and "Discovery" in the Southeast.* Lincoln: University of Nebraska Press, 1997.

Gibson, Jon L. "Aboriginal Warfare in the Protohistoric Southeast: An Alternative Perspective." *American Antiquity* 39 (January 1974): 130–33.

Goodman, A. H. and G. J. Armelagos. "Disease and Death at Dr. Dickson's Mounds." *Natural History* 94 (September 1985): 12–18.

Haan, Richard L. "'The Trade Do's Not Flourish as Formerly': the Ecological Origins of the Yamasee War of 1715." *Ethnohistory* 28 (Fall 1981): 341–58.

Hadler, Stephen C., M. De Monzon, A. Ponzetto, E. Anzola, D. Rivero, A. Mondolfi, A. Bracho, D. P. Francis, M. A. Gerber, and S. Thung. "Delta Virus and Severe Hepatitis: An Epidemic in the Yucpa Indians of Venezuela." *Annals of Internal Medicine* 100 (March 1984): 339–44.

Hahn, Steven C. *The Invention of the Creek Nation, 1670–1763.* Lincoln: University of Nebraska Press, 2004.

Hann, John. *Apalachee: The Land between the Rivers.* Gainesville: University Presses of Florida, 1988.

Hann, John, and Bonnie McEwan, *The Apalachee Indians and Mission San Luis.* Gainesville: University Press of Florida, 1998.

Harder, Ben. "The Seeds of Malaria: Recent Evolution Cultivated a Deadly Scourge." *Science News* 160 (November 10, 2001): 296–98.

Harrison, Fairfax. "Western Exploration in Virginia between Lederer and Spotswood." *Virginia Magazine of History and Biography* 30 (October 1922): 323–40.

Henige, David. *Numbers from Nowhere: The American Indian Contact Population Debate.* Norman: University of Oklahoma Press, 1998.

———. "Primary Source by Primary Source? On the Role of Epidemics in New World Depopulation." *Ethnohistory* 33 (Summer 1986): 293–312.

Hewatt, Alexander. *An Historical Account of the Rise and Progress of the Colonies of South Carolina and Georgia.* 2 vols. London: A. Donaldson, 1779.

Hickerson, Harold. *The Southwestern Chippewa: An Ethnohistorical Study.* Menasha WI: George Banta, 1962.

Hoffman, Paul E. *A New Andalucia and a Way to the Orient: The American Southeast during the Sixteenth Century.* Baton Rouge: Louisiana State University Press, 1990.

Hudson, Charles. *Knights of Spain, Warriors of the Sun: Hernando de Soto and the South's Ancient Chiefdoms.* Athens: University of Georgia Press, 1997.

———. *The Southeastern Indians.* Knoxville: University of Tennessee Press, 1976.

Hudson, Charles, and Carmen Chaves Tesser, eds. *The Forgotten Centuries: Indians and Europeans in the American South, 1521–1704.* Athens: University of Georgia Press, 1994.

Humphreys, Margaret. *Yellow Fever in the South.* New Brunswick NJ: Rutgers University Press, 1992.

Jacobson, I., and J. Dienstag. "Viral Hepatitis, Type D." *Gastroenterology* 86 (June 1984): 1614–17.

Jarcho, Saul. "Some Observations on Disease in Prehistoric North America." *Bulletin of the History of Medicine* 38 (January–February 1964): 1–19.

Jennings, Francis. *The Ambiguous Iroquois Empire: The Covenant Chain Confederation of Indian Tribes with English Colonies from its Beginnings to the Lancaster Treaty of 1744.* New York: W. W. Norton, 1983.

———. "The Discovery of Americans." *William and Mary Quarterly,* 3d ser., 41 (July 1984): 436–43.

Johnson, Jay K., and John T. Sparks. "Protohistoric Settlement Patterns in Northeastern Mississippi." In *The Protohistoric Period in the Mid-South, 1500–1700,* edited by David H. Dye and Ronald C. Brister, 64–82. Jackson: Mississippi Department of Archaeology and History, 1986.

Jones, David S. "Virgin Soils Revisited." *William and Mary Quarterly,* 3d ser., 60 (October 2003): 703–42.

Jones, Grant. "The Ethnohistory of the Guale Coast through 1684." In *The Anthropology of St. Catherines Island,* vol. 1, *Natural and Cultural History,* 178–210. New York: American Museum of Natural History, 1978.

Juricek, John J. "The Westo Indians." *Ethnohistory* 11 (Spring 1964): 134–73.

Karlen, Arno. *Man and Microbes: Diseases and Plagues in History and Modern Times.* New York: Putnam, 1995.

Keel, Bennie C. *Cherokee Archaeology: A Study of the Appalachia Summit.* Knoxville: University of Tennessee, 1976.

Kelly, John E. "The Emergence of Mississippian Culture in the American Bottom Region." In *Mississippian Emergence*, edited by Bruce D. Smith, 113–52. Washington DC: Smithsonian Institution Press, 1990.

Kelton, Paul. "Avoiding the Smallpox Spirits: Colonial Epidemics and Southeastern Indian Survival." *Ethnohistory* 51 (Winter 2004): 45–71.

Kiple, Kenneth F., ed. *The Cambridge World History of Human Disease*. New York: Cambridge University Press, 1993.

Knight, Vernon James, Jr., and Vincas P. Steponaitis, eds. *The Archaeology of the Moundville Chiefdom*. Washington DC: Smithsonian Institution Press, 1998.

Kowalewski, Stephen A., and James W. Hatch. "The Sixteenth-Century Expansion of Settlement in the Upper Oconee Watershed, Georgia." *Southeastern Archaeology* 10 (Summer 1991): 1–17.

Kupperman, Karen Ordahl. *Roanoke, the Abandoned Colony*. Totowa NJ: Rowman and Allanheld, 1984.

Lambert, Patricia M., ed. *Bioarchaeological Studies of Life in the Age of Agriculture: A View from the Southeast*. Tuscaloosa: University of Alabama Press, 2000.

Landolt, Gabriele, Alexander I. Karasin, Lynette Phillips, and Christopher W. Olsen. "Comparison of the Pathogenesis of Two Genetically Different H3N2 Influenza A Viruses in Pigs." *Journal of Clinical Microbiology* 41 (May 2003): 1936–41.

Landolt, Gabriele, Alexander I. Karasin, Melissa M. Schutten, and Christopher W. Olsen. "Restricted Infectivity of a Human-Lineage H3N2 Influenza A Virus in Pigs Is Hemagglutinin and Neuraminidase Gene Dependent." *Journal of Clinical Microbiology* 44 (February 2006): 297–301.

Larsen, Clark S. "Biological Changes in Human Populations with Agriculture." *Annual Review of Anthropology* 24 (1995): 185–213.

Larson, Lewis H. *Aboriginal Subsistence Technology on the Southeastern Coastal Plain during the Late Prehistoric Period*. Gainesville: University Presses of Florida, 1980.

———. "Functional Considerations of Warfare in the Southeast during the Mississippian Period." *American Antiquity* 37 (July 1972): 383–92.

Mackenthun, Gesa. *Metaphors of Dispossession: American Beginnings and the Translation of Empire, 1492–1637*. Norman: University of Oklahoma Press, 1997.

Mallon, Florencia. *The Defense of Community in Peru's Central Highlands: Peasant Struggle and Capitalist Transition, 1860–1940*. Princeton NJ: Princeton University Press, 1983.

Mancall, Peter. *Deadly Medicine: Indians and Alcohol in Early America*. Ithaca NY: Cornell University Press, 1995.

Mann, Charles. "1491." *Atlantic Monthly* 287 (March 2002): 41–53.

Martin, Calvin. "Wildlife Diseases as a Factor in the Depopulation of the North American Indian." *Western Historical Quarterly* 7 (January 1976): 47–62.

Mauss, Marcel. *The Gift: Forms and Functions of Exchange in Archaic Societies*. Translated by Ian Cunnison. New York: W. W. Norton, 1967.

McCrady, Edward. *History of South Carolina*. 4 vols. New York: Macmillan, 1897–1902.

McEwan, Bonnie, ed. *Indians of the Greater Southeast: Historical Archaeology and Ethnohistory*. Gainesville: University Press of Florida, 2000.

McKeown, Thomas. *Origins of Human Diseases*. New York: Blackwell, 1988.

McNeill, William. *Plagues and Peoples*. Garden City NY: Anchor Press, 1976.

McNicholl, Janet M., Marie V. Downer, Venkatachalam Udhayakumar, Chester A. Alper, and David L. Swerdlow. "Host-Pathogen Interactions in Emerging and Re-emerging Infectious Diseases: A Genomic Perspective of Tuberculosis, Malaria, Human Immuno-Deficiency Virus Infection, Hepatitis B and Cholera." *Annual Review of Public Health* 21 (2000): 15–46.

Merbs, Charles F. "A New World of Infectious Disease." *Yearbook of Physical Anthropology* 13 (1992): 3–42.

Merrell, James. *The Indians' New World: Catawbas and Their Neighbors from European Contact through the Era of Removal*. New York: W. W. Norton, 1989.

———. "Some Thoughts on Colonial Historians and American Indians." *William and Mary Quarterly*, 3d ser., 46 (January 1989): 94–119.

Merrens, H. Roy, and George D. Terry. "Dying in Paradise: Malaria, Mortality, and the Perceptual Environment in Colonial South Carolina." *Journal of Southern History* 50 (November 1984): 533–50.

Milanich, Jerald T. *Florida Indians and the Invasion from Europe*. Gainesville: University Press of Florida, 1995.

Milner, George. "Epidemic Disease in the Postcontact Southeast." *Mid-Continental Journal of Archaeology* 5 (1980): 39–56.

———. "The Late Prehistoric Cahokia Cultural System of the Mississippi River Valley: Foundations, Florescence, and Fragmentation." *Journal of World Prehistory* 4 (March 1990): 1–43.

Mooney, James. *James Mooney's History, Myths, and Sacred Formulas of the Cherokees*. Asheville NC: Historical Images, 1992.

Mooney, Timothy Paul. "Migration of the Chickasawhay into the Choctaw Homeland." *Mississippi Archaeology* 27, no. 2 (1992): 28–39.

Morgan, Edmund S. *American Slavery, American Freedom: The Ordeal of Colonial Virginia*. New York: W. W. Norton, 1975.

Muller, Jon. *Mississippian Political Economy*. New York: Plenum Press, 1997.

Neel, James. "Health and Disease in Unacculturated Amerindian Populations." In *Health and Disease in Tribal Societies*, Ciba Foundation Symposium 49, 155–77. New York: Elsevier/Excerpta Medica/North-Holland, 1977.

Neel, James V., Willard R. Centerwall, Napoleon A. Chagnon, and Helen L. Casey. "Notes on the Effects of Measles and Measles Vaccine in a Virgin-Soil Population of South American Indians." *American Journal of Epidemiology* 91 (April 1970): 418–29.

Newson, Linda. "Highland-Lowland Contrasts in the Impact of Old World Disease in Early Colonial Ecuador." *Social Science and Medicine* 36 (May 1993): 1187–95.

Nicholson, Karl G., Robert G. Webster, and Alan J. Hay, eds. *Textbook of Influenza*. Oxford: Blackwell Science, 1998.

Oatis, Steven J. *A Colonial Complex: South Carolina's Frontiers in the Era of the Yamasee War, 1680–1730*. Lincoln: University of Nebraska Press, 2004.

O'Brien, Greg. *Choctaws in a Revolutionary Age, 1750–1830*. Lincoln: University of Nebraska Press, 2002.

Paar, Karen Lynn. "'To Settle Is to Conquer': Spaniards, Native Americans, and the Colonization of Santa Elena in Sixteenth-Century Florida." PhD diss., University of North Carolina at Chapel Hill, 1999.

Parramore, Thomas. "The Tuscarora Ascendancy." *North Carolina Historical Review* 59 (October 1982): 307–26.

Pauketat, Timothy R. *The Ascent of Chiefs: Cahokia and Mississippian Politics in Native North America.* Tuscaloosa: University of Alabama Press, 1994.

Pauketat, Timothy R., and Thomas Emerson, eds., *Cahokia: Domination and Ideology in the Mississippian World.* Lincoln: University of Nebraska Press, 1997.

Paulsen, H. Jay. "Tuberculosis in the Native American: Indigenous or Introduced?" *Reviews in Infectious Diseases* 9 (1987): 1180–86.

Peebles, Christopher S. "The Rise and Fall of the Mississippian in Western Alabama: The Moundville and Summerville Phases, AD 1000–1600." *Mississippi Archaeology* 22 (1987): 1–31.

Peebles, Christopher S., and Susan M. Kus. "Some Archaeological Correlates of Ranked Societies." *American Antiquity* 42 (July 1977): 421–48.

Perdue, Michael L., and David E. Swayne. "Public Health Risk from Avian Influenza Viruses." *Avian Diseases* 49 (2005): 317–27.

Perdue, Theda. *Cherokee Women: Gender and Culture Change, 1700–1835.* Lincoln: University of Nebraska Press, 1998.

———. *Slavery and the Evolution of Cherokee Society, 1540–1866.* Knoxville: University of Tennessee Press, 1979.

Piker, Joshua. *Okfuskee: A Creek Indian Town in Colonial America.* Cambridge MA: Harvard University Press, 2004.

Polhemus, Richard R. *The Toqua Site: A Late Mississippian Dallas Phase Town.* University of Tennessee Department of Anthropology, Report of Investigations 41, Tennessee Valley Authority Publications in Anthropology, 44. Knoxville: Tennessee Valley Authority, 1987.

Potter, Christopher W. "A History of Influenza." *Journal of Applied Microbiology* 91 (October 2001): 572–79.

Powell, Mary Lucas, Patricia S. Bridges, and Ann Marie Mires, eds. *What Mean These Bones? Studies in Southeastern Bioarchaeology.* Tuscaloosa: University of Alabama Press, 1991.

Quinn, David B. *Set Fair for Roanoke: Voyages and Colonies, 1584–1606.* Chapel Hill: University of North Carolina, 1985.

Ramenofsky, Ann. "Loss of Innocence: Explanations of Differential Persistence in the Sixteenth-Century Southeast." In *Columbian Consequences,* Vol. 2., *Archaeological and Historical Perspectives on the Spanish Borderlands East,* edited by David Hurst Thomas, 31–49. Washington DC: Smithsonian Institution Press, 1991.

———. *Vectors of Death: The Archaeology of European Contact.* Albuquerque: University of New Mexico Press, 1987.

Ramsey, William L. "'All Singular the Slaves': A Demographic Profile of Indian Slavery in Colonial South Carolina." In *Money, Trade, and Power: The Evolution of a Planter Society in Colonial South Carolina,* edited by Jack P. Greene, Rosemary Brana-Shute, and Randy Sparks, 166–86. Columbia: University of South Carolina Press, 2001.

———. "'Something Cloudy in Their Looks': The Origins of the Yamasee War Reconsidered." *Journal of American History* 90 (June 2003): 44–75.

Reid, Ann H., and Jeffery K. Taubenberger. "The Origin of the 1918 Pandemic Influenza Virus: A Continuing Enigma." *Journal of General Virology* 84, no. 9 (2003): 2285–92.

Reid, John Philip. *A Better Kind of Hatchet: Law, Trade, and Diplomacy in the Cherokee Nation during the Early Years of European Contact.* University Park: Pennsylvania State University Press, 1976.

———. *The Law of Blood: The Primitive Law of the Cherokee Nation.* New York: New York University Press, 1970.

Reider, Hans L. "Notes on the History of an Epidemic Tuberculosis among North American Indians." *Indian Health Service Primary Care Provider* 14 (1989): 45–50.

Reinhard, Karl J. "Archaeoparasitology in North America." *American Journal of Physical Anthropology* 82 (June 1990): 145–63.

Richardson, Miles, and Malcolm C. Webb, eds. *The Burden of Being Civilized: An Anthropological Perspective on the Discontents of Civilization.* Athens: University of Georgia Press, 1986.

Richter, Daniel. *The Ordeal of the Longhouse: The Peoples of the Iroquois League during the Era of European Colonization.* Chapel Hill: University of North Carolina Press, 1992.

Rivers, William J. *A Sketch of the History of South Carolina.* Charleston: McCarter and Company, 1856.

Rountree, Helen. *Pocahontas's People: The Powhatan Indians of Virginia through Four Centuries.* Norman: University of Oklahoma Press, 1996.

Rutman, Darrett B., and Anita H. Rutman. "Of Agues and Fevers: Malaria in the Early Chesapeake." *William and Mary Quarterly,* 3d ser., 33 (January 1976): 31–60.

Sahlins, Marshall D. *Tribesmen.* Englewood Cliff NJ: Prentice Hall, 1968.

Salo, William, Arthur C. Aufderheide, Jane Buikstra, and Todd A. Holcomb. "Identification of *Mycobacterium tuberculosis* DNA in a pre-Columbian Peruvian Mummy." *Proceedings of the National Academy of Sciences* 91 (March 15, 1994): 2091–94.

Scholtissek, Christopher. "Source for Influenza Pandemics." *European Journal of Epidemiology* 10, no. 4 (1994): 455–58.

Service, Elman. *Primitive Social Organization: An Evolutionary Perspective.* 2d ed. New York: Random House, 1971.

Shurkin, Joel N. *The Invisible Fire: The Story of Mankind's Victory over the Ancient Scourge of Smallpox.* New York: Putnam, 1979.

Silver, Timothy. *A New Face on the Countryside: Indians, Colonists, and Slaves in South Atlantic Forests, 1500–1800.* New York: Cambridge University Press, 1990.

Smith, Bruce D., ed. *Mississippian Emergence.* Washington DC: Smithsonian Institution Press, 1990.

———, ed. *Mississippian Settlement Patterns.* New York: Academic Press, 1978.

———. "Origins of Agriculture in Eastern North America." *Science* 246 (December 22, 1989): 1566–71.

———. "The Origins of Agriculture in the Americas." *Evolutionary Anthropology* 3, no. 5 (1995): 174–84.

Smith, Marvin. *Archaeology of Aboriginal Culture Change in the Interior Southeast during the Early Historic Period.* Gainesville: University Presses of Florida, 1987.

―――. *Coosa: The Rise and Fall of a Southeastern Mississippian Chiefdom.* Gainesville: University Press of Florida, 2000.

Snow, Dean, and Kim M. Lanphear. "European Contact and Indian Depopulation in the Northeast: The Timing of the First Epidemics." *Ethnohistory* 35 (Winter 1988): 15–33.

Sousa, Alexandra, Julia I. Salem, Francis K. Lee, Maria C. Vercosa, Philippe Cruaud, Barry R. Bloom, Philippe H. Lagrange, and Hugo L. David. "An Epidemic of Tuberculosis with a High Rate of Tuberculin Agency among a Population Previously Unexposed to Tuberculosis, the Yanomami Indians of the Brazilian Amazon." *Proceedings of the National Academy of Sciences* 94 (November 1997): 13227–32.

Spiess, Arthur E., and Bruce D. Spiess. "New England Pandemic of 1616–22: The Causes and Archaeological Implication." *Man in the Northeast* 34 (Fall 1987): 71–83.

Starr, Stuart E. "Novel Mechanisms of Immunosuppression after Measles." *Lancet* 348 (November 9, 1996): 1257–58.

Stead, William, A. C. Aufderheide, J. Buikstra, and T. A. Holcomb. "When Did Mycobacterium Tuberculosis Infection First Occur in the New World?" *American Journal of Respiratory and Critical Care Medicine* 151 (April 1995): 1267–68.

Steinen, Karl T. "Ambushes, Raids, and Palisades: Mississippian Warfare in the Interior Southeast." *Southeastern Archaeology* 11 (Winter 1992): 132–39.

Swanton, John. *Early History of the Creeks and Their Neighbors.* Washington DC: Government Printing Office, 1922.

―――. *Indians of the Southeastern United States.* Smithsonian Institution Bureau of American Ethnology, Bulletin 137. Washington DC: Government Printing Office, 1946.

―――. "Westo." In *Handbook of American Indians North of Mexico,* edited by Frederick W. Hodge, Smithsonian Institution Bureau of American Ethnology Bulletin 30, 2:936. Washington DC: Government Printing Office, 1910.

Taubenberger, Jeffery. "The Origin of the 1918 Pandemic Influenza Virus: A Continuing Enigma." *Journal of General Virology* 84, no. 9 (2003): 2285–92.

Taylor, Alan. *American Colonies: The Settling of North America.* New York: Penguin Books, 2001.

Thomas, David Hurst, ed. *Columbian Consequences.* Vol. 2, *Archaeological and Historical Perspectives on the Spanish Borderlands.* Washington DC: Smithsonian Institution Press, 1989.

Thornton, Russell. "American Indian Population Recovery following Smallpox Epidemics." *American Anthropologist* 93 (March 1991): 28–45.

Trigger, Bruce. "Ethnohistory: The Unfinished Edifice." *Ethnohistory* 33 (Summer 1986): 253–67.

Usner, Daniel H., Jr. *Indians, Settlers, and Slaves in a Frontier Exchange Economy: The Lower Mississippi Valley before 1782.* Chapel Hill: University of North Carolina Press, 1992.

Verano, John W., and Douglas H. Ubelaker, eds. *Disease and Demography in the Americas.* Washington DC: Smithsonian Institution Press, 1992.

Wallerstein, Immanuel. *Capitalist Agriculture and the Origins of the European World System in the Sixteenth Century.* New York: Academic Press, 1974.

―――. *Mercantilism and the Consolidation of the European World Economy.* New York: Academic Press, 1980.

Walsh, Lorena S., and Russell R. Menard. "Death in the Chesapeake: Two Life Tables for Men in Early Colonial Maryland." *Maryland Historical Magazine* 69 (Summer 1974): 211–27.

Ward, H. Trawick, and R. P. Stephen Davis Jr. "The Impact of Old World Diseases on the Native Inhabitants of the North Carolina Piedmont." *Archaeology of Eastern North America* 19 (1991): 171–81.

———. *Time before History: The Archaeology of North Carolina.* Chapel Hill: University of North Carolina Press, 1999.

Waselkov, Gregory A. "The Macon Trading House and Early European-Indian Contact in the Colonial Southeast." In *Ocmulgee Archaeology, 1936–1986,* edited by David J. Hally, 190–96. Athens: University of Georgia Press, 1994.

———. "Seventeenth-Century Trade in the Colonial Southeast." *Southeastern Archaeology* 8 (Winter 1989): 117–33.

Watts, Sheldon. *Epidemics and History: Disease, Power, and Imperialism.* New Haven CT: Yale University Press, 1997.

Webb, Stephen Saunders. *1676: The End of American Independence.* New York: Knopf, 1984.

Welch, Paul D. *Moundville's Economy.* Tuscaloosa: University of Alabama Press, 1991.

Wesson, Cameron, and Mark A. Rees, eds. *Between Contacts and Colonies: Archaeological Perspectives on the Protohistoric Southeast.* Tuscaloosa: University of Alabama Press, 2002.

White, Richard. *The Middle Ground: Indians, Empires, and Republics in the Great Lakes Region, 1650–1815.* New York: Cambridge University Press, 1991.

———. *Roots of Dependency: Subsistence, Environment, and Social Change among the Choctaws, Pawnees, and Navajos.* Lincoln: University of Nebraska Press, 1983.

———. "Winning the West: The Expansion of the Western Sioux in the Eighteenth and Nineteenth Centuries." *Journal of American History* 65 (September 1978): 319–43.

Wolf, Eric. *Europe and the People without History.* Berkeley: University of California Press, 1982.

Wood, Peter. *Black Majority: Negroes in South Carolina from 1670 through the Stono Rebellion.* New York: W. W. Norton, 1974.

Wood, Peter, Gregory Waselkov, and M. Thomas Hatley, eds. *Powhatan's Mantle: Indians in the Colonial South.* Lincoln: University of Nebraska Press, 1989.

Worster, Donald. "Transformations of the Earth: Toward an Agroecological Perspective in History." *Journal of American History* 76 (March 1990): 1087–1106.

Worth, John. *The Timucuan Chiefdoms of Spanish Florida.* 2 vols. Gainesville: University Press of Florida, 1998.

Wright, J. Leitch, Jr. *The Only Land They Knew: The Tragic Story of the American Indians in the Old South.* New York: Free Press, 1981.

Zinsser, Hans. *Rats, Lice, and History.* Boston: Little, Brown, 1935.

INDEX

*Page numbers set in italics refer
to tables or illustrations.*

Bienville, Jean-Baptiste Le Moyne (*cont.*)
196, 197, 198; and 1704 epidemic, 190–
91, 192
Black Death. *See* plague
Black Warrior River, 136
Black Warrior River valley, 96–97, 137,
240n137
Blastomyces dermatitidus. See blastomycosis
blastomycosis, 20, 23
blood poisoning, 17
Bordatella parapertussis. See whooping
cough
Borrelia burgdorferi, 15. *See also* ticks
Brickell, John, 167, 175
Broad River, 119, 153
Brucella, 15. *See also* brucellosis
brucellosis, 14, 15
bubonic plague, xix, 29, 32, 35, 36. *See also*
plague
Byrd I, William, 109, 115, 120
Byrd II, William, 120, 126

Cabeza de Vaca, Alvar Núñez, 56, 58–60
Cahokia ceremonial center, 12, 87–88
Cahokias, 128, 229n25
Calusas, 50, 51, 186, 223, 234n11
Cartagena, 80, 81
Carteret, Nicholas, 101, 113
Casqui, 89, 90–91
Catawba River, 119, 145, 169, 173, 174
Catawbas, 71, 119, *171,* 210, 253n35; as coa-
lesced society, 145–46, 169, 174, 178,
218, 223, 245n107; struggle against Iro-
quois, 173; in Tuscarora War, 212; and
vulnerability to disease, 170; and Ya-
masee War, 215, 217
Chagas' disease, 15
Chakchiumas, 196
Charlesfort, 73, 74
Charles Town, 130, 176, 178, 213; and Car-
olina trade network, 174, 175, 179, 215,
216, 218, 220; and smallpox, 180; and
Yamasee War, 202, 205; yellow fever outbreak in, 163, *171*
Chattahoochee River, 86, 117, 125, 127,
128, 130, 133, 134–35, 140–41

Chattahoochee Valley, 133, 134, 135, 184,
185, 218
Cherokees, 94, 117, 130, 139, 168, 177, 186,
252 (Table 2); and captive taking, 104,
165; in Carolina trade network, *171,* 187,
212, 215, 220; coalescence process and
formation of, xix–xx, 119–20, 157, 163,
245n107; conquest of the Yuchis, 213–
15, 224; and Great Southeastern Smallpox Epidemic, 137, *151*; role in changing
social landscape, 140–41, 244n82,
247n159; as victims of slave raids, 125,
131–32; villages, 71; in Virginia trade
network, 120–22, 123; and vulnerability
to disease, 152–53, 158, 174–76, 178–79;
and the Yamasee War, 202, 204, 213,
215–18
Chestowee Yuchis, 213, 224
Chiaha, 61, 64, 71, 207, 208
Chichumecos. *See* Westos
Chickasawhays, 96
Chickasaws, 89, *171,* 256n125; coalescence
process in forming, 157–58, 245n107;
and English trade network, 107, 123, 138,
141, 157, 187–88, 224; Great Southeastern Smallpox Epidemic impact on, 179,
184, 185–86; settlement patterns, 97;
slave raids, 124, 128, 139–40, 149, 150,
157, 192–93, 193–94, 195–96, 197, 198–
99; and the Yamasee War, 202, 212, 216,
218
Chicken, George, 216–17, 260n204,
260n206
Chicquilousa, 124
Choctaws, 191, 192, 249n221; as French allies, 179, 186, 187, 190, 196, 198–99; and
Great Southeastern Smallpox Epidemic,
154–55; and potential alliance with English, 211–12; power of, 200, 204; protec-
tive environment of, 157, 189, 198; and
rate of population, 197–98; as result of
Native slave trade, 96, 97, 137–40,
245n107, 247n197; slave raids on, 154,
197, 198, 199; and the Yamasee War, 202,
220. *See also* Chickasawhays
clostridia bacteria, 17

Cofitachequi: chiefdom, 41, 53, 64, 71, 88, 95; plague of, 53, 54, 55–56, 61, 68, 72, 234n19

Colapissas, 192–93, 194

colonization and conquest: affecting buffer zones and exchange patterns, 85, 87, 102; biological impact of, xvii, xviii, xxi–xxii, 31, 48, 49, 77, 83, *84,* 85, 98–99, 161, 226n1; and disruption of disease ecology, 1, 3, 23–24, 42, 99, 155, 156, 157, 181, 221, 222–24; facilitated by epidemic disease, 226n1; and impact on Mississippi Valley, 194–95, 223; and introduction of firearms, 105–6, 107–8, 113; mortality rates during, xvii, xx, 158, 170, 222–23, 226n2; nonbiological impact of, xxii, 3, 19, 38, 42, 98–99, 158, 160, 161, *162, 163;* population collapse caused by, xx, 36, 46, 47, 86, 161, 226–27n5. *See also* Columbian Exchange; Great Southeastern Smallpox Epidemic; slave raids; slave trade, Native; virgin-soil epidemics

Columbian Exchange, 14, 78, 238n101; beginnings, 48–50; and the Cherokees, 176; concept of, xvii; and disease ecology, xxi, 19, 28, 29–36, 45, 181–82; diseases and Native slave trade, xx, xxii, 180; and the English, 79–80; and human-to-human diseases, 36–38; and mission system, xviii–xix, 48, 74–75, 82–85, 95, 99; and nonbiological processes of colonialism, xvii–xviii, xix, xxii, 19, 42, 160, 181–82; and Spanish explorers, 59–60, 63, 66, 72–73, 83; and the Yamasees, 180, 181–82. *See also* colonization and conquest; Crosby, Alfred; Great Southeastern Smallpox Epidemic; smallpox; virgin-soil thesis

Columbus, Christopher, 24, 47, 49

Commissioners of the Indian Trade, 205–7, 208, 210, 212, 214, 215

Coosa chiefdom, 119; collapse of, 68–69, 72, 95, 117, 121, 240n131; and European explorers, 64, 66, 94; as victims of slave raids, 243n52

Coosa River, 41, 96, 115, 121, 135, 141, 198, 213, 220, 243n52

Coosa Valley, 61, 68, 71, 94, 95, 113, 226n5, 237n69

corn. *See* maize

Couture, Jean, 139

Cowetas, 133, 134, 202, 246n134

Creek Confederacy, 119, 140, 177; coalescence process in forming, xx, 125, 147, 245n107; and disease, 157, 158; in English trade network, 135–36, 141, 157, 187–88, 212, 216, 220, 224; Great Southeastern Smallpox Epidemic impact on, 184; and population, 122, 184–85, 186; and Yamasee War, 217, 218, 220. *See also* Alabamas; Apalachicolas; Chiahas; Cowetas; Cussitas; Koasatis, Lower Creeks; Pacanas; Upper Creeks

Crosby, Alfred, xvii, 161, 176, 222, 227n1, 234n9. *See also* Columbian Exchange

Cuba, 75; and disease route to Florida, 50; and Luna expedition, 67; Narváez route from, 56, 58; smallpox in, 49; Soto expedition in, 60, 63

Cumberland Plateau, 4, 121

Cumberland River, 12, 229n35

Cumberland Valley, 20, 92

Cussitas, 128, 133, 134, 207, 246n134

Delgado, Marcus, 121–22, 136

the delta agent, 27–28. *See also* hepatitis B

Dhegiha Sioux, 91, 93

d'Iberville, Pierre Le Moyne, 139, 140, 148–49, 156, 250

diphtheria, 29

diplococci bacteria, 16

disease ecology, Southeast: and aboriginal health, 11–28; colonialism's impact on, 1, 3, 23–24, 42, 99, *151,* 156, 181, 221, 222–24; and measles, 28, 29, 36, 37, 46; of the Mississippi Valley, 62, 156–57; and mortality rates, 46–47, 157, 161; and Native vulnerability to disease, xix, 28, 46; and post-contact epidemics, 2, 3; and regional geography, 3–4; and settlement patterns, xix, 1, 2, 7–11, 16–28, 36, 46, 102, 145; slave trade's impact on, 102, 221, 222–23;

disease ecology, Southeast (*cont.*)
and subsistence routines, 4–7; and warfare, 46, 186
Dobyns, Henry, 226n4, 234n9
Drake, Sir Francis, 77, 78, 79–82, 238n93
dysentery, 161, 189, 195; and disease ecology, 54, 58, 59, 79, 156; and settlement
patterns, 16, 18

farming, 6–7, 11–12, 13, 17. *See also* agriculture; horticulture
Five Nations Iroquois, 112, 119, 123, 145,
163, 165, 173
Flavivirus. See yellow fever
Florida, 98, 130; buffer zones as disease deterrents, 233n117; Columbian Exchange
diseases in, 48, 50, 83, 85, 95, 99 161,
238n101, 250; explorers, 51–52, 56, *57*,
60, 61, 63, 67–68, 74, 81–82, 222; raiding
activities in, 118, 121, 125, 135, 154,
179–80; and smallpox, 153–54, 249n211;
Spain's arrival in, xviii, 46; Spanish mission system in, 48, 82–83, 85–86, 95, 99,
127, 153; St. Augustine, xviii, 73, 75–76,
130, 131, 134, 183, 202, 218, 223; virgin-
soil epidemics in, 80–81, 83
Folsom, Nathaniel, 154
food poisoning, 17, 54, 58, 74
Fort Biloxi, 139, 156
Fort Caroline, 74
Fort Henry, 109
Fort Toulouse, 220

Gallay, Alan, 141, 226n3, 245n107, 254n69
gastroenteritis, 17
genetic immunity, xvii, 1, 23, 227n1; and
disadvantages among Natives, 233n130;
and homogeneity, 45; lack of evidence regarding, 44–45; and malaria, 45; and virginity metaphor, 1, 43
gonococci bacteria, 16
Gordillo, Francisco, 52
Great Southeastern Smallpox Epidemic,
137, *151*; and aftershock epidemics, 160,
162, 163, 165, 176, 179, 222, 223; among
Cherokees, 152–53; and Choctaws, 154–

55; and coalescence of Native peoples,
145–46, 147, 149, 154–55, 157, 169; and
depopulation, 143–44, 147, 148–49,
155–56, 157; end of, 150, *151*; Florida in,
153–54; and Native slave trade, xviii,
144–45, 147–49, 150, 157–58, 222;
spread of, 143–44, 146–47, 150, 157–58,
163; as turning point in region, 159. *See
also* smallpox
Guales, 153, 188; and Catholic mission system, 82, 83; illness among, 75; slave raids
on, 130; and Spanish colonialism, 85, 99;
as victims of colonialism, 223

Harriot, Thomas, 78–79
helminths, 20–21. *See also* hookworm; pinworm; whipworm
hepatitis. *See* the delta agent; hepatitis A;
hepatitis B
hepatitis A, 19–20, 29
hepatitis B, 26–27, 28, 29
Hispaniola, 49, 52, 54, 80
Hitchiti, 182, 184–85, 196, 256n125
hookworm, 20–21, 230n66
horticulture: dependence on, 13–14; effects
of transition to, 6–8, 11–12, 16–20, 24–
25, 27, 38–39; region's history of, 4, 6. *See
also* agriculture; maize; subsistence routines
Houmas, 124, 156–57, 194, 195

Illinois (peoples), 140, 150, 174, 186
Illinois River, 12
influenza, 37, *162*, 222, 235n37, 250–51; as
Columbian Exchange disease, xix, 29, 36,
161; and Luna expedition, 67–68; Native
virginity to, 232n98; obstacles to spread
of, 49–50; transmission of, 62–63,
232n96
iron-deficiency anemia, 12, 13, 14, 44,
229n35
Iroquois Confederacy, 123, 168; "mourning
wars" and population movement, 92–93;
raids, 128, 144, 163, 173, 176; Tuscarora
and Algonquin refugees in, 173. *See also*
Five Nations Iroquois

virgin-soil thesis: and genetic immunity, 227n1; implications of, 1. *See also* virgin-soil epidemics; Columbian Exchange

Waniahs, 129

Waxhaws, 169, 210–11, 218, 244n71

Welch, Thomas, 138, 198, 199

Westos, 123, 130, 133; and alliance with Cherokees, 121; in Carolina's slave trade network, 127–28; defeat of, 128–29, 131; in Virginia's slave trade network, 101, 112–15, 118

whipworm, 20, 21

whooping cough, 29, 36, 37–38, 161, 232n101

women, Native: and life expectancies, 229n35; and power relations, 108, 204; and slave raids, 103, 104, 149, 159, 173, 176, 177–78, 186; Soto's abuse of, 64, 66; and transition to horticulture, 6, 7, 9, 12

Wood, Abraham, 109, 115, *116*, 117, 118, 120, 244n71

Woodward, Henry, 114, 127, 128–29, 131, 133, 134–35, 137–38

Xualla, 60–61

Yamasees, 113, 130; as Carolina allies, 170; and disease ecology, 181–82; and English slave trade, 131, 179–80, 188, 204–5; and fear of enslavement, 202–3; flight from Wesco raids, 127, 133; and losses in

Yamasee War, 218; revolt against South Carolina, 160, 202, 215; and smallpox, 179; in Tuscarora War, 181. *See also* Yamasee War

Yamasee War, *219*; and altering of social landscape, 217–18, 220; Cherokee role in, 213, 214–18; and collapse of trade relations, 187–88; end of, 220; and end to Native slave trade, xviii, 161, 220, 224, 260n3; English after, 260n216; epidemiological context of, 160–61, 163–65, *171*, 172, 175–82, 188–97, 202–4; expansion of French influence during, 220; interpretations of origins of, 258n153; tensions leading to, 223. *See also* Yamasees

Yanomami tribe, 23–24, 44

yaws, 24, 25, 64

yellow fever, 16, 76, 85, 191, 198; as Columbian Exchange disease, 29, 35–36, 77, 160–61, *162*, 250–51; and disease ecology, 31, 33–34; epidemic, 163, 164, 180; and link to Drake voyage, 81, 238n93

Yersinia pestis bacteria, 31–33. *See also* plague

Yuchis, 152, 254n52; and Carolina alliance, 130, 131–32, 133, 166, *171*, 179; Cherokee conquest of, 213–14, 216, 217, 218, 224, 247n159; and Yamasee War, 202

Yucpa Indians, 27, 28

zoonoses, 2, 14–16, 29, 31, 35, 230n44

In the INDIANS OF THE SOUTHEAST series

William Bartram on the Southeastern Indians
Edited and annotated by Gregory A. Waselkov and Kathryn E. Holland Braund

Deerskins and Duffels
The Creek Indian Trade with Anglo-America, 1685–1815
By Kathryn E. Holland Braund

Searching for the Bright Path
The Mississippi Choctaws from Prehistory to Removal
By James Taylor Carson

Demanding the Cherokee Nation
Indian Autonomy and American Culture, 1830-1900
By Andrew Denson

Cherokee Americans
The Eastern Band of Cherokees in the Twentieth Century
By John R. Finger

Creeks and Southerners
Biculturalism on the Early American Frontier
By Andrew K. Frank

Choctaw Genesis, 1500–1700
By Patricia Galloway

The Southeastern Ceremonial Complex
Artifacts and Analysis
The Cottonlandia Conference
Edited by Patricia Galloway
Exhibition Catalog by David H. Dye and Camille Wharey

The Invention of the Creek Nation, 1670–1763
By Steven C. Hahn

Bad Fruits of the Civilized Tree
Alcohol and the Sovereignty of the Cherokee Nation
By Izumi Ishii

Epidemics and Enslavement
Biological Catastrophe in the Native Southeast, 1492–1715
By Paul Kelton

An Assumption of Sovereignty
Social and Political Transformation among the Florida Seminoles, 1953–1979
By Harry A. Kersey Jr.

The Caddo Chiefdoms
Caddo Economics and Politics, 700–1835
By David La Vere

The Moravian Springplace Mission to the Cherokees, Volume 1: 1805–1813
The Moravian Springplace Mission to the Cherokees, Volume 2: 1814–1821
Edited and with an introduction by Rowena McClinton

Keeping the Circle
American Indian Identity in Eastern North Carolina, 1885–2004
By Christopher Arris Oakley

Choctaws in a Revolutionary Age, 1750–1830
By Greg O'Brien

Cherokee Women
Gender and Culture Change, 1700–1835
By Theda Perdue

The Brainerd Journal
A Mission to the Cherokees, 1817–1823
Edited and introduced by Joyce B. Phillips and Paul Gary Phillips

The Cherokees
A Population History
By Russell Thornton

Buffalo Tiger
A Life in the Everglades
By Buffalo Tiger and Harry A. Kersey Jr.

American Indians in the Lower Mississippi Valley
Social and Economic Histories
By Daniel H. Usner Jr.

Powhatan's Mantle
Indians in the Colonial Southeast
Edited by Peter H. Wood, Gregory A. Waselkov, and M. Thomas Hatley

Creeks and Seminoles
The Destruction and Regeneration of the Muscogulge People
By J. Leitch Wright Jr.

Lightning Source UK Ltd.
Milton Keynes UK
UKHW012150050821
387960UK00012B/187